Music in American Life

Volumes in the series Music in American Life
are listed at the end of this book.

RED RIVER BLUES

RED RIVER BLUES

The Blues Tradition
in the Southeast

BRUCE BASTIN

University of Illinois Press
Urbana and Chicago

Publication of this work was supported in part by a grant
from the National Endowment for the Humanities.

Illini Books edition, 1995
© 1986 by the Board of Trustees of the University of Illinois
Manufactured in the United States of America
1   2   3   4   5   C   P   5   4   3   2   1

This book is printed on acid-free paper.

Portions of this book first appeared in different form in
Blues Unlimited and *Talking Blues*.

Library of Congress Cataloging-in-Publication Data

Bastin, Bruce, 1938–
    Red River Blues.

    (Music in American life)
    Includes index.
    1. Blues (Songs, etc.)—Southern States—History
and criticism. 2. Afro-Americans—Southern States—
Music—History and criticism. 3. Folk songs, English—
Southern States—History and criticism. I. Title.
ML3521.B39   1986   784.5'3'00975   85-8571
ISBN 0-252-01213-5 (cloth : alk. paper). —
ISBN 0-252-06521-2 (pbk. : alk. paper)

*To all those magnificent bluesmen and their families
and friends who shared their music and lives with me*

Contents

Preface to the
Paperback Edition

Remarkably little new factual material has come to light since *Red River Blues* was published a decade ago. This is hardly surprising, since so few people are seriously interested in the sort of intensive research that Pete Lowry and I undertook, but also since the people we talked with are mostly gone. Of course the story continued, as more musicians were "discovered," and I'm happy to report that a number of the musicians cited in *Red River Blues* are still playing at this time. Perhaps the greatest change in the music scene during the last decade has been the emergence of the compact disc, which seems to be the popular format for future sound conservation. One wonders how many of the musicians originally documented would have dealt with *that* as a format for issuing their blues.

The most noticeable difference, without a doubt, has been the attitude toward the music in the quarter century since we first listened to Buddy Moss in Atlanta and then started uncovering bluesmen in North Carolina. Exactly twenty-one years ago, as I write this, with the help of the Students' Union at the University of North Carolina (Chapel Hill) and folklore professor Daniel W. Patterson, I put on the *first ever* blues festival in the South, predominantly featuring bluesmen whom Pete Lowry and I had located. Today, almost every cabbage patch has its blues festival, but few seek local musicians, and nobody remembers that a generation ago this simply was not done. In 1994 I was sitting in the open-air foyer of a smart Chapel Hill restaurant, redolent of professors and mixed drinks, while the public address system beamed out Chicago blues. Perhaps I was the only one to notice. It wasn't like that in my days as a student there—and I'm talking about a location I specifically chose as an "oasis" unlike anywhere else I'd visited down south. A year or two ago, in the New Orleans airport lounge, the PA system played Fats Domino, Smiley Lewis, and Professor Longhair to studied disinterest. New Orleans, of course, has since welcomed Cajuns (indeed, almost claimed them as "homegrown"), whereas in 1963, when I was trying to find Joel Sonnier's gig, we chased up Airline Hiway into the boondocks. As with blues, caveat emptor.

I was pleased with the critical reception of *Red River Blues,* especially from scholars and researchers whom I respected, and well pleased in 1987 when it won an ASCAP–Deems Taylor Award. Still, some of the response to the book was curious. A number of reviewers, apparently more comfortable with the sort of work generally published on the blues back then, wanted the more usual biographies and discographies. I saw a different need. Even so, the subject was too rich to catch all of it in this book. I published a related article on the medicine show in *American Music*[1] and have continued to share my research in other articles, record liner and brochure notes, and in the recordings themselves.

One reviewer felt my closing chapter suggested a "moribund tradition," whereas his association with D.C.-area bluesmen John Cephas, Phil Wiggins, Archie Edwards, and John Jackson suggested to him that it was a "living tradition."[2] This is really a matter of perspective—and, I suspect, distance. I don't live in Maryland, and even though I'm one of the few people to have taken John Jackson to a Chinese restaurant in London's Soho, I'll stick to my original assessment. These musicians play now for whites—often non-Americans—in concert situations. There is a raft of difference from the days of Blind Boy Fuller or even Gabriel Brown. Valerie Wilmer once told me she'd be glad never again to hear the likes of Guitar Shorty's music, as that would denote a change in social attitude. Perhaps that's optimistically simplistic, but the point is well taken. I think "tricks ain't walkin' no more."

The very title of the book led to an interesting slip by another reviewer, who miscast the subtitle as *The Blues Tradition in the Southwest.*[3] Although just about every southeastern bluesman sang a "Red River Blues" (Josh White recorded it in 1932, Buddy Moss recorded it in 1933 at his first session, and Virgil Childers cut it for Bluebird in 1938), there is no Red River in the Southeast. The Red River that most probably lent its name to this blues begins in eastern New Mexico, runs between Oklahoma and Texas, and ends in Louisiana, just north of Baton Rouge. There is also a Red River in the northern United States, unconnected to this one.

Looking back, I realize that I hadn't fully appreciated the great pleasure I'd had in getting really close to my sources, enjoying the company of those bluesmen and their friends and families. I remember well the hours I spent stopping by to shoot the bull with Willie Trice, Jamie Alston, Wilbert Atwater, Mattie Hackney, and a host of others. That time will never come again, and it remains an indelible piece of my past. I had one great advantage over American fieldworkers, of course: I was English. More than once Pete Lowry and I set out together up a path, but I was the one who knocked on the door. And what contacts we made! There was, for instance, the time we looked up Pink Anderson in 1970, with a police car escort to his door, blue light flashing. Nobody was injured going out his back door, but he'd have made a song of that event, had he been a younger man. People came to talk just because they had been part of the Normandy invasion army and had been treated well by the English. Baby Tate, who had a great time before D-Day interrupted his summer English pub performances, insisted I join him in an impromptu "Roll Me Over in the Clover," sung to an interested audience, by no means all of them under the age of ten, on the afternoon of the Pink Anderson fiasco in a shopping complex carpark in Spartanburg, South Carolina.

Armchair research can never replace the infectious pleasure of personal contact, or indeed the streetwise experiences of fieldwork at the very edges of existence. David Evans once wrote a fascinating article about the difficulties of fieldwork research that should be compulsory reading.[4] Talk to Bengt Olsson about his times in Tennessee and Alabama. Talk to Pete Lowry about his (sadly unsuccessful) endeavors to record Buddy Moss (or indeed a little experience we both had trying to work with Moss in 1972). Talk also to us about our meeting with rednecks in Edgecombe County, North Carolina, when we were trying to interview a one-time musician, Joe Black, or with Newton County, Georgia, police for "consorting with blacks" (we had just been recording Roy Dunn).

Some years ago, at an academic gathering in New Orleans to discuss R&B—none of the people who had written books on the topic, such as John Broven, Jeff Hannusch, and Tad Jones, was invited—one speaker went on at well-researched length listing archives, libraries, books, magazines, and so forth as source materials. Never once was there a mention of human resources. People had been left off the menu. Without personal contact, my own research would have been far less vivid, far less compelling. How *do* you replace memories of hearing Guitar Shorty perform at Chapel Hill's Endangered Species bar, packed with professors and "kitty money" ("Never seen so much white conscience money," said the owner)? Or watching a genuinely excited Buddy Moss play a stunning "Chesterfield" on his battered guitar one hot August afternoon at his home? Or seeing Henry Johnson play slide guitar flat across his lap, Hawaiian style, at home and some time later stroll into Chapel Hill's TV station with a petrified Elester Anderson, casually watch a quartet finish playing Mozart and pack up, then settle down to back Elester (whom he'd never before met) on "Red River Blues" (which they'd never agreed to attempt), as if he *always* played in front of a camera? Or of tracing Floyd Council via the local cab company's switch-board? Or meeting that truly larger-than-life character Peg Leg Sam?

Some commercially recorded material, originally cited in *Red River Blues* as being unissued, has now been released, usually on compact discs. Similarly, many alternative takes to issued titles have also been located and released. I wrote the notes to a Blind Boy Fuller Sony CD on which the compiler, Larry Cohn, had included previously unissued alternative takes.[5] The main changes involved the 1941 sessions of Brownie McGhee, which also involved two other major artists, Sonny Terry and Buddy Moss. A double CD now covers all of McGhee's ses-sions for OKeh-Columbia.[6] I was fortunate to have been present in the studio when the metalwork in the original, sealed cardboard contain-ers was brought up from the vaults so that, along with Larry Cohn and engineer Mark Wilder, I was the first to hear the sides since they had been made more than half a century earlier.

Seeing the release of unissued titles from one other artist's sessions gave me special delight. On page 319 I briefly discuss the Dan Pickett Gotham session(s) of 1949. A few years ago I was able to lease these titles and discovered enough unissued titles (plus four by Tarheel Slim) to release a CD, Flyright FLY CD 25. We still had very little new infor-mation about Pickett, but a lawyer from Alabama wrote to Gotham in-quiring about royalty rights on his behalf. Pickett's real name was James Founty. Heaven knows now how many college courses teach blues and how many "majors" there must be, let alone the umpteen blues societ-ies, but it took that matchless blues hunter, the German researcher Axel Küstner, to follow up the lead. Pickett has died, but I now enjoy a pho-tograph of his daughter holding my old Flyright Dan Pickett album.

The albums that carried many titles of southeastern bluesmen record-ed by the Library of Congress are long gone. Some of the most exciting titles have been reissued on *Red River Blues 1934–1943* (Travelin' Man TM CD 08). Sadly, most other albums cited a decade ago are now long out of print.

Other leads never were followed up. I'm especially sorry about the Florida jug band scene. Nonetheless, some people have continued to research the subject: Kip Lornell, especially; those pursuing the rural string band tradition that predated blues and ran parallel to it; Timothy

Duffy, who uncovered artists and information around Winston-Salem; the Durham blues festival team; and so on. I'm sure that all of these colleagues would have seen this tradition as "living." Perhaps it's only for me that "tricks ain't walkin' no more."

NOTES

1. Bruce Bastin, "From the Medicine Show to the Stage: Some Influences upon the Development of a Blues Tradition in the Southeastern United States," *American Music* 2 (Spring, 1984): 29–42.

2. Barry Lee Pearson, review of *Red River Blues* by Bruce Bastin, in *Mid-America Folklore* 18 (Spring, 1990): 65.

3. Maurice A. Crane, "Jazz and Oral History as Art Forms," *Oral History Review* 16 (Spring, 1988): 119.

4. David Evans, "Fieldworkers with Blues Singers: The Unintentionally Induced Natural Context," *Southern Folklore Quarterly* 42 (1978): 9–16.

5. *Blind Boy Fuller: East Coast Piedmont Style*, Columbia 467923 2 (1991).

6. *The Complete Brownie McGhee*, Columbia 475700 2 (1994).

Preface

In a sense this book had its origins one hot August afternoon in 1969 in Atlanta when Pete Lowry and I were interviewing Buddy Moss. Moss's chance remark about two North Carolina bluesmen friends led us to take a day off from junking for old records on our way back to New Jersey and took us to a number of people involved with blues in and around Durham, North Carolina. A series of articles in the pioneer English blues magazine *Blues Unlimited* led to a request from Paul Oliver in 1970 to write a short book in his Studio Vista Blues Paperback series. In 1972 I returned to Chapel Hill, North Carolina, to continue my fieldwork and to study the origins of blues in the southeastern states. This book is the outgrowth of all that plus subsequent work to which the unstinted assistance of a handful of selfless researchers has been added.

Pete Lowry and I have spent countless days following leads, and he has recorded more examples of the blues tradition in the Southeast than everyone else combined. My section on Virginia could never have been written without the superb fieldwork undertaken by Kip Lornell. The survey on postwar blues in Georgia would have been patchy at best without the generous assistance of George Mitchell, while much of the detailed study of blues in Durham and elsewhere in North Carolina, especially since World War II, was gladly provided by Glenn Hinson. Karl Gert zur Heide and John Cowley constantly provided obscure but highly pertinent references in print. Jeffrey P. Green has kindly produced detailed indexes to facilitate use as a reference text. This survey is of the music of the people of the region, and revealing comments within the text were provided by some of the scores of people who were good enough to be interviewed and recorded about the place of this music in their lives.

This is a history rather than an ethnomusicological survey. A number of books already exist with detailed annotation and musical analysis of specific recorded pieces by bluesmen from the Southeast, and they are available for supplementary information.[1] However, the music is aural and not transliteral. It was never written down and it was never intended to be. The really relevant way to appreciate the music is to hear it—and that usually means on record. No written annotation will fully replace the aural reception necessary to comprehend the music. Brett Sutton had this to say about black gospel music, but it is so with blues too:

> Western music could not have achieved its current level of sophistication without written music as one of its fundamental tools. Yet even in this highly developed literate tradition, certain aspects of musical performance, such as expressive variation in tempo and dynamics, tone quality and mode of attack, cannot be sufficiently represented on the printed page, and must be provided by the creative skills of the performer. . . . In folk music, where the absence of a written standard of reference and the natural fluctuation of the oral tradition place much artistic control in the hands of the performer, the personal component of the performance is perhaps even larger."[2]

We write about black folk music in the manner of western civilization's insistence that all matters of significance be documented visually. Few of the people interviewed saw their music as anything other than transitory; none saw it as art for art's sake. Its very lack of self-conscious expression, fundamental to its integrity, precludes its permanence in any form other than that in which it was created. The present study attempts to collate known elements in a format which few of the people who created the music would have been able to appreciate: it is an attempt to offer a literate study of a basically nonliterate form.

Blues in its folk form was the expression of a nearly destitute, essentially illiterate group of people. This study was not written along class lines, but it should be pointed out that black Americans did not think as a whole, any more than did white Americans. There were class divisions with different groups seeking different goals, some consciously, some unconsciously. No single body spoke for all blacks. John Hammond, well aware of a broad range of black music, has stated that "jazz and, particularly, primitive black music were too unfamiliar to the middle-class leaders of the NAACP to be anything they could take pride in."[3]

In any attempt to analyze in depth the blues tradition of the Southeast, one is always faced with the imbalance of documentation. Remarkably little contemporary written documentation has been uncovered. Where it exists, it has been incorporated in great detail, in an effort to shed as much light as possible upon the artists concerned. Thus the use of the welfare files of Blind Boy Fuller and Gary Davis enables a detailed documentation of their lives totally out of proportion to information available on many other bluesmen but also provides rare insight into the lives of professional musicians—or probably as near professional in any sense as the East Coast provided. Only in recent years have anything like systematic studies taken place, and often they were localized or centered on a given group of musicians, so certain areas or aspects have been studied in detail, but large sections of the region have not been researched at all. My personal fieldwork was confined to summer vacations from a teaching post in England; therefore I was unable to visit many areas. Despite these limitations, disparate sources have provided sufficient information for us to draw a number of valid generalizations about a regional blues tradition.

While writing this book I became aware of points made in unrelated texts which highlighted issues close to my research. One author found that "no-one remembers accurately what happened thirty or more years ago. Therefore I am not indebted for a single fact to anyone other than the authors of contemporary official letters, minutes, memoranda and records of meetings."[4] If I were to work from such information, there would be no book. Georgia bluesman Roy Dunn, asked how he could remember so much local detail, replied, "It's OK for you, you can write it down. I can't write so I have to remember." The wealth of fascinating detail which emerged from the welfare files of Blind Boy Fuller and Gary Davis brought to mind the truism of Sir Lewis Namier that "a great many profound secrets are somewhere in print, but are most easily detected when one knows what to seek."[5] Earlier use of death records had opened up an avenue of research which few had appreciated.

Nothing can replace sheer persistence based on thorough evaluation in the field. A story from World War II confirms the underlying premise of the need for practical experience:

A British mathematical physicist and an American theoretical physicist, Dr. Charles Kittel . . . had been set together . . . to work on the problem of deducing the characteristics of German magnetic mines laid at sea. . . . The data from which characteristics were to be deduced were the reports of our minesweepers as they exploded the mines. . . . Kittel wanted . . . to take a few trips on a minesweeper to sample the data for himself. The British theorist refused to do this . . . so he stuck to his desk while Kittel went out minesweeping. What Kittel immediately found was that the reports from the minesweeping crews were wildly inaccurate . . . and the only item of data on which one could rely was whether the mine had exploded to port or starboard. Simplifying all the latter reports down to this extremely limited observation, he nevertheless succeeded in deducing the answer; but the British theorist went on accepting the data as accurate and never reached an answer.[6]

Had there been the equivalents of Dr. Kittel throughout the southeastern states at any time in the half century prior to the 1960s, then this history would have been far easier to collate. Although by 1977, one writer felt able to state that "now there seems to be a researcher in every small town in Georgia . . . and both Carolinas," it was in fact the same small group of enthusiasts.[7]

Personal interviews, while a source of so much otherwise unobtainable information, provided oral, not written, evidence: written corroboration of spellings was usually impossible. Where the spelling of an artist's name is phonetic, it is shown with a preceding asterisk. *Ken *Heartsmith could have been Kent Hartsmith, but the last name of *Dallas Baldwin would appear to be accurate. Bill Henderson, though phonetic, would appear to require no asterisks. Other such names, though phonetic, have no symbol, but I would not be the first to presume the spelling of a bluesman's name. Experience has proved that written names are not always accurately spelled, especially by third parties.

For more than a dozen years this study has been in my mind. Doubtless more information will be uncovered, but certain aspects considered here are unlikely at this late date to be augmented significantly. Without the help of countless people over the years, many of whom appear in these pages, nothing would have been written. I owe them a great debt.

NOTES

1. Kent Cooper, ed., *The Harp Styles of Sonny Terry* (New York: Oak Publications, 1975); David Evans, brochure notes to *Atlanta Blues 1933,* JEMF 106 (Los Angeles, Calif., 1979), pp. 23–24; Stefan Grossman, *Rev. Gary Davis: Blues Guitar* (New York: Oak Publications, 1974); Thom Larson, *Blues Magazine* 3 (February, 1977): 34–35, 43–49; Woody Mann, *Six Black Blues Guitarists* (New York: Oak Publications, 1973); Jeff Todd Titon, *Early Downhome Blues: A Musical and Cultural Analysis* (Urbana: University of

Illinois Press, 1977); Happy Traum, ed., *Guitar Styles of Brownie McGhee* (New York: Oak Publications, 1971).

2. Joel Brett Sutton, "The Gospel Hymn, Shaped Notes, and the Black Tradition: Continuity and Change in American Traditional Music" (Master's thesis, University of North Carolina at Chapel Hill, 1976).

3. John Hammond [with Irving Townsend], *John Hammond on Record: An Autobiography* (New York: Ridge Press/Summit Books, 1977), p. 200.

4. Charles Cruickshank, *The Fourth Arm: Psychological Warfare 1938–1945* (London: Davis-Poynter, 1977), preface.

5. (Sir) L. B. Namier, *Diplomatic Prelude 1938–1939* (London: n. p., 1948), p. v.

6. R. V. Jones, *Most Secret War: British Scientific Intelligence 1939–1945* (London: Hamish Hamilton, 1978), p. 377.

7. Samuel Charters, *Sweet as the Showers of Rain* (New York: Oak Publications, 1977), p. 6.

RED RIVER BLUES

1

The Background of the Blues

In his book *Mirror for Man* the anthropologist Clyde Kluckhohn argued that "any given culture trait can be fully understood only if seen as the end point of specific consequences of events reaching back into the remote past."[1] As if taking him at his word, many who have written about blues have striven to claim origins in slavery times. "There is no indication," says Harold Courlander, "that something closely akin to blues was not sung in the towns and on the plantations in antebellum days."[2] However, he fails to give supporting evidence.

While there is unquestionable continuity in the history of black folksinging, the particular genre known as blues reflects certain circumstances in black life at the turn of the century. In the late nineteenth century, slave-song survivals remained and were the songs most commonly collected by those few persons with any interest in black secular music. Work songs continued to make the monotony of labor more palatable. Much of the black secular music of the southeastern United States reflected the white musical tradition. Black string bands using fiddle and banjo existed, playing largely for dances. Minstrel-type songs were sung, not primarily as portrayed by black-face minstrel troupes but, nevertheless, bearing some resemblance to this comic tradition. None of these branches of black secular music prefigure the beginnings of the musical tradition which finally emerged to be the blues.

The nineteenth-century forms did not suit the changes in black life. Worksongs were collective modes of expression, cast in a call-and-response pattern performed by a leader and a group and, functionally, they were strictly limited. Slave songs were neither relevant to the freedman nor a satisfactory means of expression for the new generations of southern blacks who had never experienced slavery. By the 1890s the minstrel show, with its stereotyped black caricatures, had become offensive to many blacks. Out of these disparate secular styles emerged the blues, distinctive as a musical style and rapidly becoming the chief means of secular musical expression for lower-class blacks in the early twentieth century. There is no evidence that, during the nineteenth century, blues existed in the southeastern states as a parallel development to these other styles, yet by the 1920s the blues tradition was both widespread and popular. In the years around the turn of the century this new musical tradition evolved.

A number of persons closely involved with black music have suggested the blues originated at the turn of the century. In 1940 John W. Work wrote that it was "safe to consider the blues a twentieth century product, making their appearance about 1900. Handy first heard them in 1903. . . . 'Ma Rainey' heard them in 1902 in a small town in Missouri where she was appearing with a show." In an interview with Work, she referred to lost newspaper clippings which mentioned her singing blues as early as 1905.[3] In 1917 Dorothy Scarborough also alluded to the origins of blues, stating that "for the last several years the most popular type of Negro song has been that peculiar, barbaric sort of melody called 'blues,' with its irregular rhythm, its lagging briskness, its mournful liveliness of tone." She quoted W. C. Handy as saying that "about 20 years ago [i.e., about 1897] the desire was all for coon songs. Now the tendency is toward blues."[4]

For the emergence of a blues style in the southeastern states, Howard W. Odum and Guy B. Johnson suggested a more recent date. In 1911 Odum wrote that "a study of the social songs current among the Southern Negroes shows they have arisen from every-day life, and that they portray many of the common traits and social tendencies. The majority may be said to have sprung up with comparatively recent years."[5] In this article, however, Odum does not use the term *blues*. Johnson, who undoubtedly had greater insight into the significance of blues than anyone else of his generation and was quite familiar with the music and the singers from whom he collected material, commented on the absence of early reference to blues. In his view "we have the right to suppose that if the Negro were building up a notable or distinctive body of folk songs, someone would have taken the time to observe and record it for posterity. The absence of such data makes it fairly safe to assume that the Negro, with his excellent ear for music, was doing rather successfully the prosaic thing of taking on the folk-song culture of the dominant race."[6] Rather earlier, during the mid-1920s when he was most closely involved with blues, Johnson had written that he had "frequently met the remark, after repeating the words of some late blues to a Negro laborer, 'Why, I've known a song like that for 10 years—except mine wouldn't do to put on record.'"[7] The words of these men place the origin of the blues very much in the twentieth century. Johnson later stated that he could recall no singer or musician who has learned blues from either his father or his grandfather.[8]

A review of the literature pertaining to black secular music in the late nineteenth century offers little insight into black folk music. In these years the few black writers were aspiring toward white middle-class status and were understandably uninterested in seriously considering black folk material, which might, in their own and in white eyes, reflect an inferior culture. Only sacred black folksong acquired status and respectability. It became polished and Europeanized as whites became more interested in it, and it was some distance removed from its black origins.

Many early collectors were loathe to collect black secular music. The fact that early collectors like William Eleazor Barton, James Miller McKim, and Henry George Spaulding were all ministers must have had some bearing on their attitude when they collected material.[9] To their credit, both Barton and McKim showed considerable perception, the former seeking songs as "of interest as data for study in religious and social development,"[10] but the very fact of their being ministers probably resulted in conscious censorship on the part of the singers, let alone on the part of the collectors. The general bearing of some of the well-to-do whites would have enhanced this attitude of black censorship. That conscious censorship existed on the part of most collectors is revealed by a black journal, *Southern Workman,* which had been attempting to collect black folklore since November 1893. An 1899 editorial carried this apology: "We are sorry that our desire to reproduce . . . stories as they are told . . . should have shocked the sensibilities of our readers. If the illiterate Negro, in his effort to reproduce . . . the characteristic Irish expression 'be jabbers' has twisted it into 'be Jasus' it certainly would be far from correct for us either to restore it to its original form or to suppress it altogether. . . . It is an effort to give with as absolute accuracy as we can secure, the stories, superstitions, sayings and songs of the illiterate Negro. . . . (We) are extremely sorry that offense has been given.[11]

In the nineteenth century, secular black folksongs were drawn upon only for minstrel shows. Whites insensitive to authentic features of black music made the songs into the bland, limpid melodies popular prior to the late 1890s. In his detailed study of the American minstrel stage, Carl Wittke realized that minstrel shows pictured the Negro as "a simple, somewhat rustic figure, instinctively humorous, irrationally credulous, gifted in song and dance, interesting in spontaneous frolic."[12] They staged him as a stereotype with watermelon, razor, and gaudy clothes.

The minstrel shows reached the peak of their popularity in the immediate antebellum period, but "colored performers were also much in demand in the 'seventies.'" Occasionally there was more traditional black secular music, as when some North Carolinians appeared in Cleveland in 1875 playing "upon the rude instruments of the South," giving a "ruder and more literal portrayal of the Southern Negro than that given by the Fisk and Hampton Singers."[13] By the 1880s black troupes like Callender's Original Georgia Minstrels and Henderson's Colored Minstrels had been disbanded, leaving only white imitators or black instrumentalists, who moved into the smaller, itinerant medicine shows. The withdrawal of these blacks from such shows in part reflects economic factors in the decline of the minstrel shows. They numbered twenty-three companies in 1882–83, dropping to ten by 1896 and to three by 1919. More important was the changing attitudes of blacks toward the stage stereotype. By the turn of the century blacks, who had never played a prominent role in the popularizing of the white parody of Negro songs, turned away from such music, often using it as an intensification of the rejection of black secular music, especially if they aspired beyond the lowest status.

No serious attempts were made to collect black secular songs until the first decade of this century. This material has been analyzed in some detail,[14] but little is pertinent to the emergent blues tradition in the Southeast. In 1928 Newman Ivey White published the material he had collected before 1920, still viewing it from the moralistic, middle-class white standpoint. He made two valuable contributions to the study of the emergence of blues, however. Referring to the changed role of the woman in black secular songs, he stated that women "had little place, however, in the mid-nineteenth century minstrel stage, where the songs about women were of so decidedly different a character that one is forced to conclude . . . that the Negro has changed his psychological nature since 1850,"[15] which was ultimately responsible for the change in his secular music, giving rise to diverse blues styles. He also appreciated that there were "a great number of so-called blues that do not conform to the general type. Probably many such in the present collection were not blues when collected and have since been absorbed into that category. For when most of them were collected, the recent craze for blues was just beginning to gather momentum. Any collection made since 1915 would show a much greater influence of blues upon almost all types of Negro Songs."[16]

None of the black secular songs collected in the southeastern states in the 1890s and very few of those collected in the first decade of the twentieth century offer much evidence of blues, either in verse structure or content. It is entirely possible that in the first decade of the twentieth century, blues in the southeastern states was in the first formative stage or had yet to emerge in a recognizable form. However, one collection made in Newton County, Georgia, between 1906 and 1908 by Howard Odum suggests that in Georgia, close to the deep South, blues began to emerge earlier than in the Carolinas and the upper South.[17] Publishing his findings in 1911 Odum sensed the psychological reaction of blacks to changing race relations.[18]

Three of the songs that Odum collected seem to be close to blues. In "Baby What Have I Done," stanzas such as

> Where were you las' Saturday night,
> When I lay sick in my bed?
> You down town wid some other ole girl,
> Wasn't there to hold my head,

contain a theme common to blues and Odum also states that "the same wail . . . is heard again and again."[19] "No More Good Time" has four fine blues stanzas, but the most significant of all was one taken from a singer in Newton County, "Look'd down de road," which included the couplet

> I got the blues, but too damn mean to cry,
> I got the blues, but too damn mean to cry.[20]

which must be one of the earliest songs in which the word appears. Odum makes no comment on the way the song was sung or whether it was accompanied, but here we are probably able to view the emergence of a genuine blues.

The blues, as a musical form, was almost certainly polygenetic and did not emerge everywhere at the same time. In some regions, perhaps in Mississippi, the blues probably emerged in the 1890s. It is far more probable that in the southeastern states the blues emerged only in the first decade of the twentieth century. This hypothesis is further corroborated by the statements of musicians who were playing in the first decade of this century or who learned from musicians who had formed their styles and repertoires before the advent of blues on phonograph records. When Odum was collecting in Georgia, though perhaps slightly later in the Carolinas and Virginia, the new musical style was beginning to emerge. The impetus for this came largely from sociohistorical events coinciding, as they did, with a greater availability of musical instruments, especially the guitar, and with a conscious reaction against certain aspects of black secular music of the nineteenth century.[21]

This study is not the place for a detailed analysis of blues as a genre, nor for parallel influences from field hollers as a possible source. Some investigation of hollers had been attempted in the 1950s by Ray B. Browne and Willis Laurence James but have been analyzed in more detail by Bruce Jackson.[22] In a concise history of jazz an English jazz musician and critic wrote perceptively that "there are moments when anyone setting out to discuss blues must wish devoutly that the term had never been coined."[23] Assuredly, any too-rigid definition of blues is liable to founder on the rocks of idiosyncratic bluesmen but nonetheless a working definition is required. Readers are well advised to familiarize themselves with the detailed discussion of early reports of blues as described by Jeff Titon and David Evans, whose works analyze blues in such detail as to make similar coverage here superfluous. Evans describes the general blues form as having

> one basic pattern, or an approximation of it—the twelve-bar AAB pattern. A blues in this pattern has several stanzas, each of which occupies twelve measures or "bars" of 4/4 time. These twelve bars are divided into three sections or "lines" of four bars each. The first line (A) is usually repeated as the second line (A), sometimes with a slight variation for emphasis, and the stanza ends with a different third line (B), which usually rhymes or is assonant with the first two. The entire twelve measures, however, are not devoted to the singing of these three lines. Instead, each line usually takes slightly more than two measures to sing. It is followed by an instrumental passage of slightly less than two measures as a "response" to the vocal line. The combination of three such vocal lines with their instrumental responses, each occupying four measures altogether, makes a complete twelve-bar stanza.
>
> The AAB pattern of the vocal is set off against a more complex pattern in the instrumental accompaniment. The latter consists of musical phrases whose basis lies in a harmonic sequence on tonic (I), subdominant (IV), and dominant (V) chords.[24]

Titon suggests that

> the beginning of the improvised AAB downhome song form was marked
> by the coincidence of . . . improvised AAA songs with the small number
> of three-line, twelve-bar, AAN song models whose stanzas were more or
> less in predetermined order. Singers simply added a rhyming punch line
> after repeating the first line, and in so doing they formed three-line, AAB
> songs with improvised, interchangeable stanzas. Sometimes stanzas were
> "studied" (i.e., made up) by singers in advance, to be fitted in at the proper
> moment. The new form gave the lyrics the same, circular, associative
> textual coherence the AAA songs had; stanzas could be added, eliminated,
> or interchanged without ill effect on the sense of the lyrics. . . . Perhaps
> the associative coherence was more congenial to the worldview of Black
> Belt culture than was the logical, linear, narrative structure of the ballad.[25]

A newcomer to blues can do no better than read further in the above-
cited texts while heightening personal awareness of the disparate, con-
tributing elements through continual exposure to the music itself. Any
music is a reflection of social conditions relevant to its growth, and
blues is no exception.

NOTES

1. Clyde Kluckhohn, "Mirror for Man," in *Deep Down in the Jungle,* ed.
Roger D. Abrahams (Hatsboro, Pennsylvania: Folklore Associates, 1964), p. 9.

2. Harold Courlander, *Negro Folk Music, U.S.A.* (New York: Columbia
University Press, 1963), p. 128.

3. John W. Work, *American Negro Songs and Spirituals* (New York:
Bonanza Books, 1940), p. 32.

4. Dorothy Scarborough, "The 'Blues' as Folksongs," *Publications of the
Texas Folklore Society* 2 (1917): 52–66.

5. Howard W. Odum, "Folk-song and Folk-poetry as Found in the Secular
Songs of the Southern Negro," *Journal of American Folklore* 24 (October-
December, 1911): 262.

6. Guy B. Johnson, "Negro Folk Songs," in *Culture in the South,* ed. William
T. Couch (Chapel Hill: University of North Carolina Press, 1934), p. 549.

7. Guy B. Johnson, "Double Meaning in the Popular Negro Blues," *Journal
of Abnormal and Social Psychology* 22 (April-June, 1927): 19.

8. Guy B. Johnson, conversation with the author, October 22, 1972.

9. William Eleazor Barton, "Recent Negro Melodies," *New England
Magazine,* February, 1899; James Miller McKim, "Negro Songs," *Dwight's
Journal of Music,* August 9, 1862; and Henry George Spaulding, "Negro
'Shouts' and Shout Songs," *Continental Monthly,* August, 1863, pp. 196–200,
all in *The Social Implications of Early Negro Music in the United States,*
Bernard Katz, ed. (New York: Arno Press and the New York Times, 1969).

10. Barton, "Recent Negro Melodies," p. 118.

11. Editorial, *Southern Workman* 28 (June, 1899): 201.

12. Carl Wittke, *Tambo and Bones* (Durham: Duke University Press, 1930), p. 5.

13. Cleveland *Plain Dealer,* October 19, December 9, 13, 1875; Wittke, *Tambo and Bones,* pp. 91–92.

14. Bruce Bastin, "The Origins of a Blues Tradition in the Southeastern States" (Master's thesis, University of North Carolina at Chapel Hill, 1973).

15. Newman I. White, *American Negro Folk Songs* (Cambridge, Mass.: Harvard University Press, 1928), p. 311.

16. Ibid., p. 387.

17. Guy B. Johnson, conversation with the author, October 22, 1972.

18. Odum, "Folk-song": 255–94, 351–96.

19. Ibid.: 280.

20. Ibid.: 272.

21. See also Lawrence W. Levine, *Black Culture and Black Consciousness: Afro-American Folk Thought from Slavery to Freedom* (New York: Oxford University Press, 1977); John F. Szwed, "Afro-American Musical Adaptation," in *Afro-American Anthropology,* ed. Norman E. Whitten, Jr., and John F. Szwed (New York: Macmillan, 1970); and Paul Oliver, "'Twixt Midnight and Day: Binarism, Blues and Black Culture," in *Popular Music 2,* ed. Richard Middleton and David Horn (Cambridge: Cambridge University Press, 1982).

22. Ray B. Browne, "Some Notes on the Southern Holler," *Journal of American Folklore* 67 (1954): 73–77; "The Alabama 'Holler' and Street Cries," Ibid. 70 (1957): 363; Willis Laurence James, "The Romance of the Negro Folk Cry in America," *Phylon* 16 (1955), in *Mother Wit from the Laughing Barrel,* ed. Alan Dundees (Englewood Cliffs, N.J.: Prentice-Hall, 1973), pp. 430–44; Bruce Jackson, *Wake Up Dead Man: Afro-American Worksongs from Texas Prisons* (Cambridge, Mass.: Harvard University Press, 1972). See also Peter Bartis, "A Preliminary Classification System for Hollers in the United States" (Master's thesis, University of North Carolina at Chapel Hill, 1973).

23. Humphrey Lyttelton, *The Best of Jazz: Basin Street to Harlem* (London: Robson, 1978), p. 61.

24. David Evans, *Big Road Blues: Tradition and Creativity in the Folk Blues* (Berkeley: University of California Press, 1982).

25. Jeff Todd Titon, *Early Downhome Blues: A Musical and Cultural Analysis* (Urbana: University of Illinois Press, 1977).

2

The Emergence of the Blues

As the blues began to emerge, socio-historical events reinforced the trend: not only psycho-social change on a massive scale but an increasing availability of the instrument which was to become most closely associated with the new music—the guitar. Apart from mentioning the occasional use of a banjo or fiddle, few writers at the turn of the century ever went into detail about the instruments used in accompanying black secular music. Through much of the nineteenth century the banjo was identified with black music but white banjo tunings also suggested black influence. Urban minstrel-show performers had usually tuned their banjos in a manner which made it "necessary to finger chords by pressing the appropriate frets and leaving consonant strings open." The white Kentucky banjo player Buell Kazee told Gene Bluestein that "the idea of tuning a banjo is to get as many open strings as possible. . . . A major consequence of this approach is the necessity to retune the banjo in order to play in a different key. The minstrel players achieved this by changing the fingering, which is also the practice for most guitarists. But the traditional blues guitarists habitually use open tunings—especially in 'bottleneck styles.'"[1]

Doubtless, open-tuned banjos were also suitable for blues, and some banjo blues were recorded in the 1920s. The traditional fretless banjo enabled fingers to slide along the strings, and musicians often placed a strip of metal on the neck, under the strings, to enhance the tonal quality. The banjo styles were probably introduced into the Appalachians by blacks who, by the first decade of this century, largely gave up playing the banjo in favor of the guitar.[2]

Musically, the move to guitar caused few problems. John Cohen and Mike Seeger tell us that in white music "it was Maybelle Carter who introduced the idea that the guitar could pick melody as well. She did this by having the thumb pick out the tune on the lower strings while the index finger brushed up and down across the high strings, articulating both chords and rhythm. It is interesting to note that up to this time she had played banjo: she simply transferred some of its patterns to the guitar."[3] If Maybelle Carter found that banjo techniques adapted easily to guitar, blacks were also able to use these techniques with the new instrument. Direct evidence, however, is scanty. Race phonograph recordings came only in 1920 and the recording of country blues not before 1923. Papa Charlie Jackson, when playing guitar, used a style strongly reminiscent of the banjo, which he more usually played. The twelve-string guitar style of Charlie Lincoln and Barbecue Bob from Newton County, Georgia, is a possible interpolation of a banjo style, with little adaptation, directly onto the guitar.

In black tradition the shift from banjo to guitar may have been facilitated by experience with one-stringed instruments. Many blues guitarists recall that the first instrument they ever played was homemade, either the one-stringed "jitterbug" or a crude instrument more closely resembling a guitar, both somewhat primitive and restrictive in their use.[4] Lack of frets would cause greater use of slide technique, suggesting continuity between fretless banjo and "jitterbug," or slide, guitar.

Certain tunes became well known because of their easy adaptability to open chords, like "John Henry," still a widespread number to this day. Many bluesmen in the Piedmont recall this as the first song they ever learned. In many cases "John Henry" was the only tune which these inexperienced youngsters could play with any ease. Musicians also used bottlenecks when playing their homemade guitars, and bottleneck-slide style was more common in the Piedmont than recordings have suggested. Significantly, the sleevenote writers of a long-playing album of bottleneck guitar blues have written that "the use of the bottleneck seemed to be associated with certain pieces like 'John Henry'. . . . Nearly all blues bottleneck pieces were played in the two basic open chord tunings, 'Spanish' and 'Vastapol.' The former is merely an open chord G (D-G-D-G-B-D) or open A (E-A-E-A-C♯-E) chord tuned to concert pitch, or any other open chord tuning using the same intervals between the strings. "Vastapol" is an open D (D-A-D-F♯-A-

D) or E (E-B-E-A♭-B-E) chord at concert pitch, or any open chord with comparable intervals."⁵

Many early bluesmen recall that sliding a bottleneck or knife over the strings was one of the first techniques to be learned. Howard Odum's early collection also included a "knife-song" from a singer visiting Newton County, and Odum's description shows how the instrument took over the melodic line from the voice. Those lines italicized below were the ones "sung" by the guitar:

> 'Fo' long, honey, 'fo' long, honey.
> *Law-d, la-w-d, l-a-w-d!*
>
> 'Fo' long, honey, 'fo' long, honey,
> 'Fo' long, honey, 'fo' long, honey.
> *L-a-w-d, l-a-w-d, l-a-w-d.*

Two lines are sung in harmony with the running of the knife over the strings of the Negro's guitar; while the refrain "Lawd, lawd, lawd!" wherever found is sung to the "talking" of the knife. The other two lines are sung to the picking on the guitar, as in the ordinary case.⁶

Odum's comments on Georgia singers also reveal other facts about developments in black secular music that were leading toward blues. He documents not only a transitional phase when banjos, fiddles, and guitars were all in use but also the growth of a semiprofessional class of musicians: "With a prized 'box,' perhaps his only property, such a Negro may wander from town to town, from section to section, loafing in general, and working only when compelled to do so, gathering new songs and singing the old ones. Negroes of this type may be called professionals, since their life of wandering is facilitated by the practice of singing. Through their influence, songs are easily carried from place to place. There are other 'music physicians' whose fields of activity are only local. In almost every community such individuals may be found, and from them many songs may be obtained." He differentiates between what he terms "music physicians," "musicianers," and "songsters": "These terms may be synonymous, or they may denote persons of different habits. In general, 'songster' is used to denote any Negro who regularly sings or makes songs; 'musicianer' applies often to the individual who claims to be expert with the banjo or the fiddle; while 'music physicianer' is used to denote more nearly a person who is accustomed to travel from place to place, and who possesses a combination of these qualities."⁷ To be sure, Newton County possessed a number of persons who might well have fitted Odum's definition of "music physicianer" in the decade before 1910; Buddy Keith, Sun Foster, Jim Smith, and Nehemiah Smith were all musicians who would have fitted that description. Only the first two lived to be interviewed, and neither would ever call himself a bluesman; they are remembered in other capacities, as were the Smiths. Jim Smith was instrumental in teaching a number of younger bluesmen how to play "John Henry."

The parody of the Negro in minstrelsy could be tolerated by blacks at a time of lesser social change. As social distance grew to physical and psychological distance, intensified beyond all earlier belief after 1896, this stereotyping, once tolerable as crude but harmless humor, became directly offensive. The banjo, ubiquitous instrument of the minstrel stage, embodied this stereotyping, just as later, the watermelon and headscarf would take similar roles. In the Georgia Sea Islands the term "putting on the banjo" became synonymous with ridicule, as the banjo was used to accompany songs of ridicule or criticism directed against erring members of the community.[8] By the turn of the twentieth century, blacks were reacting against the use of the banjo to parody aspects of their lives which were becoming increasingly less tolerable.

The guitars these young musicians were coming to play were made available to them by conditions of which they were barely aware: the age of the railroad and postal and mail-order expansion. The self-sufficiency, isolation, and social conservatism of the rural dweller became challenged; he was now able to participate in an existence which had been possible only for a townsman. This was partly accidental, a consequence of improved transport and postal services, and partly a result of actions directed solely to invite his participation.

From 1860 to 1910 railroad construction averaged over 4,000 miles per year. By 1900 there were almost 200,000 miles; in the following decade figures jumped 25 percent. Expansion was rapid and haphazard, with little coordinated planning. In the South the construction boom in railroads took place from 1881 to 1890, yet at this date it could still be stated that southern railroads constituted "a system of trunks with branches yet to be built."[9] The Panic of 1893 enabled J. P. Morgan to take over control of most of the southern railroads, and within ten years the Eastern Seaboard was linked to the Northeast via the Atlantic Coast Line and to the Midwest via the Louisville and Nashville, which reached Atlanta in 1904, the same year in which the Seaboard completed the line to Birmingham. For the South the main period of railroad consolidation and integration within the national network was in the years from 1893 to 1904, by which time the final network patterns were firmly established.

As the railroads offered greater interstate mobility, increased postal facilities followed. In 1871 the number of post offices had reached 30,000, and by 1901 they had reached their highest-ever peak of 76,945. The system of rural free delivery, officially suggested in 1891, became a reality in 1896. In 1897 rural free delivery served eighty-three routes and 22,272 families; by 1907 it served 37,728 routes and 3,750,000 families.

Following the improved postal services Montgomery-Ward became, in 1872, the first large concern to sell a wide variety of goods exclusively by mail. The company initially used the railroads in a novel manner by sending out "barn-storming railroad cars for several years in the nineties to display the firm's goods. The 'act' included entertainment of a minstrel variety not radically unlike the 'snake-oil' salesmen of the time."[10] In 1895 a new mail-order concern entered the field and instantly dominated it, controlling the pattern for all future development. This was the Sears, Roebuck Company, which in four years had outstripped its oldest competitor and by 1907 had annual sales of merchandise higher than that of any other concern in the United States.

The mail-order houses soon became the largest individual users of the mail: "For many years during the early stages of the development of the mail-order business (the mail-order houses) were permitted to ship their catalogs and other advertising matter as second-class at the very low second-class mail rates."[11] The postal legislation of 1879, directly and indirectly, "made possible the very existence of the mail-order magazines and this in turn opened a potent advertising medium to Richard Sears." "RFD was also of incalculable value to the mail-order business. . . . (It) contributed to the mitigation of the loneliness . . . (and) physical isolation of the settlers. . . . Country life was often tedious, neighbors distant, and amusements limited." The advent of the parcel post in 1913, following heavily contested Congressional hearings from 1910 to 1912, brought by vested interests representing, among others, merchants, department stores, jobbers, and traveling salesmen, facilitated even greater opportunities for the mail-order houses. "Parcel post was perhaps even more beneficial to mail order than the inauguration of rural free delivery had been."[12]

The financial panic of 1893 had been followed by agricultural depression, but by 1900 agricultural prosperity had partially returned. The following decade appeared in retrospect by 1920 a sort of "golden age," during which prices of agricultural products doubled. "There were few well-established farmers who could not afford spring buggies, upholstered furniture, a telephone, and even a piano.''[13] If this were true, how much more likely that cheaper, more accessible musical instruments were also available. A study of Sears, Roebuck catalogs during these years shows precisely this.

As the "golden age" of agriculture offered greater rural prosperity, figures of the phenomenal rise in sales reflected the growth of Sears, Roebuck during this period. Income from sales in 1895 had been $745,000. By 1900 this had reached over $10,000,000, and within another four years this had increased to $37,879,422—a fifty-fold increase in ten years. By 1907 sales had topped the $50,000,000 mark. A minor recession in 1908 temporarily held up progress, but the period from 1908 to 1925 was one of further boom, assisted by the introduction of the parcel post in 1913, further amended in 1917, and the increase in farm income in the years from 1915 to 1919.

The success of Sears, Roebuck may be seen in the dynamic, extravagant advertising, replete with superlatives, and, above all, in the shrewd psychology of the friendly help and advice offered to semiliterate, suspicious, timid rural folk, who had never before had dealings of this nature. The imperative, "Send No Money," penetrated every household, forcing a reaction. Sears, Roebuck aimed at a friendly personal relationship, sending chatty letters and taking a customer-is-always-right attitude. Ordering was made easy for the rural semiliterate, for instead of a set of rules, there was the informal "use the order blank if you have one. If you haven't, use any plain paper. . . . Tell us in your own way what you want . . . don't be afraid that you have made a mistake. We receive hundreds of orders every day from young and old who never before sent away for goods. We are accustomed to handling all kinds of orders. Tell us what you want in your own way, written in any language, no matter whether good or poor writing, and the goods will be promptly sent to you."[14] Contrast the imperious orders of Montgomery-Ward: "Goods shipped by express C.O.D. can be examined at the express office in the presence of the agent. Please do not abuse this privilege by disarranging the goods or occupying too much of the agent's time . . . the express companies and their representatives dislike the trouble, annoyance and risk attending it and the privilege is extended to you on the condition it is not abused. . . ." Sears, Roebuck told people how to get money orders and overcame their suspicions by such statements as, "We refer you to the Union National Bank of Minneapolis, and you are at liberty, if you choose, to send your money to them with instructions not to turn it over to us unless they know us to be perfectly reliable." The rural nature of many of the buyers was perceptively noticed and catered to by such advice as, "If you live on a rural mail route, just give the letter and the money to the mail carrier and he will get the money order at the post office and mail it in the letter for you."[15]

However, the general continued growth of Sears, Roebuck is not reflected in its sales of musical instruments, as shown by the pages of advertisements in the catalogs. The first catalog, of thirty-two pages, appeared in 1891, but musical instruments were not included until 1893, by which time the catalog had grown to 197 pages. Later that year the 1894 catalog was issued, in which instruments spread over twenty-eight pages. In subsequent years the advertising space devoted to musical instruments suggests a peak in the sale of musical instruments in 1905 or slightly earlier. The number of catalog pages devoted to musical instruments rose from twenty-eight in 1897 to sixty by 1905 but then declined. By 1915 there were fewer than in 1897 (twenty-five) and in 1925 there were twelve. By 1935 there were only eight.[16] The 1908 catalog offers thirty-one pages, consistent with the trend—a rapid decline after 1905, possibly due to the advent of the phonograph and, later, the radio.

The space given over to the sale of guitars also reflects a buildup to a peak at the same time, and again the rapid decline. "By the end of the nineteenth century, guitars were being sold through mail order houses, and larger guitar and mandolin orchestras were common."[17] Guitars may have been offered in the 1893 catalog and seem likely to have been advertised in the 1894, in view of the 22½ pages given over to musical instruments other than organs and pianos. The 1895 catalog proclaimed that "the following departments are now complete in every respect," among which they included "musical instruments," so presumably guitars were offered there. Certainly by 1897 there was a page devoted to guitars, offering a year's guarantee (later extended to a month's free trial), with prices from $3.25 to $27.00 for a Washburn. "Over a thousand samples of guitar" were offered. By 1905 there were six pages announcing guitars, including a full-page advertisement of the $2.95 model and a whole range from $4.95 to $21.00. "Sears, conscious of the great number of actual or potential guitarists in the land, laid the benison of music smack down on the bargain counter."[18] It has been claimed that "in 1905, the United States reeked with bucolic and small-town guitarists."[19] By 1908 there was one page of guitar advertisements, with illustrated models varying from $1.89 to $3.95, though the emphasis now was most strongly on mandolins and banjos. As late as 1925 there was still a single page of guitar advertisements.

Not only was the major mail-order house selling guitars at this time but it is quite possible that country and small-town stores also stocked them, having given orders either to "drummers" or traveling salesmen.

"The period from 1870 to 1900 was the great age for the drummers."[20] That country stores in some regions held musical instruments in stock is proven in an account of 1876 of an "Omnibus store," "especially characteristic of the newly settled country district of the West, yet also to be found easily within forty miles of Philadelphia itself." It describes itself as a "jewelry store, with the adjuncts of clocks, watches, violins and jews harps."[21] When guitars became popular, these too probably took their place in the country store.

Thus a number of factors coincided to make the first decade of this century the peak for the sale of guitars. By 1904 the more efficient and complete railroad system enabled the postal service, reaching its peak by 1901, to reach hitherto outlying places. Both assisted the rapidly expanding mail-order houses such as Sears, Roebuck. The sales of guitars, commencing in the 1890s, had reached their peak by 1905, in the middle of the brief period of economic prosperity for southern farmers. Thus it seems valid to deduce that a very large number of guitars were made available to a southern market during the early years of the twentieth century.

It seems unlikely that much of this market was black. What is more likely is that many of the sales failed to give enjoyment that would "last a lifetime," as the advertisement had promised. The initial delight of having the instrument, even with the month's free approval, probably soon wore off when it proved less easy to play than had been expected. No doubt in rural areas, instruments found their way into black hands, maybe more skilled and probably very eager to learn.

Until the late 1910s the main source of consumer credit was the pawnshops, which probably reached their maximum growth in 1914, slowly losing ground as newer forms of consumer credit emerged. Urban blacks could probably obtain guitars in good condition for a reasonable sum from the pawnshops. This source of supply would also have been open to rural blacks, who came into local urban centers on seasonal occasions, such as during the cotton or tobacco sales, when they would also have more money than at other times of the year. Certainly pawnshops have always offered a source for bluesmen, both to raise money and to obtain another instrument.

Not until the late 1890s and the first decade of the twentieth century was the guitar made available in quantity and at a low enough price to be sold extensively in the South and ultimately to become the instrument of blacks for blues accompaniment. This is the same period when the first blues texts were appearing in printed collections and when, according to the recollections of black songsters, they were obtaining their first guitars and learning their first blues. But the emergence of the blues in these years was also due to psychological and historical factors.

In the southeastern states, psycho-social responses to changing race relations commenced in the 1890s and were set by the middle of the first decade of the twentieth century. The blues emerged from these violent socio-cultural changes: at the turn of the century a cultural change in the life-style of the lowest class of blacks found expression in a new musical tradition. Various goals which in 1865 had seemed within the grasp of all blacks were more remote by the 1890s. Blacks found that the white man's world was not attainable in the South. The general trend of the separation of the races, which occurred after Reconstruction, became intensified, taking on a new aspect following the revived political role of the Negro in the mid-1890s. The extent to which this role was real or imagined was of less significance than the reaction it caused among southern whites. By the turn of the twentieth century, relations between the races had deteriorated to such an extent that the doctrine of white supremacy was everywhere the overriding force in southern politics. "The South, with Northern acquiescence, found and established the Negro's 'place.' "[22]

"The Negro's place, then, was humble, static and in the South. It was also on the farm."[23] Although black papers constantly emphasized black ownership, the truth was that this was the exception rather than the rule in the rural South. By the 1890s black labor was no longer as free to leave the land as it had been earlier. State laws in force from Virginia to Texas virtually operated to prevent black farmhands from leaving the land. In 1900, 75.3 percent of all black farmers were tenants or sharecroppers in the South, and as late as 1910, 78.8 percent of all blacks in the South lived in rural areas, the majority in the Cotton Belt. Once tied to the land, black farm laborers were actually dependent upon their white neighbors. Writing of events rather later in the Georgia "black belt" country, a one-time black sharecropper wrote that "like other Negro sharecroppers, we were always moving, always in hope of finding a landlord who would not take advantage of us. But we hardly ever succeeded in bettering our position."[24]

By the turn of the century, the vast majority of rural blacks were at an economic disadvantage and usually had little opportunity to better themselves. Although urban centers and industry were becoming more attractive to blacks, as John Hope Franklin pointed out, "There was a sentiment against hiring Negroes in jobs that had even the semblance of respectability. Negroes living in the cities in the South discovered that urban life could be almost as frustrating as rural life."[25]

If blacks found little assistance from industrial unions, they seemed to have been given more hope by the Farmer's Alliance. The Colored Alliance claimed a million members by 1890 and in its own right held more power than any other black organization. Southern Populists were well aware of the significance of the black vote and so, too, were blacks. The *Cleveland Gazette,* as early as 1894, had stated that "the time has come when the colored man must use to his advantage that agency, his vote, which makes him the pivot upon which turns the success or defeat of any one of the great political parties."[26] This very position as "pivot," in the election of 1892, brought both defeat for the Populist party and the realization of the fears of many southern whites of the imagined dangers of black political power. The final outcome was that the Populist party collapsed following the election of 1896, and blacks vanished from politics as a result of the tide of white supremacy and consequent disenfranchisement which came in the wake of this violent political upheaval.

With the defeat of Populism, and largely responsible for it, came the greater menace of white supremacy. "Southern racism came in on the mounting tide of national sentiment,"[27] but this adoption of extreme racism was due less to conversion to the concept of white democracy than to a relaxation of controls which had been maintained by both southern liberalism and conservatism, assisted by northern liberalism. Coming at the very time when the races were drawing further apart than at any time since the 1830s, this relaxation of controls offered a license to racism which would have been unacceptable earlier. Analyzing the origins of the 1906 Atlanta race riot, Charles Crowe observed that "the period from 1880 to 1892, which saw the most rapid advances of Negroes in the acquisition of liberty and property, was followed by an era of disfranchisement, Jim Crow laws, attacks on Negro property and education, and pervasive violence."[28] Thus the lessening of older restraints allowed the "permission-to-hate" attitude of white supremacy to emerge; it was the only formula strong enough to reconcile the estranged white classes and reunite the "solid" South.[29]

If white supremacy was not new, the extreme nature of the new "philosophy" of racism was. Racial extremism in words soon became racial extremism in deeds, and one of the more marked aspects of white supremacy was lynching. Figures for persons lynched can be used as a barometer for social tension. Between 1880 and 1886 more whites than blacks were lynched. After 1889 there was a marked increase in blacks lynched, reaching a peak in 1893. Until 1904 more blacks were lynched yearly than in any year prior to 1885. As George Brown Tindall remarked in his study of the Negro in South Carolina, "Lynching became . . . a factor in the establishment of a white terror that transformed the fluid situation created by the Reconstruction back into a rigid caste system of white supremacy.''[30]

As white supremacy gathered momentum, it brought in its wake further political and social restrictions for blacks. Disfranchisement both paralleled and preceded Jim Crow legislation. In the decade after 1895 they together wrought a fundamental change in the role of blacks in southern life. In 1890 Mississippi was the only state to disfranchise blacks before the Populist revolt. Elsewhere, disfranchisement was delayed, not because of any strong belief in black rights but for sound political reasons. White supremacy was not unacceptable to the older conservatives, but there was some concern as to which whites should be supreme. Disagreement over disfranchisement was often less concerned with whether to disfranchise blacks than with how to achieve it most effectively. In 1906 out of over 5,500 participants in legislatures in all higher and lower houses of the forty-five states, only five were black, and only one was from the South—Georgia. By 1910 white supremacy could rest easier than in 1890, for every former Confederate state had ''legally'' disfranchised the Negro.

Jim Crow legislation in public accommodation spread throughout the two decades following the Supreme Court's decision in 1890 to uphold the Mississippi statute of March 2, 1888, requiring segregated accommodations on railroads. Nevertheless, many of these legislative acts merely legalized circumstances which already existed by 1898. In 1896 the Supreme Court's decision in the case of *Plessy vs. Ferguson* that legislation is powerless to eradicate racial instincts offered positive assistance to those white supremacy elements who wanted to extend the growing racial distance. The changing pattern of race relations showed similar and largely parallel developments in social history within the southeastern states.

In his study of race relations in Georgia from 1872 to 1908, Horace C. Wingo concluded that ''until the 'nineties, rules governing such relations were inconsistent and flexible. The results were milder and friendlier relations than existed afterwards. But, state segregation statutes and extra-legal provisions appeared in the 'nineties to rigidly separate the races in practically all areas of social contact. The resulting society of apartheid was considered the final solution of the race problem.''[31] The Atlanta Riot brought southern whites to the realization of the extremity of their views, and by 1907 the majority of racists had become conservatives and former conservatives had returned to the ranks. The violence of the preceding years cooled and a new set of race relations existed, clearly demarcated and accepted by all.

Class became an important factor in black life. In discussing blacks in Philadelphia, W. E. B. Du Bois described four classes of Negroes, including

Grade 3. The poor; persons not earning enough to keep them at all times above want; honest, although not always energetic or thrifty.
Grade 4. The lowest class of criminals, prostitutes and loafers; the "submerged tenth."[32]

A white viewpoint reduced the number of classes, suggesting that "the Negro race of the South may be said to be divided into three classes— the intelligent leaders, the large middle or laboring class, and the criminal class."[33] In any consideration of race relations it will be necessary to keep in mind that lower-class black attitudes and com- ments are seldom reflected in history and that their reactions to current events, both political and economic, and their hopes have not always been those attributed to blacks in general.

If the black intellectual was frustrated in his hopes, the lower-class blacks were no less so. Indeed, their frustrations frequently had no outlet except the church, which was often inadequate to relieve the repression that some blacks felt. Moreover, for some rural blacks, but perhaps even more for the young blacks who were forced to move in order to attempt to find work, the church was no answer.

It was not easy for a black to leave the South, in which the new "place" being found for him was narrow and circumscribed. Apart from economic and legal restrictions, he had a very real attachment to the area in which he had been raised. His birthplace, with its kinship and "clan" ties, was often the only stable element in his life. Thus he found himself paradoxically bound to an existence in which he had little hope and which had become tense with frustration and fear. As the 1906 Atlanta Riot showed, it was not necessary for him to do anything except be present. That individuals—and, so far as it existed, the collective body of lower-class blacks—underwent a psychological crisis was entirely in keeping with the climate of opinion in those years. Whereas Gunnar Myrdal had believed that "after the national com- promise of the 1870s, the Negro problem dropped out as a national issue," it was really only by the turn of the twentieth century that the competitive aspect of race relations had replaced the paternalistic. "For Negroes the new order was startling, even shocking."[34]

Considering the emergence of crisis cults, Weston LaBarre observed that "only a person can be in conflict within himself over alternative cultural beliefs and behaviours."[35] Nonetheless, Alan Lomax is correct in stressing that "behavioral norms crucial to a culture are then set forth and reinforced in such terms that the whole community can accept them and join in their restatement. Singing and dancing share a major part of the symbolic activity."[36]

Describing the significance of blues to both the singer and his audience, bluesman Henry Townsend explained that

> there's blues that connects you with public life—I mean you can tell it to the public as a song, *in* a song. . . . They don't always think seriously that it's exactly *you* that you talkin' about. . . . You express yourself in a song like that. Now this particular thing reach others because they have experienced the same condition in life so naturally they feel what you are saying because it happened to them. . . . people in general they takes the song as an explanation for *themselves*—they believe this song is expressing *their* feelings instead of the one that singin' it. They feel that maybe I have just hit upon somethin' that's in their lives, and yet at the same time it was some of the things that went wrong with me too.[37]

What these new blues songs symbolized for lower-class blacks has been studied in detail. In *Blues Fell This Morning* Paul Oliver has analyzed the meaning of blues in the bluesman's attitude toward his life, his work, his hardships, and his relationships with women. In *Screening the Blues* he explained the subsurface meanings of many lyrics in more detail. In *Conversation with the Blues* he allowed the singers to express their own feelings about the meaning of blues and the personal significance of blues to them.[38] Samuel Charters described the poetic qualities of blues and something of their deeper, emotional significance in *Poetry of the Blues.*[39] Working with different types of blues singers and in different environments, both Charles Keil and William Ferris closely documented the ways in which bluesmen approached the making and singing of songs.[40] The fact that those studied by Keil were urban bluesmen with a large, commercial audience, while those studied by Ferris were rural, Delta bluesmen playing for friends, in no way invalidated the fact that they were responding in a similar manner to certain psychological stresses—or, at least, were enabling their audiences to experience tension release.

In every way these studies underpin the significance of underlying, partly subconscious reactions to tensions and pressures, loves and fears, hope and despair. Speaking for himself the bluesman also echoes the feelings and frustrations of his friends and others in his community, who may be less able to express their emotions but who respond to, and identify themselves with, his songs. The blues are a means of escape, however temporary, from problems to which there is no immediate answer. Richard Wright, commenting on blues with a perception rare among black intellectuals, rhetorically enquired,

"Could this emotional stance have been derived from a protracted inability to act, or a fear of acting?"[41] Blues was the one means of expression which served both personal and communal functions in providing focus, stability, and cohesion. As such it served the community as a "psychosocial function," much as folklorists see riddling.[42]

NOTES

1. Gene Bluestein, *The Voice of the Folk* (Boston: University of Massachusetts Press, 1972), p. 156.

2. Cecelia Conway and Tommy Thompson, "Talking Banjo," *Southern Exposure* 2 (Spring-Summer, 1974): 63–66. See also Cecelia Conway, "The Afro-American Traditions of the Folk Banjo" (Ph.D. diss., University of North Carolina, 1980).

3. John Cohen and Mike Seeger, *The New Lost City Ramblers Song Book* (New York: Oak Publications, 1964), p. 16.

4. David Evans, "Afro-American One-Stringed Instruments," *Western Folklore* 29 (October, 1970): 229–45.

5. Stephen Calt, Nick Perls, and Michael Stewart, liner notes to *Bottleneck Blues: Guitar Classics 1926–1927* , Yazoo L–1026 (New York, n.d.).

6. Howard W. Odum, "Folk-song and Folk-poetry as Found in the Secular Songs of the Southern Negro," *Journal of American Folklore* 24 (October-December, 1911): 363.

7. Ibid.: 259.

8. Georgia Writers' Project, Savannah Unit, Works Project Administration, *Drums and Shadows: Survival Studies among the Georgia Coastal Negroes* (Athens: University of Georgia Press, 1940), p. 154.

9. C. Vann Woodward, *Origins of the New South 1877–1913* (Baton Rouge: Louisiana State University Press, 1971), p. 122.

10. Boris Emmet and John E. Jenck, *Catalogs and Counters: A History of Sears Roebuck and Company* (Chicago: University of Chicago Press, 1950), p. 21. The 1897 Almanac contains pictures and descriptions of the train.

11. Paul H. Nystrom, *The Economics of Retailing,* vol. 1, rev. 3rd ed. (New York: The Ronald Press, 1930), pp. 194–95.

12. Emmet and Jenck, *Catalogs and Counters,* pp. 14, 190.

13. Harold U. Faulkner, *The Quest for Social Justice 1898–1914* (New York: Macmillan, 1931), pp. 3–4.

14. Louis E. Asher and Edith Heal, *Send No Money* (Chicago: Argus Books, 1942), pp. 5–6.

15. Ibid., pp. 3, 8, 6.

16. David L. Cohen, *The Good Old Days: A History of American Morals and Manners as Seen through Sears Roebuck Catalogs 1905 to the Present* (New York: Simon & Schuster, 1940), p.43; *1897 Sears Roebuck Catalog,* ed. Fred L. Israel (New York: Chelsea House Publishers, 1968); 1908 Sears, Roebuck catalog.

17. Cohen and Seeger, *Song Book,* p. 16.

18. D. Cohen, *The Good Old Days,* p. 43.

19. Ibid., p. 18.

20. Gerald Carson, *The Old Country Store* (Chicago: William Benton, 1969), p. 490.

21. Ibid., p. 192.

22. I. A. Newby, *Jim Crow's Defence: Anti-Negro Thought in America, 1900-1950* (Baton Rouge: Louisiana State University Press, 1965), p. x.

23. Ibid., p. 120.

24. Hosea Hudson, *Black Worker in the Deep South: A Personal Record* (New York: International Publishers, 1972), p. 13.

25. John Hope Franklin, *From Slavery to Freedom* (New York: Alfred A. Knopf, 1967), p. 400.

26. Cleveland *Gazette,* March 8, 1984, in *The Black Press 1829-1890: The Quest for National Identity,* ed. Martin E. Dann (New York: G. P. Putnam's Sons, 1971), p. 171.

27. C. Vann Woodward, *The Strange Career of Jim Crow,* rev. 2nd ed. (New York: Oxford University Press, 1966), p. 74.

28. Charles Crowe, "Racial Violence and Social Reforms: Origins of the Atlanta Race Riot," *Journal of Negro History* 52 (1968): 254.

29. Woodward, *Jim Crow,* p. 81.

30. George Brown Tindall, *South Carolina Negroes 1877-1900* (Baton Rouge: Louisiana State University Press, 1966), p. 239.

31. Horace C. Wingo, "Race Relations in Georgia, 1872-1908" (Ph. D. diss., University of Georgia, 1969). Abstract.

32. W. E. B. Du Bois, *The Philadelphia Negro* (Philadelphia: University of Pennsylvania Press, 1899), pp. 310-11.

33. B. F. Riley, *The White Man's Burden: A Discussion of the Interracial Question with Special Reference to the Responsibility of the White Race to the Negro Problem* (Birmingham, Ala.: By the author, 1910), p. 53.

34. Gunnar Myrdal, *An American Dilemma,* quoted by Bruce Jackson in *The Negro and His Folklore in Nineteenth Century Periodicals,* ed. Bruce Jackson (Austin: University of Texas Press, 1967), p. xxii; C. Vann Woodward, *American Counterpoint: The Strange Career of a Historical Controversy* (Boston: Little, Brown, 1971), p. 257.

35. Weston LaBarre, *Ghost Dance* (New York: Dell, Delta Books, 1970), p. 279.

36. Alan Lomax, *Fold Song Style and Culture* (Washington, D.C.: American Association for the Advancement of Science, 1968), p. 15.

37. Paul Oliver, *Conversation with the Blues* (New York: Horizon, 1965), pp. 164-65.

38. Paul Oliver, *Blues Fell This Morning: The Meaning of the Blues* (New York: Horizon Press, 1961), *Screening the Blues: Aspects of the Blues Tradition* (London: Cassel, 1968), and *Conversation with the Blues..*

39. Samuel Barclay Charters, *The Poetry of the Blues* (New York: Oak Publications, 1963).

40. Charles Keil, *Urban Blues* (Chicago: University of Chicago Press, 1966); William Ferris, Jr., *Blues from the Delta* (New York: Anchor Press/Doubleday, 1978).

41. Oliver, *Blues Fell this Morning,* p. ix.

42. Pierre Maranda and Elli Köngäs Maranda, *Structural Analysis of Oral Tradition* (Philadelphia: University of Pennsylvania Press, 1971).

3

The Geographical Base

The music under study naturally does not stop exactly at political boundaries, but in general it is found in the Atlantic coast states of the Southeast and has been most studied in the Piedmont belt between the mountain foothills and the coastal plain. The focal nature of the Piedmont belt is perhaps best exemplified in North Carolina, where its geographical significance had been appreciated before World War I: "Piedmont belts tend strongly towards urban development even when rural settlement is sparse. Sparsity of population and paucity of towns within the mountains cause main lines of traffic to keep outside the highlands but close enough to their base to tap trade at every valley outlet. . . . Hence they often receive their stamp from the mountains behind them as well as from the bordering plain."[1]

Given the added impetus of industrialization and the singular growth of the tobacco industry within North Carolina, these towns expanded rapidly. By 1921 the University of North Carolina *News Letter* carried a leader on "urban Carolina in 1920" which shrewdly analyzed "push-and-pull forces," observing that "our country people were lonely before but they were not acutely aware of it until rural free deliveries, automobiles, and country telephones aroused them out of social apathy." The article pointed out that 28.6 percent of the people in the state were urban dwellers; Piedmont towns like Gastonia, Rocky Mount, Winston-Salem, and Durham had experienced population growths of over 1,000 percent in the previous forty years.[2] Between 1920 and 1930 the urban population grew by 62.5 percent whereas that of rural areas by only 14.1 percent, and the Piedmont region grew by a higher rate than its flanking regions. In that decade the towns gained in excess of 300,000 people, although many in the twenty-to-twenty-nine age group left the state rather than simply drifting into towns. North Carolina was the only state in the Southeast during that decade not to register a decline in its farm population; Virginia, South Carolina, and Georgia all lost black population—both urban and rural—in that period. During the two decades to 1930 the bulk of the migrants were aged fifteen to twenty-five, and of these more were female than male, and more black than white.[3] It was no coincidence that in 1928 the R. J. Reynolds Company—one of those into which J. B. Duke's American Tobacco Company was broken in 1911 by the Supreme Court—probably made a larger profit (in excess of $30 million) than did *all* the farmers in the state.[4]

Of course the *News Letter* was white-oriented. More relevant factors than rural isolation determined the movement of black migrants to urban centers. The economic depression of the 1930s severly reduced employment opportunities, but public assistance made it easier for blacks to obtain relief. A study of black migration in and from North Carolina indicated that "North Carolina might be a clearing house for the eventual movement of Negroes to the Northeast urban centers." In the 1920s North Carolina blacks migrated to New York, Pennsylvania, and New Jersey in order of preference; by the 1930s New York still led.[5]

One of the major record producers of the post-World War II period, Jerry Wexler of Atlantic, was well aware of the migration patterns which dictated movement north for southern blacks. As he said, "From the Carolinas, Florida and Georgia, they came up to New York, giving us a mix of gospel and pop."[6] Following a route well trodden by earlier bluesmen, many key artists of the rhythm and blues scene of the 1950s were part of this movement. Wilbert Harrison and Maurice Williams of the Zodiacs were both from Charlotte. The seminal figure, Clyde McPhatter of the Dominoes and the Drifters, was born in Durham and moved to New Jersey at the age of fifteen.

Oddly, few black artists ever made commercial recordings in North Carolina during the period of the manufacture of 78 r.p.m. discs. At Okeh's sessions at the George Vanderbilt Hotel in Asheville in August-September 1925, attended by talent scouts Ralph Peer and Polk Brockman among others, only white artists were recorded. The local Asheville *Citizen* proudly and prematurely proclaimed the sessions to be "the first time phonograph records have ever been made in the Carolinas. It is customary to have the artist come to New York and the records are made there. However, the company has found the atmosphere of Asheville to be the best in the country for the reproduction of the human voice and the instrument music as well in the summer season and it is expected that the present tests being made will be so satisfactory that the company will make the majority of its southern records in this city."[7] Perhaps this was simply the writing of an overenthusiastic cub reporter; Okeh returned only once again to North Carolina—to Winston-Salem in 1927—but no black artists were recorded. Victor and Decca chose to record a few black artists in Charlotte (see chapter 11), but there the recorded story ends. Fortunately we have detailed knowledge about many North Carolina bluesmen as well as studies in depth for which there are few parallels elsewhere in the Southeast.

The shifts in population and their attendant lifestyles, seen in the growth of Atlanta and the depletion of smaller communities within easy migration distance, were simply part of the broader pattern of experience within the Piedmont belt. After the first decade of this century the cotton factories relocated in the Southeast, closer to their sources of supply, mainly along the Fall-line towns from Richmond, Virginia, through Raleigh to Columbia, South Carolina, and Augusta, Georgia, where the Piedmont belt is separated from the geologically more recent coastal plain. A commercial survey of the Southeast undertaken for the federal government by the Department of Commerce in 1927 stated that the "chief urban development in South Carolina has been in the upper piedmont region, the most important being the textile centers of Anderson, Greenville, Spartanburg and Greenwood . . . and all of them rapidly growing towns. . . . While taking on an industrial character, most of these towns are still fundamentally agricultural centers, serving a rural population largely engaged in cotton production."[8]

As a cotton-producing state only Georgia outstripped it in production among the southeastern states. South Carolina produced almost twice as many cotton bales as North Carolina, and only Georgia had more black-owned farms in the first quarter of this century, although more than half South Carolina's farms were black owned. Although blacks remained in the majority in the state in 1920, their percentage of the total state population had dropped following the great migration north from 1916 to 1918 and a continuous, though fluctuating, shift north persisted. Even the city of Charleston reflected this migration pattern, although its port facilities enabled migrants to travel by sea rather than overland. A black overall majority in the city in 1910 had become a white majority by 1920 with a population increase among blacks of only 4 percent as opposed to almost 30 percent among whites. Perhaps the 1919 race riot exacerbated this disparity.[9]

This urban drift became a flood during the 1920s. The agricultural depression of that decade hit South Carolina as hard as other states, but the boll-weevil had a devastating effect on its one-crop cotton economy, as it was unable to diversify into tobacco farming unlike Virginia and North Carolina. South Carolina experienced a marked decrease in cotton production from 1,365,000 bales in 1910–20 to 810,000 the following decade, while the price index for farmers, registered as 100 in the five years to July 1914, stood on average at 94 for the 1930s. Thus the depression of the basic economic activity enhanced the industrial aspect of the new South, with growth in centers on existing sources of supply, power, and transport facilities. As late as 1925 only 10,000 miles of South Carolina's 64,000 miles of roads were surfaced, and the new industrial towns sprang up along the Piedmont line with Greenville and Spartanburg the most important. Small wonder that tenant and sharecropper families, faced with insurmountable problems in rural areas, left the land in droves for the potential of the new towns. There the streets might not be paved with gold but conditions could scarcely be worse, and many were convinced that a new life could be forged there. Thus, land won so hard from nature was often surrendered after poor management to soil erosion and kudzu.

Georgia, at the southern axis of the Piedmont, comprises a wide range of differing geographical sub-regions, from the highly distinctive coastal belt of the Geechie region, through an extensive coastal plain which merges into the Gulf Coast plain of Alabama and West Florida in the southwest and into the low-lying swamplands of Florida to the immediate south, into the black earth of Alabama's cotton belt in the west, and northwest into the rolling hills of the Appalachian foothills. Central in the northwestern part of the state is the major route and industrial center of Atlanta, exercising a powerful human pull for the whole of the twentieth century. The city's population doubled between 1910 and 1940. Post-World War II industrialization, which has so greatly affected the Piedmont towns, has simply further enhanced Atlanta's significance and made it, like Houston in the Southwest, the gravitational center of the Southeast, far outreaching its immediate hinterland.

Florida, physically, is the southern extension of the Atlantic coastal plain, with geological links with the flat coastal regions of Georgia and the Carolinas southeast of the Fall line. Apart from the very northern counties, more akin to south Georgia, the rolling and irregular plains of the Piedmont are absent, and the soils and climate encourage an entirely different farming economy from that of the other southeastern states. Outside these northern counties, neither cotton nor tobacco dominates and rural blacks were far fewer in number than in the other states. During the period of significant rural depopulation in the early 1920s, black Florida farmers were fewer than one-tenth of those in Georgia, while the ravages of the boll weevil elsewhere had little impact on the state outside the very north. Migration to northern cities like New York was less from Florida than from the states to the north. In the forty years between 1890 and 1930 Florida shifted from a sparsely populated, almost entirely rural-dwelling state to one with three times the population, the bulk of whom lived in urban centers; Jacksonville, Miami, and Tampa had populations in excess of 100,000. The black population in 1930, constituting rather less than 30 percent of the total, was nonetheless greater than the entire population of the state in 1880.

The northern limits of the indigenous region of southeastern blues, as opposed to those centers of significance which emerged with the migration routes to New York, are understandably ill-defined. Clearly the music merges with that of neighboring regions, like the deep South, and any attempt at a purely physical limitation in relation to state lines is bound to be arbitrary. Still, a case can be made for limiting the region physically roughly along the Georgia-Alabama border, swinging to the northeast to take in the very eastern section of Tennessee. The border regions are bound to be fluid and the likes of Bill Williams of Greenup, Kentucky—although born in Virginia—and Brownie McGhee from Knoxville provide some western limits to the region. The northern limits are less distinct, but some idea can be deduced by consideration of some of the more northerly "cells" of musicians which collectively offer a definition of the northern limit. West Virginia, by and large well outside the musical confines of the southeastern blues region, has one section which clearly fits within it—the southern counties. At the end of the nineteenth century this area experienced a most significant influx of black labor which continued until the Depression. At the close of the Civil War few blacks lived in the southern counties of West Virginia; the 1870 census listed 5,540. None lived in McDowell County although by 1900 it possessed the largest and most progressive black community in the state.

In the 1870s and 1880s major railroads began traversing these
southern counties linking North Carolina and Virginia with Cincinnati.
Industry came to West Virginia and the Norfolk & Western Railroad
served as an agent for hiring blacks for work in mining and railroad
jobs and provided means for transportation there. Black labor boarded
trains in Winston-Salem, Durham, Norfolk, and Lynchburg for work
in Bluefield and Welch. By 1890 almost 19,000 blacks were resident.
That figure was to rise to over 46,000 by 1910 and almost double again
by 1930 to more than 88,000. The decline of the coal industry in the
1950s and early 1960s saw a reversal of the population shift and today
few black strongholds remain, markedly in McDowell County.[10] Thus
rather more than half the black population of southern West Virginia
moved in just at the time when the new blues music was becoming
popular, and it clearly accompanied these new immigrants. One, born
in Durham County, North Carolina, in 1896, remembered her arrival:

> They wanted people to come to West Virginia to work in the coal mines.
> They went all over hiring people; to Durham, Raleigh, Apex, New Hill—
> everywhere down in North Carolina. So my brother come up here to West
> Virginia. My mother became blind, and after awhile we moved up here
> to . . . live with my brother. . . . That first day, Momma asked for her
> harp. She said, "Children, where is my music?" We had it packed up still.
> Well, we had one of those phonographs that had a big old horn and a
> dog sitting in front of it. So she said, "Play some records then." But it
> was packed up too. She said, "Well, I don't know what I'm going to do.
> Y'all get around and let's sing." So we sang.[11]

Given such blurred parameters we can equate the vast fabric of blues
in the southeastern states with a mural, virtually none of which is visible
any more. Much of it has been completely destroyed with no hope
now of restoration; part has been completely covered with little chance
of determining with any accuracy what, if anything, remains of the
original. However, in just a few places, careful removal of the surface
layers reveals vivid glimpses of the original, sufficient for us to appreciate not only the quality of the original but also the vastness of the
area that it encompassed.

The close relationship between social stratification and musical form
will be taken up in greater detail later; now we can simply note that
whereas blues—country blues rather than the later rhythm-and-blues—
is the music of the lowest black socioeconomic order, jazz is the music
of the aspirant lower-middle class. More specifically, and moving
slightly across social boundaries, the obvious difference is in formal
music training. I know of no East Coast bluesman with the ability to

read music—perhaps the major factor in determining whether an artist ought to be considered a folk artist, in the grassroots sense. Certain aspects of rural black entertainment smudge these social boundaries. In the early days of the development of blues, the relationships between rural blues musicians and the more formal stage and show presentation of urban clubs, touring shows, carnivals, and especially jazz bands were slight. Although the smaller shows employed bluesmen, the links between rural bluesmen and jazz bands in general are far more remote than is usually acknowledged. In the entire field of commercially recorded jazz and blues before World War II, those country bluesmen who were able to blend with jazzmen or jazz bands are remarkably few. Lonnie Johnson—if he so qualifies—and Big Bill Broonzy come to mind, as does Blind Blake, but the latter's band recordings were remarkably down-home. Joe and Charlie McCoy easily bridged into the emergent rhythm-and-blues bands like the Harlem Hamfats, but these groups were as far divorced from the sophistication and discipline of the bands of Duke Ellington and Count Basie as they were from the McCoys' Mississippi blues friends like Tommy Johnson and Ishman Bracey.

The range of musical entertainment available to black southern audiences was greater than is generally appreciated. The division between rural and urban was never quite as simple as earlier critics maintained. In his classic analysis of folk culture, George M. Foster appreciated that folk society was not an isolate, but was part of a larger social unit, clearly an integral part of some cities.[12] This remains true of largely pre-industrial cities, but the industrial cities to which rural blacks flocked in the first third of this century were still much the same as the regions from which they had come. There was clearly a symbiotic relationship between the touring shows and their performers and the down-home audiences who were lucky enough to see them. Marshall and Jean Stearns' book on vernacular dance is a fine introduction to these shows, and some attempt has been made to study their influence upon the development of a blues tradition in the Southeast.[13] In oral histories jazzmen frequently refer to small touring shows which influenced their early development and in which they often later took part as they shaped their own careers. Lawrence Lucie, guitarist with Louis Armstrong among many fine bandleaders, left Emporia, Virginia, in 1927 for New York but remembered many years later that "the only professional musicians . . . we got to see were with the travelling carnivals and medicine shows. Those shows always had a guitarist with them, and I guess that was an early influence on me wanting to take up the instruments."[14]

Thus in a variety of manners influences of black secular music from these more formal shows fed back into those black audiences, who found blues to be their staple musical diet. Certainly the influences were far greater than any possibly hinted at by the formal "Negro folk songs," vehicles for the sophisticated black composers and orchestrated for choirs, for the consumption of both whites and black upper-middle classes.

Before studying the influences on the geographical distribution of bluesmen, it might be as well to preface these remarks with a few caveats about deductive reasoning from scattered sources. Studying the use of race and hillbilly recordings as sources for historical research, Otto and Burns conclude that "Afro-American attitudes toward the color differences may not have been as simplistic as the contemporary literature indicates."[15] Also, many contemporary sources await chance discovery. The following, from unlikely sources, show evidence of jug bands in the Southeast from a very early date, while no subsequent evidence has ever come down to us. Had these articles not been located, a rash writer might have been tempted to make invalid assumptions on the apparent absence of such music.

One of the popular, informative magazines of 1902, *Wide World Magazine,* carried an article on barbecues, with a photograph of "A Barbecue Orchestra At Work." It was a four-piece black band, the musicians dressed in suits and ties, comprising fiddle, two guitars—which appear to be six-stringed Stellas—and a jug. They are under cover at a white function, sitting within two or three feet of one of the tables. Although the writer informs us that "the best 'barbecue cooks' come from Georgia—old plantation negroes whose hair has turned white in bending over the smoking trenches where the meat is cooked," he is more helpfully informative in stating that "while enjoying the meal the guests listen to the music of the orchestra, or—if it be a political 'barbecue'—to the speeches of politicians. Not infrequently the dinner will have lasted over three hours before the last man rises from the table."[16] This particular function took place in Atlanta. Small surprise that almost twenty years later, bluesman Robert Hicks should be involved in similar entertainment, albeit on a smaller scale, and be given the name of Barbecue Bob. If *Wide World Magazine* was an unlikely location for a picture of a black Atlanta jug band from the turn of the century, even more unlikely was the the *Strand Magazine*[17] better known for its Conan Doyle serializations of Sherlock Holmes's mysteries, in which the article was excerpted in 1898. Many of the photographs are shared by both articles—not that of the band, however—and the photographer throughout was Howe of Atlanta. Thus the jug band dates from no later than 1898 and probably earlier.

Another *Wide World Magazine* for 1904–1905 has an excellent picture of a five-piece Florida jug band which comprised three jugs, a harmonica and jug player, and bones, all played by boys (see photograph between pp. 160–61). The detailed narrative is worth repeating in full.

> One of the familiar sights in Florida is the strange "jug bands" which are formed in nearly every district by negro boys. Perhaps the most famous of these primitive orchestras is the Palatka Jug Band, which is comprised of six little nigger boys, who go from hotel to hotel playing their weird and monotonous 'music'. Close at hand, the sounds which they draw from their large stone jugs, into which they blow or whistle, are as unlike music as could be imagined, but at a distance—the greater the better say unkind critics—the noise which they make sounds something like a brass band. The sound is said to be not at all unpleasant when the sounds are wafted on the breeze, but the nearer the jug band approaches the worse it gets, so that people generally get rid of the 'musicians' as soon as possible by giving them small coins of which they are in search. The jug band, therefore, resolves itself into a kind of musical blackmailing association.[18]

Palatka is some forty-five miles south of Jacksonville. The widespread, common occurrence of such bands at the turn of the century has never been mentioned before in the context of black secular music. Indeed, if we were to assess the degree to which black secular music was important in Florida from the number of commercial recordings made by known Florida bluesmen, we might assume that it amounted to very little. This scarcity suggests the inherent danger of attempting to assess by normal academic processes of documentation and analysis a music which did not live in such forms but which was an oral tradition, rarely documented in more permanent manner. To maintain that it did not exist because we have little physical evidence neatly begs the question. Even when a very few musicians were able to record and gain some slight recognition, it had remarkably little effect upon their lives.

The geographical distribution of bluesmen is partially related to socio-economic factors and class structure. A detailed analysis of class structure and black music with reference to Durham, North Carolina—outlined later in this study—probably held true throughout the South, although no specific research elsewhere along such lines has been undertaken. The vast majority of bluesmen were part-time musicians at best, and thus their places of residence often reflect the work opportunities available to them. In attempting to analyse "Negro music," Harold McKinney suggested that the "cultural patterns that produced blues and jazz are the result of Afro-Americans' accommodation to a socio-cultural setting established and controlled by Euro-Americans." Basing his research upon specific southern bluesmen who moved to upstate New York to find work, Kip Lornell concluded that the "uses of blues have been influenced by social changes more decisively than by economic stresses," but acknowledged that economic mobility was a lesser factor. In his *Anthropology of Music,* Alan Merriam saw music as providing "a rallying point around which the members of society gather to engage in activities which require the cooperation and coordination of the group . . . which . . . reminds them of their unity." Studies in other communities doubtless provide parallels for our present area of study. Ultimately "the folk represent an archaic way of life, the city the modern way."[19]

Superimposed upon these socio-economic factors which helped to determine the distribution of bluesmen were the policies of recording companies, the talent scouts, and Artists-and-Repertoire (A & R) men whose job it was to find and record new names. If on occasion their role was that of simply documenting what existed at a given time in a given location, more often they provided a totally distorted impression of the distribution or even the location of bluesmen, both in the specific and the general. Atlanta's undoubted significance as a route and migration center helped establish it as a center for southern recordings, but many of the bluesmen recorded there were from outside the distinctive musical region. The complete absence of recording in many other significant centers in no way reflects an absence of music. As this study reveals, many bluesmen came to record either by chance or because of particular initiative, either on their behalf or on the behalf of some talent scout or store owner. Others, for reasons of their own, did not take up firm offers to record; doubtless their numbers could be increased by competent musicians of whom we still have no knowledge.

There has been limited research into the geographical distribution of folk music and even less on black secular music by cultural geographers. Kip Lornell has taken such studies further in an investigation into the geographical perspective on blues in the Southeast as well as analyzing the spatial perspectives of Victor's field recording sessions in Bristol, Virginia, in 1928.[20] The A & R men were responsible for locating talent and supervising recording sessions. Thus, unintentionally, they produced a curiously unbalanced picture of the geographic distribution of recorded bluesmen. Lornell studies the roles of key men like Polk Brockman, who worked through a network of "jobbers" or distributors of his company's product. He was Okeh's chief talent scout for the whole South, having suggested to Okeh in 1923 that they should record the popular white Atlanta fiddler, Fiddlin' John Carson, when Brockman was still running the record retailing section of the family furniture store. One of Brockman's jobbers was Charles Rey, the Okeh distributor for Virginia, West Virginia, North Carolina, and Washington, D.C., who worked out of a store on Broad Street in Richmond. In October 1929 Brockman and Rey together set up the Okeh session there with Rey handling all the local arrangements and Brockman auditioning talent and supervising the recordings. Brockman had the final decision on who would be recorded, but it was Rey who had scouted the local talent and arranged for them to be present. He was obviously efficient, for he found enough talent for more than a hundred sides to be cut during one week. Among the black artists, predominantly from the Tidewater region, was harmonica player Blues Birdhead. Outside Atlanta, all the A & R men operated along the Piedmont industrial corridor. As Lornell remarked, if "J. B. Long had been transferred to Columbia, South Carolina, from Kinston, he would probably have continued his A. & R. work there and we would have recordings by blues singers from this area rather than Durham."[21]

Thus was established the pattern for subsequent research—following the spatial route predetermined by recorded artists. Specific areal investigations in depth in Durham, Atlanta, and Newton County, Georgia, produced an even greater imbalance in our knowledge of the regional blues scene. Only much later were studies undertaken which covered a wider brief, thanks to George Mitchell in Georgia, Glenn Hinson in North Carolina, and Kip Lornell in Virginia especially. It is much to their credit that other key sections of the jig-saw puzzle come into place. Many pieces are missing, but we are able now to obtain a better glimpse of the subject under study. Lornell's study of the Bristol sessions reveal other factors which help account for the uneven spatial distribution, such as "the home locations of the musicians, the distances they travelled to record & the regions each session drew from for musical talent." These recording centers clearly acted as functional cultural nodes,[22] and much work remains in uncovering the details of the cultural conditions which gave rise to this aspect of black music. The 1930s and 1940s produced certain noncommercial recordings which really fall outside the spatial constraints outlined above. The recordings of the Library of Congress in particular centered on penal institutions, so perhaps these might be seen as nothing less than minor nodes, while those at Fort Valley more closely equate with the publicity given an early location recording session by a major company, like

Victor at Bristol. These recordings are described in detail in the following two chapters.

As mentioned, the border regions to our study area are somewhat fluid. In some areas considerable detail about the music scene exists, but elsewhere our knowledge is so limited that perhaps it is best mentioned here, to emphasize the spatial imbalance of recorded blues and the nonlocational recording alluded to above.

Our knowledge of blues in north Georgia, above Atlanta, is minimal. Enthusiast Fred Hay located older bluesmen in and around Toccoa in the early 1970s although it is an area with relatively few blacks. Into the early 1900s a tradition of cane fife and drum music existed in Macon County, North Carolina. The bands were an integral part of certain outdoor church activities but never accompanied secular singing and dancing.[23] As Macon County is immediately across the state line, one county removed from Stephens County, of which Toccoa is the county seat, it is possible that similar music—possibly even secular—was to be heard in northeast Georgia. It is known in West Georgia, around Columbus, the only area outside northern Mississippi and southwestern Tennessee where such bands persisted at least into the 1970s. Perhaps one reason why few blacks moved down to Atlanta was that the regional focal center lay in Chattanooga. Outlining the country music scene in Tennessee, Charles Wolfe wrote that "southwest of Knoxville yet another distinct musical climate was developing in Chattanooga, which because of its location, was even more of a crossroads for different musical styles, attracting not only artists from Tennessee but also musicians from north Georgia, Alabama and Mississippi. . . . As a result of these influences, Chattanooga provided one of the most eclectic musical climates for early country music."[24] That might well have been no less true for black music.

The only black artists from north Georgia known to have been recorded and about whom information exists are Andrew and Jim Baxter, who made a number of sides for Victor in the late 1920s. They were from Calhoun, Gordon County, rather closer to Chattanooga than to Atlanta, and they were well known to members of the Georgia Yellow Hammers, a popular white group from Gordon County, who recorded extensively and with whom the Baxters traveled—in a separate car, of course—to record in Charlotte, North Carolina, and in Atlanta. Such personal information as exists comes from former members of the group. The half Cherokee Andrew Baxter "was an old time fiddler along with his other accomplishments. According to local tradition he was a proficient musician at age nine. Gus Chitwood says that he and his son James, a guitarist, often played with and for Bill

Chitwood [founder member of the Georgia Yellow Hammers] and other whites. 'They could play breakdowns; they could play blues; they could play church music; they could play *anything.*'"[25]

The Georgia Yellow Hammers recorded their second session for Victor in Charlotte in August 1927, when a number of Gordon County groups were recorded. Among them were the Baxters, who were under a management contract to the steel guitarist with the Yellow Hammers, Phil Reeve, who owned a record store in Calhoun. The Baxters recorded three sides—two blues and a fine train song, "The Moore Girl." Their session occurred at the end of the Yellow Hammers' session of August 9, and on the last Yellow Hammers' title the regular fiddler, Bud Landress, gave his place to Andrew Baxter. The band had chosen to play an instrumental, "G Rag," and Landress performed only the spoken introduction. Victor must have been well pleased with the Baxters, for their three sides, plus "G Rag," were all issued; "The Moore Girl" was backed by a spare side from Rabbit Brown's New Orleans session in March of that year.

Victor did not ask the Baxters to return with the Yellow Hammers until October 1928. This time the journey was to Atlanta. Only the last two of eight sides made were coupled for issue. "Forty Drops" is a dance piece for "set" dances. According to dancer Sidney Easton, born in Savannah in 1886, these differed from British square dances. "The colored folk used a four-four, not a six-eight tempo, four couples at a time, with lots of solo work and improvised breaks by each dancer putting together steps of his own."[26] These are the "eight-hand sets" of North Carolina. "Georgia Stomp," again with its dance calls, could hardly be further from the Atlanta stomps of Peg Leg Howell's Gang on "Peg Leg Stomp," or Macon Ed and Tampa Joe's "Warm Wipe Stomp." When "Georgia Stomp" was first issued on album in Harry Smith's American Folk Music series almost a generation ago, he said, "This performance is structurally intermediate between the early rural dance style and the syncopated urban style that was perfected about 1880."[27] Certainly it comes far closer to the fiddle music which persisted in and around the northern part of Orange County, North Carolina, in not dissimilar terrain and with a similar black-white population ratio, into the 1970s.

Whatever reasons Victor had for not releasing the other Baxter sides—all the others recorded in October by Gordon County groups were issued—they were clearly still pleased with their performances, as the Baxters returned to Atlanta with the Yellow Hammers for what were to be the final sessions for both groups. The Baxters recorded six titles, four on Wednesday, November 20, 1929, and the others the following day. All were released but in the rarest series. A photograph of the Baxters taken at a Rotary Club fish fry in 1945 showed them both looking well and fit. How long they continued to play is not known, but the black fiddle tradition persisted longer in the South than is generally appreciated.

No meaningful attempt can be made to offer even a partial appreciation of the development of blues in Florida although the snatches of information available to us permit, at least, the general placement of black secular music, especially blues, within the broader pattern of the East Coast as documented more fully elsewhere. After the fieldwork done for the Library of Congress in the 1930s, no further fieldwork was undertaken until 1978. However, Florida produced one of the two country bluesmen whose Paramount recordings of the 1920s would have been known to the majority of bluesmen: Blind Blake was one of the greatest influences from commercial record before the years of the Depression.

Blake's considerable significance in the dissemination of blues throughout the South has stimulated much investigation to determine his origins—to little effect. Even his real name provoked dissension although there appears to have been no argument that he was blind, as shown in a Paramount advertisement.[28] On occasion he is named Arthur Phelps, but copyright submissions on behalf of Chicago Music for his Paramount recordings give his name as Arthur Blake. They state his name in a variety of manners: Blind Blake ("Blake's Worried Blues"), Arthur (Blind) Blake ("Bootleg Whiskey" and "Goodbye Mama Moan"), Blind Arthur Blake ("Cold Hearted Mama Blues"), and simply Arthur Blake ("Detroit Bound").[29]

In *Country Blues,* first published in 1959, Sam Charters offered information about Blake which was clearly far from rumor:

> Arthur Blake . . . played in a rhythmic dance style with considerable inventiveness. His first record, "Early Morning Blues" and "West Coast Blues" on Paramount 12387, was advertised October 2, 1926, and it sold well. He recorded sixty-eight more blues for Paramount over the next four years. He was a heavy drinker, but his landlady, Mrs Renett Pounds, at 4005 S. Parkway, tried to watch out for him as best she could. Two of his most popular records were trio versions of "Hot Potatoes" and "Southbound Rag" with the famed clarinet player, Johnny Dodds, and the excellent drummer, Jimmy Bertrand, who played xylophone and slide whistle. Blake's guitar playing filled out the trio with a strong, swinging beat. When the sales of his records began to drop in 1929 he got in touch with a friend, George Williams, who was managing the "Happy-Go-Lucky" show, and played with the show until late 1930 or 1931, when he returned to Jacksonville.[30]

Little more than surmise has been added to that knowledge.

Some of his songs have been transcribed and annotated in detail by Woody Mann, who stated that, "playing with a terrific flair for improvisation . . . he is at once subtle and ornate. No other blues guitarist has a more complicated or sophisticated style." Even Bill Williams, a fine guitarist from Kentucky who played with Blake in the 1920s, recalled little that was factual about him, other than claiming to have taught Blake "Georgia Bound," but he did underline the above assessment of Blake, saying that "the better he felt, the better he played . . . he was crazy about the blues." Gary Davis, sparing always in his critical assessment of any musician, willingly stated, "I ain't never heard anybody on a record yet beat Blind Blake on the guitar. I like Blake because he plays right sporty."[31] Arguably the finest ragtime guitarist who ever recorded, Blind Blake was also one of the few musicians to excel in both ragtime and blues.

Kate McTell recalled that her husband, Blind Willie McTell, "brought (Blake) to Atlanta from Florida." Although one set of informative album liner notes states that Blake was "a native of Tampa whose career was frequently Georgia based," there is no reason to doubt the accuracy of the Paramount company's advertisement, printed in the Chicago *Defender*: "'Early Morning Blues' is the first record of this new *exclusive* Paramount artist, Blind Blake. Blake, who hails from Jacksonville, Florida, is known up and down the coast as a wizard at picking his piano-sounding guitar. His 'talking guitar' they call it, and when you hear him sing and play you'll know why Blind Blake is going to be one of the most talked about Blues artists in music." The following year, when Paramount mail-order businessman Fred Boerner promoted *The Paramount Book of the Blues,* with short features and photographs of its artists, the section on Blake lacked the brash, crude, hard-sell comment often found in the Chicago *Defender* advertisements: "Blind Blake . . . Born in Jacksonville, in sunny Florida, he seems to have absorbed some of the sunny atmosphere—disregarding the fact that nature had cruelly denied him the vision of outer things. He could not see the things that others saw—but he had a better gift. . . . he turned to music. He studied long and earnestly—listening to talented pianists and guitar players, and began to gradually draw out harmonious tunes to fit every mood." One possible further piece of evidence to corroborate Blake's home town is to be found on an unpublished Blake recording. An entry at the Library of Congress Copyright Office in Washington, D.C., dated February 15, 1928, is for E 686024 "Jacksonville Slide," words and melody, Blind Blake.[32]

Perhaps he should have the last word on his name too. A late Paramount recording of Blake together with Papa Charlie Jackson, "Papa Charlie and Blind Blake Talk about It, included this dialogue:

> Jackson: Say, Blake!
> Blake: What is it, boy, what you want?
> Jackson: What is your right name?
> Blake: My name is Arthur Blake!
> Jackson: Where did you get that "Arthur" at?
> Blake: Oh, I'm the author of many things![33]

Should it be needed, here is clear evidence that Blake worked the medicine show circuit like other bluesmen. He was recalled playing in 1929–30 with shows at the Pekin Theater in Savannah, Georgia, and he played with the local band led by Herman Quillion. Quillion's band, originally the Snappy Six, grew to become a larger swing band, but it is not surprising to find Blake playing in such a unit.[34] After all, he had recorded successfully with small jazz-skiffle groups in Chicago. Certainly many of Blake's numbers, like "Hey Hey Daddy Blues," substantiate the suggestion that he was accustomed to small show-stages, while others, like "Low Down Loving Gal," retain the humorous spoken introduction favored by white country artists like Uncle Dave Macon and Chris Bouchillon, who played on similar circuits.

Tracing Blake's movements, other than his short stay in Chicago, is no easy task. Widely scattered sightings have been reported by many bluesmen, and there is no good reason to doubt them. About 1922, for a period of some four months, he stayed with guitarist Bill Williams in the country outside Bristol. Williams worked as Blake's second guitarist for this period, which allowed Blake to give his undoubted showmanship free rein, playing his guitar behind his head and offering other eye-catching and show-stopping guitar stunts. He was seen in Elberton, Georgia, before 1926 by a young Baby Tate, who recalled sufficient to be able to play a remarkably accurate "Police Dog Blues" in 1970. Josh White met him in Charleston, West Virginia, and there were a number of references to him playing in North Carolina, including in Durham. In Chicago, his apartment at 31st and Cottage Grove Avenue became a meeting place for local pianists like Little Brother Montgomery and Charlie Spand, with whom Blake later recorded. Montgomery knew Blake in 1928, when they were both playing regularly on the house-party circuit, but saw no more of him after 1931. Bill Williams reported that Blake was a heavy drinker, as had his former landlady, while Montgomery recalled that the Monday "rehearsals" at Blake's apartment were helped along by moonshine. Williams assumed that Blake's over-fondness for drink had been fatal.

Disparate reports of his death helped lift him to the level of the legendary. Bob Groom stated that Blake "wandered the South in the years between the wars, spending time in Chicago while recording. He was at one time thought to have died there, but it now seems that he actually returned to Atlanta when the Depression ended his recording career and was killed there in a streetcar accident in 1941." Paul Oliver took up the legend built around his death, adding that "after 1930, Josh White saw him no more and believed that he was murdered in the streets of Chicago: Big Bill Broonzy thought that he died about 1932 in Joliet, within sight of the grim prison that featured in his blues." Pianist Blind John Davis suggested that Blake had died in St. Louis in the 1930s, but he had been told that by Tampa Red! Gary Davis heard that he had been run over by a streetcar in New York City about 1934. City records do not show his death in New York during this period, and neither did he die in Atlanta.[35] Despite the disagreements about the location, the persistent rumors of his death, often in a violent context and about the time of his last recordings, suggest a grain of truth.

Another bluesman, a stalwart of the Chicago scene in the 1920s and 1930s who also recorded extensively in the post-war period, was Tampa Red. Born in Smithville (Lee County), Georgia, just south of Americus, he grew up in Tampa, Florida, traveled throughout the South, toured on the T.O.B.A. theater circuit, and held the nickname Tampa Red before he recorded in 1928. He eventually teamed up with fellow Georgian Tom Dorsey (Georgia Tom, whom he met in 1925) in Chicago, forming one of the most famous piano-guitar duets and appearing on literally dozens of records as accompanists as well as under their own names.[36] Tampa Red is clearly the product of more than simply the state of Florida, although understandably and characteristically his performance on guitar is regionally typical, just as other southeastern bluesmen like Georgian Kokomo Arnold also reflect their origins.

With more justification one might assume that Louis Washington, who recorded twenty-two sides for the American Record Corporation in New York in 1934 both under his own name and also as Tallahassee Tight, was from Florida. Tallahassee lies in the northwestern arm of the state, which resembles the rolling plains of south Georgia rather than the coastal belt of the Gulf and the swampy lowlands of the bulk of the state. His "Tallahassee Women" suggests a town frequented by itinerant blacks, with women down in "Smokey Hollow" to cater for "spare" money. Certainly the town resembled many others within the Piedmont, for Tallahassee was a regional center for tobacco and cotton farmers in the northern part of the state. It had a large black section and the state guide for 1939 stated that "in pockets between many of the hills, and along the clay streets leading towards the Agricultural College, are Negro colonies. Crowding the rear of the Governor's mansion is the principal Negro settlement, French town."[37]

Presumably Louis Washington was from either Tallahassee or nearby, for he also recorded a "Quincy Wimmens." Quincy, some twenty miles northeast of Tallahassee, is a small tobacco center with mines and plants for processing Fuller's Earth, both of which would be likely to use transient black labor. He also recorded "Coast Line Blues," mentioning the Seaboard Air Line Railroad which ran along Railroad Avenue in the south of Tallahassee. Of the titles he recorded, half were gospel sides made under his own name. Of limited musical interest, but completely within the guitar traditions of the Southeast, Louis Washington may have the distinction of being the one recorded resident Florida bluesman of the period of commercial blues recording.

In the postwar period Florida has been a good base for many bluesmen from other regions. Some, like Big Boy Crudup, were part of the migrant fruit-picking workforce; others were part of small blues bands or traveling shows who found Florida a profitable state in which to work. Some local musicians moved out; Charlie Morris—better known as Blue Charlie or Left-Hand Charlie—moved to Louisiana, Guitar Shorty (David Kearney) and Clarence Jolly moved initially to Chicago. Those who recorded in the state for the larger companies in the 1950s were from other regions as far as is known. There were doubtless a number of small local releases, as in Georgia. The Apache label out of Crestview, near Pensacola in the very western part of the state, issued a few blues. Clifford King, a harmonica player and guitarist of limited ability, backed only by Crook Junior on drums, had a crude, down-home release but with its Jimmy Reed overtones, "Chicken Shack Boogie" could have been recorded anywhere in the South. B. B. Fleming, born in Douglas, south Georgia, about 1918, began playing guitar in the mid-1930s, reportedly playing with Buddy Moss, and can be heard in the Miami area with a modern blues band but presumably is still able to play in the regional style with which he grew up.[38]

Until research was undertaken by the North Florida Folklife Project in 1978, the only Florida bluesman located in recent years who could be considered a country bluesman was Elijah Etham, from near Bradenton, on the coast south of Tampa. His brief story was typical of so many casual musicians of more recent years, influenced not only by Blind Boy Fuller but also by John Lee Hooker and Lightning Hopkins.[39] Out of touch with playing guitar and insufficiently interviewed, he was nonetheless the only indigenous bluesman located in the state during the forty years or so since the Library of Congress trips in the 1930s. The loss to us should be obvious.

In 1978 a family group from Jonesville, near Gainesville in Alachua County, was recorded. Richard Williams had been born there in 1887 and by about 1910 was playing guitar for local parties and "set dancing." He learned blues from workers in phosphate camps in the county where he used to work and occasionally played for whites at fish fries and parties. At the latter he would play blues, but he was never asked to play for dancing. One delightful song by Williams was issued on a double album of sacred and secular black songs recorded in the state in 1978 and 1980 and released by the Folklife Program of the Florida Department of State.[40] Named "Old Forty," the song is a gently sung and beautifully picked version of "I Want to Go Further on Down the Road," so commonly found in the Southeast. In fact it has an uncanny resemblence to the obscure version recorded by Robert N. Page for Victor in Charlotte, North Carolina, in 1927.

Richard Williams, another survivor of the pre-blues performers, makes one wish that musicians like him could have been recorded in their prime. Although his daughter, Ella Mae Wilson, was able to sing blues accompanied by her father, they were hesitant and his delicate guitar picking was not heard to its best effect. Nonetheless, this playing is entirely within the East Coast idiom with far more ties to Georgia and the Carolinas than to the states to the west. A cousin of Richard Williams, Robert Dennis, was born about 1914 in the small community of Half Moon, Alachua County. His guitar playing was rather like Williams's and his voice was obviously past its prime, but he must once have been a fine bluesman. His "Early One Foggy Morning" is a good, personal blues, making full use of floating blues lines. Also recorded in 1980 was "Polk County Blues," described in the next chapter. It had been recorded, unaccompanied, from Philip Anderson during the Library of Congress fieldtrip in 1935. One version of "Polk County Blues" recorded in 1980 was collected from Willie Gillard, who was born in Charleston, South Carolina, in 1910. He moved to Florida to work the orange groves of Sorrento in Lake County before settling eventually in Tampa. Although he is clearly well past his prime, his guitar playing remains well within the idiom, and it is clear that the song was widespread within the state.

Other bluesmen recorded by the Folklife Program were originally from out-of-state, but Emmett Murray, born in 1911 in Moultrie,

Georgia, some forty miles above the state line, moved to Florida in the 1930s and settled to work the cane fields around Pahokee on Lake Okeechobee. Recorded in 1980, his most interesting song is "Old-Time Rounders," sung rather as an accompanied worksong. Murray used to learn blues from 78 rpm discs, but one wonders if this was where he learned his versions of "She's a Fool, She Ain't Got No Sense," otherwise recorded by the Alabama guitarist Ed Bell and Big Boy Crudup as "I'm Gonna Dig Myself a Hole," The latter would have been easily heard, but then Crudup did make his living in later years, and certainly in the 1950s, acting as courier for an agency shipping in migrant labor to Florida for fruit picking.

In retrospect, it is unfortunate that the recording of these Florida blues musicians came so late, for they are really little but shadows of the performers they must once have been. However, the recordings do underline most clearly that the bluesmen were there and that they fitted entirely comfortably within the broad fabric of southeastern blues.

No research whatever has been undertaken into the blues tradition along the South Carolina coast or with special reference to the urban center of Charleston. That such a tradition existed further south in and around Savannah has been slightly documented, and there is sufficient evidence to suggest a parallel existence around Charleston. In 1862 St. Helena Island became the center of the Port Royal Experiment, a northern abolitionist scheme to educate blacks and provide a solution to the "Negro problem." Songs were avidly collected from the area, many of them published in the 1867 *Slave Songs of the United States,* and St. Helena Island remained of interest to anthropologists and folklorists, including Guy Johnson, who recorded many cylinders of songs on the island but lost them to the ravages of mould. Marshall and Jean Stearns sought the origins of early black dance along the Georgia coast. The Charleston is clearly one dance originating within the region. Although it sprang upon a delighted world in the 1920s, its origins were far older, as claimed in a letter to the *New York Times* in 1926 by Will Marion Cook, a formal black bandleader and composer who was as well versed as any other in the changing musical styles of the times, and in black musical roots: "The 'Charleston' has been done in the South, especially in the little islands lying off Charleston, S.C., for more than forty years to my knowledge. The dance reached New York five years ago. In Harlem any evening a group of negro children could be seen 'Doin' the Charleston' and collecting pennies." Cook had been upset by a *Times* article crediting George White and his Scandals with the creation of the Charleston and Black Bottom as dances and ended his letter with considerable dignity, commenting upon the white music scene: "Why, with their immense flocks of dramatic and musical sheep, should they wish to reach out and grab our little ewe lamb of originality?"[41] Chris Smith, pianist and composer of "Junk Man Rag," "Ballin' the Jack" (another dance), and "Down in Honky Tonk Town," was born in Charleston in 1879.

Undoubtedly the most important jazz nursery in the country existed in Charleston from the late 1890s until well after World War II. The Jenkins Orphanage on Franklin Street gave an enormous number of black youngsters their first introduction to musical instruments, and thanks to their early tutoring, many of them like Jabbo Smith and Cat Anderson became highly significant jazzmen in later life. A less important member was Thomas Henry Delaney, born in the city in 1889. At the Jenkins Orphanage he formed the Springfield Minstrels and toured in the early 1920s up the East Coast as part of the song-and-dance team of Mitchell and Delaney. As Tom Delaney, he recorded for Columbia in 1925 as a singer. Delaney also played the piano but did not record in this capacity unless he is the pianist on the 1929 Bertha Odaho sides for Columbia. She claimed that he was and that he wrote the songs. His "Down Home Blues" became a huge success for Ethel Waters, whose manager he became.[42]

Trumpeter Bubber Miley, who was once replaced in Duke Ellington's band by Jabbo Smith, was born in Aiken, South Carolina, closer to Augusta than to Charleston and only a few miles from the birthplace of bluesman Julius Daniels, probably within the same year. Miley, born April 3, 1903, was brought up in a "musical family. His father played the guitar, filling Bubber's home life with the blues. His mother and three older sisters all sang." It is probably no coincidence that Ellington specifically incorporated Miley's muted blues playing in his compositions and that Miley took the incomparable solo in the blues tone poem "Black and Tan Fantasy." He told his biographer, Roger Pryor Dodge, that he used to keep a small reed organ which "he used to play on while humming blues."[43] (Dodge was a noted authority on dance, a dancer himself in the 1920s, and his wife accompanied on piano some superb examples of Miley's blues trumpet playing, which I heard on unissued home recordings made in the 1930s.)

From Sumter, north of Charleston, came such diverse bluesmen as the obscure young harmonica player Edward Hazelton, who turned up on Skid Row in Los Angeles in 1960. Guitarist C. C. Richardson was born in Sumter on December 18, 1918. He lost a leg following an accident but worked a Silas Green show in 1932. Restarting to play in 1965 he has made some home-produced records and played a few

festivals.[44] Drink Small, a guitarist now resident in Columbia, has also
played a few festivals and recorded.[45] Another guitarist from near
Charleston was Ed Green, born in 1890. By 1903 he was touring with
John J. John's carnival, reputedly the largest in the South at that time.
In the years that followed he played churches, dances, and house-rent
parties, maintaining a fairly active career as a musician. His career is
described in more detail in the liner notes accompanying an album with
his one issued recording. "South Carolina Blues," a raggy little dance
tune, no doubt typifies his early style.[46]

We know the general boundaries within which the blues developed
and flourished, and we have noted, with a cautionary warning, the
uneven documentation available. Let us now turn to certain areas in
which we are able to probe in considerable depth.

NOTES

1. Ellen C. Semple, *Influences of Geographical Environment* (New York:
Holt, 1911), pp. 527–28.

2. E. C. Branson, "Our Rapidly Growing Cities," University of North
Carolina *News Letter,* December 14, 1921. Actually Durham was only 964
percent; Gastonia was over 5,000 percent.

3. Horace Hamilton, *Rural-Urban Migration in North Carolina 1920 to
1970,* Agricultural Experimental Station of North Carolina State Bulletin 295
(Raleigh, 1934), pp. 19, 20, 26, 44, 65.

4. Samuel Huntington Hobbs, Jr., *North Carolina: Economic and Social*
(Chapel Hill: University of North Carolina Press, 1930), p. 141.

5. James Joseph Maslowski, "North Carolina Migration 1870–1950" (Ph.D.
diss., University of North Carolina at Chapel Hill, 1953), pp. 163, 186, 258.

6. Arnold Shaw, *Honkers and Shouters: The Golden Years of Rhythm and
Blues* (New York: Collier, 1978), p. 415.

7. Asheville *Citizen*, August 26, 1925, quoted in Charles Wolfe and Tony
Russell, "The Asheville Sessions," *Old Time Music,* 31 (Winter, 1978/79): 6.

8. John M. Hager, *Commercial Survey for the South East* (Washington, D.C.:
Department of Commerce, 1927), p. 144.

9. Arthur I. Waskow, *From Race-Riot to Sit-In: 1919 and the 1960s* (New
York: Doubleday, 1966), p. 14.

10. Randy Lawrence, "Black Migration to Southern West Virginia,
1870–1930," *Goldenseal* 5 (October-December, 1979): 30–31.

11. Randy Lawrence, "'Make a Way Out of Nothing': One Black Woman's
Trip from North Carolina to the McDowell County Coalfields," *Goldenseal*
5 (October-December, 1979): 29.

12. George M. Foster, "What Is Folk Culture ?" *American Anthopologist*
55 (1953): 159–72.

13. Marshall and Jean Stearns, *Jazz Dance: The Story of American Vernacular Dance* (1968; rpt., New York: Schirmer, 1979); Bruce Bastin, "From the Medicine Show to the Stage: Some Influences upon the Development of a Blues Tradition in the Southeastern States," *American Music* 2 (Spring, 1984): 29–42.

14. Laurie Wright, "Rhythm Is My Business: An Interview with Lawrence 'Larry' Lucie," *Storyville* 96 (August-September, 1981): 218.

15. John Solomon Otto and Augustus M. Burns, "The Use of Race and Hillbilly Recordings as Sources for Historical Research: The Problem of Color Hierarchy among Afro-Americans in the Early Twentieth Century," *Journal of American Folklore* 85 (October-December, 1972): 355.

16. Day Allen Willey, "Barbecues and How They are Conducted," *Wide World Magazine* 9 (April-September, 1902): 189–90. I am indebted to Jeffrey P. Green for locating this and the following two sources.

17. John R. Watkins, "Barbecues," *Strand Magazine* 16 (July-December, 1898): 463–68.

18. "A Florida Jug Band," *Wide World Magazine* 14 (October, 1904-March, 1905): 414.

19. Harold B. McKinney, "Negro Music: A Definitive American Expression," *Negro History Bulletin* 27 (February, 1964): 120; Christopher Lornell, "The Effects of Social and Economic Changes on the Uses of Blues," *John Edwards Memorial Foundation Quarterly* 11 (Spring, 1975): 47; Alan P. Merriam, *The Anthropology of Music* (Chicago: Northwestern University Press, 1964), p. 227; Charles Keil, *Urban Blues* (Chicago: University of Chicago Press, 1966); Alan Lomax, *Folk Song Style and Culture* (Washington, D.C.: American Association for the Advancement of Science, 1968); William Ferris, Jr., *Blues from the Delta* (New York: Anchor Press/Doubleday, 1978); David Evans, *Big Road Blues* (Berkeley and Los Angeles: University of California Press, 1982); Ralph Beals and Harry Hoijer, *An Introduction to Anthropology* (New York: Macmillan Co., 1971), p. 224.

20. George O. Carey, *Sounds of People and Places: Readings in the Geography of Music* (Washington, D.C.: University Press of America, 1978); Doug Langille, "The Spatial and Diffusion of a Culture-Specific Artform: The Geography of Blues" (Bachelor's thesis, University of Guelph, Toronto, n.d.); Kip Lornell and Theodore Mealor, "Piedmont Blues: The Spatial Perspective on the Recording Industry in the Southeastern United States," paper read at the South East Association of American Geographers (SEDAAG), Atlanta, Ga., November, 1981; Kip Lornell, "Spatial Perspectives on the Field Recording of Traditional American Music: A Case Study from Tennessee in 1928," *Tennessee Folklore Society Bulletin* 46 (1981): 153–59.

21. Lornell and Mealor, "Piedmont Blues": 7–8, 15.

22. Lornell, "Spatial Perspectives": 158; Terry Jordan and Lester Rowntree, *A Thematic Introduction to Cultural Geography* (New York: Harper & Row, 1979), pp. 13–15.

23. Glenn Hinson, brochure notes to *Eight-Hand Sets and Holy Steps: Traditional Black Music of North Carolina*, Crossroads C-101 (Raleigh: North Carolina Museum of History, 1978).

24. Charles K. Wolfe, *Tennessee Strings: The Story of Country Music in Tennessee* (Knoxville: University of Tennessee Press, 1977), p. 49.

25. Gene Wiggins and Tony Russell, "Hell Broke Loose in Gordon County, Georgia," *Old Time Music* 25 (Summer, 1977): 13–21. See also Gene Wiggins in *The Devil's Box* 11 (March, 1977): 19–20, for an earlier version and Tony Russell, "Andrew and Jim Baxter," *Talking Blues* 4 (January-February-March, 1977): 5.

26. Stearns, *Jazz Dance,* p. 23.

27. Harry Smith, brochure notes to *American Folk Music,* vol. 2, *Social Music,* Folkways FP 252 (New York).

28. *The Paramount Book of Blues* (Port Washington, Wis.: New York Recording Laboratories, 1927), p. 15, in Jeff Todd Titon, *Early Downhome Blues: A Musical and Cultural Analysis* (Urbana: University of Illinois Press, 1977), p. 80.

29. Arnold S. Caplin, liner notes to *Blind Blake 1926–1930,* Biograph 12003 (New York). Copyright renewals in London in 1955 and 1956 are in the name of Blake Alphonso (or Alfonzo) Higgs. This was a confusion with the proper name of the Bahamian singer, also named Blind Blake. John H. Cowley to the author, August 24, 1983.

30. Samuel B. Charters, *The Country Blues* (London: Michael Joseph, 1960), p. 37.

31. Woody Mann, *Six Black Blues Guitarists* (New York: Oak Publications, 1973), p. 8. Pages 10–21 carry transcriptions of Blake's songs. Titon, *Early Downhome Blues,* pp. 76–77, 79, duplicates two of these. Stefan Grossman, *Rev. Gary Davis: Blues Guitar* (New York: Oak Publications, 1974), p. 13.

32. Kate McTell interviewed by Anne Evans in Wrens, Georgia, June 27, 1977; Stephan Calt, Nicks Perls, and Michael Stewart, liner notes to *The Georgia Blues 1927–1933,* Yazoo L-1012 (New York); Chicago *Defender*, October 2, 1926; Titon, *Early Downhome Blues,* pp. 78, 80; John H. Cowley to the author, January 21, 1979.

33. Stephan Calt, liner notes to *Blind Blake: No Dough Blues 1926–1929,* Biograph 12031 (New York).

34. Thanks to David Evans and Karl Gert zur Heide.

35. Bob Groom quoted by Caplin, *Blind Blake,* Biograph 12003; Paul Oliver, liner notes to *Blind Blake,* Jazz Collector Records JFL 2001 (London); Karl Gert zur Heide to the author, August 1978; Grossman, *Rev. Gary Davis,* p. 13. Grossman quotes Davis as saying it was "a year before I came to New York City in 1930." Davis first went there to record in 1935, so it is probably a mistranscription—hence the date of 1934 in the text. Calt, *Blind Blake,* Biograph 12031; investigation of Fulton County (Atlanta), Georgia, records by the author, August 1970.

36. Jim O'Neal, liner notes to *Tampa Red: Guitar Wizard,* RCA AXM2-5501 (New York).

37. Federal Works Agency, Works Project Adminstration (Federal Writers Project), *Florida: A Guide to the Southernmost State* (1939; rpt., New York: Oxford University Press, 1965), p. 275.

38. *Living Blues* 21 (May-June, 1975): 54.

39. L. S. Summers and Bob Scheir, "Florida Blues: Elijah Etham," *Living Blues* 5 (Summer, 1971): 17.

40. *Drop On Down in Florida: Recent Field Recordings of Afro-American Traditional Music,* Florida Folklife LPs 102, 103 (White Springs, Florida, 1981), contains a detailed brochure.

41. Elizabeth Jacoway, *Yankee Missionaries in the South: The Penn School Experiment* (Baton Rouge: Louisiana State University Press, 1979); William Francis Allen, Charles Pickard Ware, and Lucy McKim Garrison, *Slave Songs of the United States* (New York: A. Simpson, 1867); Guy Benton Johnson interviewed by the author in Chapel Hill, North Carolina, October 22, 1972; Stearns, *Jazz Dance;* Will Marion Cook, *New York Times,* December 26, 1926, courtesy Klaus Kuhnke, Archiv für Populäre Musik, Bremen. Karl Gert zur Heide to the author, April 17, 1980.

42. John Chilton, *A Jazz Nursery: The Story of the Jenkins Orphanage* (London: Bloomsbury Book Shop, 1980); Sheldon Harris, *Blues Who's Who* (New Rochelle, N.Y.: Arlington House, 1979), pp. 152–53.

43. Roger Pryor Dodge, "Bubber Miley," *Jazz Monthly* 4 (May, 1958): 6, 7; Dodge interviewed by the author in New York City, April 30, 1964.

44. *One String Blues,* Takoma B 1023 (California); Jean-Claude Arnaudon, *Dictionaire de Blues* (Paris: Filipacchi, 1977), p. 213.

45. Drink Small, *I Know My Blues Are Different,* Southland SLP-1 (Atlanta, Ga.).

46. Bruce Bastin, brochure notes to *Another Man Done Gone,* Flyright LP 528 (Bexhill-on-Sea, England, 1978), pp. 12–13.

4

Noncommercial Recordings:
The 1920s and 1930s

In 1927 Carl Engel, chief of the Music Division in the Library of Congress, first called attention to the "pressing need for the formation of a centralized collection of American folk-songs."[1] Soon after Engel's call the Archive of American Folk-Song was set up with Robert Winslow Gordon as its first archivist. An enthusiastic amateur collector, Gordon had become interested in folklore through influential scholars like Barrett Wendall and George Lyman Kittredge at Harvard before World War I, and was collecting by the early 1920s. In 1925 he collected songs on cylinder in Asheville, North Carolina, and by Christmas of that year had filled almost 300 cylinders. However, he decided to move to Darien, on the Georgia coast north of Brunswick, where, by May 1926, he had made 550 recordings. This helped foster Engel's interest in a documented body of folksongs, and on July 1, 1928, Gordon became a salaried representative of the Library of Congress with a brief to acquire material.

Within two months of his appointment Gordon had traveled some 5,000 miles and recorded "box-pickers," as he wrote Engel.[2] The material which has survived appears to be unaccompanied, however; and the black material recorded, including secular songs, is outside a discussion of the evolution of blues. Some of these sides have been gathered together on album.[3] Gordon's position continued until the summer of 1932, when lack of funds prevented its extension, although he remained until the end of the year indexing the vast collection. The Archive was revived in 1933 under John Avery Lomax, who became honorary consultant and curator. Looking back in 1938, Harold Spivacke, then chief of the Library's Music Division, recalled that "at this time, the Library acquired and placed at (Lomax's) disposal a portable recording machine. Since then, the Archive has emphasized the use of phonograph records in collecting folk-songs whenever possible, because of the greater accuracy of this method over that of aural transcription alone."[4] We must be eternally grateful that the older method of collection was thus replaced and John Lomax blazed an unparalleled trail in his search for American folk music. This is not the place for a detailed appraisal, but the importance of his role cannot be permitted to pass without comment.

In December 1934, having recorded extensively since his post with the Library of Congress, particularly in his home state of Texas in November, Lomax came to Georgia. He had experienced great success recording in the penitentiaries, where he felt that the older black ballads might have survived with the minimum of modification. Thus in Georgia he followed the pattern which had been successful elsewhere and arrived at Bellwood Prison in Atlanta, where he recorded guitarist Jesse Wadley on December 11. One of Lomax's more inspired ideas, to request the inmates to sing a song outlining the reason for their presence in the penitentiary, produced some truly remarkable and personal blues. Wadley gives some detail of the process of his sentence, naming officials as well as his girlfriend:

> Judge read my verdict, rocked in his easy chair;
> Judge read my verdict, rocked in his easy chair.
>
> Said, "I'm sorry, Jesse Wadley, you can't have no mercy here."
>
> Mr. Whitney come got me, Dad Campbell carried me down for trial;
> Mr. Whitney come got me, Dad Campbell carried me down for trial.
>
> Ollie hung her head and cried like a baby chil'.[5]

Recorded in Atlanta but entitled "Alabama Prison Blues," it suggests that Wadley was more than familiar with the penal system.

Four days later Lomax was at the State Farm in Milledgeville, a huge, 4,000-acre complex with some 1,000 inmates, mostly white. The 1940 state guide described the prisoners who, "though well cared for, receive no wages for the labor required of them," giving some idea of the true nature of southern correctional agriculture at the time. More accurate portrayals of the barbarity of some penal establishments exist.[6] In Milledgeville Lomax recorded an excellent guitarist, Reece Crenshaw, who performed "Trouble" in answer to Lomax's question as to why he was in jail. At the end of the song he was joined by another singer, identified by Crenshaw in the final stanza: "If anybody ask you who composed this song, tell him Cool Breeze and his companion been through here and gone." His other known song was the regular request from Lomax, "John Henry," a fine, if less individual, performance. An unidentified track exists at the Library of Congress which might be by Crenshaw; a guitar solo accompanied by dancing, it suffers from such speed fluctuations that it remains unissued.[7] These were the most interesting recordings by Lomax in Georgia from a blues standpoint, but perhaps his finest East Coast recording that month took place in North Carolina.

Although the Central Prison in Raleigh permitted "no visitors except prisoners' relatives,"[8] Lomax nonetheless recorded there on December 19, 1934, obtaining two songs from a singer whom he incorrectly called Blind Tom, only to be corrected instantly by the singer to Blind Joe. "When I Lie Down" is perhaps the nearest approach to the guitar style of Blind Blake achieved by a near-contemporary performer, while the other song was obviously sung in accordance with Lomax's perceptive request. "In Trouble" is a magnificent personal blues relating in graphic detail the background of his prison sentence. There is no reason to doubt the autobiographical detail in his telling lyrics:

> The first time I was ever in trouble was 1934;
> The first time I was ever in trouble was 1934,
>
> When that high sheriff come rolling up to my mother's door.
>
> Yes, he took out his papers and he began to read;
> Yes, he took out his papers and he began to read,
>
> He said, "I got you charged here, Joseph, of bigamy."[9]

It has been suggested to me that this might even have been Blind Joe Walker, a Greenville, South Carolina, musician whose brother recorded.[10] At that time Joe Walker was living with his mother, Lucy, his father having died, and he might well have been involved in a bigamous relationship, having once lived with Mary Davis—Gary Davis's first wife—and eventually leaving a widow in Greenville, Beulah, who died in March 1972, just too soon to have been able to elaborate on the speculation.

The following year the Library of Congress undertook further fieldwork in Georgia and also in Florida. This time it was not John A. Lomax who went along, but his son Alan, on his first field trip without his father. Alan took with him a "new and improved recording machine," obtained in May 1935. It was probably no accident that the 1935 expedition commenced fieldwork close to where Robert Gordon had worked in the middle-late 1920s—in the Geechie region of Georgia, where residents still speak Gullah, an old mixture of native

African and possibly nineteenth-century English. As late as 1976 the Sea Island Language Project was set up to teach English as a second language to Gullah-speaking persons and to encourage preservation of the dialect.[11]

Lomax had not gone alone: the other members of the fieldtrip were a black folklore student, Zora Neale Hurston, and a white professor of English at New York University, Mary Elizabeth Barnicle, who had an interest in linguistics and ballads. Lomax was to provide the technical expertise.

Hurston was a remarkable black scholar and writer whose folklore fieldwork has been too much neglected.[12] Born in Eatonville, Florida, in 1901, she grew up in an all-black town with fierce personal racial pride. Progressing through a series of colleges, she studied under anthropologists Ruth Benedict and Franz Boas, through whom she obtained a scholarship from Columbia University in 1927 to undertake fieldwork in Florida, including the collection of songs. In February 1927 she left for a six-month stay in central Florida, but her intellectual, academic background was quite unsuited to the work and she had not thought about the approach necessary to obtain significant material. Nonetheless she learned greatly from the experience and a second trip in the winter of 1927–28, again under Boas's supervision, was more successful, resulting in articles, published in the *Journal of Negro History* and *Journal of American Folklore,* on dance songs and tales in the Bahamas and hoodoo lore in New Orleans. During this second trip she managed to enter the society of the people from whom she was to collect and acquired material which was ultimately to be shaped into her collection of narrative tales, *Mules and Men.*[13]

She also gained an insight into and a liking for black secular music when one of her Eatonville tale-tellers asked her: " 'Why don't you go down 'round Bartow and Lakeland [east of Tampa] and 'round in dere—Polk County? Dat's where they really lies up a mess [tell tall tales] and dat where dey makes up all de songs and things like dat.' Bubber Mimms, a guitarist, added: 'Ah learned all Ah now 'bout pickin de box in Polk County.' "[14] The black section of Lakeland was in the north of the town, where citrus workers and fruit packers lived on streets with such unofficial names as Voodoo Corner, Jonk Street and Careless Avenue. Here Hurston roomed and entered the rough jook joints where "the guitars cried out 'Polk County' and 'Red River' and just instrumental hits with no name, that still are played by all good box pickers."[15] "Singing, laughing, cursing, boasting of last night's love, and looking forward to the darkness again . . . Polk County. After dark, the jooks. Songs are born out of feeling with an old beat-up piano, or a guitar for a midwife."[16] Hurston entered the life with enthusiasm and provided us with the first-ever description of a jook joint: "The jook was in full play when we walked in. The piano was throbbing like a stringed drum and the couples slow-dragging about the floor were urging the player on to new lows. 'Jook Johnnie . . . jook it Johnnie! Throw it in the alley!' . . . Somebody had squeezed the alcohol out of several cans of Sterno and added sugar, water and boiled-off spirits of nitre and called it wine . . . the pay-night rocks on with music and gambling and laughing and dancing and fights."[17]

Hurston was now experienced in collecting material and once chided her fellow Harlem Renaissance intellectual, Langston Hughes, when they were listening to the songs of turpentine and dock workers in Savannah. Hughes had been upset that the "songs they sang we had heard before and they were not very good songs," but he was rebuked by Hurston, who said, "You can't just sit down and ask people to sing songs for you and expect them to be folk-songs, and good ones, and new ones."[18] This experience allowed her "to select the area and contact the subjects" in 1935, although by then she had become less interested in the academic approach of folklore, feeling that it was "almost useless to collect material to lie upon the shelves of scientific societies."[19] Her biographer noted that "her career as a folklorist ended when she finished with her field notes, and after the fall of 1932 she usually conceived of herself as a creative writer—even when writing about folklore."[20] Nonetheless, Lomax was to see her as indispensable, feeling that she was "almost entirely responsible for the success" of the first part of the field trip to Georgia and Florida.

Barnicle's suggestion that Hurston accompany them paid off immediately as Lomax's enthusiastic letter to Oliver Strunk, chief of the Library's Music Division, conveys: "(We) met in Brunswick, Ga., on June 15th and began our search for folk songs there. Through Miss Hurston's influence we were soon living, in an isolated community on St. Simon's Island, on such friendly terms with the Negroes as I had never experienced before. This community is a settlement of Negroes that has remained practically static since the days of slavery. We rented a little Negro shanty and sent out the call for folk singers. The first evening our front yard was crowded." More recently, Lomax recalled the event: "I went to the sea islands to meet my friend Mary Elizabeth Barnicle, and she brought Zora Hurston along with her. We lived together in Frederica in a little shack and recorded sea island music and stories for two or three weeks and then moved on to Eatonville where we recorded the people who figured so importantly in Zora's books. . . . In those days the blues were one of the best recorded musics. So we seldom bothered to record the blues singers that turned up. We were interested in the older level of secular music."[21] St. Simon's Island is one of the remote sea islands which, together with those along the South Carolina coastline, had attracted folklorists for years. The pioneer *Slave Songs of the United States,* published in 1867, had drawn from the region. Robert Gordon had recorded around Darien in 1926, Guy Johnson had worked on St. Helena Island in the 1920s, and the Federal Writers Project closely documented African retentions in the black subculture around Savannah.[22]

During the short stay in 1935 much of the recording took place in Frederica, an old, once-flourishing seaport which had fallen into decay. A number of persons were recorded, but the bulk of the sides were drawn from the Davis family, especially from John and Robert, who played guitars. Together with guitarists Bill Tatnall, Brewster Davis, John Brewster, and Henry Blue, they made a variety of recordings, a good many of them blues or dance pieces, breakdowns, two-steps, and guitar pieces referred to as "jooking." Although the recorded sound quality was rather poor, the music clearly differs considerably from that of the northern part of the state. Lomax was well aware of this and wrote that they had made "records of what is called 'jooking' on the guitar. The 'jook' is the saloon and dance hall of this part of the South, and 'jook' music furnishes the rhythm for the one-step, the slow drag, and other dances of whiskey-filled Saturday nights. At St. Simon's Island we were lucky enough to find still current and popular an early and primitive type of guitar playing, in which the drum rhythm is predominent, that was the forerunner of the more highly developed and sophisticated 'blues' accompaniments so popular over the South today."[23] We are fortunate not only that Lomax documented this music at that time but that it has persisted to the present in south-central Georgia in Houston County, in the playing of guitarist James Davis.

This "drum rhythm" can be heard in the 1935 recording of Bill Tatnall's "Fandango" and Robert Davis's "Poor Joe Breakdown," the latter appropriately accompanied by his foot-tapping. John Davis's version of "John Henry" is very primitive and reflects the variety of styles in which the tune can be played. Writing about him in 1941, the Lomaxes described John Davis as "the best man, the biggest drinker, the most powerful argufier, and the best singer in Frederica."[24]

The area, and Davis in particular, made a considerable impression on Lomax for, when he returned to fieldwork in the South after a good number of years—having collected in Europe in the 1950s—preparatory to publication of his work on cantometrics and choreometrics,[25] it was to St. Simon's Island that he returned, in 1959. Robert Davis had died in 1953, but John Davis was still alive, and he and many others were recorded and even featured on film.[26] This time Lomax was concerned with work and group songs, and from the trip came the discovery of Bessie Jones, who, together with the Georgia Sea Island Singers, has represented black folk music both sacred and secular—but without blues—for the past twenty years. Big John Davis died in 1972. His brother, Peter, whom Lomax in 1959 acknowledged having previously known, claimed to the author that he had been recorded earlier.

As Hurston had been allowed to select the area of study, it was logical that she should choose her home town of Eatonville, Florida, especially as she had been highly successful gathering material for *Mules and Men.* The book contained one Bubber Brown, based on local guitarist Gabriel Brown, who was in Lomax's words, "better even than Lead Belly although of a slightly different breed."[27] Sometime during late June 1935 they recorded a number of aluminum discs for the Library of Congress from Gabriel Brown and neighbors Rochelle and John French. All of these have been issued on album, in the notes to which they have been described in detail.[28]

Recording problems which began in Frederica followed them to Florida, and some of the discs possess flaws. Also, as is the case with many Library of Congress recordings, many songs start late or finish abruptly. Obviously, since the discs were expensive and limited in supply, the collectors had to be sparing in their use, so on occasions only a part of a song would be recorded. Sometimes the machine was started late as a musician suddenly began to perform without warning or before the operator was ready; sometimes the disc simply ran out before the end of the song and thus a truncated version was all that remained. The summer heat added to the problem. In the older days commercial recording companies often ran into trouble with wax masters and tried to avoid summer tours.[29] Nonetheless the detailed session(s) recorded a wide repertoire, the like of which was rarely documented on commercial recordings.

Both John and Alan Lomax were anxious to record black ballads, including "John Henry," whose "career" had been well documented although no one has ever explained the popularity of the song to the present day.[30] An archetypal blues among East Coast musicians, it was twice recorded by Gabriel Brown—a slide version in the key of E and a finger-picked version in the key of C in which he neatly bends the notes with his fretting fingers in the manner of a slide. The latter is certainly an archaic version, and we must be grateful that Lomax and Hurston requested different tunings and playing styles from Brown. Older songs, gospel songs, and blues were recorded from Brown and

Rochelle French, and both men were allowed to perform rather unusual compositions of their own before finishing with what the fieldnotes list as a "vulgar semi-ballad," "Uncle Bud." Two superb long pieces were recorded—"Education Blues" and "Talking in Sevastopol." The fieldnotes state that the former was in C and the latter in E; on both Brown played slide guitar with a knife while Rochelle French played "straight." This was not the end of Brown by a long way: by 1943 he was recording in New York City, carving out a brief career for himself in the North. These recordings, true always to his Florida roots, are more appropriately covered in the section on northern migration.

Leaving Mary Elizabeth Barnicle and Eatonville, Hurston and Lomax headed south for Lake Okeechobee in the Everglades, where sessions took place in two communities on the south shore of the lake, at Belle Glade and Chosen. At the former a truly remarkable session took place within the last few days of June, 1935. Recorded in the open air, according to a photograph taken at the time, it involved one of the finest small jook bands ever to be documented, comprising harmonica players Booker T. Sapps and Roger Matthews and guitarist Willy Flowers.

Belle Glade is the center of the region's seasonal crop-picking, and the perceptive 1939 state guide even incorporated Hurston's description of the scene, vividly depicted in her novel *Their Eyes Were Watching God,* published two years after she had recorded Sapps and his friends: "Day by day now the hoards of workers poured in. Some came limping in with their shoes and sore feet from walking. . . . They came in wagons from way up in Georgia and they came in truck loads from east, west, north, and south. Permanent transients with no attachments and tired looking men with their families and dog flivvers. All night, all day hurrying to pick beans. . . . People ugly from ignorance and broken from being poor."[31] Sapps and his friends had come from a few miles up the lakeshore at Pahokee, of which the state guide observed that "from Christmas to April, Pahokee is a 24 hour town; long trains of refrigerated cars roll out for northern markets day and night; the streets are noisy and crowded; bars, restaurants and gambling houses are seldom closed." Little surprise that during the seasonal fruit-picking period folk songs were "as thick as marsh mosquitoes," as Lomax reported to the Library of Congress.[32]

We are introduced to the Booker T. Sapps session, all of which is available on album together with more detailed notes, through his fine version of a train imitation on harmonica.[33] Roger Matthews uses another standard number—"The Fox and Hounds"—to introduce his harmonica skills, but Sapps runs the session and everyone seemed content to permit it. A very long, two-part "Alabama Blues" introduces Flower's superb slide guitar with both harps in uncanny unison behind Sapps's wild vocals. Incorporating the "Rolling and Tumbling" motif common enough further west in Alabama and Mississippi, Flowers drives them at almost breakneck speed. Flowers's beautiful yet anguished quitar playing on "Levee Camp Holler" must vie with Gabriel Brown's as the finest playing recorded on the whole expedition. A wide range of song types within a mere eleven titles culminated in the superb "Boot That Thing," which the field notes term a "two-step." These numbers deserve far wider recognition, and we must be thankful once more that between them Hurston and Lomax knew where to find such fine music and were able to document it. They located Sapps and his friends at a labor camp at Belle Glade with great ease. Lomax recorded a little, asked about blues, whereupon the group was pointed out to them immediately. They might have done as well had they read the *Everglade News* for June 28, 1935, which carried an article about a local talent contest at the Belle Glade theater. One section read that "an added prize and one which was not in the competition for prizes was that of five colored boys who presented the music and dancing. Two harmonicas and a guitar furnished the music while two of the group did single and double dancing numbers."[34] Given the nature of the music and the instrumentation, it is hard not to presume that this was Booker Sapps's little group.

Writing back to the Library of Congress on August 3, Lomax referred to the expedition as the "most exciting field trip" he had ever made. Although various recordings for the Library were made in Florida over the next four years, few could be termed blues. One splendid unaccompanied exception was recorded by John Lomax at the State Farm in Raiford, some forty miles southwest of Jacksonville, in May 1936. Ozella Jones sang "Prisoner Blues," and when *Our Singing Country* was written, the Lomaxes had this to say of her: "If Bessie Smith enthusiasts could hear Ozella Jones or some other clear-voiced Southern Negro girl sing the blues, they might, we feel, soon forget their idol with her brassbound, music-hall throat. The blues sung by an unspoiled singer in the South, sung without the binding restrictions of conventional piano accompaniment or orchestral arrangement, grow up like a wild flowering vine in the woods. Their unpredictable, incalculably tender melody bends and then swings and shivers with the lines like a reed moving in the wind. The blues then shows clearly their country origin, their family connection with the 'holler.'"[35] Written in 1941, not long after the trendy patronizing of Harlem artists, including Bessie Smith, by the New York intellectual clique characterized by Carl Van

Vechten, this was a brave—if ignored—statement. Ozella Jones's "holler" quality is clear in her compelling delivery, almost paradoxically defiant to the end. Almost as interesting is the fact that she had copied, unappreciated at the time, Barefoot Bill's 1930 Columbia recording of "Bad Boy"—an intriguing example of oral transmission of material, modified to suit the new singer.

Nineteen thirty-six saw two trips to Virginia by John Lomax to record black music for the Library of Congress, again in penal institutions. He was accompanied by Harold Spivacke, later chief of the Library's Music Division. Two years later Spivacke wrote to Lomax about their trip to the Virginia State Farm at Lynn, on the James River.

> The Warden had expected us and prepared for us a reception in typical Hollywood fashion. He and his family were sitting on the veranda of his house while on the lawn in front he had a Negro quartet which burst into song the minute we appeared. On the steps of the house was sitting a blind Negro strumming a battered banjo. On hearing the quartet you said something to me about "trouble ahead" which I did not understand but which became perfectly clear to me later. . . . the Warden's quartet was very poor; and I admired your tact in getting rid of them after half an hour or an hour and at the same time obtaining from the Warden permission to roam the yard at will. But it was when you sat for over two hours with the blind Negro [Jimmie Strothers], just getting acquainted, that I realized what a consummate artist you are.[36]

This was perhaps the first written assessment of the qualities of John A. Lomax as a collector. Even with hindsight it is difficult to appreciate just how incisive he was, especially given the fact that he was a southerner, born during Andrew Johnson's presidential term of office, making him in his seventieth year when he recorded in Virginia.[37] The events of their recording trips have been analyzed in great detail in the brochure notes to an album which included the best blues recorded in East Coast penitentiaries between 1934 and 1936.[38]

While Lomax was off searching for other singers and songs older than the more current blues that Jimmie Strothers was singing, Spivacke recorded Strothers performing a wide variety of songs accompanied on banjo: "Keep Away from the Bloodstained Banders" and "We Are Almost Down to the Shore" were released on album by the Library of Congress.[39] For his final number Strothers chose a brilliant blues, sung to his own guitar accompaniment, which ran for almost six minutes, ending with the stanza:

> I done played this piece, babe,
> Till my fingers got sore.
> Now there ain't nothin' doin',
> I ain't gonna play no more.

Nor did he. This was "Goin' to Richmond," and we must be thankful for Spivacke's good sense in not trying to cut short the performance. It was, after all, the longest blues yet recorded, affording a little more insight into the singer's approach to his song and its contents.[40] The following day—somewhat surprisingly, it being a Sunday—Strothers recorded "Poontang Little Poontang Small." Its existence was not generally appreciated until its appearance on album, for it was listed only on the check sheet of bawdy titles at the Library of Congress, not in the usual files. To its credit, the Archive of Folk-Song has never attempted to discourage the collection of such material, nor to destroy it once collected.

Snippets of information about Strothers have appeared. Benjamin A. Botkin stated that "Blind Jimmie Strothers learned his hearty minstrel style of gospel-singing while traveling with a medicine show," while John Lomax explained how "Big Jimmie Strothers" became blind: "Years ago an explosion in a mine destroyed his sight. Afterwards he earned a living as a street-corner entertainer. Now, grown old, his favorite songs are spirituals."[41] If so, they did well to record "Richmond Blues" from him, to say nothing of "Poontang." Listening to "Tennessee Dog" one can imagine a really lively performance, perhaps somewhat akin to one by Uncle Dave Macon.[42] Spivacke later recalled that Strothers was at the State Farm because he had murdered his wife with an axe.[43]

The trip on which Spivacke accompanied Lomax was not the first visit to collect convict music in the state. In his 1936 report to the Librarian of Congress Lomax observed that "though the Virginia Negroes do not sing folk songs so readily as their brethren further South, my visits to the headquarters penitentiary at Richmond and to the beautiful farm up the James River, both under happy auspices, added some interesting music to the collection."[44] That was certainly true and not simply of the Strothers titles.

His first visit had been on the weekend of May 30–31, 1936, when he visited the state penitentiary in Richmond. This time the warden made no attempt to set up the type of music which he assumed Lomax would want to hear, as Warden R. R. Penn was to do a fortnight later at Lynn. In Richmond Lomax recorded a number of bluesmen, which might account for the different direction of his attempts on Spivacke's trip. Indeed, prior to their compilation for issue on album in 1979, these sides had never been properly documented. Many supposedly unaccompanied items actually feature one or more guitars, but one man had such a fine voice that Lomax recorded many unaccompanied sides from him. In *Our Singing Country* Lomax mentions "Willie

Williams, who could sing, holler at his mules ('Don't 'low me to beat 'em, got to beg 'em along'), or lead spirituals with equal power and fervor, and in another book he refers to a "Wee Willie Williams (nearly seven feet tall and as big as a mountain)," who might well be the same man.[45] "Red River Runs" is an eclectic blues, the only one of Williams's titles to feature an instrumental accompaniment. On the original aluminum disc Lomax identifies the full title as "Tell Me How the Red River Runs" and gives the probable personnel: Williams's vocal is accompanied by himself and J. Brown on guitars, although the file information suggests that Jimmie Owens may play one of the guitars. Owens played and sang on two other titles, "John Henry" and "Not Satisfied." In the latter, an excellent regional blues featuring gently complementary guitars, Owens is backed by Brown, while in the former, an especially interesting, long version, Owens plays the guitar flat across his lap, using a bar slide. It makes interesting comparison with other versions made in Georgia in 1934 and 1935. Another song by Owens, of which there is no trace at the Library of Congress, was "Georgia Land," transcribed and annotated in *Our Singing Country* as a "sinful reel."[46]

A more sophisticated singer than either Williams or Owens was J. Wilson, whose "Barrel House Blues" reveals a large, shouting voice, although the guitarists—aurally the same men who backed Williams—are traditional enough. James Henry Diggs recorded "Freight Train Blues" backed not only by two of these three guitarists but also, as Lomax announces on the disc, "an unknown person playing a fine bugle," somewhat in the style of cornettist Baby James, who can be heard on a number of 1929 Paramount recordings.

Not all the titles Lomax recorded in May were blues. "Poor Farmers," recorded from Lemuel Jones, is a most interesting unaccompanied protest song, similar to many collected by Lawrence Gellert, unreleased until the Blue Ridge Institute's superb compilations of Virginia folk music commenced in the late 1970s.[47] The song "I Used to Work on the Tractor," recorded in June from Strothers, is also a bitter comment on the exploitive ways of a contractor named Mike Hardy, paralleling similar songs of protest in white music often associated with mill work and coal mines.[48] Perhaps Virginia blacks sang less readily for Lomax than people he found elsewhere, but he was absolutely correct when he stated that his 1936 trips had "added some interesting music to the collection."

Further recordings were made for the Library of Congress in the southeastern states in the late 1930s, but apart from Blind Willie McTell's session, covered in chapter 8, few were of secular music much related to blues. In July 1937 some recordings were made in Charleston's Hibernian Hall of a folk play with a black cast from Wadmalaw Island. A trio of guitar, washboard, and washtub bass recorded "John Henry" and "Corrina," but the disc, AFS-1047, is missing from the Library of Congress vaults. The same group—or at least the same instrumentation—provides the music for some dances later in the play, but none appears to be of any blues significance. In 1939 some performances which included banjo and bones accompaniment were recorded at Brevard Plantation, Adams Mill, near Columbia. Among them were traditional pieces like "Fox Hunt" and medicine show numbers like "Since I Got Mine." In Florida in the early summer of 1939 guitarists Leroy Smith and Lonnie Thomas were recorded behind singers William Johnson and Joe Brown respectively on just three titles, while the fiddle-guitar duet of Fred Perry and Glenn Carver cut half-a-dozen titles. The lone Smith and Johnson title was made at Belle Glade, while the others were recorded at Raiford State Farm.

By the late 1930s the Archive of Folk-Song had initiated the practice of lending its recording machines to collectors already in the field and supplying them with the necessary discs. The records made with the equipment remained the property of the Archive, which prepared duplicates for the collectors.[49]

LAWRENCE GELLERT

Born the son of Hungarian immigrants in 1896, Lawrence Gellert grew up in New York City, but as a result of ill health in the early 1920s, he moved to Tryon, North Carolina, in Polk County just over the state line from South Carolina. To Gellert it was "a northern oasis in the midst of southern prejudice." Gellert took up residence with a black woman and obtained the status of an insider, which no other collector had been able to achieve. He commenced recording black protest songs, both accompanied and unaccompanied, as early as 1924. Understandably, Gellert consciously protected the anonymity of his informants, but the years and location of his blues recordings were known in many instances, although the wealth of accompanied recordings only became known with the release in 1984 of fifteen blues, recorded between 1924 and 1932 in South Carolina and Georgia.[50] This recent discovery of an alternative source to commercial blues recordings and to field recordings for the Library of Congress under the more obvious physical restrictions of a prison setting, made at the very time when blues was becoming a dominant black secular music, offers a new area for research.

Perhaps Gellert had sociopolitical motives for collecting black protest songs as he did: one of his brothers, Ernst, had been murdered in jail while awaiting trial as a conscientious objector during World War I, and another brother, Hugo, was involved with the socialist magazine *New Masses*. While he was still recording black work songs and protest songs, Gellert had some of them written out and printed in issues of *New Masses* in the early 1930s. Nancy Cunard, long-time champion of the black man, included them in her book, published at personal expense in 1934.[51] These songs remained but tantalizing references until the release of an obscure album on the Timely label in 1973. Entitled *Negro Songs of Protest* [*sic*], it included eighteen recordings made by Gellert in the Carolinas and Georgia between 1933 and 1937. The initial album was a cheap affair, possibly of no more than 100 pressings, with no album jacket, a poorly cyclostyled, one-sided page of notes, and no date, but it was later reissued with better packaging and excellent notes.[52]

The majority of the work songs printed in *New Masses* came from South Carolina and from the Piedmont—Greenville, Spartanburg, Travellers Rest, and Gaffney—but Gellert ventured as far as Sumter and Beaufort on the coast below Charleston to collect material, as well as going into northeast Georgia around Greensboro. Since he made no distinction between localities in one state and the next, evidently parochial distinctions within the regional framework did not strike him. At least half of the songs on the album were recorded in the Greenville, South Carolina, county jail. Although most of the songs on the album are given no location, a number clearly stem from Georgia.

Half a century later it is hard to appreciate how difficult and dangerous his work must have been. Most of his singers were prisoners on gangs. The somewhat paternal nature of Georgia's penal establishments given in the 1940 state guide conflicts with Gellert's recollection: "Near Augusta, Georgia, I hung around a chain-gang for days. One of the Negro convicts somehow aroused the wrath of the guards. Two of them went for him, pummelled and kicked him until he lay still and bleeding on the ground. 'Isn't there a law of some kind against a guard beating a prisoner?' I asked a third guard lolling on the grass beside me, watching the proceedings. 'Hell,' he answered, 'there ain't no law for niggers. We has to use our own judgement.' And he showed me the horrible abrasions and ring sores, brass knuckles had caused in the exercise of 'good judgement.' 'We ain't allowed to use no whips no more,' he explained."[53]

Gellert's empathy was immediately obvious, for the singers pulled no punches in their lines: the face of Uncle Tom was not to be seen.

Niggers ain't got no justice in Atlanta,
Down in Georgia where you better live right . . .
Lord you better not gamble and you better not fight.
Niggers ain't got no justice in Atlanta. . . .
Well, he lockin' up the niggers, let the white folks go.
Niggers ain't got no justice in Atlanta.

The only one of the songs on this album which had a guitar accompaniment was "Mr. Tyree." Tyree was a little-loved Atlanta prison guard, to whom the convict requests, "Mr. Tyree, please let my pardon go,/ If you let me out of Bellwood, I won't return no more."[54] Bellwood Prison Camp, where Lomax recorded Jesse Wadley, is probably now Federal Prison Farm No. 1, in the southeast of the city. Built in 1902 it is a massive edifice partly constructed from granite hewn by inmate labor from Stone Mountain and not to be confused with the county jail, known as "Big Rock," which was located just below Decatur Street at 208 Hunter, until demolished in 1969.

Understandably, these songs were well known to other singers. During his December 1934 trip to Georgia penal institutions, John Lomax recorded two versions from convict groups—"I Promised Mr. Tyree" in Bellwood and "We Don't Get No Justice in Atlanta" a few days later in Milledgeville.[55] Behind the singer on "Mr. Tyree" is an excellent guitarist who takes extended solos, showing himself to have been well aware of the more sophisticated licks of Lonnie Johnson. He was obviously not a simple country blues guitarist, and one wonders about his identity and why he did not record commercially.

Prior to Gellert's death in 1980 the wealth of his recordings remained unknown. But in 1982 another album of work songs recorded by Gellert was issued. On this second album the "Mr. Tyree" guitarist returns to accompany a powerful blues: "Gonna Leave Atlanta" includes a forceful indictment of life there: "I'm gonna leave Atlanta; I don't want to see this white man's town no more,/ Cause hard time got here and prosperity is slow." A second guitar-accompanied title, a version of the black ballad "Delia" featuring a different guitarist, also appears on the album. Between them, the two guitarists promised great things. In the album notes Bruce Conforth mentions "500 acetate and aluminum recordings" that Gellert had made, revealing the treasure trove of new material available to add to our knowledge and understanding of black secular music in the 1920s and 1930s.[56]

Correspondence with Bruce Harrah-Conforth led to the issue of fifteen more of Gellert's guitar-accompanied titles in 1984.[57] They constitute the most remarkable aural document of the music from South Carolina and Georgia to have been issued for years. Four titles, recorded in Greenville, South Carolina, in 1924, are among the earliest country blues recorded; they may even predate commercial recordings of country blues, which began in that year. Nine titles were recorded in Atlanta in 1928 and 1929 and a tenth in 1932; all feature the "Mr. Tyree" guitarist, who appears not to sing. On "Gonna Leave from Georgia" this guitarist is backed by two others; Gellert appears to call them a "string band" on the acetate sleeve. This may be the Star Band—an Atlanta string band with a fluid personnel—which is discussed in detail in chapter 8.

This album will doubtless provide endless speculation as to the identity of the singers and guitarists, so it is tempting to commence now. The singer on "Black Woman," recorded in Atlanta in 1929, sounds remarkably like Jesse Wadley (see note 5 below), who was in Bellwood Prison in Atlanta five years later. Perhaps the most revealing is the guitarist on "Six Months Ain't No Sentence," recorded in Greenville, South Carolina, in 1924. He plays in a manner strongly reminiscent of Buddy Moss almost a decade later. For me the pick of a fine crop is the sole representative from Spartanburg, South Carolina, recorded in 1929. "I Been Pickin' and Shovellin'" is performed by a highly skilled and well-practiced singer-guitarist—yet further evidence of the fact that the best did not always record commercially. He may have been Blind (or Slim) *Littlejohn (see chapters 11 and 15).

EDWIN KIRKLAND

While on the faculty of the University of Tennessee between 1931 and 1946, Edwin Kirkland made some field recordings on acetates in the Carolinas in the late 1930s. Some of the recordings were by black artists; those made in North Carolina were blues, mostly guitar-accompanied. The most significant sides were made in December 1937 at Walnut Grove, Stokes County, some fifteen miles above Winston-Salem. Three titles were recorded from singer-guitarist Arthur Anderson, including that title beloved of collectors, "Lost John," and two titles were recorded from singer-guitarist Preston Fulp, accompanied by Wheeler Bailey on guitar. "That'll Never Happen No More" is a nice blues, and Fulp was still able to play it well in 1984! In the same month Kirkland recorded an unidentified singer at Danbury Prison, a few miles north of Walnut Grove, close to the Virginia state line. At the time of writing some of Kirkland's material is in preparation for release through the Tennessee Folklore Society with notes by Kip Lornell, who provided the above information.[58]

As many noncommercial recordings of the 1920s and 1930s from the Library of Congress, Lawrence Gellert, and Edwin Kirkland have recently come to light, perhaps it is an omen that such material from the 1940s will come to light too.

NOTES

1. Carl Engel, *Report of the Librarian of Congress for the Fiscal Year Ending June 30, 1928* (Washington, D.C.: Library of Congress, 1928), p. 143, in Harold Spivacke, "The Archive of American Folk-Song in the Library of Congress," *Southern Folklore Quarterly* 1 (March, 1938): 31.

2. Debora G. Kodish, "'A National Project with Many Workers': Robert Winslow Gordon and the Archive of American Folk Song," *The Quarterly Journal of the Library of Congress* 35 (October, 1978): 229.

3. *The Robert Winslow Gordon Collection 1922–1932,* Library of Congress AFS L68 (Washington, D.C., 1978). Almost all titles were recorded near Darien, but two were from Brickton, North Carolina, recorded December 1925. Debora Kodish to the author, August 28, 1978. See also Robert Winslow Gordon, "Negro 'Shouts' From Georgia," *The New York Times Magazine,* April 24, 1927, in Alan Dundes, ed., *Mother Wit from the Laughing Barrel: Readings in the Interpretation of Afro-American Folklore* (Englewood Cliffs, N.J.: Prentice-Hall, Inc., 1973), pp. 445–51.

4. Spivacke, "The Archive of American Folk-Song": 32.

5. Jesse Wadley, "Alabama Prison Blues," AFS 71-B-3 on *Red River Runs: Library of Congress Field Recordings from the South-eastern United States,* Flyright-Matchbox FLY 259 (Bexhill-on-Sea, England, 1979). Besides more detailed notes by the author the album includes many songs by Reece Crenshaw, Blind Joe, Robert and John Davis, Bill Tatnall, Ozella Jones, Jimmie Owens, Willie Williams, J. Wilson, James Henry Diggs, and Jimmie Strothers, all mentioned in this chapter.

6. *Georgia: A Guide to Its Towns and Countryside* (Athens: University of Georgia Press, 1940), p. 183; Paul Oliver, *Blues Fell This Morning: The Meaning of the Blues* (New York: Horizon Press, 1961).

7. Unidentified, "Stock-time," AFS 260-B-2.

8. Federal Works Agency, Works Project Administration (Federal Writers Project), *North Carolina: A Guide to the Old North State* (Chapel Hill: University of North Carolina Press, 1939), p. 246.

9. Blind Joe, "In Trouble," AFS 269-B, *Red River Runs,* Flyright 259.

10. Bob Groom to the author, April 4, 1980.

11. Elizabeth P. Latt, "Beaufort Project Teaches English, Preserves Gullah," Atlanta *Constitution*, February 28, 1977.

12. Much information concerning the 1935 trip has been published in the inset brochure notes by the author to the albums of material recorded on the trips. Her excellent biography is Robert E. Hemenway, *Zora Neale Hurston: A Literary Biography* (Urbana: University of Illinois Press, 1977).

13. Zora Neale Hurston, *Mules and Men* (Philadelphia: J. B. Lippincott, 1935).

14. Ibid., p. 79.

15. Ibid., pp. 87–88.

16. Zora Neale Hurston, *Dust Tracks on a Road: An Autobiography* (London: Hurchinson, n.d.), pp. 94–95.

17. Hurston, *Mules and Men*, p. 185, and *Dust Tracks*, p. 97.

18. Lanston Hughes, *The Big Sea* (New York: Hill & Wang, 1940), p. 297.

19. Hurston, *Dust Tracks*, p. 134; letter to Rosenwald Fund, December 14, 1934; Hemenway, *Zora Neale Hurston*, p. 207; Robert Hemenway, "Zora Neale Hurston and the Eatonville Anthropology," in *The Harlem Renaissance Remembered*, ed. Arna Bontemps (New York: Dodd Mead, 1972), p. 208.

20. Hemenway, *Zora Neale Hurston*, p. 160. Tony Martin, *Literary Garveyism* (Dover, Mass.: The Majority Press, 1983), p. 27, observes that Hurston was writing for Marcus Garvey's influential weekly *Negro World* before her involvement with *Opportunity* and *Crisis*, and the Harlem Renaissance.

21. *Report of the Librarian of Congress for the Fiscal Year Ending 30 June 1935* (Washington, D.C.: Library of Congress, 1935), p. 159. Alan Lomax to the author, 28 June 1983.

22. William Francis Allen, Charles Pickard Ware, and Lucy McKim Garrison, comps., *Slave Songs of the United States* (New York: A. Simpson, 1867); Guy B. Johnson, *Folk Culture on St. Helena Island, South Carolina* (Chapel Hill: University of North Carolina Press, 1930); Savannah Unit, Georgia Writers Project, Works Project Administration, *Drums and Shadows: Survival Studies Among the Georgia Coastal Negroes* (Athens: University of Georgia Press, 1940).

23. *Report of the Librarian of Congress . . . 1935*, p. 159.

24. John A. Lomax and Alan Lomax, *Our Singing Country* (New York: Macmillan, 1941), p. xii.

25. Alan Lomax, *Folk Song Style and Culture* (Washington, D.C.: American Association for the Advancement of Science, 1968).

26. Edmund Carpenter, Bess Lomax Hawes, and Alan Lomax, *The Georgia Sea Islands*, 1963. This is a twelve-minute black-and-white film.

27. Hemenway, *Zora Neale Hurston*, p. 212.

28. *Out in the Cold Again: Library of Congress Field Recordings from Florida by Gabriel Brown*, Flyright-Matchbox SDM 257 (Bexhill-on-Sea, England, 1975).

29. Gayle Dean Wardlow, "Garfield Akers and Mississippi Joe Callicott: From the Hernando Cottonfields," *Living Blues* 50 (Spring, 1981): 27.

30. Richard M. Dorson, "John Henry," *Western Folklore* 24 (1965): 155–63, as "The Career of 'John Henry,'" in Dundes, *Mother Wit*, pp. 568–77.

31. Zora Neale Hurston, *Their Eyes Were Watching God: A Novel of Negro Life* (Philadelphia: J. B. Lippincott, 1937), p. 196.

32. *Florida State Guide*, p. 475; Alan Lomax to Oliver Strunk, August 3, 1935.

33. Bruce Bastin, brochure notes to *Boot That Thing: Library of Congress Field Recordings from Florida by Booker T. Sapps, Roger Matthews and Willy Flowers,* Flyright-Matchbox SDM 258 (Bexhill-on-Sea, England, 1975).

34. Alan Lomax to the author, June 28, 1983; *Everglade News,* June 28, 1935; Kip Lornell to the author, March 25, 1981. Research by Lornell suggested that Flowers was a resident of Belle Glade, where he died in 1965.

35. Lomax and Lomax, *Our Singing Country,* pp. 364–65.

36. John A. Lomax, *Adventures of a Ballad Hunter* (New York: Macmillan, 1947), pp. 157–58.

37. John A. Lomax was born September 23, 1867, and died January 26, 1948.

38. *Red River Runs,* Flyright 259.

39. *Afro-American Spirituals, Work Songs, and Ballads,* Library of Congress AAFS L3 (Washington, D.C.), and *Negro Religious Songs and Services,* Library of Congress AAFS L10 (Washington, D.C.).

40. Jimmie Strothers, "Goin' to Richmond," AFS 749-B, on *Red River Runs,* Flyright 259, and *Folk Music in America,* vol. 2, *Songs of Love, Courtship and Marriage,* Library of Congress LBC-2 (Washington, D.C.: 1977). See David Evans, "Techniques of Black Composition among Black Folk-Singers," *Journal of American Folklore* 87 (July-September, 1974): 240–49, and Jeff Todd Titon, "Thematic Pattern in Downhome Blues Lyrics," *Journal of American Folklore* 90 (July-September, 1977): 316–30.

41. B. A. Botkin, brochure notes to *Negro Religious Songs,* AAFS L10; John A. Lomax, spoken comment to Jimmie Strothers's "The Blood-Strained [*sic*] Banders," on *The Ballad Hunter Part 7,* Library of Congress AAFS L52 (Washington, D.C.: 1958).

42. *Red River Runs,* Flyright 259; *Virginia Traditions: Non-Blues Secular Black Music,* Blue Ridge Institute BRI 001 (Ferrum, Virginia).

43. Richard K. Spottswood, brochure notes to *Folk Music in America,* vol. 2, LBC-2, p. 3.

44. *Report of the Librarian of Congress for the Fiscal Year Ending 30 June 1936* (Washington, D.C., Library of Congress, 1936) p. 148.

45. Lomax and Lomax, *Our Singing Country,* p. xiii; Lomax, *Adventures,* p. 199.

46. Lomax and Lomax, *Our Singing Country,* pp. 284–85.

47. Lemuel Jones, "Poor Farmers," AFS 729-A-1, on *Virginia Traditions,* BRI 001.

48. John Greenaway, *American Folksongs of Protest* (Philadelphia: n.p., 1953).

49. Spivacke, *The Archive of American Folk-Song,* p. 32. This practice continues to the present, and the author was glad to make use of the Archive's Nagra machine to record Frank Hovington in 1975.

50. Bruce Harrah-Conforth, notes to *Nobody Knows My Name: Blues from South Carolina and Georgia 1924–1932,* Heritage Records HT 304 (Crawley, Sussex, England, 1984).

51. Ibid.; *New Masses,* November 1930, January 1931, May 1932; Nancy Cunard, ed., *Negro: Anthology Made by Nancy Cunard, 1931–1933* (London: Nancy Cunard at Wishart & Co., 1934), pp. 366–77.

52. *Negro Songs of Protest,* Timely Records TI-112 (New York, 1973) reissued as *Negro Songs of Protest,* Rounder 4004 (Somerville, Mass.).

53. Cunard, *Negro,* p. 376.

54. *Negro Songs of Protest,* Rounder 4004.

55. Convict group, "I Promised Mr. Tyree," AFS 254-B-1, Bellwood Prison Camp, Atlanta, Georgia, c. 11–12 December 1934; convict group, "We Don't Get No Justice in Atlanta," AFS 263-B-3, Milledgeville, Georgia, c. 15 December 1934.

56. Bruce Conforth, notes to *Cap'n You're So Mean: Negro Songs of Protest,* (Somerville, Mass. 1982).

57. *Nobody Knows My Name,* Heritage 304. See also Bruce Harrah-Conforth, "Laughin' Just to Keep From Cryin'" (Master's thesis, Indiana University, 1983).

58. Kip Lornell to the author, 13 March 1984, and 20 April 1984.

5

Noncommercial Recordings: The 1940s

In the late 1930s Lawrence Gellert's field trips ended, and by 1940 the Library of Congress was less involved in field recordings in the Southeast. The only known field recordings from the Southeast during the 1940s were made at an unlikely venue at first sight—a black teachers' college in central Georgia. Fort Valley State College in Perry County, south of Macon, was actually a focal center for the rural black community, having held since 1915 an annual Ham and Egg Show, later co-ordinated by the county agricultural agent and sponsored by the college and local businesses. By 1937 an arts festival was begun, including some musical events, and made part of the festival. Horace Mann Bond, the president of the college, inspired by the singing in a rural church, decided to add a folk music festival in 1940. The director of the Third Annual Arts Festival, Edgar Rogie Clark, sent out a letter to "the musicians and music lovers of the State"to the effect that

> on behalf of the Arts Department, and the Administration, we are happy to extend [an invitation] to all players and singers of Negro work songs, ballads and folk blues to participate in a special program on Saturday night, April 6, 1940 at 8:00 p.m.
>
> For this parade of secular folk music we wish to invite all banjo players, guitar players, jug bands, fiddlers, mouth organ, harp players and string bands to come to Fort Valley State College on April 6th.

Fortunately the county agent, Otis O'Neal, was extremely supportive, and he helped spread the word so that genuine folk performers came. The magnitude of this event is hard to appreciate forty years later: there has never been a comparable example of a black folk music festival run entirely by blacks. Incongrously, President Bond was considered a member of the "followers of the Tuskegee educator"—Booker T. Washington—the "Uncle Toms" of the period.[1]

Lawrence Gellert said of black colleges: "Hampton, Fisk, Tuskegee and others in the South, have compiled volumes of plantation melodies from time to time. The songs were taken down from students who were freshly arrived from folk-lore productive areas. However, with endowment from white corporations and individuals their main revenue, and the wish to live in peace with white residents in the area where the institution was located, it is understandable that the songs are carefully chosen and edited to make certain that there was no danger of antagonizing either the sponsors or the Southern whites."[2] He might have added that the vast majority of black academics were not in the slightest interested in this music. Indeed, it is hardly less true today. What Fort Valley was attempting in 1940 was remarkable enough, but how much more so that Edgar Clark could have written: "Some people look down on some of the folk music. This type of music may be what polite society calls gutter songs. Often these 'gutter songs' or blues, as they are rightly called, are the very essence of Negro life; songs that men and women sang in their America. There is a human stir in them all. . . . Some made new songs, some changed old songs, and they are carried from place to place today. We at Fort Valley wish to keep these dying and forgotten songs of the Negro by presenting them as art—Negro art songs." Clark's "art songs" were the songs of the people, not the polished "art songs" of the Harlem intellectuals. Nine years later Clark wrote that at first he was not in favor of the folk music festival, "but since that time I have observed how little that we really know about our own folk culture as compared to other ethnic groups, that I decided I would to do something about it."[3] One can hardly imagine a more enthusiastic and dedicated advocate. A truly remarkable man from Atlanta, he was only twenty-three years of age in 1940. He left the college in 1943, and his whereabouts were traced too late for him to be interviewed. He was murdered in Detroit in 1978.[4]

The 1940 folk festival was a success, but because the agricultural show brought in blacks from the entire region, it was decided in 1941 to integrate it partially with the Ham and Egg Show, rather than incorporate it with the arts festival. It was fully integrated in 1942 and became highly acclaimed. The March 1944 issue of the *Peachite,* the college magazine, includes supportive comments from prominent black and white scholars of black folk life. W. C. Handy attended the opening ceremony at which "so many variations of the *Saint Louis Blues* were played by admiring, sometimes barefooted, guitarists and harmonica players, that Mr. Handy wept with joyous laughter and at the end he took out his gold trumpet and played [it] and the folk loved it." Handy saw the importance of the "Fort Valley Rural Folk Festival," as he called it, as it "presented from year to year the people who are making a new form of music in their own tradition without the influence of radio and records." John W. Work saw its significance in bringing "such inimitable music as 'Gus' Gibson, 'Bus' Ezell, and Samuel Jackson . . . to the attention of America, and in the same action proving to these musicians that their appreciative audience extends far beyond their own church or corner storefront where they previously sang and played." His is an important point: all those musicians interviewed who had performed at the festival. were proud of their small niche in local history. Gus Gibson was able to hear his recorded songs placed on album; Jack Hudson was able to gather his family and excitedly point out his photograph and that of fellow-guitarist Edward Slappy in the *Peachite.* From the establishment world of black intellectualism, composer William Grant Still and author and poet Langston Hughes added their supportive comments. So too did Thomas W. Talley, a collector of black folk tales, Louise Pound of the American Folklore Society, and Howard Odum, who turned down an invitation to attend the opening festival.

According to the *Peachite,* "From the first the festival fell naturally into the evening devoted to secular performers, principally guitarists and banjoists (Note: we have never had a fiddler) and a Sunday afternoon (reaching to unpredictable hours, also, of the evening) for religious groups. Each year increasing numbers have taken part. On the secular evenings, we have had guitarists, banjoists, pianists, harmonic [*sic*] players, jug bands and artists with washboards, 'quills,' saws, bones, and improvised one-string instruments." That really is a remarkable statement. Many of these folk instruments have seldom been recorded. The banjo was subsequently assumed to have vanished by that time from the black tradition. The Greek syrinx or quills— variously termed reed-pipes or panpipes also—are hollow reeds of graduated lengths bound together to form a musical wind instrument. Quills players have been recalled by a number of persons but rarely recorded. Commercial recordings were made by Big Boy Cleveland for Gennett in 1927 and by the Texan Henry Thomas for Vocalion between 1927 and 1929, and recordings were made in north Mississippi for the Library of Congress in 1942. The only named Fort Valley festival performer on quills was a young Perry County man, Willie J. Burden, a possible suicide from a gunshot wound in 1959 at the age of 35. If by 1944 the festival did not have a fiddler, they were still around and appeared there as late as 1953, when Elbert Freeman brought his five-piece band from Monticello, having played the previous year with a guitarist. In 1951 an Oglethorpe fiddler named J. D. Smith had taken part—his second festival—but although a resident of that town since 1927 he probably was not a folk artist. Registration notes state that he "plays mainly from sheet music" and one of his two performances was "The Mocking Bird." However, his accompanying guitarist, Willie C. Towns, played "John Henry" as a solo piece. The fiddle tradition persisted even longer, and Elbert Freeman was recorded as late as 1967.[5]

The first festival recordings were made in 1941 by John Work from Nashville's Fisk University. The preliminary contest was held at 5:00 PM and the final took place at 7:30 PM on Thursday, March 6, with "Mr. W. C. Handy, Mr. Alan Lomax guests." Unfortunately, Work's name was omitted from the official program, whereas Lomax did not attend. On the Friday the festival winners were presented after lunchtime barbecue and Brunswick stew and a spiritual by Sam Jackson's group. Probably those who recorded did so afterwards, before they headed home, although the religious component of the festival was broadcast on the Sunday over radio station WMAZ. Those recorded by Work were eventually copied by the Library of Congress and allocated their AFS disc numbers between 5147 and 5167.

Recorded were guitarists Sonny Chestain, Allison Mathis, Gus Gibson, and Buz [*sic*] Ezell, who also played rack-harp. Harmonica player Jesse Stroller and pianist Charles Ellis were also recorded, as were banjo player Sidney Stripling and the Smith Band, comprising guitar, bass, banjo-mandolin, and kazoo. The band was from Macon, and Blind Billy Smith—as the *Peachite* called him, although he was listed differently almost every time he participated—was a good friend of Blind Willie McTell in the 1950s and generally known around Atlanta as Blind Cliff.[6] Allison Mathis—or Anderson Mathis, as he is probably more accurately named in a later listing—was a superb guitarist, playing slide in a manner reminiscent of Fred McMullen or Curley Weaver. He performed a powerful "Bottle Up and Go," transformed into his own piece, and was supported by the fine harp of Jesse Stroller on two other numbers. Chestain recorded a rough but highly appealing "Po' Boy," which has distinct stylistic similarities with the similarly tuned "John Henry,"

recorded by John Davis from St. Simon's Island in 1935. Buster Ezell
was something of a local character and was still playing at the festival
in 1953. Pianist Charles Ellis performed one pleasant number with no
particular regional distinctiveness, while the Smith Band recorded two
titles—a fine "Fort Valley Blues" and "Smithy Rag," a spirited version
of the 1918 popular song "Hindustan."

The field notes are specific about the instrumentation of the Smith
Band and the upright bass is bowed. In one musical combination or
another Clifton William Smith returned year after year and as late as
1951, as C. W. Smith, was playing guitar along with Bamalama on jug
and rubboard, keeping up-to-date with "Boogie Woogie." In 1942
William C. Smith was playing banjo and an undated festival lists Clifton
Smith's "string ensemble" from Macon. Jack Hudson, a festival participant born in 1909, remembered Blind Cliff's string band from Macon.
A thoughtful annotator in 1951 added a note that C. W. Smith and his
accompanist lived at 64B Tindall Heights, Macon, stating that Smith
played guitar, mandolin, and banjo and had traveled with string bands
from "Cuba to Canada."

The 1941 festival judges were invited back the following year, but
Tuskegee's William L. Dawson only arrived in time to judge the
religious festival on the Sunday. Absent were Howard Odum, Guy
Johnson, and Zora Neale Hurston, but "William C. Handy of New York
City" was back as "Chief Judge"; the other two were John Work and
Willis Lawrence James of Atlanta's Spelman College, who had recorded
two "folk" songs in the accepted white style for Paramount in 1927.
Linton Berrien, then director of music at Fort Valley State College, sent
a letter to faculty staff stating that "our Festival had now become an
established tradition. We at Fort Valley must keep alive these dying
and forgotten songs, ballards [*sic*], work songs, melancholy melodies,
'gutter songs,' or blues . . . performed on guitars, mouth organs, jug
bands, by string bands, railroad gangs, peach orchard groups. . . . We
must keep these songs, games, and tales alive by presenting them."
Prizes were now offered. First prize for the best string band was $10.00
with $5.00 for second best. For best banjo, guitar, harp, and fiddle,
there were first prizes of $7.50 and further prizes of $5.00 and $2.50
for each instrument with a prize of $5.00 for the best novelty instru-
ment, "jug, washboard, bottle, etc." The festival was also carefully
organized "in order to prevent long-drawn out [*sic*] performances of
mediocre performers." Brief tryouts before a judge took place in Room
16, and those who passed went into Room 14 before going on into
the auditorium, each with a card showing "name, place, sponsor, if
any, and air to be played." Tryouts were on Thursday, March 5, from

5:00 to 7:00 PM with the main festival commencing at 7:30 PM so there was little time for delay. The memorandum regarding the handling of the crowd included an order that "a space of about seven rows back on the right hand side of the auditorium (as one enters from the front) should be reserved for white visitors."

A list of the 1942 secular performers exists:

Guitar.	Fred Lindsey	Fort Valley
	Willie Chasteen [*sic*]	Macon
	Ernest Poole	Macon
	Joe Holmes	Macon
	John Amica	Fort Valley
	Grace Lindsey	Fort Valley
	Emmitt Matt	Andersonville
	Mose Hill	Perry
	Buster Ezell	Fort Valley
	Guss Giberson [*sic*]	Fort Valley
	Bob Roberts	
	Anderson Mathis	Perry
	Jack Hudson	
Harmonica.	Jessie [*sic*] Stroller	Fort Valley
	Johnnie Lee Thomas	Griffin
	Sarah Jessie	Fort Valley
	Tobe Jackson	Hawkinsville
	Leroy Ellis	Marshall
		[possibly Marshallville]
Soloists.	Mary Perry	Americus
	William C. Smith	Riverside
	Snead	Montezuma
String Bands.	Dise Williams & Charlie Jenkins	Byron
	Sneeze, Sanders, Duffy	Montezuma
Banjo.	David Hillman	Riverside

The 1941 winners were back: Ezell, Mathis, Stroller, Gibson and John Thomas. Other names were to become more familiar, and some were to record the following year. Jack Hudson's name was hurriedly added in longhand to the list, but the name of his hometown—Fort Valley—was omitted. Bob Roberts might have been from out-of-state, for his residence was simply "523 Army Lot, Macon Street," which could well have referred to nearby army camps like Fort Benning or Camp Wheeler, as Edgar Clark had gone out of his way to invite wartime groups of soldiers to the festival.

The 1943 festival, held on Friday, March 5, and Sunday, March 7, was again recorded. Willis James recorded AFS discs 6986 to 6993, of which the first half were of secular music. These comprised two sides by Buster Brown, a harmonica player from Cordele, three by Buz

Ezell accompanied by his own guitar, one by Gus Gibson, and a rag by James Sneed's band. With the exception of one by Ezell, all these sides have been released on album.[7] Buster Brown and Ezell both sang topical songs about the war, and Ezell's "Roosevelt and Hitler" became a firm festival favorite. However, there were traditional themes—a faster-tempoed "I'm Gonna Make You Happy" by Brown, Sneed's "Southern Rag," and Gibson's "Milk Cow Blues" (not the song associated with Georgia guitarist Kokomo Arnold). Although the field notes by Lewis Jones and Willis James list "Milk Cow Blues" as "sung by Gus Gibson (?) with guitar by Will Chastian (?)," Gibson maintained that he had played the guitar and that Chastain had not been present. James Sneed might well be the person whose "tin-can band" was recalled by Atlanta guitarist Buddy Keith, but the *Peachite* tells us rather more about his guitarist partners, J. F. Duffy and Alvin Sanders, who were peach orchard workers. "The audience loves them because of their talent and their intensely interesting personalities; they achieve a personal, natural, human balance which is above mere comedy and which might well be the ambition of more famous artists. Sanders and Duffy never fail to 'set-off' an unrestrained current of response from the audience when they sing."

The elimination contest for new performers took place as usual at 5:00 PM; "all new performers and those who entered last year who did not win prizes" were auditioned for some to join the winners of the previous year in the final, starting at 7:00 PM. Money appears to have been tighter, for there was no second prize for string bands and the three prizes for other categories were reduced to $5.00, $2.50, and $2.00. Folk tales was an additional category and the poster proudly proclaimed that "Records Will Be Made of all Performers' Music."

A list of artists without their instruments was given:

Fort Valley	Edward Slappy
	Gus Gibson
	John Amica
	Bus Ezell
	Lester Jolley
	Jackson Hudson
	Lewis Clayton
	Charlie Smith
	Walter Baldwin
	Ulysses Knight
	George Lumpkin
Byron	D. Williams & C. Jenkins

	Will Chasteen
	Chovie Hill
Marsha[ll]ville	Harvey Oglesby
Powersville	John H. Graces [*sic*]
Americus	Pearly Brown
Cordele	Buster Brown
Hawkinsville	Tobe Jackson

Pearly Brown, no relation to Buster, remained a blind religious street musician into the 1970s in Americus and Macon. However, other artists were present, some of whom were also recorded. In 1972 Pete Lowry and I located a washboard player, Arthur "Popcorn" Glover, who claimed to have been recorded in a guitar-and-washboard duet with Blind *Simon *Davis, with whom he played for many years.[8] There seems to be no reason to doubt that he recorded; he made no other such claim. Incidentally, we located him two years before we were even aware that college files remained on some festivals, but on checking we found an undated sheet listing the names of "Mr. Eddie Buckeye Bryant and Mr. Arthur Glover (washboard), 312 Clark Street, Milledgeville," which was where Roy Dunn had taken us to find him. This sheet almost certainly referred to 1943 as Gus Gibson was listed with "Milk Cow Blues," corroborating his statement that Will Chastain was not present. Fort Valley guitarist Jack Hudson, with no prompting, remembered the words of Gibson's song, made at the same time that Hudson recorded "Chain Gang Blues" and "Baby You Think I'm Crazy about You, You Better Change Your Mind" for a Miss *Reed. In 1974 Hudson recalled both songs—which were listed on the sheet with Gibson's—and his uncle was even able to quote lines from the former.

Also on the list was Will Chasteen from Byron, who played two titles, one of which was "Poor Boy," and one wonders if he might not have been the Sonny Chestain who recorded this title in 1941. Alvin Saunders from Henderson and Duffy (variously named Jeb, Zebe, and Zeke) were listed as performing two titles, one of which was the rag recorded with James Sneed in 1943. Duffy's name was most probably Jeb, as the field notes list him as J. F. Duffy. Buster Brown is listed as performing "I Got My Questionnaire" and "Come Back Baby," surely the ones he recorded. Dess [Dise?] Williams and Charlie Jenkins were the guitar-harmonica couple listed as a string band in 1942, and they played "John Henry" and "Lost John." Photographs of Hudson and Edward Slappy, taken at the 1943 festival, appeared in the 1944 *Peachite,* and on the sheet of titles performed, Slappy is credited with three blues. Hudson recalled that Slappy also recorded. Finally Ezell—

variously credited as Buz, Bus, and even Bux—was listed as playing "The Story of Joe Louis," which was recorded from him in 1943.

Other snippets of information exist about the 1943 performers. John Amica was shown playing banjo, which he subsequently denied ever having played. Buster Brown also played harmonica in a quartet which included "trap drums." Harvey Oglesby was elsewhere stated to have been from Nashville, but as this is close to the Florida state line, Marshallville seems more likely. V. L. Holmes brought a harmonica-guitar duet from Thomaston, but J. Merritt's string band from the same town appears not to have arrived.

Perhaps Willis James arranged for more titles to be recorded than the Library of Congress checklist suggests. There are some discs of religious songs, not all of which were copies, held at the college and entered in the Library of Congress files, made later in the year by James.[9] It is also possible that Edgar Clark recorded some himself. Despite his initial reluctance he quickly became involved in the folk festivals and by the end of the decade had not only formed the New York Folklore Council but was making lecture tours with color slides and recorded music. He even offered to bring his recording machine to the 1949 festival, by which date he had undertaken field trips in Mississippi, Georgia, South Carolina, and Louisiana, all with no outside funding.

Life magazine published photographs of the 1943 show and even quoted from Buster Ezell's "Roosevelt and Hitler."[11] Other photographs were made available to the *Peachite* and included Jack Hudson, Edward Slappy, Buster Brown (twice), Sanders and Duffy, as well as a remarkable shot of two young boys playing one-stringed instruments, using a bottle to slide over a wire.

In 1974 Pete Lowry and I made a brief search to locate survivors from these early festivals, as well as a check of Houston and Perry County death records. While we found no trace of many performers, we quickly realized how parochial these events had been. Within a few hours, we had located John Amica, Jack Hudson, and Gus Gibson still living in or close to Fort Valley. Finding Gus Gibson truly was a shock, as the *Peachite* had reported his death some time after the 1943 festival. Tobe Jackson (born 1908) had died in 1972; John Henry Grace (born 1905) had died in Powersville a few months earlier, in March 1974; and Chovie Hill (born in Houston County in 1896) had died in 1961. Interviews revealed that Buster Ezell, Jesse Stroller, Dise Williams, Alvin Sanders, Will Chastain, and Lewis Clayton were all dead.

The 1944 festival began on March 3 and included choirs, glee clubs, and quartets. Of the listed performers, only Buster Ezell, Tobe Jackson, and Alvin Sanders were back; nothing was ever heard again of Sanders's old partners, Sneed and Duffy. This time Sanders was teamed with pianist Curtis Daniels, and they played "Southern Rag." Some of the new performers were clearly from the folk idiom. Nathan Jefferson, born in 1902 in Fort Valley, where he died in 1966, played harmonica and Virgil Harris, a guitarist from Zenith, played two blues. Emanuel Green, a Fort Valley guitarist known to Jack Hudson, was also present. However, a change of taste is represented by two trumpet-playing entrants, one of whom played "Sweet Slumber" and "Star Dust." Doubtless Hoagy Carmichael would have been pleased—after all, W. C. Handy had brought white pianist J. Russel Robinson with him in 1941—but it seems some distance from President Bond's initial concept. Interestingly, the main guest speaker was Ralph McGill, liberal, antiracist editor of the *Atlanta Constitution,* while in the local *Leader-Tribune* the following week, Otis O'Neal, the black agricultural agent, thanked "the white people of the community whose interest and financial support have encouraged the continuation of the event for so many years." Of passing interest, the festival poster stated that the 1944 winners would be recorded.

Secular music seems to have been a staple part of the festival for a further decade. Although details are either unavailable or unascribable to particular years, circumstantial evidence is strong. For example, in 1945 the C. W. Smith "string ensemble" might not have come from Macon, for a scribbled note states "boys scattered but will try to get some." The $10.00 prize that year was won by Glover's String Band, which comprised, at least, "Popcorn" Glover on washboard and George Anderson, a banjo player who roomed with him in Milledgeville. Clay Wade's band was unable to attend because of illness. Apparently the 1945 festival featured a new harmonica-guitar duet from Fort Valley—Jesse Stroller and Charlie Smith, both of whom had attended before, the former recording in 1941. There might be a connection with the Smith and Harper who recorded for ARC in Augusta in 1936. "Poor Girl" has two men singing in unison, very much like Buddy Moss and Josh White on their 1935 ARC sides. Presumably one plays guitar and the other harmonica, the former reminiscent of Moss, the latter in the same regional style as Jesse Stroller. A second guitar is added on both this title and "Insurance Policy Blues," a slightly slower number with fine slide guitar, in the style of McMullen, Weaver, and Allison Mathis. As harmonica players are called "harpers," it is just possible that Smith might be the guitarist. If so, Smith and Harper might be Charlie Smith and Jesse Stroller from Fort Valley, with another local man—maybe Allison Mathis. After all, a main road links Macon with Augusta, and other artists at the sessions had come to Augusta from Atlanta and Charleston.

Familiar names appeared at this 1945 festival: James Merrit, V. L. Holmes, John Amica, Joe Holmes, Gus Gibson, Buz Ezell, John Lee Thomas—who wanted to play saw as well as harmonica—and the one-man band from Byron, Chovie Hill. Some new names appeared as the festival's fame spread. Americus guitarist Bosey McDonal was too sick to attend, but Clarence and Willie Price, a guitar-banjo duet from Cordele, were there, as were Sweet Little, a guitarist from Eatonton (recalled by Roy Dunn), Julius Gipson on washboard from Milledgeville, Grady Mathis, a Fort Valley harmonica player, and guitarists Wesley Jackson from Macon and James Hopkins from Donaldsonville. Willie J. Burden, who appears to have been in the army, appeared playing quills. The festival was also broader in scope, for the *Leader-Tribune* promised that "on Friday night [March 9] there will be exhibitions of children's folk games, the usual guitarists and banjoists and other folk performers, possibly a railroad section gang singing railroad songs and a 'liar's contest' featuring local story tellers in folk tales."[12]

By the early 1950s the festival was dying. Nineteen fifty-four saw the last secular folk festival and the following year the last of sacred music. Changing attitudes among students caused it to close, for students so ridiculed folk artists that they refused to attend.[13] Registration sheets exist dated Friday, March 30, 1951. Dolphus "Gus" Gibson played an "original composition," "Boogie Blues," and "Step It Up and Go," and an Oglethorpe harmonica player won $3.00 with "Mama Blues" and "Good Morning Little Schoolgirl." The remarkable Buz Ezell had updated "Roosevelt and Hitler" to "Great Things Are Happening in Korea" and reworked his 1941 "Boll Weevil." He also performed "The Story of Truman and Staff" and "A Robber of the First National Bank 1951." He must have been a fascinating balladeer and it is clear why he worked for many years with John Robinson's six-ring circus, playing guitar as he had done since the early years of the century.

The name of Raymond Bronson from Lumpkin had been forwarded by the local vocational agricultural instructor,[14] so Otis O'Neal's 1942 directive to scout for local talent still held good. Other sponsors are on file: the Macon County Schools suggested a gospel quartet, the Rising Four, and Noamon Grubbs, a guitarist. A faculty member of Savannah State College recommended a local man, Richard Grayson, who could "play a solo on a saw with remarkable ability."[15] Also present were Fort Valley guitarists Ausby Alexander and David E. Lockett, and Blind Billy Smith from 1941 was back as C. W. Smith on guitar with Bamalama on "jug and rubboard," who must have been the man recalled by a Savannah informant as "a guy in Florida who danced on his hands. And he would use a jug, washboard, or anything else to make music with. . . . It must have been about (1955 or 1957). They called him Bamalam, because of him beating on that old washboard that they used to have to wash clothes. He used to make music with that thing. And he could take a jug and blow it, you know. He'd draw peoples. . . . But he was an elderly man when he was doing that."[16]

The 1952 festival was held on March 27 and 28 and the "oldest participant who never misses," Buz Ezell, was back with two titles which won him $20.00. So too were guitarists Ausby Alexander—with Mose Smith on spoons—and David Lockett, and they won $10.00 and $5.00 respectively. Another guitarist, Major Vance from Perry, won $6.00, and the string band which won $20.00 comprised Artis Ford and Elbert Freeman from Monticello. Their selections were "Shoe Shine Boy" and "Tennessee Waltz."

In 1953 the festival was held on Friday, March 27, and Ezell was again there. Moses Smith was back playing "clay spoons" with George Smith, a blind player. Charlie Jenkins, absent for some years, was back playing harmonica, but his old partner Dise Williams had been replaced by Will Chastine [*sic*]. Jenkins, listed as having played harp since 1940, was still around—though not interviewed—in 1974. Gus Gibson played two songs, including "Sweet Honey Hole" (probably the Blind Boy Fuller song), and a note stated that he had been there since the first festival. Ausby Alexander was back with another local guitarist, Philip Stevens, playing a current Little Walter hit, "Sad Hours." Perry guitarist Isiah King also played juke-box hits with Rosco Gordon's "No More Dogging" and "A Bald-Headed Woman," clearly from Lightning Hopkins. Whoever completed the registration blank had added two lines of the song: "I don't want no woman with her hair shorter than mine, She jus' make trouble buying wigs all the time." W. C. Handy's comment that performers played "without the influence of radio and records" clearly no longer held good.

The augmented Freeman String Band from Monticello played "Blues–Freeman Arrangement" and "Down Yonder," made famous by the white Georgia fiddler Gid Tanner. Elbert Freeman was on fiddle and Ortis [Artis?] Ford, presumably the man who accompanied him the previous year, on guitar, joined by Nathaniel Ford on electric guitar, Howard A. Smith on piano, and Alfred Johnson on bass. Freeman and

Nathaniel Ford were recorded fourteen years later when, among tunes played at the 1952 and 1953 festivals, they recorded "Blues" with fine, rough, alley fiddle from Freeman, closer to Eddie Anthony's style than on his other pieces, such as "John Henry" and Fiddlin' John Carson's "Old Hen Cackled."[17] Both men are now dead.[18] Nathaniel Ford might be the man recalled by Roy Dunn as a member of a band which played around Machen and Shady Dale (Henry County), to the north of the county seat of Monticello. Along with Joe *Buck, *Bo Harris, Will *Sanders, and a father and son, *Em and Edward *Sanders, was *Namon Ford. Somewhere between Dunn's pronunciation and my transcription in 1972, Nathan could easily have become Namon—again it was two years before the college files came to light. Perhaps Alvin Sanders of the Sneed band was related to these men too.

The 1954 festival was held on Friday, March 12, and only Jack Hudson and Edward Slappy are known to have attended—at least their names are written on the back of an announcement sheet of that year. The following year the *Leader-Tribune* stated simply that "President C. V. Troup and members of his staff at the college . . . are lending their co-operation as usual to make this agricultural event a success."[19] However, Bill Mathis was chairman of the festival committee in 1955 and the blind Americus singer, Pearly Brown, had been invited to attend, for in a letter to the college, he promised to bring "the Lord's work and electric guitar."[20]

Thus ended a truly fascinating decade and a half of festivals at Fort Valley. Apart from a few recordings at Virginia's Hampton Institute, they constitute the only known noncommercial recordings of blues in the Southeast from the 1940s. They provide the link between pre- and postwar recordings and offer unparalleled evidence of both persistence and change in the music. With no preconceived notions— although a few performers appear to have tried to guess the possible tastes of the judges—these musicians clearly played the music with which they were most familiar. Many of them, like Buz Ezell and the fascinating Smith band, were effectively professional. The very persistence of the older black secular traditions might well have been enhanced by the principles under which the festivals were conducted, but it is probably fair to assume that little ground had been given in the direction of newer black secular sounds when the Smith Band played "Boogie Woogie" or when Artis Ford and Elbert Freeman played "Shoe Shine Boy." If by 1953 Little Walter and Lightning Hopkins hits were being played, that is really little different from Alison Mathis performing "Bottle Up and Go" in 1941, provided it remained some distance from a straightforward copy.

What really does strike one forcibly is that the earlier secular sounds were alive and well throughout the 1940s and into the 1950s. Gus Gibson was still performing Blind Boy Fuller numbers into the early 1950s—doubtless in his very personal manner—and new performers still came forward. The reason for many older performers failing to attend in the 1950s was the changing attitude of the college students, which terminated the festival. When Elbert Freeman and Nathaniel Ford recorded, more than a dozen years after the festival had ceased, they showed no modern musical influences. When three former musicians at festivals were interviewed in 1974, there was nothing to suggest that any significant musical changes had entered their lives before they ceased to play. When Pete Lowry recorded "Popcorn" Glover on washboard behind Atlanta bluesman Frank Edwards in 1972, it was a conscious attempt to try to recreate Edwards's 1941 recording session.[21] "Popcorn" fitted in easily enough and there was no reason to assume any great changes in his playing style or preferences in the thirty years since he appeared at Fort Valley.

Apart from the unique setting of the Fort Valley festivals and the abundance of information they provided, they also point out very effectively that the apparent shift in black secular music as reflected in commercial recordings—or lack of them—can be very misleading, if commercial recordings are our sole arbiters of changes in taste. Of course the music was changing, but change did not necessarily register with everyone, and the older black secular music styles persisted long after critics blandly assumed them to have disappeared.

NOTES

Much of this material is held by the Music Department of Fort Valley College, Georgia, and I am indebted to Bill Mathis for permission to use it. Some was published in a three-part article in *Blues Unlimited* 111 (December, 1974-January 1975): 11–13, 112 (March-April, 1975): 13–16, 114 (July-August, 1975): 20–21.

1. Roi Ottley, *"New World A-Coming": Inside Black America* (Boston: Houghton-Mifflin, 1943), p. 238.

2. Lawrence Gellert, brochure notes to *Negro Songs of Protest,* Rounder 4004 (Somerville, Mass.).

3. Edgar Rogie Clark to J. W. Freeman, February 2, 1949.

4. Wendell P. Whalum, Morehouse College, Atlanta, to the author, February 5, 1979, and Estas Smith, Jackson State University, Miss., to the author September 12, 1978; Eileen Southern, *Biographical Dictionary of Afro-American and African Musicians* (Westport, Conn.: Greenwood Press, 1982), p. 71.

5. In Monticello, Georgia, by John Burrison of Georgia State University, April 8, 1967.

6. David Evans, brochure notes to *Atlanta Blues 1933,* JEMF 106 (Los Angeles, Calif., 1979).

7. *Fort Valley Blues,* Flyright-Matchbox SDM 250 (Bexhill-on-Sea, England, 1974). The Smith Band's "Smithy Rag" is on *Red River Runs,* Flyright 259 (Bexhill-on-Sea, England, 1979).

8. Pete Lowry, "Doin' the Piedmont," *Blues Unlimited* 100 (April, 1973): 23.

9. Library of Congress copies are dated June 1943. A different Fort Valley copy is dated June-July 1943. Willis James was the director of the Fort Valley Peach Folk Festival held at the college on August 1, 1943, but only gospel groups attended and were recorded that summer.

10. Edgar Rogie Clark to J. W. Freeman, February 2, 1949.

11. *Life,* March 22, 1943.

12. Fort Valley *Leader-Tribune,* March 1, 1945. A Wesley Jackson became a frequent rhythm-and-blues session guitarist in Atlanta in the 1950s.

13. Bill Mathis interviewed by Pete Lowry and Bruce Bastin in Fort Valley, Georgia, August, 1974.

14. Maulvin Engram to J. Walker Freeman, March 27, 1951.

15. Mrs. Mavis Walker Donnelly to Dr. C. V. Troup, February 26, 1951.

16. Reverend Patrick Jones interviewed by David Evans and Anne Evans in Statesboro, Georgia, April 23, 1975.

17. *Another Man Done Gone,* Flyright 528 (Bexhill-on-Sea, England, 1979).

18. David Evans to the author, September 15, 1977.

19. Fort Valley *Leader-Tribune,* March 3, 1955.

20. Pearly Brown to the Department of Music, Fort Valley State College, February 24, 1955.

21. Frank Edwards, *Done Some Travelin',* Trix 3303 (New Paltz, N.Y., 1973).

6

Atlanta Strut: The Pianists

One group of musicians who clearly had the scope and opportunity to perform across the range of black music in the South were the pianists. Little Brother Montgomery well exemplified this, playing solo piano in turpentine camps, working with blues guitarists like Big Joe Williams, and playing in a wide variety of bands, many of them his own.[1] Perhaps one of the best-known pianists to come from Georgia was Thomas A. Dorsey, "Georgia Tom" until his entry into church life caused him to revert to his full name. Born in 1899 in Villa Rica, halfway between Atlanta and the Alabama state line, he moved to the city about 1910. He remembers little of the music of those days but clearly there "wasn't many pianos."[2] He recalled a number of pianists in Atlanta who used to play at the 81 Theater on Decatur Street, where most of the out-of-town black shows played when they stopped over. Ed Butler usually played piano for these shows, but about 1912 Eddie Heywood, Sr., took over the stool before moving to New York to appear either with his band or in an accompanist's role on a number of records in the 1920s.

Others were no more than names Dorsey recalled: Edgar Webb, who died young, Long Boy, Lark Lee, James Henningway [*sic*], and Nome Burkes. However, Dorsey left Atlanta about 1915 and eventually settled in Chicago, so it is difficult to see where these pianists fitted into the local blues scene, if indeed they could be termed blues pianists.

Dorsey's recollections were very general and while he stated that he "got (his) blues experience when (he) was a young boy about 10 at the old 81 Theater,"[3] he remembered Lark Lee only as "a great piano player, in his style, in his way" while others were "the highbrows over around the college there, now, I didn't know any of those fellows around over there, because that was off limits. Nome Burkes, he was pretty well up there, but he was making some money."

There is nothing to suggest that these pianists were strictly bluesmen in any sense and considerable evidence to suggest that soon after the Atlanta Riot of 1906, when it might be presumed that blacks would have regrouped and become less factional, there was a distinct pattern of higher society players which the teenaged Dorsey was unable to see. He often played at parties at which "there'd be maybe three or four piano players there, or five," but not guitarists and fiddlers as "they didn't use them (then). Only used 'em in the country—the fellows where there wasn't no pianos, they'd pick 'em. And they could play them too. But you didn't see 'em too often in town. There they used piano."[4] Clearly two levels of musicians existed, and the urban pianists did not mix with the influx of rural musicians, although serious rural depopulation was almost a decade away. Since these rural musicians themselves grouped into various "sets" and some considered themselves "above" the rougher set of Peg Leg Howell, it is hardly surprising that the more sophisticated urban musicians, performing usually at clubs and elaborate parties, mixed little if at all with the rougher immigrants.

One of the pianists Dorsey recalled was James Hemingway, variously spelled Heminway and Hemenway, remembered also by two other Georgia-born pianists, Rufus "Speckled Red" Perryman and Horace Malcolm.[5] Hemingway clearly traveled a good deal. Speckled Red recalled him playing in the taverns and bordellos in Detroit with such pianists as Will Ezell and Charlie Spand. Spand might have been born about the turn of the century in the small Georgian town of Ellijay, near the Tennessee state line, and may well have been the Charlie Spann remembered around Atlanta. Speckled Red was born in Hampton, Georgia, in 1891 or 1892 and moved to Atlanta in 1917, marrying and moving to Detroit, where he stayed until 1927.[6] Thus he must have met "the 375-pound James Hemingway," whom he described as being "big and fat and his belly would rub against the keyboard," sometime in the 1920s in Detroit, although he also appeared in Chicago and New Orleans during those years.[7] Horace Malcolm, born in Atlanta in 1910, moved with his family to Chicago in 1919 and only then began to learn to play piano. He began playing house parties about 1924. Malcolm learned from neighborhood pianists, but he particularly stressed Hemingway's influence, stating that he learned the style used on the Harlem Hamfats' "Root Hog or Die" from him, although this was not recorded until 1937. New Orleans cornetist Punch Miller recalled that Hemingway played piano to his accompaniment of Billy and Mary Mack's first Okeh release, recorded in New Orleans on January 22, 1925. They "had a boy who died, from Atlanta, Georgia,"he said, "James something, he was a dope fiend too, died. James Hemingway. He was a good piano player."[8] The Chicago *Defender* in 1927 described Mary Mack's new show, "Pickings from Dixie," which opened at the Monogram Theater. The accompanying jazz band included James Hemmingway [*sic*] on piano and a New Orleans violinist, O'Neil J. Levasseur.[9]

Speckled Red's brother, Willie "Piano Red" Perryman, entered the Atlanta picture at a later date. A measure of his distance from the general run of country bluesmen was that he knew relatively few of them, although he was the only Atlanta musician ever to recall Eddie Mapp's guitarist, Guy Lumpkin.[10] Richard M. Jones maintained that Ferdinand Morton took the nickname "Jelly Roll" from an Atlanta pianist of that name, and Morton certainly worked with singer Ida Cox at a theater there in 1920.[11] Harlem stride pianist Willie "The Lion" Smith recalled a boogie pianist named "Peachtree," who might have been from the city, and Buddy Moss remembered Bell Street Slim as a "wild piano player" who "conked out."[12] Piano Red remembered Soap Stick,[13] and the Atlanta-born dancer Henry Williams stated that "Nob Derricot played low-down piano" there.[14]

Pianists with the touring show and local jazz band scenes overlapped while some early Atlanta pianists were fine exponents of ragtime and the cakewalk. Perry Bradford, best known for his involvement in the recording of Mamie Smith's "Crazy Blues," which sparked the entire commercial blues scene in 1920, moved to Atlanta in 1901 when he was six. He learned to play piano when young and remembered Paul Turner and Frank Rachel trying to absorb piano licks whenever a piano and cakewalking contest was held.[15] Rachel died in Atlanta in 1911.[16] Jelly Roll Morton told Alan Lomax that Racheal [*sic*] was "supposed to be the tops in Atlanta."[17] Graham Jackson, an Atlanta pianist who took over the 81 Theater piano stool from Heywood but whose fame came largely from being a favorite performer of President Franklin D. Roosevelt, remembered Atlanta pianists like Hemingway, whom he called "outstanding," Perry Bradford, Paul Turner, Ed Butler, Harvey

Quiggs, and Baby Grice, who actually came from Pensacola, Florida.[18] Asked if he recalled a Jelly Roll besides Morton, Jackson chuckled and said, "On Decatur Street there were a lot of them."[19]

Another pianist, little-known but a stalwart of the black entertainment scene, was Troy C(alvin) Snapp. He accompanied Ma Rainey, perhaps the finest female country blues singer and herself a Georgian, in the early 1920s before she came to Chicago to record for Paramount in 1923 and before she used Georgia Tom Dorsey to back her.[20] By late 1923 Snapp was touring with the "Stepping Along" company as part of a five-piece band; from 1926 to at least 1929 he led the Whitman Sisters' Musical Comedy Road Show. They had been partly responsible for the cakewalking craze which had struck Atlanta in 1906 and which Perry Bradford so enthusiastically remembered. In 1927 Snapp recorded with members of the Road Show behind Kid Brown and Ernest Michall for the Black Patti label, possibly as Snapp's Ginger Snaps on one title. He also backed singer Mattie Dorsey on four titles for Paramount. By 1932 he was back in Atlanta, still directing the band traveling with the troupe, which retained its Atlanta roots.[21]

Female blues singer Cleo Gibson made one coupling for Okeh in Atlanta in 1929 accompanied by her Hot Three, which included Atlanta pianist J. Neal Montgomery. In the past much speculation centered on Gibson's identity, suggesting that the name masked a better-known singer, possibly even Bessie Smith.[22] However in 1924, when Boissey De Legge's Bandana Girls Company played the Dudley Theater in Petersburg, Virginia, Cleo Gibson was in the cast.[23] According to *Billboard,* "Gibson and Gibson, the lady being Cleo Sephus," appeared at the Frolic Theater in Birmingham on October 8, 1923, and the woman sang blues.[24]

Although J. Neal Montgomery accompanied several blues singers, not all the Atlanta sessions attributed to him were in fact by him. Four sides, recorded by Okeh two days before the Cleo Gibson sides, were by Waymon "Sloppy" Henry, aurally an older vaudeville performer. The Chicago *Defender* of December 19, 1925, carried a picture of Henry, wearing a top hat, on page 5. He was never listed as a resident in Atlanta; Georgia Tom met him in Memphis in 1927, which suggests that he recorded on occasions when his touring company was in town. His first coupling in 1924—one side a rag—had been accompanied by Eddie Heywood, and a fascinating 1928 session found him teamed with the very rural guitarist Peg Leg Howell and fiddler Eddie Anthony, plus another guitarist. The March 1929 sides with J. Neal Montgomery included the Georgia blues "standard" "Some Sweet [Cold] Rainy Day." Whether or not Montogomery played on the single David

Pearson title later that month, he did not play on the Columbia sides of Lillian Glinn made in April 1929; the accompanying group was white.[25] Perry Bechtel, the guitarist, was to record again in the following year for the same company, backing other blues singers.[26]

Taylor Flanagan, the pianist with guitarist Perry Bechtel's Orchestra, went on to record for Columbia in 1931. Dan Hornsby, a member of the orchestra, was also a talent scout for Columbia. The band had just returned from a long stint in the North when the Lillian Glinn sessions were arranged. Her manager, R. T. Ashford, who was responsible for bringing Blind Lemon Jefferson to record, was shrewd enough to ensure that her appearance in cities like New Orleans, Atlanta, and her home town, Dallas, coincided with touring Columbia recording units.[27] Perhaps Hornsby had little prior notification that Glinn would be in Atlanta in early April, since he had himself just returned to the city. Perhaps Montgomery's regular ten-piece band was out of town: *Billboard* for August 17, 1929, reported that Montgomery's orchestra was playing at Rockaway Beach, New York, and at Atlantic City, New Jersey, for the 1929 summer season.[28] Hornsby needed to look no further than his own band and brought in a trumpet player from Charlie Troutt's Melody Artists who had also recorded for Columbia. Pete Underwood plays the very fine, black-sounding horn.[29]

Another musician who adds a little more to our picture of the Atlanta piano scene is Edgar Battle, a multi-instrumentalist—although mainly trumpeter—born there in 1907. By 1921 he was playing with pianists J. Neal Montgomery and Harvey Quiggs before going on to work theaters in Atlanta with Eddie Heywood's band and then to tour with carnival bands.[30] He recalled Quiggs's band with which he played at the Atlanta Roof Gardens in 1921, describing Quiggs as "the Art Tatum of his days, a fantastically gifted pianist, whose style stemmed straight from Blind Tom; his band played ragtime, blues, Dixieland, as well as ballads."[31] Blind Tom had been a virtuoso pianist of slavery times.[32] Quiggs was Battle's cousin; another talented relative was pianist Pomp Timmons.[33]

Perhaps as further evidence of the polarity of jazz and blues within Atlanta, an interview of Atlanta-born trombonist J. C. Higginbotham, published in *Downbeat* in 1964 by critic George Hoefer, makes no reference to the lower level of blues playing in the city. Referring to Higginbotham in the jazz sense as a "blues player" who played—in all probability—in J. Neal Montgomery's band at the Atlanta Roof Gardens, Hoefer understandably makes no further comment upon blues in the city. Perhaps the trombonist says it all when he says that his "family owned a restaurant and was fairly well-to-do."[34]

If that was the experience of one Georgia trombonist—or more accurately perhaps that of his interviewer—it was not one shared by another, born only six years later. Trummy Young was from Savannah, which quite clearly had a flourishing music scene on a number of levels. Being a seaport it was a "good-time town," and Young recalled not only touring stars like Ma Rainey, Bessie Smith, and Ida Cox but also "local talent including many blues guitar players, church music where 'they hollered and jumped all night,' and hot pianists such as 'Eagle Eye' Shields, who went on to lead a good band in Jacksonville."[35] In an almost identical biography, Stanley Dance states: "Many musicians who were not born there, nevertheless made it their home. In the countryside around were numerous turpentine camps, and these attracted blues singers, who entertained the workers in the juke joints. On Saturday nights, all these people came to town, and Young soon became familiar with the basic blues. In fact, while still quite small, he used to lead one of the singers around. His name was Blind Willie, and after taking him to wherever he was to perform, the boy would find somewhere to rest until he was told, 'It's time. to take Willie home!'"[36] This might even have been Willie McTell, who frequently played in the area, although he was well able to get around on his own.

In July and August 1927 the Victor mobile recording unit toured the South from Bristol, Tennessee, through Charlotte to Savannah, where in late August they recorded a gospel group—the Jacksonville Harmony Trio—two other singers, and a remarkable pianist, Sugar Underwood. Underwood played on the harmony trio's sides and also backed Ruby Houston, a female vacalist, on one title which was never issued. Although Underwood has been rather cursorily dismissed as a "black-key piano player" by clarinettist Ed Hall of the city's Ross De Luxe Syncopators, who had recorded on the previous day, his piano solos, "Davis Street Blues" and "Dew Drop Alley Stomp," demand attention. The titles suggest a Jacksonville, Florida, origin for him, as does his presence with the trio. Davis Street runs northward, parallel to the railroad tracks through Jacksonville's downtown area; Dew Drop Street runs east-west in downtown Jacksonville, so presumably the Alley title refers to this or to a small street running off it.[37] A different, possibly local, pianist was used to back the other singer, L. C. Prigett. Clarence T. Walker is a good pianist in the James P. Johnson tradition, but the male Prigett sounds to be from the vaudeville circuit and the issue of his "Frogtown Blues" on the reverse of Julius Daniels's old country piece, "Can't Put the Bridle on That Mule This Morning," makes an odd coupling.

Savannah also produced pianist Arthur H. Gibbs (born 1895), who went to New York in 1913 with a dance band.[38] His 1923 recordings for Victor show little blues influence. Sidney Easton, born in Savannah in 1886, appeared in carnivals, vaudeville and minstrel shows,[39] and even in films in the 1940s.[40] In October 1926 he recorded a vocal duet with Elizabeth Smith for Victor in New York, accompanied by Georgia guitarist Bobby Leecan. Two days later, Margaret Johnson recorded his "When a 'Gator Holler Folks Say It's a Sign of Rain," a powerful blues full of folk elements and suggestive of a Geechie origin with the "'gator" reference and her intonation. Here is a clear overlap between musical levels. Perhaps the reverse title, "Graysom Street Blues," locates it in Savannah. The city's sports stadium on Highway 80 is the Grayson Stadium.

Quite evidently there were differing levels of musical entertainment in black secular music into which blues found its way. The influences of traveling shows must not be undervalued. The major recording artists of the period traveled extensively throughout the South, and especially the Southeast, and artists like Bessie Smith were on the road for weeks at a time.[41] The relationships between class and black musical tastes are mentioned in greater detail in chapter 12, with specific reference to Durham, North Carolina, but the Atlanta pianists draw into focus the significance of their city to all musicians, among them the bluesmen.

NOTES

1. Karl Gert zur Heide, *Deep South Piano* (London: Studio Vista, 1970).
2. "Georgia Tom Dorsey," *Living Blues* 20 (March-April, 1975): 17.
3. Ibid., p. 18.
4. Ibid. p. 20. See also Arna Bontemps, "Rock, Church, Rock !" in *Anthology of American Negro Literature,* ed. Sylvestre C. Watkins (New York: Random House, 1944), pp. 425–32.
5. Bob Koester, "The Saga of Speckled Red," *Jazz Report* 2 (January, 1962): 14. Paige Van Vorst, "The Harlem Hamfats (Part 1)," *The Mississippi Rag* 4 (February, 1977): 8.
6. David Mangurian, "Speckled Red," *Jazz Journal* 13 (June, 1960): 3, states Perryman was born in 1891; Koester, "Speckled Red": 15, states 1892. Both state October 23 but Koester gives birthplace as Monroe, Louisiana. Only Newton County separates Henry County from Walton County, Georgia, which has a Monroe township.
7. Rudi Blesh, *Shining Trumpets: A History of Jazz* (London: Cassell, 1949), p. 304.
8. Punch Miller interviewed by Richard B. Allen in New Orleans, April 4,

1957. Tape copy deposited at the William Ransom Hogan Jazz Archives, Tulane University.

9. Chicago *Defender*, May 21, 1927.

10. Karl Gert zur Heide to the author, April 5, 1978.

11. Laurie Wright, *Mr. Jelly Lord* (Essex, England: Storyville Productions, 1980), p. 3.

12. Roger Brown to the author, October 30, 1978.

13. Karl Gert zur Heide to the author, November 2, 1978.

14. Marshall and Jean Stearns, *Jazz Dance: The Story of American Vernacular Dance* (New York: Macmillan, 1964), p. 70.

15. Perry Bradford, *Born With the Blues* (New York: Oak Publications, 1965) p. 19.

16. *Freeman,* May 29, 1911. Courtesy Lawrence Gushee.

17. Alan Lomax, *Mr. Jelly Lord* (London: Cassell, 1952), p. 121.

18. Karl Gert zur Heide to the author, September 4, 1980. Baby Grice was Thomas Grice.

19. Roger Brown to Karl Gert zur Heide, January 4, 1978.

20. *Record Research* 67 (April, 1965): 12.

21. Karl Gert zur Heide, "Clyde, Mike and the Whitman Sisters," *Footnote* 8 (February-March, 1977): 16–22.

22. John Baker, *Record Research* 87 (December, 1967): 8.

23. Chicago *Defender*, February 2, 1924.

24. *Billboard,* October 27, 1923.

25. Jeff Tarrer, *Storyville* 83 (June-July, 1979): 167–68.

26. Bruce Bastin, *Storyville* 85 (October-November, 1979): 12.

27. Paul Oliver, liner notes to *Lillian Glinn,* Vintage Jazz Music VLP 31 (London, 1978).

28. Walter C. Allen, *Record Research* 93 (November, 1968): 5.

29. Tarrer, *Storyville,* p. 167.

30. Albert McCarthy, "Notes on Two Neglected Jazzmen," *Jazz Monthly* 6 (January, 1961): 11.

31. Bertrand Demeusy, "Edgar 'Puddinghead' Battle," *Jazz Statistics* 29 (October, 1963): 2.

32. Tom Stoddard, "Blind Tom—Slave Genius," *Storyville* 28 (April-May, 1970): 134–38.

33. McCarthy, "Notes," 11.

34. George Hoefer, "The Early Career of J. C. Higginbotham," *Downbeat* 31 (January, 1964): 19.

35. Charles E. Martin, "Trummy Young: An Unfinished Story," *The Second Line* (Summer, 1978): 30.

36. Stanley Dance, *The World of Earl Hines* (New York: Chas. Scribner's Sons, 1977), p. 22.

37. Eric Townley, *Tell Your Story: A Dictionary of Jazz and Blues Recordings 1917–1950* (London: Storyville Publications, 1976), pp. 87, 93.

38. *ASCAP Biographical Dictionary,* 3rd ed. (New York: ASCAP, 1966), p. 259.

39. Stearns, *Jazz Dance,* pp. 23, 71. *ASCAP Biographical Dictionary,* p. 195, gives date of birth as 1896.

40. Dr. Klaus Stratemann, *Negro Bands on Film,* vol. 1, *Big Bands 1928–1950* (Lübbecke, Germany: Verlag Uhle & Kleimann, 1981), pp. 65, 76.

41. Bruce Bastin, "From the Medicine Show to the Stage: Some Influences upon the Development of a Blues Tradition in the Southeastern States," *American Music* 2 (Spring, 1984): 29–42; Doug Seroff, "Blues Itineraries," *Whiskey, Women, and . . . ,* 11 (June, 1983): n.p.

7

Goin' to Town

With its range of geographical complexity and persistent rural isolation, the musical variations within Georgia are considerable. In the first
third of the twentieth century, prevailing economic conditions
throughout northeastern Georgia brought musicians schooled in all
these variations into Atlanta.[1]

In every Georgia county except two, the number of black farm
owners increased between 1910 and 1920 but declined sharply in
1920-25, when blacks suddenly began migrating from farms in greater
numbers than in the earlier migration during the war years of 1915-16.
The panic of 1921 coincided with the spread of the boll weevil and
the depletion of land through poor husbandry, an overworked cotton
monoculture, and soil erosion. It is hardly surprising that Georgia failed
to ride out these troubles, despite the supposed boom of the Coolidge
Era, as Atlanta was mainly dependent on agriculture. Not only was
cotton unable to withstand the economic collapse of 1929 but people
who had quit farming later moved to Atlanta in search of jobs and relief
benefits. The population of the city grew from under 155,000 in 1910
to 200,000 in 1920, swelled to 270,000 by 1930, and topped 300,000
by 1940, more than doubling in thirty years, despite the estimate that
between 1920 and 1940 half of Georgia's young people had left the
state because of lack of job opportunities.[2] Small, locally prosperous
market towns of that period like Shady Dale (Jasper County) and

Willard (Putnam County), both east of Atlanta, are virtual ghost towns today.

That Atlanta was not to be the Mecca for the rural underprivileged soon became apparent. City planners at the time were well aware that while the population had grown 59 percent in the twenty years to 1920, the city's territory had increased by over 140 percent. It was "urban growth on a grand scale, but it was often chaotic and without visible design"—urban sprawl which would eventually lead to severe urban renewal. In 1920 the Atlanta *Journal* appreciated that the city's "very progress will become a penalty,"[3] and the city planning commission's annual report for 1922 introduced the first zoning law, altering informal Jim Crow arrangements into a formal pattern of residential segregation for "the promotion of public peace, order, safety and general welfare."[4] Whereas Atlanta's Ku Klux Klan members "rarely engaged in public demonstrations prior to 1920," by 1922 the Klan was marching in the Labor Day parade, replete with drum and bugle corps, and in September of that year the population elected a Klan mayor, adding to Klan successes at state level for governor, a senator, and a superior court judge.[5]

Within a decade Atlanta experienced the compression of a flood of rural, undereducated workers into specific urban areas. A perusal of the city's statistical information based on the 1930 census tracts offers interesting reading. Tract F-33, roughly encompassing Decatur Street in the south and Auburn Avenue in the north in a half-moon shape, enclosed much of the area inhabited by bluesmen and their associates. With a nonwhite population of 98.2 percent, it featured among the highest rates of homicide and police arrest. It also featured the worst rate of residential structures in good condition and in 1937 held one of the highest rates of W.P.A. employable relief cases. Transitory or permanent, these people brought with them such aspects of their sub-culture as would facilitate this traumatic shift in life-style, and a series of unmistakable schools or cells of musical styles grew up within the general regional blues framework.

NEWTON COUNTY, GEORGIA

Many of the musicians who made Atlanta their home originally came from small communities located in and around Newton County, some thirty miles to the southeast. In Newton County between 1906 and 1908 sociologist Howard W. Odum began to collect texts of black secular songs.[6] Without doubt he was the first serious scholar to turn his attention to black folk music, especially the secular, rather than to the bowdlerized stage performances generally perpetuated by established academic institutions. Some of these institutions, notably Hampton Institute, were also interested at times in documenting the grass roots of black music but, by and large, the respectability of the black middle class operated against such an approach. Much of Odum's work in Newton County was set out in considerable detail in the *Journal of American Folklore* for 1911.[7] Of his collected song texts, forty-three were from Newton County residents and twenty-two from visitors to the county; the remainder largely came from earlier work he had undertaken in Mississippi.

With hindsight it is easy to bewail the fact that Odum took down only song texts, never the melodies, let alone the names and more detailed locations of the singers. However, this was typical of folkloric interest at the time, and to be fair one should stress that very few persons have ever been equipped technically to transcribe the complexity of the simplest blues, let alone been so competent in an age without the advantage of constant playback on a tape recorder. Apart from that, formalized western musical notation cannot easily cope with the written transcription of blues. At the time no one was in any way interested in the vehicles of the texts, the singers, and it is only the western tradition of biographic approach which dictates the very type of study attempted in these pages. Thus we do not know the sources of songs Odum collected from visitors to Newton County. "One More Rounder Gone" might well have all the hallmarks of a Blind Willie McTell precedent; "Nobody's Bizness But Mine" and "Honey Take a One on Me" (from a county resident) became widely-spread songs and were heavily recorded, while "Lilly" has a reference to Bell Street, presumably in Atlanta.

Odum became professor of sociology at the University of North Carolina at Chapel Hill, involving himself off and on to the end of the Depression with black folklore, often in conjunction with the equally remarkable sociologist Guy Benton Johnson. Odum received sabbatical leave for the second half of 1928, and a note among his unpublished papers states that "he traveled around the South, gathering material for a book, and apparently did not keep copies of the letters he wrote."[8] One presumes he visited Newton County again—his son was still sheriff of the county in 1972—but whether or not he revisited any of his informants of twenty years earlier may never be known. Surely, if the life histories of other Newton County and neighboring artists can be generalized, some of his earlier informants would have moved to Atlanta at the beginning of the 1920s.

While some well-known Georgia bluesmen of the 1920s moved to Atlanta, their contemporaries stayed behind. "Sun" Foster and George White both lived in Newton County at Porterdale and were playing guitar by the time these early Georgia bluesmen were forming their styles and repertoire. Foster was born on Christmas Day 1894 in Henry County, raised near McDonough, and moved into Covington, Morgan County, in the summer of 1915. He had been playing banjo since about 1903, but by the time he moved to Morgan County he was also playing guitar, on which he had been proficient for some three years. He remained on the fringe of the music scene at the time, knowing Curley Weaver all his life, as well as Barbecue Bob and Eddie Mapp. He was in frequent demand for playing at parties, for both whites and blacks. "They'd come get us and carry us off. We'd have a party five nights a week, every night. . . . We'd just pass the hat round and whatever they took up they'd give to us. Ten dollars back on down to one dollar; anything they could get up." Probably this very informal method of payment failed to suit the likes of Weaver and Mapp, who, like other professional musicians, carefully rationed their music for specific returns. "Candy Man" was probably the first tune that Foster was able to play, but while he could pick well, he was also capable, like the majority of East Coast guitarists, of playing with a slide, using a pocketknife with the guitar slung flat across his lap in Hawaiian style. "I played with a slide too, played Spanish, C-natural they call it. Vastopool. Tune the guitar in four or five different tunings for different kinds of music. . . . I used to make music." Besides the better-known musicians, Foster also recalled other fine local musicians of those early days, some of whom were corroborated from other sources. Two older guitarists were Jim Smith and Nehemiah Smith—not related, "just friends and good friends at that."[9] *Buck Smith and Tom Smith also played guitar but were not as influential in the area as Jim and Nehemiah. Three brothers, *Si, *Homer, and *Washy *Vandergriff, all played stringed instruments.

George White, Foster's brother-in-law, was born on December 29, 1901, in Jackson, Butts County, moving to Newton County to the immediate north when he was five. He tended to play as much on his own as with Foster for parties, but they often played "set-dances" (square dances) in which they'd alternate as caller and guitarist. He had received his first guitar when he was twelve, learning to play from his step-father's brother, Joe Berry, and to play banjo from an older brother, Worthy White. "Candy Man" was also the first piece that he picked, "starting out in C-natural," but played slide on tunes like "John

Henry." He was at pains to point out that "you wouldn't call 'Candy Man' and 'Atlanta Favorite Rag' [the second tune he learned] blues . . . it's just got a beat for you to dance by," going on to state that "you can take 'Let the Deal Go Down'; I used to sit up all night and play hit for people to dance." That was back before he played with Sun Foster, not long after Odum had written down the words to that song and a mere year or so after he published them.

George White played frequently and traveled a good deal, around Griffin, Monroe, McDonough, and "near up to Atlanta" in the days before hardtop roads. "I played just about as much for one color as I did the other," he recalled and, like Foster, was in sufficient demand for whites to come from as far as Luella and Griffin to collect them to play, arriving about 7:30 in the evening and expecting them to play all night until, around 4 o'clock, "in went the floor." Around Christmas time they played six nights and never missed. Sometimes they would play first of all at a drug store until nine or ten at night and then go to some white home to play out the night. He "played all night long a million nights."[10]

White and Foster taught Curley Weaver to tune his guitar when he was still at school and helped him with other tunes. He knew both Nehemiah and *Judd Smith, frequently playing with them both, as well as other musicians whose names came from no other source. *Maylon *Parker and John *Hardeman played guitar, *Vine *Hardeman played fiddle, while *Jesse *English played banjo. Like many other musicians, White also sang in a quartet broadcasting in Covington for some eight years until the group, the Willing Five, folded in the 1940s. All the men worked at the local cotton mill.

George White's wife, who had been listening to the conversation with interest but no comment, suddenly filled in details of musicians her husband had overlooked. Her one-armed brother, Robert Smith, played harmonica with George White; another harmonica player was Pete *Coleman, who "could really make it blow." Both men are dead. Two others, contemporaries of Curley Weaver, lived in nearby Covington. Herman Jordan was, by all accounts, a fine guitarist but was also a heavy drinker and had been hard hit by Curley's death. Willie C. "Dusty" Rhodes, born in Newton County in 1910, could play both piano and guitar, the latter in a style very like Weaver. Neither man was easy to locate or, when located, easy to interview to any purpose. Jordan was never recorded despite a number of attempts, but David Evans recorded Rhodes in 1977.

This shows some of the breath and depth of secular music and the number of fine, hitherto unknown musicians in just one small area in the early years of this century. From this Newton-Walton-Morgan area came a group of talented musicians who moved to Atlanta in the 1920s—among them Peg Leg Howell; Robert and Charlie Hicks, who became better known as Barbecue Bob and Charlie Lincoln; Curley Weaver; and Eddie Mapp. Not necessarily better than those who remained behind, they represent a remarkable body of blues proficiency. But they were quite distinct from one another, and the differing styles of these five guitarists from within a few square miles of northeastern Georgia emphasize the inherent danger of classifying musicians too rigidly. Peg Leg Howell's group with their rougher, rural heritage did not really fit with the smoother guitar style of Buddy Moss and Curley Weaver. The twelve-string guitar style of the Hicks brothers—probably a Newton County style—had nothing in common with the more melodious style of Blind Willie McTell. Indeed, the oft-mentioned twelve-string guitar school in Atlanta was less a school of shared musical characteristics than a number of idiosyncratic musical styles loosely grouped within the broader pattern of the Piedmont Blues.

INTO ATLANTA

Among the bluesmen working in Atlanta, Ed Andrews probably has the distinction of being the first country blues singer to be recorded commercially on location, in April 1924.[11] Georgia-born Reece Du Pree, who claimed to have written "Shortenin' Bread," had recorded "Norfolk Blues" about two months before, but not on location.[12] Although Du Pree's voice is more obviously that of a stage performer, he is accompanied by two country blues guitarists. The first recorded country blues guitar without a vocal was "Guitar Blues," played by Sylvester Weaver in November 1923. No relation to Curley Weaver, for many years before he moved to Louisville Sylvester Weaver was thought to be from Georgia. He was, however, born in Louisville in 1897 and died there in 1960.[13] Weaver's "Guitar Rag" inspired a whole generation of white guitarists, and his "Smoketown Strut" of 1924 produced widely imitated runs in white music.

Pioneer recording agent Polk Brockman probably was responsible for Ed Andrews being recorded; occasionally he would "accost musicians on the street."[14] When Okeh released Andrews's recording, the Chicago *Defender* ran a drawing of Andrews with the caption, "Right where blues songs were born is where Ed. [*sic*] Andrews was singing 'em and playing 'em when the special Okeh Recording Expedition discovered him."[15] Clearly Okeh presumed Andrews to be an Atlanta resident, but he was outside the main stream of Atlanta artists of the 1920s and may well have been only a transitory figure.

The common feature of the city's blues scene was its mobility. While many musicians lived there for years, many others passed through, stopping over briefly as part of the general migration pattern—rural to urban, deep South to the northern East Coast cities like New York. Nineteen twenty-four, the year in which Andrews recorded, was the only year he was listed as being a city resident, living at the rear of 322a Holcombe Avenue. Nineteen twenty-four also marks the beginning of the influx of rural musicians.

Atlanta rapidly became a center for blues recording, featuring not only Georgia artists, but also artists from other southern states, a blues melting pot. The Mississippi Sheiks, the Memphis Jug Band, Blind Willie Johnson from Texas, Ed Bell from Alabama, Willie Walker and Pink Anderson from South Carolina, among many, all recored there. Following the Ed Andrews session, Columbia and Okeh recorded sessions there on eighteen occasions between 1925 and 1931, making it their favorite location in the South. Victor and Bluebird recorded there twelve times between 1927 and 1941. Brunswick's first field trip in 1928 was to Atlanta. The American Record Corporation never bothered to record under field conditions there but took its Georgia artists to New York.[16]

PEG LEG HOWELL

Among the bluesmen who were to record in Atlanta in the 1920s, first to arrive was Joshua Barnes Howell, known as Peg Leg because of a shooting accident in 1916. He came in seven years later, in 1923, from Madison, county seat of Morgan, where he had worked at a fertilizer plant. Born in the adjoining county to the south, in Eatonton, on March 5, 1888,[17] he grew up with the music of the preblues period, and aurally his style is an older blues form. Perhaps these origins helped cement the friendship with fiddler Eddie Anthony, thought by Buddy Moss to have been from Macon. Howell gathered about him a group of musicians, named on his second Columbia recording session as his "Gang," which included Anthony and guitarist Henry Williams, who recorded with him and appeared in the one photograph of Howell dating from the 1920s, other than the formal snapshot in the Columbia catalog in which Howell, resplendent in moustache, white shirt and tie, vest, and jacket, is topped off by what appears to be a white fez. The sales blurb alongside states "the loss of a leg never bothered 'Peg Leg' as far as chasing around after blues is concerned. He sure catches them and then stomps all over them."[18]

Howell was the first local country bluesman to be recorded in Atlanta by Columbia, in November 1926. He was spotted playing on the streets accompanied by mandolinist Eugene Pedin, who was not required for the session. Howell recalled that "Mr. Brown—he worked for Columbia—he asked me to make a record for them. I was out serenading, playing on Decatur Street and he heard me playing and taken me up to his office and I played there."[19] Wilbur C. Brown, who became assistant manager of the studios,[20] arranged for Howell to cut four titles for which he received the princely sum of $15.00 per side, although he had to wait until December 11 for payment on the first pair and until the new year for payment for the others. "New Prison Blues" and "Fo' Day Blues" went on sale in February 1927; the other coupling was released in May,[21] by which time Howell had already been back to record six more titles with Anthony and Williams. They obviously sold well, for he was to make seven further sessions. Columbia also tried to promote sales in those magazines which reached a black market: in a June 1928 edition of the *Bookman,* Abbe Niles wrote, "Give me a jazz record with strangeness and humor, or with wit, or with honest slapstick. . . . Therefore I shall holler for such fox-trot records as Columbia's of the raucous, ginny voices and felonious fiddling of Peg Leg Howell and his Gang in 'Too Tight Blues.' "[22] One can imagine many jazz musicians cringing at the thought that their music should be confused with the rough music of the Gang.

This rough music clearly reflected some rough experiences. Williams apparently died in jail in January 1930, serving time for vagrancy—whatever that might have meant at the time. In 1927, when he first recorded, the city directory lists ten Henry Williamses, all black, all laborers, as well as others with other occupations. In 1929, however, one roomed at the rear of 316 Martin across the street from Eddie Anthony and close to the blues center of town. Court records show a number of charges attributable to that Henry Williams including driving without a license, possession of intoxicating liquor, playing skin game—Howell, solo, recorded "Skin Game Blues" on November 9, 1927—intoxication, and vagrancy.[23] This would seem to fit the man who recorded, recalled vaguely by a number of Atlanta bluesmen but clearly by none.

Life was also tough for Howell. J. B. Howell, convict Number 4B236 of the River Camp in Atlanta, wrote on September 22, 1932, to George Maddox, possibly the judge who sentenced him:

> I have made four mt 10 days on a six month sentence and I am asking you Dear Sir Will you let me out as I have a sick wife at home and no one to see after her. I had a talk with Mr. Thompson to Day. he is willing

for me to go. he told me to write you. If you will please let me out and Ill guarntee you Ill never Come Before you again. please Sir let me out on the sake of and old mother and a sick wife. Thare no one to see after Them. I was sent up for whiskey But Ill never come Be fore you any more. Ive got another means for sus port. I see wood and coal as fall is Come-ing in I can make it all OK.[24]

One wonders whether a white bootlegger would have received six months. When Howell sang "New Prison Blues," "Ball and Chain Blues," "Rock and Gravel Blues," and "Skin Game Blues," it was from personal experience. If he really intended to "susport" his family sell-ing wood and coal when the fall came, he probably also knew about "Broke and Hungry Blues." When released from jail he "went back to making moonshine whiskey."

In 1963 Howell was located in Atlanta by three local enthusiasts—Jack Boozer, Roger Brown, and George Mitchell. He was ill and died soon after recording an album on April 11, 1963—about a month after he was located—in an Atlanta studio. As he had not played since 1934, when Eddie Anthony had died, the album makes difficult listening and is of no practical value in attempting to identify regional characteristics.

When not playing solo, Howell usually recorded with Anthony and Williams, but other members of his Gang also appeared on record, although not always credited. Two mandolin players were Eugene Pedin and Jim Hill, although it seems that only Hill recorded, on the final session in April 1929. Howell stated that he had also recorded with Ollie Griffin on banjo in the Gang. In fact, no Howell sides feature banjo; "Banjo Blues," unfittingly, is a fiddle and guitar duet. Griffin, a fine Atlanta musician and a multi-instrumentalist, was also a member of the Star Band, a similar loose aggregation of musicians, where he often played guitar. Roy Dunn remembers him as a fiddler and pianist; Frank Edwards felt he was a better pianist. Presumably, Ollie Griffin plays the unattributed second fiddle behind Anthony on Howell's "Broke and Hungry Blues" and "Rolling Mill Blues," recorded on April 10, 1929. It has been suggested that the accompaniment to the unissued Okeh session of December 9, 1930, in Atlanta by Brothers Wright and Williams is aurally Henry Williams's vocal with Eddie Anthony on one of the two fiddles.[25] Perhaps Griffin plays the other. Two other Atlanta guitarists, Jonas Brown and Charlie Rambo, both of whom played with Griffin in the Star Band, stated that Griffin had recorded on violin with Howell.[26] However, he might even have been the unknown second guitarist on the August 1928 session of Sloppy Henry, which appears to have Howell and Anthony present.

Indeed, this type of music must have been popular—allied as it was with the rough fiddle music and hokum sides by such white Georgia artists as Gid Tanner, Lowe Stokes, and Clayton McMichen—for Anthony and Williams recorded two sides for Columbia without Howell present, while Anthony recorded two sessions for Okeh under the name of Macon Ed, together with Tampa Joe, who might have been different men on each occasion. Aurally, Barbecue Bob might be present on some, notably "Try That Thing." For what it is worth, Roy Dunn knew a light-skinned guitarist from Madison—where Howell was living immediately before he left for Atlanta—by the name of Tampa Red but not the famous bluesman resident then in Chicago. Maybe Tampa Joe became Tampa Red when the latter's records began to sell. Blues history contains a good many fakes: the South had fake Little Walters, Sonny Boy Williamsons, Elmore Jameses, and Muddy Waters in the 1950s. Frank Hovington, a Delaware songster, heard Blind Boy Fuller in Philadelphia a good decade after his death.

The other group of Walton-Newton County performers also recorded heavily in the 1920s and the guitarists especially make a fascinating study.

BARBECUE BOB AND LAUGHING CHARLEY LINCOLN

As if to underline the variety of styles within the broad spectrum of Piedmont blues, within a year or so of Howell's arrival in Atlanta, Robert Hicks from adjoining Walton County had moved in too. As Barbecue Bob he was to become the most heavily recorded Atlanta bluesman of the 1920s and a steady seller for Columbia until his premature death in 1931. Furthermore, the set of musicians with whom Bob mixed were entirely separate from Howell's Gang.

The Hicks family was originally from Clarke County, of which Athens is the county seat, although the father, Charlie Hicks, had come from Morgan County to the south. He married Mary Harris of Clarke County, but they soon moved to Walton County, where they settled in Walnut Grove, a small community above Porterdale. Their elder son, Charlie, was born on March 11, 1900, about the time that they moved. A second son, Robert, was born exactly eighteen months later, on September 11, 1902, and their last child, a daughter named Willie Mae, was born some years later.[27] Although very fond of her brothers, Willie Mae Jackson was unable to recall much of their early musical upbringing apart from the fact that "neither of them had much education and they picked up music for themselves." One of Robert's friends, Albert Noone Hill, remembers they were at school together some three months in the summer and about four months in the winter, perhaps closely linked to work in the cotton fields. Charlie left school after third grade to work on a farm. He began to play guitar about the age of sixteen, and Robert must have been quick to follow suit. Charlie bought his first guitar from money he had saved picking cotton, and as there were no musicians in the family—although his father sang a little—he looked to a neighbor to help him to play. This was Savannah Weaver, known to her friends as "Dip,"[28] the young mother of Curley Weaver, who was six years younger than Charlie but was to join the same set in Atlanta.

Unfortunately we have no idea of Dip Weaver's style, but Robert's guitar sounds as if a banjo tuning and strumming style had been transposed to guitar. His plangent, highly idiomatic style is one Curley Weaver used on some of his recordings, such as the Columbia version of "No No Blues" from 1928. Only Charlie Hicks, recording as Charley Lincoln, and the obscure Willie Baker ever played in like style. It would appear that this is directly attributable to Dip Weaver's influence possibly compounded by the use of a twelve-stringed guitar, itself an unusual and complex instrument to choose when six-stringed Stellas were available from Sears Roebuck by mail order for $1.98 in 1908, although Piano Red remembered that Charlie also played a six-stringed guitar.[29] Perhaps the twelve-stringed guitar lent itself more readily to the "flamming" style of the Hicks boys, somewhat in the manner of clawhammer banjo. It might seem odd that two boys from another family should follow Dip Weaver's style when her own son tended not to. However, as a boy Curley Weaver came under the influence of Nehemiah Smith, a fine guitar picker, and by the time he came to record, for the same company that Barbecue Bob was recording for, Robert had already recorded at eight sessions and his first release had been something of a southern "hit." Doubtless no one wanted a Barbecue Bob sound-alike, and while Weaver showed he could play in his mother's style—he remade "No No Blues" for the American Record Corporation four years later, still sounding like Robert—he clearly wanted to be known as a picker and was careful all his life to play in that manner.

Younger than the Hicks boys, Curley Weaver was nonetheless playing guitar when he was ten. He teamed up with an exciting young harmonica player from Social Circle, Walton County, who came to live on the Smith farm in Newton County, between Walnut Grove and Almon, about 1922. He was Eddie Mapp, a superb performer, and he and Weaver played for country dances and frolics before he left for Atlanta about 1925. A Newton County resident well remembered Mapp: "He used to get to blowin' in Covington and folks would get to crowdin' around and if they didn't give him no money, he'd just walk on away. But he sure could blow a harp. . . . I didn't know where he stayed but he used to be in Covington about every Saturday night."[30] Robert Hicks often ran with both Weaver and Mapp before moving to Atlanta. By the time of Mapp's tragic death in 1931, his mother had moved to Stone Mountain, but he still has relatives in Newton County, in Newborn. Albert Noone Hill and Edward "Snap" Hill, friends of the Hicks and Weavers from school days, well recalled Mapp, although he was not close to them.[31] They remembered that he always played on his own in Covington but never sang. They instantly recognised his solo recording, "Riding the Blinds," made in early 1929 in New York. The record, made for the QRS company, is extremely rare and cannot have sold much in the South, let alone survived for anyone to recall clearly what it sounded like. It was played on a cassette with no introduction or prompting, immediately after a Barbecue Bob title—which they knew and with which one female member of the household sang along on the opening stanza with complete accuracy— so they can hardly have expected to hear a Mapp recording. Like other talented musicians who recorded little, their songs are well remembered by local residents who knew them in their prime.

Charlie Hicks was the first to move into Atlanta, in 1923. He married and settled down to a steady job, only playing music on the side. Robert moved to Atlanta the following year, staying for only a few weeks in the early days, probably with Charlie, before returning to his parents' home, which was then in Lithonia, a small town in Dekalb County, about halfway between Walnut Grove and Atlanta. Robert, too, married but the marriage was unsettled and his life rather different from his brother's. Charlie, a quiet man who did not make friends readily, kept much to himself and was quite unlike the person he portrayed on some of his recordings as the extrovert "Laughing Charley." He worked first in a metal factory, then in a bakery on Highland Avenue, and finally at a paint factory, whereas Robert took odd jobs, including one at the Biltmore Hotel. Robert relied more on his playing and was an easygoing, personable man who took life none too seriously. He finally went to work at Tidwell's Barbecue in Buckhead—an Atlanta suburb some five miles north of Downtown—where he sometimes played for the patrons, as did Blind Willie McTell in later years. Some of the patrons carried him off to after-hours parties when work was over.

One way or another Robert came to the notice of Columbia record scout Dan Hornsby, who, interviewed in 1951 on behalf of the Atlanta *Journal,* recalled that both brothers were working at the drive-in, singing as they worked. No one else reported Charlie working alongside Robert there and Hornsby's recollections were not always accurate.[32] The outcome was a session for Columbia in Atlanta, during a recording tour which took them on to New Orleans, on March 25, 1927, two weeks before Peg Leg Howell made his first recordings with his Gang. Hornsby decided to use Robert's job at the barbecue pit as a gimmick, dressed him in chef's white with a high hat, and named him Barbecue Bob.[33] It stuck for his entire recording career: out of more than fifty sides issued, only two records bore his real name—his one gospel coupling (Blind Lemon Jefferson and Charley Patton had pseudonyms applied to their religious issues) and an odd 1930 coupling in which his brother's name appeared correctly for the only time, "Darktown Gamblin'—The Crap Game" and "Darktown Gamblin'—The Skin Game." If Robert's real name was to be used for his religious sides, one can but marvel at the logic of issuing the latter coupling under his real name too.

"Barbecue Blues" with its attendent gimmicks ensured sufficient sales for him to be brought back within three months for another session, for which he had to travel to New York by train. Trains would have been familiar enough to most musicians traveling from Covington to Atlanta in the 1920s, for there were no hardtop roads and no one owned a car. On the train journey Robert composed "Mississippi Heavy Water Blues," which described the almost annual bursting of that river's banks following spring meltwater from the mountain regions brought down by a myriad feeder streams. The flood of 1927 was one of the worst, and drastic action was necessary to avert future floods on the same scale.[34] In New York he stayed at Mamie Smith's apartment, cutting four titles on each of successive days including the one he had worked out on the train, and Columbia found themselves with a large seller for a southern country bluesman. "Mississippi Heavy Water Blues" was so well known it was even mentioned by the preacher at Robert's funeral in Walnut Grove.

Robert had made his name and was to be recorded every time Columbia came to Atlanta with a mobile unit, with at least two groups of sessions every year under his own name plus a few others on the side. Whether or not Hornsby had seen both brothers at Tidwell's, Charlie too was soon recording for Columbia, his sides being issued as by Laughing Charley and Charlie (Charley) Lincoln. No one was able to explain the pseudonym, but since Lincoln was the maiden name of Eddie Mapp's mother, it might have been a nod of acknowledgement to a friend. Over the next three years both brothers recorded, although Charlie saw only three more records released from three sessions and was not called upon to record at the December 1930 sessions, which were to be his brother's last.

Two obscure sessions saw the brothers in accompanying roles. On April 21, 1928, immediately following two sides recorded by Robert, a young female blues singer, Nellie Florence, also recorded two titles. Robert's guitar is clearly audible, as is Charlie's laugh on "Jacksonville Blues."[35] The lyrics reveal that her man lives in Jacksonville, not the singer herself. In fact she was probably an old girlfriend from Walnut Grove who had been brought along for a session by Robert; his sister remembered a girl of that name who went to school with her brothers. The singer is obviously trying to harden the timbre of her voice—and sounding good at it. Robert at least was pleased enough to encourage her with, "Ah, sing it, Miss Nellie, sing it!" on "Midnight Weeping Blues." Charlie had obviously come along to enjoy the session; he did not record, and his voice is well off mike when he laughs. However, he laughs loud and clear at the same line on two occasions, and one wonders if it first happened by accident and was then built into the finished take by the engineer.

More important than the pleasant Nellie Florence session were the superb sides made during the December 1930 sessions by the Georgia Cotton Pickers. For many years collectors had been under the impression that the two guitarists on the session could be chosen from Barbecue Bob, Curley Weaver, and Fred McMullen—the latter because of the 1933 Georgia Browns session for ARC. It was also presumed that the harmonica player on the Georgia Browns session was Eddie Mapp. In typical reserved English style, Godrich and Dixon, whose blues discography is essential to any understanding of the music, had stated relative to the Georgia Cotton Pickers that "the hca [*sic*] appears to be the same as the one heard accompanying the Georgia Browns (see Curley Weaver)."[36] They were correct.

An interview with Buddy Moss established that it was he who had played harmonica on both sessions and that the guitarists for the 1930 session had been Robert Hicks and Weaver. Close analysis of the four titles clearly establishes that Weaver plays lead throughout, singing on "She Looks So Good," while Robert plays second guitar—perhaps because his style was so recognizable—and sings lead vocal with Moss on harp. Perhaps there was a conscious attempt to have Moss sound like Mapp, for Snap Hill recognized Robert's singing but thought the harmonica was by Mapp. He had not appreciated that Moss played harp and simply stated that the "boy sounds just like Eddie Mapp!" It was Moss's first session and a further example of a friend of Robert's recording for Columbia. Willie Mae Jackson first met Buddy Moss in

1930 when he came out with her brothers to Lithonia. He had met Robert when he was staying at 318 Felton Drive N.E. in Atlanta, when Moss was at 229 Corley—by coincidence where Mrs. Jackson was living when interviewed.

The Georgia Cotton Pickers' sides, like their 1933 "covers," are brilliant small band recordings entirely typical of the music of many a dance or party. If any music conjures up the atmosphere of a country jook, it must be these sides.

Riding high on a recording career as Robert was doing meant little when the Depression struck. After December 1930 Okeh-Columbia returned only once to Atlanta, ironically just two days after Robert died of pneumonia, brought on by influenza. In his analysis of Robert's role on his final sides, Pete Lowry states that they "indicated that Robert was capable of more that just distinctive frailing. He appears to have died just when his ability as a guitarist was broadening in scope, for death came on October 21, 1931, a year after his wife had passed away and two years after the loss of his mother."[37] It is remarkable to realize that he was just twenty-nine years old when he died, for he had become a stalwart on the recording scene. Although he had been living at 314½ Harris Street N.E., he died at his father's Lithonia home.

Charlie had always been close to his brother and they had both been hard hit by their mother's death in 1929, but with Robert's death he went to pieces. "He was just a different Charlie altogether," as his sister recalled. His marriage broke up, and he separated from his wife, who later died of pneumonia also. Soon after this, in 1935, his father died, and Charlie became an alcoholic. Quiet when sober, the latent danger his mother had noticed in him as a child began to manifest itself when he was drunk. Having already "cut" two or three persons, he "got in trouble Christmas Day, 1955." According to Charlie he was on Old Wheat Street behind Auburn Avenue, a tough sector of town, when he intervened to stop a man beating his wife. The man threw beer bottles at him so Charlie shot him. Every other witness stated that Charlie "shot him for nothing." Despite his defense attorney's request that Charlie should plead guilty, he did not and received twenty years in Cairo Prison, in Grady County near the Florida state line. In jail he continued to play his guitar—which his common-law wife received after his death—but he would only perform religious songs to atone for his guilt. Hoped-for parole after seven years failed and he became dispirited and nervous, hoping that he might be transferred, but in September 1963 he suffered a brain hemorrhage and died. By a remarkable chance, the only other person to know of his guitar-playing in jail was Mississippi bluesman Big Joe Williams, who met him when

Charlie was a trustee.[38] He remembered him as the only twelve-stringed guitarist he knew in Georgia but had not realized he was Charlie Lincoln.

Although a number of Atlanta bluesmen recorded using twelve-string guitars, in itself an unusual enough feature, the highly idiomatic guitar style of the Hicks brothers was rarely to be heard elsewhere. Willie Baker and George Carter appear to be from Georgia. Baker is the greatest enigma of them all, recording in 1929 for Gennett in Richmond, Indiana. He is reported to have been a resident of Patterson (Pierce County) in the southeast of the state, to the northeast of Waycross. Both Baker and Barbecue Bob used open G tuning; the latter's "Waycross Georgia Blues" of April 1928 may offer up a clue. His sister recalled that he rarely traveled far from home—although Big Bill Broonzy claimed to have met him in Chicago[39]—but he did make a few trips with a medicine show, one of which took him to Waycross. As Patterson is a mere seventeen miles away, Baker probably saw and heard him play, and a rival company found it convenient to have a performer who could "cover" such a style. In fact, the second song recorded by Baker was Curley Weaver's "No No Blues" (October 1928), which was in that style, and Baker's fourth title, "Sweet Petunia," had been the reverse of Weaver's issue. It seems that there was considerable difficulty in recording that song, for it took four session attempts before a satisfactory version was obtained in March 1929. The company also made three attempts to record "No No Blues" before it gave up and issued the first attempt. It has been suggested that because of Baker's able ragtime work on "Rag Baby," recorded at his last session, he was the originator of the style.[40] By that date Barbecue Bob had made thirty-two sides, Charlie Lincoln all but his last two sides, and Weaver had cut "No No Blues." It does seem excessively late for the originator to enter the field.

Of George Carter, who recorded four sides for Paramount in 1929, nothing is known. He sounds to be one of the Atlanta group although his playing is less close to that of the Hicks brothers. On hearing a title by Carter, Snap Hill, who knew all three men who had learned from Dip Weaver, said, "He's from Atlanta!" He knew nothing of him but was familiar enough with the style. No one else could hazard a guess as to whom he might have been.

One of the twelve-stringed guitarists who lived for a while in Atlanta and aurally has a style linked to the city is the Georgian, Emery Glen. At least, that was how he was credited on his two released couplings, recorded for Columbia on November 7, 1927, although he was listed in the files as Blind Emery Glenn. He has a languid vocal delivery and his guitar style is somewhat in the Barbecue Bob mold but subdued and very much secondary to his performances. "Fifth Street Blues" might refer to the city, and of the three streets of this name, the most obvious is to the north of Ponce De Leon Avenue. The city directory names him Emory Glenn and he shows up only in 1935, rooming on Yonge Street, which runs north from Decatur. Two years later he had moved to the heart of the blues scene, to 189 Houston, N.E. half way between Yonge and Fifth Street. He died in 1942.

An Uncle Bud Walker played twelve-stringed guitar on two songs recorded in Atlanta in 1928 for Okeh. His origins are unknown: no Bud Walker was ever listed as a resident, but the name Uncle Bud might refer to an old folk song and not be his true name.[41] His playing in no way resembles the other men from the city. The liner notes to two albums on which these titles have been reissued state that "Walker's jagged phrasing seems indicative of Texas rather than of the Delta bluesman. His heavy strumming summons another twelve-string specialist, John Byrd, to mind."[42] (Byrd was from Mississippi). "Although somewhat like riffs are executed by Charlie Patton . . . and Robert Wilkins . . . Walker's upstroke-downstroke ('cha-poong') picking motions are atypical in the blues idiom."[43] Like many others who recorded in Atlanta, Walker could have come from miles away.

The most famous of the twelve-string guitarists was Blind Willie McTell, companion for many years to Curley Weaver after his set had broken up with the deaths of Robert Hicks and Eddie Mapp. Indeed, it is Weaver who provides the link between the older school of playing, as portrayed by the Hickses, and the younger set which was to group itself around Buddy Moss in the early 1930s.

CURLEY WEAVER

Curley James Weaver was born on March 25, 1906, to Jim Weaver and Savannah Shepard of Newton County, and grew up on the farm of a cousin, Tom Brown, at Liviston Chapel just outside Porterdale. Curley's mother played guitar and piano in church—he learned some "good songs" from her, even if he only ever recorded secular ones—and probably had more influence on the sons of her close friends, the Hicks. Curley began to learn the local secular songs at an early age, by which time he had moved with his parents to Almon, a small community on the Atlanta side of Porterdale. He had an easy disposition and made friends readily. By the time he was ten Curley was playing guitar; about that time his mother was teaching the older Hicks boys, with whom Curley was always to keep in close touch.

There was much music to be heard in Newton County and close by, as has been documented earlier. Sun Foster remembers that Curley learned from *Judge (Judd?) Smith, an older man than Foster (born 1894) and Nehemiah Smith. Both men were recalled by Blind Buddy Keith, resident in Atlanta since 1924 but born in Newton County in 1894. Keith was from Mansfield in the south of the county but saw fit to mention no musicians from there. He well remembered the Smiths and *Spencer *Wright as fine guitarists from around Covington and Porterdale. Keith also knew Robert Hicks in those days, and in view of the reputation that Keith has among neighbors and Atlanta bluesmen, young Curley may well have learned some from him too. A measure of Keith's ability was that in his later years he only ever played with Blind Willie McTell, who used to take Keith his guitar to get it repaired, a job he was still capable of doing when first interviewed in 1972.

Musical Smiths predominated in the area. Keith recalled also Jim and *Doc Smith—the former taught Roy Dunn in his early days near Covington—while *Buck and Tom Smith were remembered by Foster and George White, both of them playing in the first decade of this century. Some of them must have been related to Judge (Judd) and Nehemiah! Roy Dunn, who knew Curley well from the mid-1930s, felt that, more than anyone else, Nehemiah Smith was responsible for Weaver's skill as a musician in his early years. Even with that extensive list the names of Weaver's mentors are far from exhausted. George White was taught by guitarist Joe *Berry, who died as recently as 1969-70. He was "all the time pickin' at home, y'know," so it is quite possible that Weaver knew Berry too. Both White and Dunn thought that in later years Weaver learned much from Harry *Johnson, a fine guitar and mandolin player by all accounts. They became firm friends and frequently played together. Another close friend of Weaver's in his Covington days was guitarist Charlie Jackson, who apparently never moved to Atlanta.

In this environment Weaver's playing flourished. Together with the Hicks brothers and Eddie Mapp, he formed a close relationship. Mapp moved into Newton County about 1922-23 and came to know the other two families well. The song for which Mapp was best remembered locally was "Careless Love," which he eventually recorded with guitarist Slim Barton for QRS in 1929, and it is interesting to note that Odum had collected "Kelly's Love" in Newton County back in 1906-8, perhaps even from the same source.

Before long the country offered less to these restless musicians than did Atlanta. Aged nineteen, Weaver followed the Hicks brothers to town, acting out a pattern which became well set—away from the depleted countryside into the brash, noisy city with its totally new way of life. During these years many of Weaver's other musical friends came to town—Buddy Moss, Buddy Keith, Harry Johnson, Johnnie Guthrie, and Blind Willie McTell.

Once Barbecue Bob's position was established with Columbia, he arranged for Weaver to record, in October 1928, immediately prior to two tracks by himself. On "No No Blues," whether by choice or in deference to Barbecue Bob, he played in the same flailing guitar style and was occasionally to return to the format, notably in "Tippin' Tom" and "Birmingham Gambler" and a remake of "No No Blues," from the January 1933 sessions for ARC. Although he did not stay with Columbia—which after all had Barbecue Bob, Charlie Lincoln, and Peg Leg Howell on their books from Atlanta—his 1928 session marked the start of an extensive recording career which has never received due credit. In May 1929 Weaver, Mapp, and Guy Lumpkin all recorded in Long Island City, New York, for QRS. Mapp and Lumpkin recorded one solo each, backing each other; the two performances were coupled for issue. Mapp also backed Weaver on one side of his release and played on five of six titles made by Slim Barton and James Moore, who may not have been from Atlanta. Art Satherley might have been responsible for these sessions, as he was at one time a scout for QRS,[44] but researcher Gayle Dean Wardlow stated that the sessions were arranged by Harry Charles, who had been on the staff of Columbia's Atlanta Studio.[45]

In 1930 Barbecue Bob brought Weaver back to Columbia to record the Georgia Cotton Pickers' sides along with a young Buddy Moss. Weaver also gained a reputation as an accompanying guitarist, and he was used to support two female singers, Ruth Willis and Lillie Mae. Music may well have been his full-time employment despite his appearance in the city directory for 1929 as a laborer living at 144 Fulton S.E., the street next to that on which Moss lived later, although 144 has vanished under the Atlanta Stadium. Down the same road in 1929 lived an Anderson Mapp at 132.

By 1933 Weaver was close friends with Moss and Blind Willie McTell. Barbecue Bob was dead and his brother never to recover from this loss so soon after his mother's death. Within the month of Robert's death Eddie Mapp was "found dead in street: brachial artery left arm—severed," as his death certificate baldly states. He had been killed on the corner of Houston and Butler, in a rough section of town where bluesmen often gathered to play, on November 14, 1931. Piano Red stated that "a woman stabbed him with a knife at a liquor house. Got him right in the heart," which may not have been totally inaccurate.[46]

No one in authority seemed very concerned, and the body was shipped back to his mother in Stone Mountain. Very possibly he was older than the twenty years given him at death, but he might well have been only fourteen or fifteen when he first came to town. Adulthood comes very early in certain environments. His was one of the very few bluesmen's death certificates to read "musician" as an occupation, which denotes a degree of professionalism rare in those days. Thus the three great Newton County friends with whom Weaver had begun to meld his style were dead or demoralized before he was to make his own distinctive mark upon the Atlanta blues scene.

Weaver ran with a number of different sets of musicians in Atlanta. Sometimes he would play with Buddy Moss, fiddler Eddie Anthony (but never Peg Leg Howell), and harmonica player Slim *Kirkpatrick. However, Weaver only roomed in Atlanta—in 1933 he was staying at the rear of 62 Butler N.E. very close to where Mapp had been killed—and he returned most weekends to Almon, where he teamed up with Harry Johnson or backed Charlie *Stinson, a good singer who used to stay at Jack Wright's pool hall in Covington. Perhaps a measure of this friendship was an unissued title at the January 18, 1933, ARC session, "Charlie Stimpson," which might even be the correct spelling. Sadly it does not appear to have survived, while many others unreleased at the time have. In 1933, at the peak of his recording career, he was listed as a musician for the first time in the city directory. This phase of his life linked him with Blind Willie McTell and the set in which he regularly moved.

In mid-January 1933 Weaver traveled to New York with Buddy Moss, Ruth Willis, and the shadowy Fred McMullen, a superb guitarist with a delicate touch. The sessions spanned four days commencing Monday, January 16, with almost three dozen sides recorded, although a number of McMullen's were remakes. Fittingly, Moss's "Bye Bye Mama," the first title recorded, features two of the guitarists and Ruth Willis makes some comments. From then on the tracks are divided up at random with Ruth Willis's seven titles in a row on Tuesday being the longest run by any of them. The guitarists take turns backing one another, in no set pattern, although nowhere do all three play at once. Although the A&R man's file notes offer some hints,[47] only a brave person would state with certainty which two guitarists are present.

The initial session brought Weaver's remake of his first Columbia title, "No No Blues," and McMullen's first named appearance on record. His first title, "Poor Stranger," was remade later, so the first of his titles to be issued was a version of a Mississippi song, itself an interpretation of Tommy Johnson's "Big Road Blues." McMullen's

"Wait and Listen," played immaculately with bottleneck yet with intricate fretting, is magnificent. Unfortunately only five of his sides were released. The other titles apparently did not survive, but an unissued take of "Wait and Listen" does exist. Ruth Willis fared worse than McMullen—only two of her titles were released—whereas Moss's sides placed him firmly on the map for ARC, and he was to be one of their most reliable sellers. Weaver recorded a few, including some in the style of Barbecue Bob, but most notable of them all was the Georgia Browns' session, the final titles to be recorded apart from a lone unissued Willis. Only the 1930 Georgia Cotton Pickers and perhaps the Booker T. Sapps session in Florida in 1935 can match these for vigor and vitality.

In an obvious attempt to emulate the Columbia recordings of three years previous, the Georgia Browns recorded six titles, and how better to do it than to use two of the same musicians, Weaver and Moss? The first two titles recorded, "Tampa Strut" and "Decatur Street 81" (the theater address), are superlative instrumentals; one can see why Moss rated Weaver as the best guitarist playing at the time. "Next Door Man" and "Joker Man Blues," the two songs with Moss's vocals, were not issued immediately and later came out only on Vocalion, as distinct from the bevy of simultaneous issues on Banner, Melotone, Oriole, Perfect, and Romeo. Even then they identified Moss as Jim Miller. Interestingly, a second take of "Joker Man Blues" survived and has been made available on album. Slightly slower that the issued take, it has an impromptu "Aw, shucks, play that thing!" from someone at the very end, which might have told against its issue.

Within eight months Moss and Weaver were back in the studio, Moss to establish himself as the definitive East Coast bluesman until he was replaced by Blind Boy Fuller. Fred McMullen apparently moved on. He was listed only once in the Atlanta city directory, in 1932. The ARC files name him as MacMullin, although the company issued him as McMullen. Perhaps it is fitting that we don't even know how to spell his name. Moss remembered little of him and felt that he might have returned to his home town of Macon. There is no record of his death there in Bibb County.[48]

The only other person interviewed who knew McMullen, Kate McTell, claimed that McMullen introduced her husband to Moss. "Buddy saw (McTell and Weaver) playing together . . . and he was playing with Fred McMullen, I believe. Buddy Moss was at the 81 Theater. Then Willie asked him . . . would he like to record some records. . . . That's how he met him, through Fred McMullen."[49] She also hinted that Georgia White wrote songs for McMullen.[50] She was from Sandersville, halfway between Augusta and Macon; Moss was born near Augusta, where McTell had once lived, and McTell attended blind school in Macon.

Blind Willie McTell replaced McMullen for the September 1933 sessions. McTell had recorded four sides with Weaver in October 1931 for Okeh—two under one of his pseudonyms, Georgia Bill, and two accompanying Ruth Willis. By this time he had been recording regularly for some four years. The September 1933 sessions lasted a full week from Thursday the fourteenth, although there were no recordings made on the weekend and on Wednesday. More than forty different titles were recorded, many of them having more than one take. By remarkable good fortune many of these unisssued sides—both titles and unissued alternative takes—were kept by Art Satherley, A&R director of the sessions, who eventually placed them with the Country Music Foundation in Nashville and the John Edwards Memorial Foundation at the University of California at Los Angeles. Sixteen of these previously unissued sides are now available for comparison with the issued material and substantially increase our understanding.[51] Three previously unissued Weaver titles, "You Was Born to Die," "Dirty Mistreater," and "Empty Bedroom Blues," place him firmly in the forefront of Georgia bluesmen. On the last two titles Moss apparently plays second guitar, but on the first title McTell's twelve-stringed guitar is much in evidence. These three recordings carry far more emotional conviction than do the bulk of Moss's titles from the same sessions, although Moss became the steady seller, whereas Weaver recorded only one further session before World War II, in the middle of the 1935 Decca session by McTell.

In Atlanta Weaver continued to play with Moss but ran with a wider group of musicians including Harry Johnson. Roy Dunn, born in 1922, had moved into Covington and met Weaver in 1935. He remembered that even in the late 1930s "Candy Man" and "Come On Down to My House Baby" were still great favorites in the set. Then Weaver was playing a good deal with Jonas Brown, reputed by many Atlanta musicians to have been a better guitarist than most of the local men who recorded. Weaver and Jonas Brown often played in a trio with the eccentric "Bo Weevil," about whom stories are legion. No one knew his real name, but it might have been Freeman Walker.[52] His repertoire was broad, and like McTell, in his later years he played on the streets for whites. He lived in a shack made of old boxes on Houston and Butler at "Armor Junction," so named because of the nearby location of the Armor Agricultural Chemical Plant, and was an "everyday friend" of McTell. He was murdered in 1957 by a local whore.

Although Snap Hill claimed that Weaver regularly played on the sidewalks and in friends' houses but never in clubs, Kate McTell remembered him playing with Blind Willie for whites at the Pig 'n' Whistle drive-in on Ponce De Leon Avenue. Johnnie Guthrie, born in Walton County in 1915, ran across Weaver in the 1930s in Covington. They remained friends for years; in the 1950s they joined Buddy Moss to form a trio which played as far away as Greensboro, where Moss's sister Louise Lawrence lived, some thirty miles east of Covington. Guthrie remained Moss's second guitarist until about 1972. Although Weaver never took part in Charlie Rambo's Star Band, a string band with varing personnel, he was well acquainted with most of the musicians who participated, among them Ollie Griffin, Jonas Brown, and Frank Edwards.[53] Ruth Willis, with whom Weaver had recorded, rented rooms in Rambo's home until she died in 1962. Of all the Atlanta bluesmen, Curley Weaver associated with more sets of musicians than any other.

A rumor persists that Blind Boy Fuller was in the Atlanta vicinity shortly before he died. Ernest Scott (born 1917) learned a great deal from Buddy Moss but plays in a remarkably accurate representation of Fuller's guitar style—in itself no great surprise in the late 1930s. Scott claimed that he met Fuller in Chicago and that Fuller accompanied him to Atlanta.[54] Fuller's last session, only months before his death, was in Chicago in June 1940. Of Fuller's eleven trips to various cities to record, this was the only one to Chicago, a fact which Scott, illiterate and unpredictable, cannot possibly have known. Other than stating that he also played with Weaver, Scott makes no claim to have played with any other bluesmen of note, not even McTell. His story gains credence from another bluesman, Robert Fulton, who came to Atlanta in 1939 from Warrenton, midway between Greensboro and Augusta. He claimed that he saw Fuller in Warrenton and Thomson and that Fuller played with Weaver. Fulton, who played with Buddy Moss and recorded in 1954 in Atlanta with Big Boy Crudup, is a highly articulate man, and his other information is accurate and unsensational. Perhaps Fuller was in the area and did play with Weaver; it would have been logical. It might even explain the presence of a card from a Chicago photography company and a button from a Chicago racetrack among Weaver's effects, in the possession of his half-brother, Eddie Carquitt. Since there is no evidence to suggest that Weaver ever went to Chicago, perhaps the momentos were from Fuller. Baby Tate remembered Fuller coming through Greenville, South Carolina—in the late 1930s, he thought. Piano Red also met Fuller in Greenville when he "was with a carnival . . . in the early 1930s."[55] Fuller was not known otherwise to have traveled with a show; perhaps the events simply coincided. Although Fuller was in Columbia, South Carolina, in October 1938, according to his welfare files he was back in Durham, North Carolina, two days later, so he had no chance then to travel in Georgia. Perhaps, after all, he did travel with Ernest Scott. Unfortunately, Buddy Moss was away from Atlanta between 1936 and 1941, when Fuller died, so the fact that he knew nothing of the "rumor" does not disprove it.

In the 1940s and early 1950s Weaver continued to shuttle back and forth between Almon and Atlanta, playing with Harry Johnson and Herman Jordan, who perhaps remained closest to Weaver's style. Despite his friendship with Weaver, Jordan thought Johnson the best of the local guitarists. Jordan, Newton County-born, began finger-picking about 1939 when he was seventeen and used to broadcast over WMOC (now WGASS) in Covington. Another radio station set off the next phase in Weaver's life.

A somewhat surprising move by the New Jersey-based Regal label brought Fred Mendelsohn to Atlanta in 1949 in search of country blues talent: he recorded McTell, Weaver, Frank Edwards—an idiosyncratic guitar and rack-harp player who had recorded in 1941 for Okeh—and Little David Wylie. Wylie recalled Weaver as being instrumental in arranging the session, but as Edwards laconically commented in 1972, "we all knowed about it, all of us together," as Mendelsohn had advertised over the air for bluesmen. Following tests made at a hotel, the final tracks were cut in a studio at 441 Edgewood Avenue in August,[56] but only eight sides were ever issued on 78 r.p.m. discs. Six sides of McTell were issued—four of them gospel—and two of the four that Wylie made were also released, perhaps because he had something of the flavor of John Lee Hooker, then a popular bluesman. The other material remained unissued for years but is mostly now on album.[57]

Although Weaver is present on many of McTell's sides, four titles were recorded with his vocal lead. "She Don't Treat Me No Good No More," issued in 1964, featured a hummed chorus with excellent support from McTell, who also seconds Weaver on "Brownskin Woman" and "Keep On Drinkin'," both in the regular mold of both men. "Wee Midnight Hours" has a duet vocal with McTell singing the falsetto part to Weaver's lead. Logically Weaver was chosen to support Edwards's erratic rhythmic lines; in "Love My Baby," Weaver sings in his typical high voice over edgy, plangent electric guitar with sharp, swinging notes from Edwards's harp. Weaver's acoustic guitar softens the edges and provides a firm base for Edwards. It is perhaps the most exciting of all the pieces recorded by Mendelsohn.

Within a year of the Regal sessions Weaver recorded for Bob Shad's

Sittin' In With label, presumably in New York. The whole session remains obscured but it could be a session, apparently within three months of the Regal one, when Weaver, Wylie, Harry Johnson, and Atlanta's Washboard Sam reportedly traveled to New York to record.[58] Although Wylie did not think the material had been issued, Weaver's four SIW titles were probably from this session. To confuse matters further, Wylie called Harry Johnson *"Slick" Johnson, but no one else ever used that name. In Houston in 1951 a Harry "Slick" Johnson recorded a number of titles, of which only one record was released. Aurally the guitar work is typically Texan and the uninteresting vocalist, in typical Houston period style, is unlikely to be the Harry Johnson whom Georgia musicians recalled never sang.

Only Weaver's sides were issued on SIW; Wylie remembered that only Weaver ever received payment; perhaps this was why. "My Baby's Gone," much in the manner of Moss's "Hard Road Blues," was backed by an exuberent, boastful, dance-rag version of "Ticket Agent." The second, later, coupling backed a moody remake of his 1930 Georgia Cotton Pickers' "Some Rainy Day" with a superb version of "Tricks Ain't Walkin' No More," referring to tough times facing streetwalkers in the Depression. To "turn a trick" was common whorehouse language, but producer Bob Shad, evidently perplexed by the phrase, issued it as "Trixie." Good as Weaver was as a bluesman in 1933, he also brings a seasoned talent to such songs as "Ticket Agent" and "Trixie." The latter is hard to equal for its sheer joy. Both songs show Weaver, released from McTell's twelve-stringed guitar, to have been McTell's superior at this time. He was after all only forty-four and at the peak of his skills.

Unfortunately, these solo sides in 1949 were to be his last. By the late 1950s Weaver and McTell stopped traveling and McTell turned more toward church music. By 1959 Weaver totally lost sight in the one eye which had always been poor, and the sight in the other was fast deteriorating. In August of that year McTell died, soon after Weaver had returned to Porterdale. Initially he lived in Sun Foster's home but later moved to Almon, staying with his half-brother. Here he died on September 20, 1962, was taken to the Sanford-Young Funeral Home on S. West and Clark in Covington, and buried in the quiet rural churchyard in Almon.

Ten years later when collecting information on Weaver and his associates I heard not one unpleasant word about him. People recognized his music with unaffected delight and remembered him with affection. It is fitting to leave the final word to Buddy Moss: "I think (people) liked Curley best [of Barbecue Bob, McTell, and Weaver].

Curley was a guy, he could really raise behind you and he could take up the slack. You didn't have to wait for him."[59]

NOTES

1. Bruce Bastin, "Atlanta Blues," in brochure notes to *Atlanta Blues 1933,* JEMF-106 (Los Angeles, Calif., 1979), pp. 1–2.

2. G. S. Perry, *South East Post,* August 22, 1945.

3. Blaine A. Brownell, "The Commercial-Civic Elite and City Planning in Atlanta, Memphis, and New Orleans in the 1920's," *Journal of Southern History* 41 (August, 1975): 342.

4. Ibid.: 359.

5. Kenneth T. Jackson, *The Ku Klux Klan in the City 1915–1930* (New York: Oxford University Press, 1970), pp. 31, 37–39.

6. Guy Benton Johnson, interview with author, October 22, 1972, Chapel Hill, North Carolina; George B. Tindall, "The Significance of Howard W. Odum to Southern History: A Preliminary Estimate," *Journal of Southern History* 24 (August, 1958): 285–307.

7. Howard W. Odum, "Folk-song and Folk-poetry as Found in the Secular Songs of the Southern Negro," *Journal of American Folklore* 24 (October–December, 1911): 255–94, 351–96.

8. Odum Papers, 1920–37, Southern Historical Collection, University of North Carolina at Chapel Hill.

9. Sun Foster, interview with author, August, 1972, Porterdale, Newton County, Georgia.

10. George White, interview with author, August, 1972, Porterdale, Newton County, Georgia.

11. Tony Russell, "The First Bluesman?" *Jazz and Blues* (June, 1972): 15. However, see chapter 4 concerning Lawrence Gellert's 1924 recordings.

12. E. Simms Campbell, "Blues," in *Jazzmen,* ed. Frederick Ramsey, Jr., and Charles Edward Smith (1939; rpt. New York: Harvest/Harcourt Brace Jovanovich, 1977), pp. 117–18. D'Pree [*sic*] told Campbell, a black cartoonist with *Esquire* magazine, that he had sung on board ship in 1905 and at "pound parties." Quoted in E. Simms Campbell, "Blues Are the Negroes' Lament," in *Esquire Jazz Book,* ed. Paul Eduard Miller and Ralph Venables (London: Peter Davies, 1947), p. 63.

13. Paul Garon and Jim O'Neal, "Kentucky Blues Part Two: The Sylvester Weaver Scrapbook," *Living Blues* 52 (Spring, 1982):15–22; Guido Van Rijn and Herb Vergeer, notes to Sylvester Weaver, *Smoketown Strut,* Agram AB 2010 (Netherlands, 1982).

14. Roger S. Brown, "Recording Pioneer Polk Brockman," *Living Blues* 23 (September–October, 1975): 31.

15. Chicago *Defender,* June 21, 1924.

16. John Godrich and Robert M. W. Dixon, comps., *Blues and Gospel Records 1902–1942* (London: Storyville Publications, 1969), pp. 11–25.

17. Peter J. Welding, "I'm Peg Leg Howell," in *Nothing But the Blues,* ed. Mike Leadbitter (London: Hanover Press, 1971), p. 258. Samuel B. Charters, *The Country Blues* (London: Michael Joseph, 1960), p. 104, gives Howell's birthplace as "outside Coredele, Georgia, south of Macon."

18. Roger S. Brown, "Atlanta Odds and Ends," *Living Blues* 14 (Autumn, 1973): 28.

19. Welding, "Peg Leg Howell," p. 258.

20. Charles Wolfe, "Columbia Records and Old Time Music," *John Edwards Memorial Foundation Quarterly* 14 (Autumn, 1978): 118–25, 144.

21. Chris Albertson, *Bessie* (New York: Stein and Day, 1972), p. 165. "Fo' Day Blues" is transcribed in Jeff Todd Titon, *Early Downhome Blues* (Urbana: University of Illinois Press, 1977), pp. 125–26.

22. Charters, *Country Blues,* p. 103.

23. Roger Brown to the author, December 18, 1978.

24. Brown, "Atlanta Odds and Ends," p. 29.

25. Tony Russell to the author, February 21, 1979.

26. Roger Brown to the author, October 30, 1978. The two titles in question can be heard on *Peg Leg Howell (1928–1929),* Matchbox MSE 205 (Badminton, England, 1982).

27. Mrs. Willie Mae Jackson, interview with author, August 15, 1970; Willie Mae Jackson to the author, undated but after August 20, 1970; Willie Mae Jackson to Roger Brown, Roger Brown to the author, December 18, 1978; Willie "Piano Red" Perryman interviewed by Roger Brown, Atlanta, July 25, 1972.

28. Pete Lowry, "Some Cold Rainy Day," *Blues Unlimited* 103 (August–September, 1973):15; idem. "Atlanta Black Sound: A Survey of Black Music from Atlanta during the Twentieth Century," *Atlanta Historical Bulletin* 21 (Summer, 1977): 94.

29. Willie "Piano Red" Perryman interviewed by Roger Brown, Atlanta, July 25, 1972. Roger Brown to the author, December 18, 1978.

30. Mrs. Susie Foster interviewed by the author, August 1972, Porterdale, Newton County, Georgia.

31. Albert Noone Hill and Edward "Snap" Hill interviewed by the author, August 14, 1970, Decatur, Dekalb County, Georgia.

32. *Melody Maker,* May 26, 1951. Miss Alma Jamison of the Atlanta Public Library interviewed Hornsby on behalf of Mr. Don Carter of the Atlanta *Journal.* Hornsby reported Charlie Hicks's nickname as "Catjuice Charlie," a pseudonym masking a number of different persons, and "Too Tight Henry" as being Henry Townsend. He was Henry Castle. However, he correctly remembered the name of the barbecue drive-in and Lithonia, where the Hicks brothers' parents lived.

33. Barbecue Bob, "Barbecue Blues," Columbia 14205-D (143757), recorded

March 25, 1927, in Atlanta, is transcribed in Titon, *Early Downhome Blues,* pp. 105–7.

34. Pete Daniel, *Deep'n As It Come: The 1927 Mississippi Flood* (New York: Oxford University Press, 1977).

35. Bruce Bastin, *Talking Blues* 7 (October-November-December, 1977): 8. "Jacksonville Blues" is transcribed in Titon, *Early Downtown Blues,* pp. 72–73.

36. Godrich and Dixon, *Blues and Gospel Records,* p. 250.

37. Peter Lowry, "Georgia Cotton Pickers," *Blues Unlimited* 90 (n.d., 1972): 14.

38. Pete Lowry, *Some Cold Rainy Day,* p. 15.

39. William "Big Bill" Broonzy, "Baby, I Done Got Wise," in Art Hodes and Chadwick Hansen, eds., *Selections from the Gutter: Jazz Portraits from "The Jazz Record"* (Berkeley: University of California Press, 1977), p. 58.

40. Bernard Klatzko, liner notes to *Sic 'Em Dogs on Me,* Herwin 201 (New York).

41. Mack McCormick, brochure notes to "The Bawdy Song," in *Unexpurgated Folk Songs of Men,* Raglan unnumbered (Calif. [?], 1960).

42. Nick Perls, liner notes to *Mississippi Moaners,* Yazoo L-1009 (New York).

43. Stephen Calt, Jerome Epstein, Nicks Perls, and Michael Stewart, liner notes to *Going Away Blues (1926–1935),* Yazoo L-1018 (New York).

44. Tony Russell, "Q.R.S.," *Old Time Music* 26 (Autumn, 1977): 19–20.

45. Kip Lornell to the author, March 25, 1981.

46. Brown, "Atlanta Odds and Ends," p. 29.

47. Bruce Bastin and John Cowley, "Uncle Art's Logbook Blues," *Blues Unlimited* (June–July, 1974):12–17.

48. Vital Records Division, Macon-Bibb County Health Department to the author, August 13, 1970.

49. Kate McTell interviewed by David Evans, Wrens, Georgia, January 19, 1976.

50. David Evans, "Kate McTell Part I," *Blues Unlimited* 125 (July–August, 1977):11.

51. *Atlanta Blues 1933,* JEMF 106 (Calif., 1979); Bruce Bastin, "Unissued Art Satherley Blues," *Talking Blues* (July–August–September, 1977): 6–8.

52. Tom Pomposello, "Charles Walker: Blues from the Big Apple," *Living Blues* 18 (Autumn, 1974):14.

53. For more on the Star Band see chapter 8, pp. 140–42.

54. Roger Brown to the author, December 18, 1978.

55. Robert Springer, "The Blues Gives Them Inspiration You Know," *Blues Unlimited* 126 (September–October, 1977): 20.

56. Mike Rowe, "Fred Mendelsohn," in Leadbitter, *Nothing But the Blues,* p. 223.

57. *Living With the Blues,* Savoy 1600 (Newark, N.J.: 1964), contains titles

by all the artists. *Blind Willie McTell 1949,* Biograph 12008 (New York) includes Weaver in accompaniment. *Sugar Mama Blues 1949,* Biograph 12009 (New York), had titles by them all. *Love Changing Blues 1949: Blind Willie McTell—Memphis Minnie,* Biograph 12035 (New York), has Weaver backing McTell on two titles.

58. Peter Lowry, "David Wylie," *Blues Unlimited* 102 (June, 1973): 10.

59. Robert Springer, "So I Said, 'The Hell With It,'" *Blues Unlimited* 117 (January–February, 1976): 20.

8

Down in Atlanta, G.A.

BUDDY MOSS

In the years between Blind Blake and Blind Boy Fuller, Buddy Moss was the most influential East Coast bluesman and in Atlanta was very much center of a set which included both Weaver and McTell. Born in Jewel, Hancock County, Georgia, on January 26, 1914, he was christened Eugene but was always known around Atlanta as Buddy. Hancock County had a very high percentage of blacks, and some hints at black music, particularly a fiddler named Alfred Thomas who would "lay the fiddle down on his lap and play it," emerged from an article on the white Cofer Brothers.[1] About 1918 Moss's parents moved to Augusta, and as a teenager Buddy joined the increasing flow into Atlanta. Arriving in 1928 he soon came to know the Walton-Newton County musicians in town, becoming firm friends with Curley Weaver, whose guitar style was similar to that Buddy heard when he was growing up, although at the time he played only harmonica, in a style remarkably close to Eddie Mapp's. He much admired Blind Blake's playing, and while Moss first learned from Barbecue Bob, in January 1933, when he first recorded on guitar, his style certainly owed more to Blake.

In 1930 Barbecue Bob brought Weaver and Moss to the Campbell Hotel to record as the Georgia Cotton Pickers. It is stunning to think that Moss was just short of his seventeenth birthday when he made these magnificent examples of small-band blues. Eddie Mapp was the same age when he recorded, if the age on his death certificate is to be believed. Nothing more is heard of Moss on record until the January 1933 sessions in the company of Weaver, McMullen, and Ruth Willis. To Moss fell the honor of recording the first title, under his own name, on which Ruth exhorts him to "play it for Miss Willis!" Born in 1898 she was rather older than one might expect from her voice, but she was one of the finest female country blues singers. In 1933 she was working as a maid and was still working as "a domestic" when she died.[2] Whereas the other artists' records from these sessions are scarce at best, the Moss sides are more commonly found, albeit seldom in good condition. Pressed on poorer quality material, these discs sold for thirty-five cents during the Depression years and were rapidly torn up by the steel needles. All of Moss's eleven titles were released, again quite unlike the others.

In September of that year, together with Weaver and McTell, Moss again recorded. Weaver more often than McTell backed Moss, and recently discovered alternative takes make interesting comparisons with the issued versions. However, two takes of "Back to My Used To Be," neither of which were originally issued, are virtually identical. Moss clearly prepared his songs very carefully, which no doubt made him an easy man to record. Again the sides sold well, for it was Moss alone whom ARC recalled for sessions the following summer, from which seventeen of the eighteen titles recorded were released. Recording alone, his singing style became rather more bland, reminding one of Josh White. Hardly surprising then that when Moss returned almost exactly a year later in August 1935, he was teamed with Josh White and they accompanied one another. Buddy's contracts for 1934-35 show he was paid $5.00 per selection recorded, whether on his own sides or in accompaniment with White. His final session was on August 28, 1935, at which time he signed a new contract for one year at a flat payment of $10.00 per selection. He was obviously set to become a major race recording artist, whatever one might think of the small fee, but Buddy was not to return.

To use every bluesman's phrase, he "got into trouble" and went to jail. It destroyed his chance of real fame and he remained, understandably, embittered about it. He didn't lose his friends; Roy Dunn remembers passing him cigarettes via a warden while he was still in Atlanta's Big Rock Jail awaiting trial, before spending the next five years in jails in Greensboro and Warrenton. His recording contract shows that he was paid an advance of $25.00 on December 19, 1935, and this could well have been to help with legal expenses. It is our collective loss that he never did complete the session. Roy Dunn maintains that he played himself out of jail, which is partly true. He was in fact released on parole in 1940 or probably early in 1941, on the word of James Baxter Long, at that time "manager" of Blind Boy Fuller. Long had attempted to secure Moss's release in 1939, offering work and a recording contract, but apparently the parole board underwent reelection before his plea could be considered, and he had to submit again the following year. Long recalled that after Buddy "had served four or five years of his sentence, his two sisters hired a lawyer to seek parole for him. The Parole Board turned them down . . . six months (later) Mr. Art Satherley of Columbia Records asked me to see if I could work for his parole which I did."[3] It is interesting that the request for Long to intercede came from Moss's old A&R director at ARC, Art Satherley, who had not in fact defected to another company. Brunswick Record Corporation, a sister subsidiary to ARC, bought Columbia and Okeh in 1934. ARC-BRC were in turn bought by the Columbia Broadcasting System in 1938 and constituted as the Columbia Record Corporation. Satherley was simply seeking his old recording star. Whatever Satherley's motives, and indeed Long's—for the latter if not both of them must have been well aware by the winter of 1940 that Blind Boy Fuller was dying—it was a shrewd move to involve Long, for he was ultimately successful in obtaining parole for Moss.

Buddy Moss left Georgia for Elon College, just west of Burlington, North Carolina, where he worked—and at first lived—in the Long home for ten years. He left suddenly in March 1951; the date is fixed firmly in Mrs. Long's mind as it was two weeks before her daughter's wedding. Perhaps the terms of Moss's parole involved his being indentured to Long for as many as ten years; certainly the Longs never had cause to complain about Gene, as they called him. Nonetheless one can well appreciate the frustration Moss felt and can hardly be surprised at a hurried exit. At Elon College he made few close friends but got on well with the two Trice brothers from Durham, Willie and Richard—great friends of Fuller, who died in February 1941, just too late for Moss to meet him. Although knowing Moss to be a withdrawn man, both Trice brothers remembered him with affection. When talking about North Carolina—studiously avoiding discussing his time with Long—Moss recalled them with great warmth, and were it not for Moss's initial suggestion of where to search for them,[4] this book would never have been written.

Moss soon came to know Brownie McGhee, living then in Burlington, and traveled with him and his sidemen, Jordan Webb and Robert Young, as well as Fuller's old sidemen, Sonny Terry and Oh Red, recording with them for Columbia in New York in October 1941. These sides show that Moss's playing and singing had lost nothing during his years in jail; indeed, his own session produced tracks which rank among his finest. "Unfinished Business," with only his guitar in accompaniment, and "Joy Rag," with Brownie McGhee surprisingly on piano, were rush released in November 1941, with a further coupling issued in December. Only one more coupling was to be issued, leaving seven titles unreleased. A test of "Baby You're the One for Me," in the author's collection, is a superb number featuring Moss instrumentally at his finest. Clearly factors other than musical prevented the issue of the remaining titles.

The Imperial Japanese Navy cared nothing for Moss's possible return to recording fame: Pearl Harbor destroyed his chances. Not only did the sessions drop away but the shortage of shellac, required for other wartime needs, meant that the industry went through a restricted phase, further exacerbated by the Petrillo recording ban of 1943, and the majority of his recorded sides were never issued. Disillusioned, Moss remained in North Carolina while McGhee and Terry moved to New York and subsequent international fame. Moss finally returned to Atlanta, saddened by his missed opportunities, fully aware that his own musical talents were the equal of McGhee's. Although he participated locally in the folk revival boom of the early 1960s, his interviews of recent years reflect this bitterness.[5] He played small black country parties well into the 1970s with local bluesmen like Roy Dunn and Johnnie Guthrie, and he attended festivals and concerts when he felt like it.

At the instigation of John Hammond of CBS he recorded again in May 1966 in Nashville, but the session was never released.[6] The following month he performed for the Folklore Society of Greater Washington with John Jackson on second guitar and the concert was released on album.[7] When I heard him at his Atlanta home in 1969, his playing was nothing short of brilliant. A fine singer and magnificent guitarist when at his best, Buddy Moss fully deserved the real break that constantly eluded him. He died in October 1984.

BLIND WILLIE MCTELL

The most remarkable Georgia bluesman was undoubtedly Blind Willie McTell. An artist of immense musical stature, playing a twelve-stringed guitar with dexterity and sensitivity across a great range of music, he was heavily recorded over a period of almost thirty years. Known to every musician in Atlanta, stories about him are innumerable, often in the realm of legend, but hard facts about his life were lacking until recently despite exhaustive research by a number of persons.[8]

Rumor had long had it that he was from Statesboro, partly because of his 1928 Victor recording of "Statesboro Blues" and partly because of an interview in 1940 with John A. Lomax on behalf of the Library of Congress. However, what he actually said to Lomax was that he "growed up down in south Georgia. Statesboro, Georgia, was my real home. I were born at Thomson, Georgia, a hundred and thirty-four miles from Atlanta, thirty-seven miles west of Augusta."[9] Not only does this more accurately state his birthplace but it also highlights McTell's remarkable grasp of detail. He was an extremely intelligent, highly articulate man, full of confidence. A photograph taken of him in the early 1930s, posed against an idyllic garden scene of ornamental bushes and descending stairway such as might be found in the better plantation homes, has him nattily dressed in suit, vest, white shirt and tie, pointed-toed shoes, and a snazzy flat cap. Everything about his appearance was sharp: immaculate creases in his trousers, tie well knotted, watch chain just visible above his twelve-stringed Stella guitar, held authoritatively ready, as if about to commence playing. People not given to speaking in awe of anyone at all spoke of McTell in hushed tones. Buddy Moss spoke with disbelief at McTell's ability to get around despite his blindness. When they were recording in 1933 in New York, McTell—who had attended blind school there in the late 1920s—blithely led Moss and Weaver through the city's subway system. Moss, one noted, did not hesitate to follow and accept his directions. One of McTell's cousins called him "ear–sighted," and this blindness-heightened sense of hearing, together with a stubborn independence, enabled him to undertake a lifestyle which would have been too adventurous for most sighted persons. Unlike other musicians who became blind in later years, like Blind Boy Fuller, McTell was blind from birth, thereby partly accounting for his independence of spirit.

Willie Samuel McTell was in fact born almost ten miles south of Thomson in McDuffie County, out in the country, not very far from where Buddy Moss was born. The exact date of his birth remains obscure but 1898 is likely, probably in May. One complicating factor in earlier attempts to trace his history was that his father's name was McTear or McTier. Locally it appears there is no difference in pronunciation, with the emphasis on the first syllable, as if it were Mack. Around 1907 he moved with his mother to Statesboro, which he always considered to be his home town. He probably began to play guitar soon afterwards. Both Willie's parents played guitar, and his mother was especially proficient. An uncle, Harley McTear, also played, as did

Josephus "Seph" Stapleton, who like McTell had only just moved in to Statesboro. All these helped him to play.

In 1940 McTell reminisced of these early days with Lomax. "I'm talking about the days of years ago. Count from 1908 on up to the original years. Back in the years of those days blues have started to be original, in 1914. From then until the war time people always had times from blues on up to original blues. Then on up to 1920 they changed blues. After then there was more blues. After then it became the jazz blues, some like this (he plays in triple rhythm)." With difficulty he is trying to explain to Lomax—who had a far greater appreciation of blues than McTell could have forseen—the changes which had overtaken blues in a relatively short period. In his view, the blues originated between 1908 and 1914, then the migration during the war years caused a shift in approach. Interestingly, the only other date given is 1920, the year of Mamie Smith's "Crazy Blues," which sparked off the entire race record industry and opened up to rural listeners the more sophisticated stage mannerisms which they would otherwise have heard rarely if at all. It is quite clear in his mind that in the thirty years or so prior to the interview, various changes took place in what in black secular music we loosely term as blues. In view of his considerable grasp of minutiae, we would do well to accept his statements at face value.

Although McTell appears only to have been recorded playing a twelve-stringed guitar, he was remembered by a contemporary, still singing his songs in the mid-1970s, as playing a six-stringed guitar when a young man in Statesboro.[10] His widow recalled him playing a variety of other instruments. "He could blow a harp. No piano. He couldn't play piano. But he could blow a harp. And I believe he played a banjo. A violin . . . I thought he played real good (on) the violin. And he could play an accordion." Two white men in Savannah who knew McTell as a young man corroborated this. Cliff Hobbs recalled him on banjo while Oliff Boyd remembered him on "guitar and bazooka, I mean, a little old horn looking thing that you hum in, and he'd play 'em together sometimes. . . . Used to cost a dime in the ten cent store."[11] It is worth noting that McTell was shown as playing both guitar and kazoo in the accompaniment to Alfoncy and Bethenea Harris's Victor recording of "This Is Not the Stove to Brown Your Bread," cut in Atlanta in November 1929 according to Rust's *Victor Master Book,* although the Victor files used for the third edition of the standard blues discography lists only McTell's guitar.[12] Although Alfoncy Harris recorded in Texas and traveled to California, an Alphonso (Alphonzo) Harris was living between 1927 and 1929 in Atlanta, in the same area as McTell, at one time living on Old Wheat Street where Charlie Hicks lived.

In the interview with Lomax McTell stated that he quit playing guitar for eight years, presumably from 1914 to 1922, when he attended the blind school in Macon, Georgia. As he was reported playing with the John Roberts Tent Show in 1916 and 1917, he was evidently never far from music. He clearly played, and may have had some formal training, during his three years at the Macon blind school, which was attended by another fine, blind Georgia singer and guitarist, the white Riley Puckett.[13] Incidentally, Puckett's powerful guitar solo, "The Darkey's Wail"—one of only two solos recorded by him, the other being a rag—was learned from a "darkey in Atlanta," as he informs us on the disc. McTell attended other blind schools in New York and Michigan, but only for a short time; he was back within three years to record in Atlanta, as he proudly told Lomax: "I continued my playing up until Nineteen and Twenty-Seven, the 18th day of October, when I made records for the Victor Record people. And from then up until 1932 I played with the Victor people alone, by myself. But in the period of time of 1929 I made records for the Columbia people, changing my name to Blind Samuel. . . . And after then I worked with the Vocalion people of 1933. . . . Picked up another job with Decca Record Company. . . . And after the period of time I returned, back to Augusta, Georgia, where they had moved the machine, where they made a gang of blues there in the summer, in the June of 1936."[14] All of this had been unerringly accurate, even to the Vocalion date of 1936, although until recently discographies had always listed the recording date as July 1. We should have known better than to doubt Willie McTell!

Shortly after Howell and Barbecue Bob started with Columbia, this remarkable man began his career recording for Victor. Proud of the fact that he had been recorded "alone, by myself," McTell remained so through eight sessions over the next four years, broken only late in 1931 when he added Curley Weaver on second guitar. The recordings of those years span a wide range of songs: superb blues by any standards like "Statesboro Blues," raggy numbers like "Atlanta Strut" and "Georgia Rag," the Newton County favorite "Come On Round to My House Mama," and show numbers like "Razor Ball" and "Southern Can Is Mine."

McTell was constantly on the move. Relatives remember him playing towns throughout the state, and he followed "medicine shows, carnivals, and all different types of funny little shows." He followed the winter tourists to Miami, traveled with Weaver to Nashville, and knew the great religious singer, Blind Willie Johnson, who recorded for Okeh in Atlanta when McTell was recording as Blind Sammie, and they traveled and played together. McTell's repertoire had to be broad enough to appeal to a white audience, and he even recorded a "Hillbilly Willie's Blues" for Decca. Someone who sang with him outside the splendid Jaekel Hotel in Statesboro recalled, "We was singing all kinds of blues and ragtime. It wasn't too much to 'em. We sang a spiritual every now and then, you know. We used to sing 'Shanty Town.' We had that one (we) used to sing together."[15] The pattern was much the same by the late 1950s, although the blues content was probably even more reduced, when he used to wander among the parked cars and their often teenaged white occupants in Atlanta's Pig 'n Whistle drive-in on Ponce De Leon Avenue.

Naturally McTell played with other fine guitarists in rural areas who were never to be recorded. One such musician, who resisted all McTell's efforts to induce him to record, was Lord Randolph Byrd, better known locally by a number of other nicknames, among them Blind Log. Although Victor actually visited his home town of Savannah in 1927, they were never to repeat the trip. Within two years McTell was recording also for Columbia and well recalled Frank Walker, the manager, and Henry Charles, his assistant, more than twenty years later.[16] Walker was primarily concerned with Columbia's expansion into southern music and supervised the 15000-D series, specifically for white country artists.[17] By the time McTell recorded for Walker, the Depression was about to break. Tuesday, October 29, 1929, was the day when the New York Stock Exchange traded 16,000,000 shares, the worst in its history. McTell recorded the following day. Two titles were coupled in January 1930 for issue, with an initial pressing of 2,205 being followed by a further one of 2,000, average for the time. Of the remaining four titles, two were never issued and the other two were released at the end of May 1932, shortly before the demise of the Columbia 14000-D series. Only 400 were pressed. Indeed, by that release date McTell had been twice recalled to the studio by Columbia—in April 1930, when slightly fewer than 1,000 copies of the coupling then made were pressed, and in October 1931, when six sides were made in total. Four were issued on Okeh and two on Columbia, for which an meager initial pressing of 500 was made.[18] It was to be the last field trip undertaken by the company.

McTell was back recording for Victor in February 1932. Four titles were issued as by Ruby Glaze—Hot Shot Willie. The identity of the female singer remains in doubt, although Ruby Glaze might be a pseudonym for Kate McTell. David Evans has suggested this is unlikely as Kate and Willie did not marry until January 1934;[19] however, Ruby Glaze's spoken interpolations on "Searching the Desert for the Blues" sound very similar to Kate's spoken parts on the 1935 "Ticket Agent Blues." On "Lonesome Day Blues" McTell says, "Sing it girl!" and were it Kate, she would only have been twenty. They met at her 1931 high school graduation reception from Paine College, Augusta, before Kate went on to Washington High in Atlanta to complete twelfth grade the following year. Thus she was physically in Atlanta at the time of this session.[20] Victor was scrupulously careful to ensure that McTell continued to receive royalties from these sides until 1937, presumably on the strength of their reissue on the Bluebird label.

As McTell told Lomax, he "started out under Mr. Ralph Peer of 1619 Broadway of New York" [Victor] and "after a period of time worked under W. R. Calaway and Mr. A. E. Satherlidge [*sic*] of 1776 Broadway of New York." The latter ushered in the September 1933 recordings with Buddy Moss and Curley Weaver, but whereas Moss's and Weaver's sides—apart from some under the pseudonym of Jim Miller—appeared on assorted ARC labels like Banner, Melotone, Oriole, Perfect, and Romeo, McTell's only appeared on Vocalion. McTell recalled that he "worked for the Vocalion people of 1933. Taken up for odd job. They pay me a small sum of money of fifty dollars a week, but they was getting all the records of blues that they can, which we call the 'alley.'" However, the very first title recorded—which appears not to have survived—was a religious piece, "Lay Some Flowers on My Grave," as were the first two titles recorded the following day at his session. Vocalion might well have tried to record all the blues they could, but they were unable to issue them. Those not issued until 1979 stand up perfectly well with those chosen for issue at the time, and these probably sold poorly for they are uniformly rare. Some songs appear part of a common pool, for both Moss and McTell recorded "Broke Down Engine," and "Lord Send Me An Angel" had been recorded by McTell as "Talkin' to Myself" in 1930, although the opening stanza is identical to that of a 1927 recording, Bert Hatton's "Freakish Rider Blues." Speculation as to the origins of blues lyrics is highly specious, but it is worth noting that McTell recorded songs earlier associated with other Georgia singers like Bumble Bee Slim and "Sloppy" Henry. Even more interesting is that his later sessions in 1940, 1949, and 1956 show how songs shifted within McTell's own creative capacity, providing a remarkably detailed view of a folk artist reworking his own material.

McTell married Kate in 1934 and stayed in Atlanta with Curley Weaver and his current girlfriend, Cora Thompson, at 381 Houston

Street, N.E. The following year Decca took them to Chicago to record; Willie was then "under Mr. Dave Kapp of 666 Lakeshore Drive, in Chicago, Illinois." Some of the songs were conscious remakes of titles left unissued by Vocalion, such as "Lay Some Flowers on My Grave," while "Lord Send Me An Angel" became "Ticket Agent Blues," the song for which Weaver was best known around his home town, but on which he was curiously absent. On "Let Me Play with Your Yo-Yo," McTell mentions both "Papa Weaver" and "Miss Cora," however. Kate recalled that Mayo Williams "came down, and picked us up and drove us to Chicago. Me and Willie, Buddy Moss, Curley Weaver, and Gladys Knight." Although Moss was a good friend, he was absent and a slip of the tongue (or in transcription) probably gave the name of the more recent popular singer from Atlanta instead of pianist Georgia White. She had already recorded for Decca and was to record again in the same month as McTell and Weaver. A Decca publicity photograph has her seated with Bumble Bee Slim (Amos Easton), born in Georgia in 1905.[21] Kate McTell knew he was from "Brunswick, Georgia, but he was living in Atlanta. . . . made some records with us."[22] Easton recorded for Decca in Chicago in the same month as the McTells and Georgia White, accompanied by an unknown pianist.

Kate McTell is to be heard on six of her husband's Decca sides. On "Ticket Agent Blues" she offers some rather self-conscious comments, but she sings on four gospel numbers. Having joined the Spread Chapel A.M.E. Church in Stapleton, Georgia, at the age of twelve, she had sung in quartets. In Atlanta she was a member of the Big Bethel Church on Auburn Avenue, the base of Atlanta's most-recorded artist, the Reverend J. M. Gates.[23] The finest of Kate's gospel titles is "God Don't Like It," with Willie singing the second part to some of his finest slide guitar. Interestingly, Decca saw fit to issue three of Kate's songs in their first two couplings; two of the remaining three titles were not issued until the 1970s.[24]

McTell's final session before World War II came in June 1936 in Augusta, with W. R. Calaway as recording director. If the location seems random—unless it was due to the fact that Calaway and Art Satherley's wife owned a motel in town—the selection of artists was no less so. There were two previously unrecorded duets, only one of which was secular, a dance–jazz band comprising members of the Jenkins Orphanage in Charleston, South Carolina,[25] Atlanta's Piano Red, and McTell. They recorded at radio station WRDW during Kate's summer vacation and stayed with Kate's aunt, whom Vocalion reimbursed for expenses. Kate thought her husband had been paid $300.00, but Red remembered it differently. "(Willie) took me . . . to see a man named Calloway [*sic*] to record for ten dollars."[26]

Possibly Red was known to Calaway through his brother Rufus, "Speckled Red," but Piano Red maintained that it was McTell who suggested the idea: "I had knowed (McTell) like a couple of years and he asked me why didn't I try to get on records. I told him I didn't know how to contact nobody. He'd say, 'Well, I know a guy if you write him.' He'd sit down and told me what to say, just like he was writing. . . . told him I was Rufus' brother and naturally Rufus had made some records for him. . . . He told Willie he was coming down, had someone to tell me to get something together and he would put me on."

Although they all traveled from Atlanta together, they hadn't rehearsed together because, as Red recalled, "Willie and me wasn't going to play together anyway. Willie was supposed to have his session and I'd have mine."[27] However, that was not to be. Kate recalled that Willie only had one disagreement with a record company, and that was over the Augusta sessions. "He wanted to make his records just with his guitar, and they had this . . . Piano Red. And Willie couldn't play with him. He couldn't keep up with him, you know. He played so fast."[28] Why Calaway chose to record them together will never be known. Perhaps he hoped to produce a piano-guitar duet to replace Leroy Carr and Scrapper Blackwell, who had fallen out some eighteen months previously. For the only time in McTell's recording career he was teamed with a pianist, and a none too subtle one at that. However enthusiastic one might be about Red's playing, it would be difficult to select a rougher pianist to team with McTell.

Between them Willie and Red recorded twelve titles. Four are listed in the files as by Blind Willie and Piano Red, with vocals by McTell; six are listed as by Piano Red alone; the first two recorded, on June 26, are listed as by Piano Red and Partner, a neat reversal of Vocalion's credits of some of McTell's 1933 titles, released as by Blind Willie and Partner. A curious circumstance surrounded one title, "Married Life's a Pain." Big Bill Broonzy had recorded it for ARC in Chicago more than two months previously, duly crediting Willie McTell as the writer. McTell had never recorded it before, so perhaps Big Bill learned it from McTell in 1935 when he was in Chicago to record for Decca. One wonders what Kate McTell thought of the title.

Of the twelve sides, none were issued and apparently none survived. In an interview in 1972 Red suggested that the recording equipment at Augusta in 1936 was not working properly; five years later he added that the master discs may have melted in the heat. Perhaps this is true, since none of the Carolina Cotton Pickers' fourteen sides made at the same time were issued either; the band had to record again the following year while on tour in Birmingham. Portable recording equipment was always liable to suffer difficulties, especially in the heat of a southern summer. In 1935 the Library of Congress team in Georgia found it difficult to maintain constant speed on their machine due to either overheated bearings or poor lubrication, but they were amateurs. After Augusta the Vocalion unit went to Hattiesburg, Mississippi, where they recorded over seventy sides, so any mechanical problem was soon ironed out. However, the following year on location in Dallas many of Vocalion's recordings proved to be faulty. Unfortunately, out of all the McTell recordings Calaway was unable to salvage anything. One blues coupling did emerge from Augusta—Smith and Harper's fine "Poor Girl" and "Insurance Policy Blues." One issued title was recorded each day of the weekend of 27-28 June, but the group remained in town until July 2 to cut a further unissued title.

McTell did not record again for more than a dozen years. Although Decca's J. Mayo Williams wrote to him on September 27, 1937, in reply to a letter from McTell, informing him that he would be in Atlanta in October and would stop by to see about possible additional recordings,[29] nothing appears to have come of this. It is odd that Williams should have been interested, for six sides remained unissued from the 1935 Decca session. McTell continued to travel widely, taking Kate when she was on vacation from Grady Hospital, where she was training to be a nurse. They visited New Orleans, California, and New York, where they sang with Josh White at Small's Paradise, a haven for South Carolinians.

Early in 1940 they were living on Felton Drive in Atlanta, up the road from where Barbecue Bob was living when he became ill and died. Later that year they moved to 211 Butler N.E. near the city center, close to where Eddie Mapp had been killed.[30] On November 4 Ruby Lomax spotted McTell playing at the Pig 'n' Whistle, and in typical McTell fashion he climbed into the Lomaxes' car and directed them back to their hotel, correctly indicating the turns and all the stoplights en route. He agreed to return the following day to record. Certain writers infer that McTell was dissatisfied with Lomax's minimal payment for recording, but Lomax had clearly stated that all he could offer was one dollar and taxi fare, and McTell was under no illusions. He probably understood Lomax's role and sensed a chance to state his piece, which he generally did very soundly. Having played for whites for years, he was adept at providing what they wanted, so many of his songs were spirituals or narrative ballads. In the Lomaxes McTell had met perhaps the one white couple who knew enough about blues not to be upset by indelicate lyrics, but Lomax was far more interested in recording ballads, which he felt were fast dying away—a happy coincidence, for otherwise much of this other side of McTell's repertoire would have been lost.

Gradually McTell began to travel less and became more involved with religious music. He toured with a group of religious singers and even sang in the tenor section of the Glee Club of the Metropolitan Atlanta Association for the (Colored) Blind.[31] I was shown a store–front church on Highland Avenue, opposite the bakery where Charlie Hicks once worked, where McTell sang on Sundays. Sister Susie Weaver Young, an amazing eighty-year-old singer who was still preaching and banging her big bass drum under the viaduct on Decatur Street in 1972, remembered McTell teamed up with another guitarist, playing only religious songs. The other, rather obviously, was known as Little Willie. Originally from Florida, he played his guitar flat, Hawaiian-style across his lap. McTell and Little Willie could be heard over WEAS Decatur and out on Auburn Avenue, where Little Willie sometimes played electric guitar, hooked up to Big Hank's place. At the August 1949 Regal recording session, the last seven out of seventeen songs were religious, most of them of recent popularity.

McTell may have persuaded Fred Mendelsohn, whose idea it was to record country blues, to record sacred material. It was probably as well that he did for only four records were released, three of them by McTell, and two of those were religious couplings. All are extremely rare and sales must have been poor. The first coupling was issued as by Blind Willie. The next gave him his full name, spelling it Blind Willy McTell. For the secular coupling Regal dropped the idea of giving him a name at all and accurately labeled it Pig 'n' Whistle Band. "A to Z Blues" turned up on album in the 1960s, credited to Pig 'n' Whistle Red.

Mendelsohn explained why a white record producer from the North should have sought out country blues in Atlanta during a rhythm and blues boom. "I always liked blues," he said, "heard it on the radio. . . . (and) worked in a drug store in a black neighborhood in Brooklyn. . . . In 1949 three of us—the Braun brothers and myself—started a rhythm and blues label in Linden, New Jersey. . . . With the Brauns, I went down to Atlanta. We brought along our own Magnarecord recorder and rented. . . . an empty store."[32] This was the studio recalled by David Wylie at 441 Edgewood Avenue.[33] Another probable reason for recording Atlanta artists was that Zenas "Daddy" Sears, Atlanta's first rhythm 'n blues disc jockey on WAOK, carried a big audience. Mendelsohn admitted that "in Atlanta, if Zenas Sears played your record, it was a hit—automatically a hit. He was on every night and he had a tremendous following."[34]

Owner of WAOK in 1974, Sears well remembered McTell,[35] not from the Regal session but from one for another newly formed rhythm 'n blues company, Atlantic Records of New York, founded in 1947 by Ahmet Ertegun in partnership with Herb Abramson. Ahmet and his brother Nesuhi were avid jazz fans and appreciated blues. When they heard about McTell from their Atlanta distributor, they arranged a session late in 1949 at WGST, where Sears was then working. On Christmas Eve 1949 the trade magazine *Billboard* announced that Atlantic had signed "Blind Sammy." The Erteguns must have been pleased with their material, for McTell was in fine form, although it must have been his professionalism which shone through: Sears recalled that "we had a lot of problems and we were there all night. Willie was in constant pain and drunk a great deal. He'd keep falling into the mike and we'd have to set him up again." There were a number of short, false starts to songs—which were never issued—so Sears's comments seem accurate. Although fifteen sides were recorded, Atlantic found it viable to issue only one disc, as by Barrelhouse Sammy (The Country Boy), and it is a rare issue. One song, "Broke Down Engine Blues," hearkens back to his final Columbia session in 1931; "Kill It Kid" he recorded for Lomax in 1940. Thanks to Pete Lowry the remaining titles were issued on album in 1972, and Nesuhi Ertegun was certainly pleased at their eventual release.[36] Titles ranged from ballads like "Little Delia" to gospel songs, remakes of old recorded numbers like "Razor Ball," and unissued titles from commercial sessions like "On the Cooling Board," as well as versions of songs from sources as widely spread as Pine Top Smith, Blind Lemon Jefferson, and Charlie Spand.

Good though these songs were, they were not the type to appeal to the new generation of black record buyers. Zenas Sears assessed it accurately: "There was no sophistication about Willie at all—he played and sung, period. . . . He worked primarily in a restaurant here called the Blue Lantern as a car hop. . . . He always performed for whites up through the 'fifties as he couldn't sell records [to blacks] at that time."[37] He continued to play for his friends, but the time was past when he could expect to play predominently for blacks and the time had not yet come when whites would appreciate black music presented at the coffee bar and on the concert stage. When that time came, McTell was dead; otherwise he would have made a good living.

In the 1950s McTell became even more involved in religious music, also singing over WGST. Around 1957 he informed Kate, from whom he had grown apart over the years, that God had called him to preach. Kate, living then in Augusta, reported him as saying, "I don't sing the blues any more or play blues. . . . All I sing now is spirituals. I've given myself to the Lord. . . . This is my favorite song now, 'I'm Sending Up My Timber.'"[38] This was one of the titles which he recorded for Regal but which remained unissued for years. The incident took place soon after what was to prove to be his very last recording session in September 1956.[39]

The session came about when Ed Rhodes, a young record shop manager, was playing a disc by the twelve-stringed guitarist Leadbelly and was informed that a black performer was playing like that in a nearby parking lot. It was McTell, playing at the Blue Lantern on Ponce De Leon Avenue. McTell was at first reluctant to record again but came to trust Rhodes and finally allowed about an hour of music to be recorded. Of the nineteen titles, oddly none were religious numbers, but there were plenty of the sort which he used to regale his Blue Lantern audiences, as will as some of his old pieces like "Kill It Kid," "Dyin' Crapshooter's Blues," and "Pal of Mine" from Regal. There were also new songs like a version of Blind Blake's "That Will Never Happen No More." The tapes remained in a cupboard, almost forgotten, until Rhodes read Sam Charters's book, *The Country Blues.* Charters takes up the story: "[Rhodes] flew to New York in 1961 with the tapes. . . . [which] were sad to hear, despite the insight they gave into McTell's last years as an artist, because they showed so clearly how little he had been able to use his great blues talent in his years of street entertaining. For Rhoades [*sic*] they had a particular poignance, for he was suffering from the same eye trouble that had blinded McTell, and as his own sight got worse he felt closer and closer to his memory of McTell."[40] Although we never find out the cause of this "same eye trouble" which had afflicted McTell since birth but Rhodes only during adulthood, we are fortunate that Charters saw to it that thirteen of these songs were released on album.[41] Although the only evidence to suggest this was McTell's last recording session was a file card, dated October 1960 and marked "deceased," at the Lighthouse for the Blind in Atlanta, it was accurate enough. McTell had died on August 19, 1959.

David Evans's detailed analysis of McTell's life and songs needs no further statement here,[42] but perhaps one simple testament to McTell's music may be extracted, given by Naomi Johnson, who first met McTell in Statesboro in 1936:

He played a hymn, "Amazing Grace," and it sounded like a church full of people. Peoples now fram the guitar, but he played! . . . it was the most beautiful thing that I ever heard. I think he had something like a thimble on his hand. It was metal. I don't think I've ever, since he left, heard a guitar sound like he did. He could really make it talk. And he could play that "Amazing Grace." You just couldn't hardly stand it. It sound like people used to sing, something like fifty or sixty years ago, with that harmony in it. They don't have the harmony in it today. . . . But now he had a blues, but I don't know too much about the blues. But he never did play what you might call a hard blues or a swing blues. He always played something mellow.[43]

That last line is an epitaph in itself.

THE OTHERS

There were, of course, other bluesmen in Atlanta, some of whom recorded but many more who did not. Some, like Rufus and Ben Quillian, were in no way part of the blues mainstream but belonged to the slightly sophisticated, close-harmony group of performers, and some were individual bluesmen, like Frank Edwards, who recorded, and Buddy Keith, who did not. Men like Roy Dunn, who did not record until the research period of the 1970s but who knew the earlier bluesmen, help to tie together a vast array of loose ends.

Peg Leg Howell's Gang included a number of musicians at various times, among them Henry Williams, Eddie Anthony, Jim Hill, and Ollie Griffin, all of whom recorded. It is hardly surprising that the personnel for the Gang was fluid. Much the same could be said of the set associated with Buddy Moss in the mid-1930s, and for that matter with other similar groups of musicians in other cities. In Atlanta there was yet another group of musicians who formed a loosely composed string band, the Star Band.[44] Although it did not record as a unit, a number of its members recorded at one time or another.

The Star Band usually comprised five or six performers with a variety of instruments: fiddle, six- and twelve-stringed guitars, bass, rubboard, harmonica and jug, and occasionally even a brass or reed instrument. They were popular throughout the 1930s and probably later, playing for dances, both black and white. They played blues as well as a wider range of music and could in all probability have compared well with groups like the Memphis Jug Band, Jack Kelly's South Memphis Jug Band, or the Knoxville-based groups of Carl Martin and Howard Armstrong like the Four Keys and the Tennessee Chocolate Drops. The Star Band traveled and are remembered playing in Rome, Georgia, and across into Alabama and Tennessee. Although musicians joined with them for a few days and passed on, there was always a nucleus to the band: Jonas Brown and his one-legged brother *Hollis on guitars, Ollie Griffin on fiddle, Big Cliff Lee on twelve-stringed guitar and bass fiddle, and Charlie Rambo, who played fiddle, mandolin, and guitars. Others who played with them with some regularity were Leroy Dallas on rubboard and guitar; Georgia Slim, who recorded for ARC in Birmingham, Alabama, in 1937; and Frank Edwards, who played with them about 1938, on guitar and harmonica. Edwards often went on the road with members of the band, notably Georgia Slim—probably George *Bedford—and Leroy Dallas, who was to record in New York after World War II. In later years a short, hump-backed guitarist living in East Point named Johnny Price played with them, sounding very much like Curley Weaver. Originally from Cuthbert, Georgia, Price died in 1960 aged 55.

Charlie Rambo was the one surviving core member of the Star Band capable of being interviewed; Jonas Brown was relocated in 1972 but was totally incapacitated by a stroke. Born in Atlanta—a rare distinction—in 1912, Rambo was playing guitar about 1920. Interviewed in 1971 he had not played in years but had clearly once been a remarkable musician. He probably played most stringed instruments; he even once used to play a one-stringed instrument.[45] In 1971 he had a personally-built eight-stringed guitar with both bottom strings doubled, a twelve-stringed guitar, plus an old Gibson harp-guitar which he used to play. Oddly the 1920s duo of Sam Moore and Horace Davis recorded on octa-chorda (an eight-stringed guitar) and harp-guitar.[46] For his own amusement Rambo made guitars, which he would not sell, and his home was full of small objects which he had made from wood, plastic, and pieces of junk. Most appeared to have no function other than the decorative. His eight-stringed guitar was decorated with Kennedy half dollars but played perfectly well.[47] A superb photograph taken of him in 1933 shows him in his best outfit, holding a steel National guitar, obviously decorated by himself with additional ornaments.[48] Frank Edwards, in typical laconic manner, said that Rambo "couldn't sing ne'er a lick," which he freely admitted, leaving the role to another band member. He tended to perform across the other sets of Atlanta musicians, playing a few times with Weaver and even playing on Fraser Street with Peg Leg Howell. He was one of those who reported that Ollie Griffin and another fiddler, other than Eddie Anthony—"who played all the time!"—had recorded with Howell.

Although they did not record, Jonas Brown and Clifford Lee are recalled by the majority of Atlanta bluesmen as being among the finest; Brown was probably more bluesmen's first choice than any other artist, known or otherwise. Roy Dunn remembers Jonas with Curley Weaver when he first arrived in Covington in 1935. He was a "big, heavy-set man with a lot of gold in his mouth . . . about the darkest man I ever seen in my life," and Rambo remembered him as a "long, tall dark feller." Big Cliff Lee, born in the 1890s, was recalled by Buddy Moss as "having fingers like hammers," but he was capable of superb finger-picking. According to Dunn, Jonas Brown ran with a set of musicians which included Buddy Moss, Buddy Keith, Blind Willie McTell, Bo Weevil, *Bunny *Tiller, and Paul *McGuinnis. The versatile *Bunny *Tiller, who played with Weaver and Moss as well as with Roy Dunn, began playing washboard but switched first to harmonica and then to guitar. *McGuinnis has not been seen since 1940 when he roomed for some six months with Dunn.

Two members of the Star Band who did record were Leroy Dallas and Frank Edwards.[49] Edwards was born at Washington (Wilkes County) in 1909 and began performing as a guitarist in the mid-1920s. About 1934 he saw a white man play guitar and rack harmonica; intrigued, he also began to play both. Although based in Atlanta from 1938, Edwards was never seriously one of the local blues scene. He traveled considerably before returning to Georgia: he met Tampa Red in St. Augustine, Florida, in 1926, soon after he had begun to play; worked medicine shows, theaters, and jukes, while riding freight trains over much of the country; spent two years in New York state; was in Los Angeles in 1944; and knew many diverse blues artists, among them Howard Armstrong in Knoxville, Tennessee. Armstrong's guitarist, Carl Martin, taught Edwards some guitar techniques. While in Yazoo City, Mississippi, he met Tommy McClennan, then a recording artist for Bluebird, and they traveled to Chicago, where Edwards recorded eight sides in May 1941 for Okeh, thanks to Frank Melrose, the Chicago session "fixer" and publisher.[50] For the session, Tampa Red suggested backing him with a washboard, so Washboard Sam provided the rhythm and perhaps the off-mike comments on "We Got to Get Together," the only one of the issued titles to remain in Edwards's repertoire. His first release came in August 1941, and a second in December, but war presumably prevented the release of the other four titles.

Back in Atlanta he met Willie McTell for the first time in 1943 and finally settled in the city. In 1949 he was one of the group who recorded for Regal, but his two sides were only issued much later on album.[51] Located in 1971 he recorded an album the following year,[52] although finding musicians who could stay with his odd time was difficult. In an attempt to return to the "feel" of his 1941 sides, a washboard player was added—Arthur "Popcorn" Glover, who had recorded at Fort Valley.

Rufus and Ben Quillian were born in Gainesville, northeast of Atlanta, on February 2, 1900, and June 23, 1907, respectively and like many Georgians moved to Atlanta.[53] Rufus was a good pianist, playing around Atlanta for dances with a small group, including guitar and drums, and in Eddie Heywood Senior's band. Thus he was well outside the general pattern of Atlanta bluesmen and certainly would never have classed himself in that category, being more in line with those Atlanta pianists who never did record. His brother Ben worked with him at the Terrace Dry Cleaning plant, along with another migrant from Gainesville, guitarist James McCrary—"not exactly a musician," as Ben said, "but he could strum pretty good." They had a spot over WATL radio as the Blue Harmony Boys and were proud of writing their own material. Some titles were bluesy, but "most of them were kinda indecent for that day but . . . not today! We were a little ahead of our time. That's about all they wanted from us was jumping little songs, "Tight Like That," "Dirty But Good," "Keep It Clean!" . . . We had a lot of fun, played a lot of house-parties, small dances."

Between 1929 and 1931 the Quillians recorded a number of sides, first for Paramount as the Blue Harmony Boys and later for Columbia under their own names. They appeared to have been brought to New York to record, initially it seems by Gennett on behalf of Paramount, for that company had closed its New York studio by the end of 1926. In fact, on this trip Ben stayed in Atlanta while Rufus played piano on the session and sang in duets and trios with a Brother Jackson and an unnamed person. As McCrary did not play on these sides it is possible that Rufus was the only one to have traveled up from Atlanta. Six of the eight sides recorded were issued late in Paramount's series, all of them credited to Quillian as writer. Doubtless as a result of the session they were recorded when Columbia next came to Atlanta on a field trip. The first Paramount release had been advertised in the Chicago *Defender* of March 15, 1930,[54] and must have been played over WATL. Dan Hornsby was still scouting for Columbia, for when the brothers came to record, the less proficient McCrary was replaced by Perry Bechtel, who had played on the Lillian Glinn sides. Only two titles were made; the initial pressing of "Keep It Clean" and "Good Right On" went on release in November 1930. Another session, again with Bechtel, took place on Sunday, December 7, 1930, when four very un-Sunday-like songs were recorded: "Working It Slow," "Satisfaction Blues," "I Got Everything," and "It's Dirty But Good." Obviously the pattern fitted well. As on the Glinn sides, Bechtel has denied his presence, but the same highly proficient guitarist is present on them all. Further, Ben Quillian recalled: "I was on all the Atlanta sessions but some of the recordings we made in Atlanta James McCrary wasn't playing on them. . . . he sang with them but there was a white fella we met down there in the studio—he was playing the guitar. Yeah, and he was really good. But I heard him later on the radio. I can't think of his name, they call him 'The Man With A Thousand Fingers.' He was really good on the guitar and he could just pick up anything you start.'' Bechtel broadcast regularly over Atlanta radio stations and was considered one of the finest guitarists around by Adam C. ''Duke'' Welborn, who ran one of the hottest of all East Coast dance bands, the Atlanta Footwarmers. He later managed the Phil Spitalny Orchestra, whose star soloist was Perry Bechtel.[55] An album was issued in the early 1960s of Bechtel playing banjo; in the liner notes he is described as ''The Man with 10,000 Fingers.[56] He clearly improved with the years.

The two new Columbia records were each pressed in initial quantities of only 700, and yet when Columbia/Okeh made its last trip to the city in October 1931, the Quillians were once more recorded, on the same day as McTell, Weaver, and Ruth Willis. For the first time James McCrary was present and so credited on the labels of ''Workin' It Fast'' and ''Holy Roll,'' the only two of the four sides to be issued—a pressing of 600 in January 1932. Only Rufus's piano is to be heard in accompaniment but the song formula held good to the bitter end. For Rufus the end was not long in coming. Separated from his wife in 1939, he went to California but returned to die in south Atlanta in 1946, still the tailor he was when the recording career ended. Suffering from complications following pneumonia, he was operated on but died six days later on January 31. A peeved note from the coroner appended to the death certificate stated: ''This case was referred to me after *burial*. I can add nothing to facts stated hereon.'' Fortunately, at the time of writing, Ben Quillian and his wife are alive and well in St. Louis.

Many other bluesmen came to Atlanta, some of them Georgians, a few of whom recorded there and passed on into continued obscurity. Henry Lee Castle, born in Georgia in 1899, recorded a very graphic two-sided ''Charleston Contest'' for Columbia in Atlanta in 1928 but moved to Helena, Arkansas, in the 1930s before dying in Chicago in 1971.[57] Although Castle was not part of the true Atlanta scene, Dan Hornsby remembered him in 1951, but was not sure whether he was a city resident.[58] Others might well have been resident for a while. Hornsby also recalled two artists, Ed Bell and Pillie Bolling, who proved subsequently to have been from Greenville, Alabama.[59] Kokomo Arnold and Hudson Woodbridge (Tampa Red) were but two of the Georgia artists to leave the state to record extensively. Guy Lumpkin, vaguely recalled by Piano Red, was remembered by Kate McTell as being from

New Orleans, although she met him only in Atlanta.[60] Many others who recorded with Atlanta bluesmen remain obscure. To my knowledge no one ever recalled the likes of Slim Barton, Clarence and James Moore, Lillie Mae, Ruby Glaze (although a James Glaze once lived at the same house as McTell), Billy Anderson, and Troy Ferguson. Still, they may have come from far afield.

Other musicians of similar or earlier generations left Georgia, and their music is not regionally distinctive. Marshall Owens, born there about 1890, moved to Alabama, possibly Mobile, as a boy, and his recordings from 1932 denote an Alabama source.[61] Jesse Fuller, born in the last years of the 1890s in Jonesboro (Clayton County), just south of Atlanta, did not record until 1955, by which time he had long been a resident of California, following a life of travel. As a boy he heard his first guitar blues—"frailing blues," perhaps like the Hicks brothers—in Stockbridge (Henry County), adjoining Newton County. Moving to Red Oak in the southwest outskirts of Atlanta, he learned to play banjo from a brother-in-law, Melvin Moore. He used to travel to McDonough (Henry County) to hear blues, where many others recalled fine musicians from the past, but eventually took off on his travels, which modified his style. By no means a Georgia bluesman as such, he plays a twelve-stringed guitar.[62]

Some bluesmen who moved to Atlanta never did record. Blind Buddy Keith, who was playing guitar in 1907 when he was thirteen, arrived in Atlanta on July 4, 1924, and "stayed ever since." At his peak he had been by all accounts a very fine guitarist and in his old age was zealously guarded by his neighbors, who showed him great respect. Had it not been for Roy Dunn he would never have been found. Keith, who died in 1976, recalled bluesmen not remembered by others—*Clint *Weaver, a fine guitarist from Covington, and guitarists Willie *Sapp and Buddy *Rowe, from Atlanta and Covington respectively. Charlie "Roach" *Seats played such good harmonica that the white family for whom he worked took him with them to play on their Florida vacations. Roy Dunn also remembered guitarists Charlie *Howard and Charlie Brown, who burned to death in a fire. *Aubert *Prince, a straws and rubboard player from Farrer, Willie Lee *McGuire, a fine Morgan County guitarist who was parolled after seven years of a life sentence, and Augusta guitarist Eddie Lee *Johnson— "another Blind Lemon"—simply start a list which is almost endless and little more than a string of names and instruments played, dredged up from memories hazed by time.

But the list proves beyond the slightest doubt that the music was that of innumerable poor blacks, out of which but a few ever became professional in any sense. These men, whose names appear above in print perhaps for the first time, about whom little else is known, were considered by people whose knowledge of the music scene at the time was too thorough not to be accepted at face value, to be the equal of and often superior to some of the great names of recorded blues in the city. That ought not to surprise us. It was, after all, a grass-roots music, ephemeral and transitory, never intended to be caught, let alone assessed by whites who lived too late to hope to understand fully the ramifications of the social pressures which gave it birth.

NOTES

1. Gene Wiggins, "Not Very Aristocratic," *Old Time Music* 26 (Autumn, 1977): 5-7.

2. Ruth Willis died on March 5, 1962, of a heart attack.

3. J. B. Long to the author, September 18, 1975.

4. Bruce Bastin, "Rich Trice," *Blues Unlimited* 68 (December, 1969): 7-8; idem. "Willie Trice," *Blues Unlimited* 69 (January, 1970): 8-9.

5. Valerie Wilmer, "Buddy Moss," *Melody Maker,* July 15, 1972. For more on Moss and McGhee see chapter 15.

6. Marshall Frady, "Lonesome Traveler," *Atlanta* 6 (August, 1966): 35-41.

7. Buddy Moss, *Rediscovery,* Biograph BLP-12019 (New York).

8. Peter B. Lowry, "Blind Willie McTell," *Blues Unlimited* 89 (February-March, 1972): 11. The definitive work, from which some details are drawn for this chapter, is David Evans, "Blind Willie McTell," brochure notes to *Atlanta Blues 1933,* JEMF-106 (Los Angeles, 1979), pp. 6-24.

9. Blind Willie McTell, "Monologue on History of the Blues," Library of Congress AFS-4072-A-1, recorded November 5, 1940, in Atlanta.

10. Clarence McGahey, interviewed by David Evans and Anne Evans in Thomson, Georgia, September 10, 1975.

11. Kate McTell, interviewed by David Evans in Wrens, Georgia, January 19, 1976. Cliff Hobbs and Oliff Boyd, interviewed by David Evans and Anne Evans in Savannah, Georgia, March 1975.

12. Brian Rust, *The Victor Master Book Volume 2 (1925-1936)* (Pinner, England: own publication, 1969), p. 320. Robert M. W. Dixon and John Godrich, *Blues and Gospel Records 1902-1943,* 3d. ed. rev. (Chigwell, England: Storyville Publications, 1982), p. 300.

13. Charles K. Wolfe et al, *Riley Puckett (1894-1946)* (Bremen: Schriften des Archivs für Populár Musik, 1977), p. 4. See also John A. Burrison, "Fiddlers in the Alley," *Atlanta Historical Bulletin* 21 (Summer, 1977): 76.

14. Blind Willie McTell, "Monologue on Life as Maker of Records," Library of Congress AFS 4072-A-2, recorded November 5, 1940, in Atlanta.

15. Willie Hodges, interviewed by Anne Evans in Statesboro, Georgia, August 22, 1975.

16. *Melody Maker and Rhythm*, May 26, 1951.

17. Charles Wolfe, "Columbia Records and Old-Time Music," *John Edwards Memorial Foundation Quarterly* 14 (Autumn, 1978): 118-25, 144.

18. Dan Mahony, *Columbia 13/14000-D (Numerical Listing)* (Stanhope, N.J.: Walter C. Allen, 1961). All subsequent Columbia pressing figures and issue dates are from this source.

19. David Evans, "Kate McTell Part 1," *Blues Unlimited* 125 (July-August, 1977): 4.

20. David Evans, "Kate McTell Part 2," *Blues Unlimited* 126 (September-October, 1977): 8-10.

21. Paul Oliver, *The Story of the Blues* (London: Barrie & Rockliff, 1969), p. 108.

22. Kate McTell, interviewed by Anne Evans in Wrens, Georgia, September 10, 1975.

23. Evans, "Kate McTell Part 2": 10.

24. "Don't Let Nobody Turn You Round," *Blind Boy Fuller—Blind Willie McTell,* MCA 3523 (Japan), also includes two otherwise unissued McTell titles from these sessions, one with Curley Weaver on second guitar—"I Got Religion, I'm So Glad," MCA 3530 (Japan). All four are on Blind Willie McTell, *Blues in the Dark,* MCA 1368 (Universal City, Calif., 1983).

25. Bruce Bastin, "A Note on the Carolina Cotton Pickers," *Storyville* 95 (June-July, 1981): 177–82.

26. Robert Springer, "The Blues Gives Them Inspiration You Know," *Blues Unlimited* 126 (September-October, 1977): 20.

27. William Lee Perryman, interviewed by Karl Gert zur Heide in Bremen, West Germany, October 1, 1977.

28. Kate McTell, interviewed by David Evans in Wrens, Georgia, September 10, 1975.

29. Evans, "Blind Willie McTell," p. 15.

30. John A. Lomax's notes on the record jackets; John H. Cowley to the author, January 21, 1979.

31. Lowry, "Blind Willie McTell," p. 11.

32. Arnold Shaw, *Honkers and Shouters: The Golden Years of Rhythm and Blues* (New York: Collier, 1978), p. 353.

33. Peter Lowry, "David Wylie," *Blues Unlimited* 102 (June, 1978): 10.

34. Shaw, *Honkers and Shouters,* p. 354.

35. Mike Leadbitter, "Mike's Blues," *Blues Unlimited* 105 (December, 1973–January, 1974): 28.

36. Blind Willie McTell, *Atlanta Twelve String,* Atlantic SD 7224 (New York).

37. Leadbitter, "Mike's Blues," p. 28.

38. Kate McTell, interviewed by David Evans in Wrens, Georgia, January 19, 1976.

39. Michael Ruppli, *Prestige Jazz Records 1949–1969* (Denmark, n.p., 1972), p. 27.

40. Samuel Charters, *Sweet as the Showers of Rain* (New York: Oak Publications, 1977), pp. 130–31.

41. Blind Willie McTell, *Last Session,* Prestige-Bluesville 1040 (Bergenfield, N.J.).

42. Evans, "Blind Willie McTell," pp. 22–24, plus song texts, pp. 25–29. For musical notation plus texts see Jeff Todd Titon, *Early Downhome Blues* (Urbana, University of Illinois Press, 1977), pp. 104–5, 127–28. For tablative notation see Woody Mann, *Six Black Blues Guitarists* (New York, Oak Publications, 1973).

43. Evans, "Blind Willie McTell," p. 23.

44. Pete Lowry, "Atlanta Black Sound: A Survey of Black Music from Atlanta during the Twentieth Century," *Atlanta Historical Bulletin* 21 (Summer, 1977): 99–102.

45. David Evans, "Afro-American One-Stringed Instruments," *Western Folklore* 29 (1971): 229–45.

46. Brian Rust, comp., *Jazz Records 1897–1942,* rev. 4th ed. (New Rochelle, N.Y.: Arlington House, 1978), p. 1094.

47. Kip Lornell, "Three Weeks in Atlanta," *Talking Blues* 1 (April-May-June, 1976): 10.

48. Lowry, "Atlanta Black Sound," p. 101.

49. For more on Leroy Dallas see chapter 18.

50. Pete Lowry, "The Frank Edwards Story," *Blues Unlimited* 99 (February-March, 1973): 10–11.

51. *Living With the Blues,* Savoy MG 16000 (Newark, N.J.); *Sugar Mama Blues 1949,* Biograph BLP 12009 (New York).

52. Frank Edwards, *Done Some Travelin',* Trix 3303 (Rosendale, N.Y., 1973).

53. Bruce Bastin, "Blue Harmony Boys: Rufus and Ben Quillian," *Blues Unlimited* 113 (May-June, 1975): 21; Mike Rowe, "The Blue Harmony Boys—the Unusual," *Blues Unlimited* 123 (January-February, 1977): 23–25. All Ben's quotations are from Rowe.

54. Max E. Vreede, *Paramount 12000/13000 Series* (London: Storyville Publications, 1971), n.p.

55. Bruce Bastin, "Atlanta Footwarmers," *Record Research* 67 (April, 1965): 13; Duke Welborn, conversation with the author, Greenville, South Carolina, 1965.

56. *The Banjo Style of Perry Bechtel,* RCA Camden CAL-871 (New York), reissued as Perry Bechtel, *Plectrum Banjo,* Banjar BR 1785; *Cadence* 6 (September, 1980): 25.

57. Jim O'Neal and Steve LaVere, "Too Tight Henry," *Living Blues* 34 (September-October, 1977): 17.

58. *Melody Maker and Rhythm,* May 26, 1951.

59. David Evans, liner notes to *Let's Get Loose: Folk and Popular Styles from the Beginnings to the Early 1940s,* New World NW 290 (New York, 1977); Don Kent, liner notes to *Ed Bell's Mamlish Moan,* Mamlish S-3811 (New York, 1981).

60. Kate McTell, interviewed by David Evans in Wrens, Georgia, January 19, 1976.

61. Don Kent, "Marshall Owens," *Living Blues* 26 (March-April, 1976): 7.

62. Valerie Wilmer, "Jesse Fuller," *Jazz Journal* 12 (May, 1959): 4. See also Richard Noblett and John Offord, " 'I Got a Mind to Ramble and I don't Want to Settle Down,' An Interview with Jesse Fuller, 22nd October 1965," *Blues World* 25 (October, 1969): 10–12, and *Blues World* 26 (January, 1970): 21–22.

9

Goin' Down in Georgia:
Georgia Blues Today

Today the Georgia blues scene is fragmentary and, apart from the occasional festival, there is little obvious opportunity for playing other than for family and friends. Understandably many performers in recent years have given up playing and are unlikely to be coaxed back. Nonetheless detailed investigation by a dedicated handful of researchers has uncovered a wealth of blues talent to further prove the wide, grassroots extent of the music. Foremost among these active researchers were George Mitchell and Pete Lowry. Mitchell has been active in searching out bluesmen ever since the early 1960s when as a high school student he relocated Peg Leg Howell. He eventually settled in West Georgia and undertook the only research ever there, mainly within a fifty-mile radius of Columbus. A number of albums of music Mitchell recorded in the region in 1969-70 have been issued, as well as albums of material recorded in the late 1970s when he became actively involved with the Georgia Grassroots Festival, of which he was director.[1] Mitchell continued to be the most involved fieldworker in the state and, in October 1984, was coordinator of the National Downhome Blues Festival in Atlanta, and also of an earlier festival in Columbus, Georgia, which featured predominantly local bluesmen. Mitchell's on-going research constantly adds to any study of the current blues scene in the state and perhaps at some future date his work, now mainly in the lower Chattahoochee Valley, can extend the coverage of this chapter. Pete Lowry's extensive research and recordings took place in the early-to mid-1970s, mostly in Atlanta and to the east.

SOUTH AND WEST GEORGIA

Mitchell's work has clearly shown that the southwest section of the state is a transition zone for blues within the deep South. Much of the material shows distinct musical links with the sounds of the Piedmont, as with George Henry Bussey of Waverly Hall and Bud Grant of Thomaston. Buddy Hubbard from La Grange played his slide guitar in a style similar to those recorded at Fort Valley and on the coast. The smoother style of the Carolinas and northeast Georgia existed side by side with the rougher, more plangent style of the southern part of the state. Perhaps Mitchell's most interesting discovery was the presence of a fife-and-drum tradition in the country between Waverly Hall and Talbotton, northeast of Columbus.[2] Until recently it was assumed that the tradition of fife-and-drum music was uniquely that of north Mississippi around Senatobia. However, bands have been recorded in the 1970s in Tennessee,[3] and the tradition existed in both Virginia and North Carolina, although in the latter, it apparently existed only for religious functions. The similarities of the music of the Senatobia and Waverly Hall groups hints that the music was probably more widespread than is appreciated. A possible link between the regions came from Willie Guy Rainey, born in Calhoun County, Alabama, in 1901. He recalled that people would give a barbecue "and they'd beat the pan, blow a cane with six holes in it—call them fifes. They'd blow them things—we didn't have anything else."[4] A further example of an Alabama fife tradition is a ten-note panpipe, now in the Smithsonian Institution, made by Joe Patterson of Ashford, Alabama, close to both Georgia and Florida state lines.[5] The Georgia fife-and-drum group was essentially a family band comprising J. W. Jones on bamboo cane fife and his brother James on kettle drum, with the bass drum played by either a younger brother, Willie C. Jones, or a cousin, Floyd Bussey.

A good example of the older style of the middle-south Georgia blues is to be found in the playing of Dixon Hunt, although past his peak when he was recorded. Born in the mid-1890s he was playing by his early teens, first on banjo and later on guitar, and warmly recalled his early days: "I went and made music in every frolic they gave. I used to go all over the country—all over Marion County, Columbus, Sumter

County, all down in there, everywhere. We'd play from Saturday morning till Sunday night, slam on into Sunday, picking guitars and having fun. I wouldn't miss a Saturday night making music and frolicking. Back then, I was just about the best boy there on guitar."

The parochial nature of Hunt's performing territory, little more than sixty miles from end to end, is typical of the Southeast. Artists of undoubted ability seldom ranged more than a few miles from base even though, like Hunt, they played "everywhere." Hunt's style lived on in that of Cliff Scott, a neighbor half his age, in the small community of Draneville, northwest of Americus; "Sweet Old Tampa" is a fine example. However, by the time researchers Jim Pettigrew and Paul Dingman relocated Scott in 1976, he had sold his guitar.[6] Other performers in this urgent, middle-south blues style include Jim Bunkley and Green Paschal, both of Talbot County, as well as men located and recorded in the late 1970s, like James Davis, William Robertson, Jimmy Lee Williams, and John Lee Ziegler.[7]

Jim Bunkley was one of only two west Georgia bluesmen recorded at any depth by Mitchell in 1969, when there were plenty of bluesmen—always one per small town—even if they only knew, and performed well, one or two songs. Within ten years few remained playing, although those who did—and were recorded—were still highly proficient. Bunkley was born in 1912 in Geneva (Talbot County) and began playing about 1920. "Everyone in my family could play—we had five boys and four girls. My mother and father could play. We could play fiddles too." As a young man he won local contests held in a theater in nearby Junction City, and he still played well in 1969. Unfortunately, he was killed in a car crash the following year.

George Henry Bussey was the other Talbot County bluesman recorded in depth, at Waverly Hall. Born in adjoining Harris County, he grew up heavily influenced by Blind Boy Fuller's records. By the time Mitchell located him, he was a woodworker and had given up playing in 1955. A quiet, reserved man, he agreed to practice and recorded only when he felt competent.

Talbot County was home to many bluesmen besides those named above. Emmit Jones, a neighbor of Bunkley, was recorded singing with him. Harmonica player Golden Bailey, who performed at the 1976 Atlanta Grassroots Festival, is also from Geneva.[8] Jessie Clarence Garman, born in Talbot County in 1928, recorded a superb "Going Up the Country" for Mitchell in Thomaston. A guitarist since 1937, he epitomized another change in the performing role of the active bluesman—playing in a rock 'n' roll band. Although he used to sing "nothing but blues," he claimed to have forgotten all his old songs, with the exception of the one recorded. It was certainly our loss. Mitchell also recorded fiddler George Hollis, much in the style of Elbert Freeman.

Mitchell of course recorded bluesmen from other counties. Bud White, then about forty years of age, played guitar and harmonica in Richland (Stewart County), south of Columbus; he learned "Sixteen Snow White Horses" from a traveling bluesman from Florida. Born in 1924 in Thomaston (Upson County), he was playing guitar by the age of twelve, "mostly little frolicking pieces . . . just for someone to dance off. Buck dances." Like Bussey and others, he shows the influence of Fuller in his playing.

In the late 1970s Mitchell returned to the region to locate active bluesmen for the Grassroots Festival and to follow up leads from Jim Pettigrew. In 1976 Pettigrew had located one of the finest Georgia bluesmen of recent years in Bronwood (Terrell County), just south of the one small Georgia town which was to become known to millions throughout the world—Plains. A good guitarist but a vocalist possessed of great range and control, he is a highly superstitious man. He uses a pseudonym, William Robertson, because he is afraid that his photograph or knowledge and mis-use of his name will injure him through "evil spells." Born around 1922, he farmed all his life until forced to retire with a back injury, which he is convinced has not healed because of hoodoo. He is unable to climb the steps of his porch without assistance and has to pause when speaking to regain his breath, but his voice on record certainly doesn't sound like that of a sick man.

He was playing by the age of five.

> I started off playing one string . . . put me a wire up side of the house. And I played that with a bottleneck. I put some bottles up side of the house with a strand of wire across them. . . . When I was 12 years old, I come in playing a real guitar. I started off ragging it, playing them rag pieces. My father and uncle played—they said they were about the best, but they had done left from around here by the time I started playing. . . . But a heap of people what caught the pieces that they played, they played 'em and I caught 'em from them.[9]

Robertson played "just about any occasion" for both whites and blacks. Some of his songs were traditional to the locality: "True Love" was known to Cliff Scott, who lived some twenty-five miles away, and both men played "Pole Plattin'," a song used for May Day celebrations, performed in the same strummed manner. Robertson even claimed that his frolicking songs were really "round-dance" songs. Perhaps his music was far enough away from the bustling interstate highways 85 and 75 to change too rapidly. As he pointed out, "There wasn't no radio around here then. We only had record players, you know, the kind that you fold up like a suitcase. It was a long time before there was any radio in these parts.''[10]

Although the most interesting of the local musicians discovered in the later 1970s, Robertson was not the only one. In and around Manchester, immediately north of Talbot County, live J. C. Rush, George Denson, and Willene Terry. Rush occasionally still plays guitar and harmonica at frolics and fish-fries; Denson is an older bluesman, who taught Terry and has now "crossed over" to the church. Guitarist Jimmy Jordan and his neighbor James "Tip" Neale live in Americus. Shot in the left hand and arm in 1978, Jordan may well never play again, but Neale is one of the few medicine show performers still musically active.

Neale was born in 1906 in Eufaula, just across the Chattahoochee River state line in Alabama. He joined a medicine show at the age of twenty and spent the next forty years traveling in such shows as those of Silas Greene and the Rabbit Foot Minstrels. He plays jew's harp—a haunting snatch of his jew's harp can be heard on the Georgia Grassroots album—and washboard, which he claimed first to have played when he knew blues guitarist Tampa Red. "We started going to town and playing around them filling stations. And the white folks see us and that rubboard and all those pots and pans and things I had to put on it. And I got more money out of the clowning than he did out of the guitar."[11] Perhaps this *was* the famous Tampa Red, from Smithville, Georgia. Neale's account is set before he joined the medicine show about 1926, the same year in which Frank Edwards met Tampa Red in St. Augustine, Florida.[12] While Tampa Red claimed to have teamed up with Georgia Tom Dorsey "around 1925,"[13] they did not record together until 1928. Neale quit working medicine shows as late as 1970.

One obscure record by a Georgia bluesman from southwestern Georgia was discovered as late as 1972 in a pile of second-hand records in Nashville. Dating from 1953 and made for the Trepur label in La Grange, it featured the vocal and slide guitar of Robert Lee Westmoreland on "Hello Central, Please Give Me 209" and 'Good Looking Woman Blues,'' the latter with an excellent vocal and impassioned slide guitar. It was the only blues recorded for the label as it sold so poorly for the owner, Rupert McClendon, one of the white McClendon Brothers who had recorded for Bluebird. Interviewed by Pete Lowry, McClendon recalled nothing about Westmoreland and had last heard of him in the mid-1960s around Griffin, midway between Macon and Atlanta.

In 1966 another bluesman made a down-home recording at a Columbus studio. McKinley James was born in Macon in July 1935 but was raised in Macon County, Alabama. Neighbors Willie Gardsen and Bo Bo Brown helped him learn to play guitar. His opportunity to record came when a teacher in an adult education program heard him playing at a graduation party: "Tuskegee Boogie," with rack-harp and Elmore James-styled slide guitar, went down well, and a music professor at Tuskegee helped him arrange the session.[14] The reverse of the record, "Ain't Gonna Pick No Cotton," has a guitar line strongly reminiscent of the lead guitar on Betty James's 1961 New York recording of "I'm a Little Mixed Up" and is entirely within the Piedmont tradition. Fellow Macon County, Alabama, guitarists Albert Macon and Robert Thomas perform today in the general regional style found in southwest Georgia.

John Lee Ziegler was one of many Houston County musicians who attended the Fort Valley festivals. Born in Kathleen, where he still lives, on April 12, 1929, he is a left-handed guitarist who plays "upside-down," learning to play about 1945 from a brother-in-law who was a professional musician. He later learned about open tunings and within two years was playing fish-fries and parties. Although he drew upon popular bluesmen like John Lee Hooker and once played in a band in New York, he is very much a bluesman in the local tradition. His slide pieces like "Poor Boy" and "John Henry" are typical of the region, and his own numbers like "If I Lose Let Me Lose" reflect nothing of the newer influences at work when he began to play. Performing today, usually with spoons player Rufus Jones, he finds more work than he cares to take on. "All the people round here, Macon, Hawkinsville, they say I'm about the onliest one around here, about the best. A lot of the people come out to hear me play."[15]

Another Houston County bluesman from Henderson is perhaps the only remaining country bluesman in Georgia who plays regular gigs for a black audience. James Davis is two years younger than Ziegler, and his playing is a remarkable example of the persistence of the "drum music" tradition documented on the coast but doubtless common through south-central Georgia. Davis's father and uncle were well known locally for their drumming at church picnics and house parties, using nothing but a bass drum and kettle drum. There may well be some link here with the Waverly Hall fife-and-drum tradition. Today Davis plays guitar backed only by a drummer. The local people still refer to the music Davis plays as "drum music" and the dance as a "drumbeat." Davis mused, "I was born around here, been here all my life. My daddy was a drummer all his life and I inherited it from him. When they didn't have nothing but the rural school, he used to beat for the children's playdays, school close, and all that kind of stuff." Every Friday night a large rickety room in Perry, the county seat, is transformed into a dance hall. No admission is charged, but vodka and beer sell for seventy-five cents and there is a broad cross-section of people of all ages, meeting to dance and socialize. On Saturday nights he often plays the Jazz Inn in Elko, where John Lee Ziegler occasionally performs. Fifty cents will gain you admission.

> I get a crowd of people every time I play. Not too many people playing the blues around here now . . . but people here, all they want to know is where I be playing at. I don't have to worry about the crowd, they'll be there! Sometimes there be over 150.
> The people round here call it the old country drumbeat. They like that old country-style playing. A lot of them say they'd rather hear my playing than hear them piccolos [juke-boxes].[16]

He was recorded with both his drummers. Eddie Releford was his first choice and the two can be heard playing "James' Boogie" and "Old Country Rock"—not the William Moore Paramount tune. "Good Morning Little Schoolgirl," with Ulysses Davis drumming, is obviously learned from record.

Mitchell also traveled through the southern counties trying to trace bluesmen. In Bainbridge he located a pianist-singer, Andrew Jones. Born about 1894, Jones used to play both clubs and parties and claimed to have been taught by a pianist from Columbus. The only other bluesman to have been recorded to date from the very southern Georgia counties is Jimmy Lee Williams, who was born in Poulan, Worth County, between Albany and Tifton. A farmer who owns his land, he lives in a remote part of the country. He learned to play guitar in 1941 and by the following year was playing for all-night Saturday frolics, at which he would earn maybe ten dollars plus as much as he could eat and drink. For a while he played a rack-harmonica, spurred on by the success in New York of his nephew, Buster Brown, whose story belongs to those who migrated to the urban complex. His highly idiomatic "Hoot Your Belly and Give Your Backbone Ease" is regionally representative. Emmett Murray, born in 1911 in Moultrie, Colquitt County, Georgia, adjoining Worth and Tifton counties, moved in the 1930s to Florida, where he was recorded in 1980 (see chapter 3).

Other than Mitchell's, only one piece of research had ever been carried out—a follow-up to the Tifco issue of "Wild Women" and "Kokomo Me Baby," featuring Danny Boy and His Blue Guitar, backed by another guitar, a harmonica, and drums. Pete Lowry traced the owner of the label and the story of the recording emerged.[17] The session had been cut in Atlanta in 1958 in Bill Lowery's studio. Lowery, who was to become an important factor in the pop music boom in Atlanta in the 1960s, had established a music publishing business in the city in 1952 and owned the National Recording Company. The Danny Boy session was made just before the boom broke, as he explained. "In the fifties we were primarily country music orientated. We published a lot of big sellers, but none of them were Atlanta artists. We didn't get into pop or rock and roll until 1956. . . . The music business in Atlanta didn't really start moving until '59 or '60."[18] Lowery cut the session as a favor; Tifco otherwise released only country artists. Held on a Sunday, the session started badly when the black harmonica player turned up without an instrument. A borrowed one was out of tune and some reeds stuck but there was no alternative but to use it. Danny Boy sang and played rhythm guitar, the lead guitarist and drummer were supplied from the Lowery camp, then into rock and roll. The fine guitarist heard throughout was one of Lowery's highly successful white rockers, Jerry Reed. A truly integrated session—only Danny Boy and his harp player were black.

COASTAL GEORGIA

In 1959 Alan Lomax returned to the Georgia sea islands, which he had first visited almost twenty-five years before. None of the "drum music" recorded earlier was documented on this trip; indeed, no instrumental music was recorded at all. There was no reference as to whether this music had persisted but, remote as the islands were, times might have overtaken them. In his liner notes to one of the albums of the music recorded, Lomax wrote the following:

> Mrs. Maxfield Parrish . . . is directly responsible for the authenticity of the material in these two albums. . . . She became seriously interested in their music . . . (and) formed an organization of singers called the "Spiritual Singers of Georgia." Each member of the singers received a button which distinguished him as a "Star Chorister" and signified that he was a folk singer and dancer in the great tradition of the region. . . . The chorus performed for the visitors and tourists who by then had begun to stream onto St. Simon's Island. . . . Thus, through the heritage of this group of true Negro folk singers, which still performs regularly at the Cloisters Hotel on Sea Islands, there has lived on until today a remarkable body of songs sung in authentic ante-bellum style. After the death of Mrs. Parrish the supervision of the group was taken over by Mrs. Margaret Case, librarian at the Cloisters.[19]

Therein lie a number of reasons why "drum music" may well have gone into hiding, although it had not died out elsewhere along the coast in the 1950s. Marshall and Jean Stearns, hoping to find early black dancing styles and the accompanying music for their definitive study of vernacular dance, had gone to St. Helena Island in 1951. After an initial lack of success "we had walked outside the shack for a breath of fresh air when suddenly we heard the sound of African drums. We rushed inside and there, in the middle of the creaky wooden floor, were two young men dancing."[20] The Stearns had studied African drumming with an African drummer so were well familiar with the sounds; Marshall had written perhaps the best brief history of jazz.[21] Had they gone to St. Simon's Island they might have discovered that the music was still there. After all, Zora Neale Hurston, in *Mules and Men*, has one of her characters say about whites: "You see we are a polite people and we do not say to our questioner, 'Get out of here!' We smile and we tell him or her something that satisfies the white person because, knowing so little about us, he doesn't know what he is missing. . . . He can read my writing but he sho' can't read my mind. I'll put this play toy in his hand, and he will seize it and go away. Then I'll say my say and sing my song."[22] Hurston was herself faced by this on her first fieldtrip to Florida. It is a very arrogant fieldworker who would maintain he has never experienced it.

Between Lomax's two trips, the very detailed Federal Writers Project study, published in 1940, reported on "drum music," including its use at a Daddy Grace religious service: "At first the procession is orderly and fairly quiet, but as time passes, the music becomes increasingly loud. Above the brass instruments the steady throb of the drum can be heard . . . the pulsating rhythm of the instruments increases in tempo. . . . The steady, insistent sound of the drum urges them on." The drum clearly had a series of social functions including being used at funerals, warning people of recent death, and literally drumming people out of a community as in military tradition.[23] The "pulsating rhythm" remained in the secular tradition for dancing, as in the music of James Davis.

Both George Mitchell and David Evans uncovered musicians along the Georgia coast and Evans's research into Blind Willie McTell unearthed a considerable amount of information about one of McTell's old playing partners from Savannah, Blind Log. Born Lord Randolph Byrd and blind, he acquired a number of nicknames, among them Blind Log, Lloyd, Lord, and Loss, and a reputation as a fine musician and singer. A left-handed guitarist before a stroke in 1964 stopped him from playing, Byrd started out playing traditional songs like "John Henry" using a bottleneck, but he soon switched to using a metal car bushing, as the glass often cut into the bass strings. First he played with local guitarists like Bubba Johnson, Stokes, Dink Williams, who moved to Miami, and pianist Blind Ivory Moore. He traveled widely, not only within the state, and accompanied McTell for two or three years after 1928. McTell's nickname in the Statesboro-Savannah area was Blind Doog; two musicians named Blind Doog and Blind Log were easily remembered. Before he joined McTell he also knew Benny and Pauline Parrish, two blind religious singers, who recorded as Blind Benny Paris and Wife for Victor in Atlanta in 1928. He claimed that Benny died in 1938 or 1939 and that both he and his wife are buried in Screven County, where Log was living when he had his stroke. It is unfortunate that he was never persuaded to record when at his peak, but a remote chance exists that some tapes survive, made by his son in the mid-1950s containing, among some of his best songs, a "ring play," "Little Sally Walker."[24]

One of the bluesmen with whom Blind Log used to perform was Dave Coney, now deceased, whose son Ira lives in Metter, just west of Statesboro. A guitarist who came under many more recent influences, having played with a band in Miami and worked in the Bahamas, he knew both Log and McTell and performed at the 1976 Grassroots Festival.[25] Also featured at a later festival was Savannah guitarist Embry Raines, originally from Upson County, around Thomaston. Of the men located by Evans in 1976-77 in the area, only Raines was really capable of public performance, but Ray Lewis and Harry Fields had obviously been fine players in their day.

One survival of the small washboard and jug bands which were once very popular among white audiences as well as black is the Washboard Band from Brunswick. It offers "blues, jazz, folk, and pop," according to the Georgia Grassroots Music Festival's *Dictionary of Down Home Musicians,* but it lies closer to the more sophisticated washboard bands popular in the early 1930s, like the Washboard Rhythm Kings, than to the local "drum music." Originating in 1922 with Bill Sprig-gin on mandolin and rubboard, Bowen King on bass fiddle, and Robert Avery and Jim Killens on guitars and vocals, it was probably then closer in musical context to Blind Billy Smith's (Blind Cliff's) band from Macon, which recorded at Fort Valley. In 1978 the Brunswick band comprised its leader, Charles Jones, Sr., on bass-fiddle, kazoo, and vocals; his son, Charles, Jr., on rubboard; Will Daniels on piano; and Jim Bryant on guitar. Daniels and Bryant were born in 1916.[26]

IN AND AROUND ATLANTA

A number of bluesmen remain in and around Atlanta, some of whom continue to perform. Some were located by George Mitchell, a few by others, but the majority were found by Pete Lowry during his periodic research trips in the 1970s. The musicians in and around Newton County have been discussed earlier in detail. The main town to the immediate north is Athens, home of the University of Georgia. Twice scholars there have been involved in research in the area, and Art Rosenbaum, teaching in the Department of Art, is currently active. The first person to collect there was Bill Koon, in 1965.

Koon lived in Lexington to the southeast. In the summer of 1965 he met and recorded Eddie Lee "Mustright" Jones, a fine, if rough, country singer and guitarist. Koon had no intention of issuing any material, but David Evans arranged for the best to be edited and released on album in 1974. Koon's description of his introduction to Jones shows the unexpected opportunity which the good fieldworker is quick to grasp. All collectors of black material have similar stories, and Evans put together some of his own experiences with a view to assisting future collection in the field.[27] Koon recalled: "I saw (him) sitting on his front porch playing a guitar. . . . When I approached him Eddie Lee stopped playing and, despite my urging, would not resume, saying simply that he didn't know how to play. Since I was studying blues guitar, I asked if I might play a bit, and he agreed. I sang some forgotten blues, using the best licks from the Jerry Silverman blues instruction book, upon which Eddie Lee yelled to his wife, 'Lord, listen here. He plays just like one of the hillbillies on the TV.' Since that afternoon I've never attempted blues again. But it broke the ice."[28] Jones was again recorded in 1977 and performed a concert in Athens in 1980.[29]

Immediately east of Athens is the small community of Winterville, where Neal Patman was born in 1926. He lost his right arm when he was seven but a few years later began to play harmonica when his father bought him one for Christmas. Playing somewhat in the style of Sonny Terry, he has performed at concerts in Athens and at the Grassroots Festival.

Mitchell located a number of bluesmen in and around Atlanta in the late 1970s, most notable being Willie Guy Rainey, who now lives in Palmetto, southwest of the city. Born in Calhoun County, Alabama, in 1901, he moved to Atlanta in 1906. Today he plays guitar and piano on sporadic gigs around Atlanta but clearly remembers the early days of his music. "I first started playing violin, but now I can't strike a

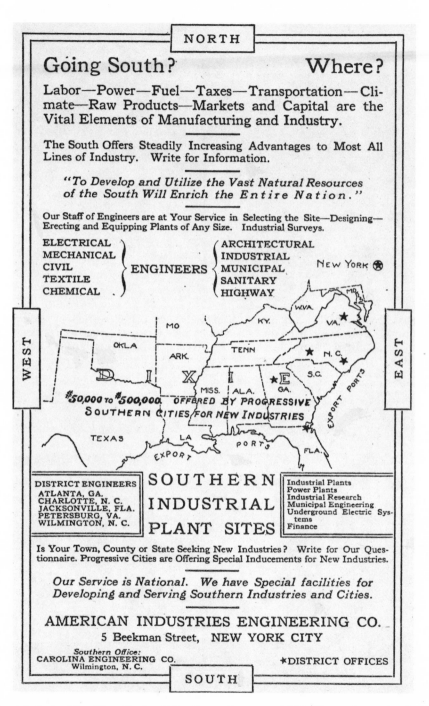

Ad from *The Blue Book of Southern Progress,* 1923 (from the author's collection).

Sharecropper picking cotton near Chapel Hill, North Carolina (photo by Marion Post Wolcott, 1939, from the collection of the Library of Congress, courtesy of the Southern Historical Collection, University of North Carolina at Chapel Hill).

Country store, Person County, North Carolina (from the collection of the Library of Congress, courtesy of the Southern Historical Collection, University of North Carolina at Chapel Hill).

Palatka Jug Band, Florida, 1905 (from *World Wide Magazine,* October 1904–March, 1905).

"A Barbecue Orchestra at Work" (from *World Wide Magazine,* April-September, 1902).

Blind Blake

WE have all heard expressions of people "singing in the rain" or "laughing in the face of adversity," but we never saw such a good example of it, until we came upon the history of Blind Blake. Born in Jacksonville, in sunny Florida, he seems to have absorbed some of the sunny atmosphere — disregarding the fact that nature had cruelly denied him a vision of outer things. He could not see the things that others saw—but he had a better gift. A gift of an inner vision, that allowed him to see things more beautiful. The pictures that he alone could see made him long to express them in some way — so he turned to music. He studied long and earnestly — listening to talented pianists and guitar players, and began to gradually draw out harmonious tunes to fit every mood. Now that he is recording exclusively for Paramount, the public has the benefit of his talent, and agrees, as one body, that he has an unexplainable gift of making one laugh or cry as he feels, and sweet chords and tones that come from his talking guitar express a feeling of his mood.

Blind Blake ad (from *The Paramount Book of Blues,* 1927).

Free Will Offering Benefit American Red Cross

GUITAR PLAYERS, BANJO PLAYERS, STRING BANDS, MUSICIANS OF ALL KINDS WANTED! ALSO STORY TELLERS

CASH PRIZES

THE FORT VALLEY STATE COLLEGE FESTIVAL OF OLD TIME MUSIC
FRIDAY, MARCH 6, 1942

PROGRAM

5:00 P. M.	Elimination Contest for New Performers. All new performers and those entered last year who did not win prizes are asked to be present promptly at 5:00 P. M. for a contest to pick out the best for the evening.
7:00 P. M.	Final Festival Contest. All winners from last year and special features invited to participate.

PRIZES
FOR BEST STRING BAND
$10 Cash for First Prize   **$5 Cash for Second Prize**
FOR BEST BANJO, GUITAR, HARP, FIDDLE PLAYER
$7.50 First Prize $5.00 Second Prize $2.50 Third Prize

For the Best Novelty Instrument, Jug, Washboard, Bottle, Etc.—$5.00

Prizes for the Best Group of Musicians and for the Best Individual

Also This Year—Persons to Tell F

PLEASE PASS THE WORD ON TO MUSICIANS IN THIS LI

Records Will Be Made of all Perfor

William C. Handy, Composer of St. Louis Blues,

OTHER PRIZES OF ALL DESCRI

For Further Information Address Lint
Festival Director, Fort Valley State College,

THE 1942 FOLK FES

Friday, 1:30, March 6	Friday, 7:00, March 6
Children's Games	Instrumental Folk Music Program
	Folk Tales

Ad from Fort Valley Folk Festival (from the author's collection), and performer Elbert Freeman, 1967 (courtesy of John Burrison).

Ad for "Barbecue Blues" by Barbecue Bob (from the Chicago *Defender*, May 21, 1927).

Ad from the Chicago *Defender*, June 21, 1924 (courtesy of Karl Gert zur Heide).

Peg Leg Howell, 1963 (courtesy of George Mitchell).

Charlie Rambo, 1933, a member of the Star Band (courtesy of Peter B. Lowry).

Blind Willie McTell, ca. 1950 (courtesy of Hazel McTear and David Evans).

David Wylie, ca. 1974 (courtesy of Peter B. Lowry).

Buddy Moss, 1933 (courtesy of Paul Oliver).

Curley Weaver, Ruth Willis, Fred McMullen, and Joshua White, 1933 (courtesy of Pau Oliver).

tune on it to save my life. . . . Back then, they'd be playin' violin, beatin' dishpans—they'd just have a frolic when they could.''[30] Mitchell also located and recorded Alfred Barnett playing blues harmonica on the streets of East Point and in 1978 located a number of railroad section gang callers who still worked for the Georgia Railroad, five of whom—William Lotts, Pope Maddox, Fred Daniel, William Brightwell, and Robert Thompson—lived in the Stone Mountain–Redan–Lithonia area immediately east of the city.

However, Mitchell did his initial research in the city in 1963 when he arranged for Peg Leg Howell to record and also made a few recordings of other bluesmen, including some duets between Willie Rockmore and Bruce Upshaw. Upshaw was a harmonica player from Montgomery, Alabama, but Rockmore was from Newton County, born there on February 2, 1921. Like his more illustrious neighbors, he moved to Atlanta but was living in Decatur when he died on August 26, 1971. On "Love Her with a Feeling" the two sound much in the pattern of Blind Boy Fuller, but a short "Got the Stuff Right Here" is a splendid cameo, highly reminiscent of the 1933 Georgia Browns with Rockmore playing guitar in the style of Curley Weaver.[31]

Without doubt the most important of the bluesmen Pete Lowry located was Roy Dunn, a veritable mine of information about the region to the east and southeast of Atlanta, whose recollections of artists known and unknown and willingness to lead us to other bluesmen and informants provided more information than all other oral sources put together. Born in Eatonton (Putnam County)—Peg Leg Howell's birthplace—on April 13, 1922, Dunn moved to Kelly (Jasper County), just south of Covington in 1931. There he came under the influence of Jim Smith, who taught him to play traditional numbers like "John Henry" in open tuning. In 1935 he moved to Covington, where he befriended Curley Weaver and Jonas Brown. From a large and musical family, young Roy learned a wide range of music. His father, four uncles, and some aunts all played instruments, as did two brothers, who joined Roy and a third brother to make up a family vocal quartet. Playing guitar and singing, he joined and toured with half a dozen gospel groups, among them the Victory Bond Gospel Singers, dated neatly to World War II. An inveterate traveler, he spent some time in jail, fortunately (his word!) learning to drive heavy road-making equipment and improving his guitar style, both of which helped him on his release in 1960. Although at first glance Dunn seems a robust man, he was permanently disabled in a disastrous car accident in 1968. Carefully nurtured by Lowry, he recorded a fine album at various sessions between 1971 and 1974.[32] He performed along with other Atlanta artists at the March 1973 Blues Festival sponsored by the University of North Carolina at Chapel Hill, has made frequent appearances at clubs and festivals around Atlanta, including the Grassroots Festival and the 1980 Piedmont Arts Festival, and has appeared on WRFG-FM's *Living Atlanta Project* with Buddy Moss and Frank Edwards.[33]

Lowry recorded many other Atlanta musicians between 1972 and 1978. Clifford Lee "Sam" Swanson, born about 1925, is a fine harmonica player who lived across the road from Frank Edwards, who accompanied him on some sides. Robert Fulton, a guitarist and harmonica player in more modern style, had been first recorded on a session with Big Boy Crudup in Atlanta in 1954. Two of the four titles issued at the time plus a third previously unissued title were released in 1965.[34] Lowry also recorded pianists Eddie Lee Person and Tommy Lee Russell, a member of a talented musical family. Tommy Lee was born on September 11, 1925, in Vienna (Dooly County [*sic*]), immediately east of Americus. His father Charlie played piano, as did his mother Mattie. Moving to Atlanta in 1929, he played with a guitarist cousin, Earl Russell, who died in 1957, as well as with a number of Atlanta pianists like *Wiley *Cook, "Chicken" and "Farmer," and "Skeeter" from Savannah. Much in the barrelhouse tradition, his playing, tempered by his stints with larger Atlanta bands, also reflects a degree of sophistication. Like Frank Edwards and Roy Dunn, he appeared at the 1973 Chapel Hill festival. At that time his mother, well into her seventies, was able to sing and play guitar with sufficient vitality to make one appreciate that in her day, in the chorus line of the 81 Theater behind the likes of Bessie Smith, she must have been an excellent entertainer. Her older son, Charlie Russell, was born in Cochran (Blechley County) southeast of Macon in 1920 and played guitar and rack-harp. Tommy Lee and Mattie are both dead, but one day it will be good to hear a Russell Family album.

Also from Eatonton were guitarists *Link *Paul—whom Roy Dunn remembered about 1930 playing slide guitar—and one Rogers. Another fine guitarist from the town whom Lowry recorded in some depth was Ernest Scott, born March 18, 1917. Although his father, Riley Scott, played banjo and guitar, he taught him little, but soon after he started playing for a living in 1940 he ran across Curley Weaver. A very talented musician, Scott drank extremely heavily, which contributed to his death in January 1977, and sessions reflected this before too long. However some titles are truly superb, and on best recorded evidence he can be ranked with the finest from Atlanta.

Other musicians Roy Dunn recalled really make little more than a long list but one worth appending here: guitarists Edward *Knowle, William Henry *Jolly, Dick Martin from Morgan County, and O. T. from Good Hope in Walton County, Joe Louis *Madison and Big Joe *Sammy from Dublin and Sammy *Philips from Villa Rica. Harmonica players included Nathaniel Willis from Birmingham, Alabama, Moses *McNeil from Monticello (Jasper County), and R. W. Lawson, who went to the State Mental Hospital in Milledgeville. A far from complete list, it still offers some idea of the immensely rich heritage from which a few men came to be recorded. We can but hazard a guess at what was lost to us.

NOTES

1. Two albums initially issued in England were reprogrammed. *Georgia Blues*, Revival RVS 1007, included sides by George Henry Bussey, Jessie Clarence Gorman, Bud Grant, Buddy Hubbard, Willie Rockmore, Cliff Scott, and Bud White. Gorman, Rockmore, Scott, and White were reissued on *Georgia Blues*, Rounder 2008 (Somerville, Mass.), with titles by the Georgia Fife and Drum Band, Bud Grant, George Hollis, Dixon Hunt, and Green Paschal. *George Henry Bussey: Jim Bunkley*, Revival RVS 1003, was reissued on Rounder 2001 with two extra titles by each. Titles recorded at the Georgia Grassroots Festival in Atlanta in 1976 and 1977 were issued on an untitled, unnumbered album in 1978, containing titles by James "Tip" Neal, Embry Raines, Willie Guy Rainey, the Washboard Band, and John Lee Ziegler. William Robertson, *South Georgia Blues*, Southland SLP-5 (Atlanta, Ga.).

2. *Traveling through the Jungle: Negro Fife and Drum Music from the Deep South*, Testament T-2223 (Calif.). This includes Mississippi sides.

3. Bengt Olsson, liner notes to *Old Country Blues*, Flyright 537 (Bexhill-on-Sea, England, 1979); Jim O'Neal, liner notes to *Homesick James: Goin' Back Home*, Trix 3315 (Rosendale, N.Y.).

4. Valerie Wilmer, "Still Got the Blues: Georgia Bluesmen Talking," *Blues Unlimited* 133 (January-February, 1979): 16.

5. Presented by Alan Lomax in 1964, it was featured in an exhibit, "The Harmonious Craft, American Musical Instruments," Renwick Gallery, Smithsonian Institution, Washington, D.C., September 29, 1978–August 5, 1979.

6. Jim Pettigrew, "Me Cryin', Ooo-hooo: Do They Sing the Georgia Blues Anymore?" *Browns' Guide to Georgia* (July-August, 1976): 42–43.

7. *Georgia Blues Today*, Flyright 576 (Bexhill-on-Sea, England, 1981), has tracks by all these artists.

8. *Living Blues* 32 (May-June, 1977): 40.

9. See David Evans, "Afro-American One-Stringed Instruments," *Western Folklore* 29 (1971): 229–45; William Ferris, *Blues from the Delta* (New York:

Anchor Press, 1978), pp. 37–38, 62; George Mitchell, liner notes to *William Robertson*, Southland SLP-5.

10. Pettigrew, "Me Cryin'": 41.

11. George Mitchell, "James 'Tip' Neale," Atlanta *Gazette*, October 13, 1976.

12. William Bentley, liner notes to Frank Edwards, *Done Some Travelin'*, Trix 3303 (Rosendale, N.Y.).

13. Jim O'Neal, liner notes to Tampa Red, *Guitar Wizard*, RCA AXM2-5501 (New York).

14. John G. Allinson, "The McKinley James Story," *Blues Unlimited* 135/136 (July-September, 1979): 12–13.

15. Wilmer, "Still Got the Blues": 21. See also Val Wilmer, "Still Got the Blues," *Observer Magazine* (UK), December 17, 1978, pp. 33–39.

16. Ibid., p. 17.

17. Pete Lowry to the author, August 1978.

18. Jim Pettigrew, Jr., "From Rhythm 'n' Blues to Disco," *Atlanta Historical Bulletin* 21 (Summer, 1977): 122.

19. Alan Lomax, liner notes to *Georgia Sea Island*, vol. 1, Prestige-International 25001 (Bergenfield, N.J.).

20. Marshall and Jean Stearns, *Jazz Dance: The Story of American Vernacular Dance* (New York: Macmillan, 1968), p. 36.

21. Marshall Stearns, *The Story of Jazz* (New York: Oxford University Press, 1956).

22. Zora Neale Hurston, *Mules and Men* (Philadelphia: J. B. Lippincott, 1935), pp. 18–19.

23. Savannah Unit, Georgia Writers Project, Works Project Administration, *Drums and Shadows: Survival Studies among the Georgia Coastal Negroes* (Athens: University of Georgia Press, 1940), pp. 48–49, 62, 154–55.

24. Randolph Byrd, interviewed by David Evans in Savannah, Georgia, January 17, 1976, and September 14, 1976.

25. Ira "Tiny" Coney, interviewed by David Evans in Portal, Georgia, January 15, 1976.

26. *Living Blues* 32 (May-June, 1977): 40; Robert Springer, "Georgia Blues Today," *Blues Unlimited* 131/132 (September-December, 1978): 37.

27. David Evans, "Field Recordings with the Phonograph in Mind," *John Edwards Memorial Foundation Quarterly* 14 (Summer, 1977): 89–93. See also Bruce Bastin, "The Historical Research of Blues and Pre-Blues in the Southeastern United States," lecture to conference on "Popular Music in the Americas," at the University of Warwick, England, November 20, 1982. This is scheduled for publication in a book containing all the lectures, to be published by Cambridge University Press.

28. Bill Koon, liner notes to *Yonder Go That Old Black Dog: Blues, Spirituals and Folksongs from Rural Georgia by Eddie Lee Jones and Family*, Testament T-2224 (Calif., 1974).

29. David Evans to the author, September 15, 1977.

30. Wilmer, "Still Got the Blues": 16.

31. "Love Her with a Feeling" on *Georgia Blues*, Rounder 2008; "Got the Stuff Right Here" on *Another Man Done Gone*, Flyright 528 (Bexhill-on-Sea, England, 1979), which also includes one title by Bud Grant.

32. Roy Dunn, *Know'd Them All*, Trix 3312 (Rosendale, N.Y.).

33. *Blues Come to Chapel Hill*, Flyright 504 (Bexhill-on-Sea, England, 1974); *Living Blues* 43 (Summer, 1979): 8; 48 (Autumn, 1980): 37.

34. "Big Boy" Crudup, *Rhythm and Blues*, Vol. 4, RCA RCX(UK) (Ep) 7161.

10

Greenville Sheik

By 1930 Greenville, South Carolina, had become the most populous city in the state, numbering 117,009 persons. During the previous decade the population of the entire state had increased by only 55,041 and more than half of these were in Greenville. Significantly the state's twelve Piedmont counties showed a population gain of over 66,000 while the remaining thirty-four counties—some 75 percent of the area—showed a loss in excess of 11,000. As the major industrial center of the Piedmont, Greenville saw an influx of black labor. By 1930 only about a third of the city's blacks were native. Ten percent had come in from other states while some 60 percent had moved in from other South Carolina counties. Black communities sprang up in Bucknertown, Meadow Bottom, Little Texas, and the very rough Dirty Thirty district.

Among the families to move to Greenville was that of George and Lucy Walker. From Laurens, thirty miles to the south, came Gary Davis and also a very young Pink Anderson with his family, although they moved to the other major industrial city on this axis, Spartanburg, some twenty-eight miles to the northeast. The Tate family moved to Greenville from Elberton, Georgia, some fifty miles away, with their son, a ten-year-old youngster, Charles Henry.

A string band tradition existed well before World War I throughout the region, and a black fiddle tradition had been well documented in

the state before the end of slavery, including a ball held on a plantation near Columbia at which "the whole music consisted of two violins
and a tamborine."[1] Further recollections came from ex-slaves, interviewed in the mid-1930s: "C. B. Burton (Newberry, South Carolina),
We danced and had jigs. Some played de fiddle and some made whistles
from canes, having different lengths for different notes. . . . Peggy
Grigsby (Newberry, South Carolina), The old folks had corn-shucking,
frolics . . . and quilting. . . . When dey danced, dey always used fiddles
to make music."[2] From this string band tradition, which appears to
have died out earlier than in North Carolina, came two superb and
locally influential guitarists, Gary Davis and Willie Walker, both blind.
Davis was born in Laurens, near Newberry, in 1896, and played in a
string band in Greenville about 1912.

Yet another fine guitarist, Josh White, was born rather too late to
be part of the string band tradition. Probably the best known of the
Greenville school, White rose to fame not as a bluesman—in which
capacity he is remembered by black musicians—but as a folk artist far
removed from these origins and ambiguously involved in social
radicalism in New York City. Born to the Reverend Dennis and Daisy
White on February 11, 1914, Joshua Daniel White became one of the
significant influences on East Coast bluesmen in the early 1930s in the
period between Blind Blake's Paramount recordings and those of Blind
Boy Fuller. Josh White's early years were harsh. Ugly childhood
experiences—seeing his father beaten by the police and unjustifiably
committed to an asylum, where he died, and witnessing a lynching
in Waycross, Georgia—made sure that he would speak his mind at a
later date if he were ever in the position where he could be heard.
A studiously strict religious upbringing ensured that young Josh would
either follow suit or reject his doctrinal lessons entirely; paradoxically,
he did both.

When he was about eight years old, Josh received his mother's permission to travel as lead boy with a blind Greenville street singer, John
Henry "Big Man" Arnold, who weighed "260 to 270 pounds." Arnold
paid Daisy White $4.00 a week for Josh's service, which probably
helped overcome her religious doubts about her son's tough task. Josh
and Man Arnold headed south, probably in 1922, where they were
witnesses to the lynching. Beaten by police in Jacksonville, Florida,
and jailed "'cause they thought I had run away from home," Josh was
doubtless glad to get back home. His mother's "contract" with Arnold
meant that he was also hired out as lead boy to other blind singers—
Columbus Williams; Archie Jackson; Joe Taggart, who was not a Green-

ville native; and Joe Walker, Willie Walker's brother. Three of these
men influenced White's music considerably. His biographer states that
"Blind Joe Walker was to be a major influence on Josh, as was Archie
Jackson. Jackson fashioned his finger picks from the metal of sardine
cans, giving his guitar a strong metallic clang that would carry the sound
far."[3] Joe Walker had a fine reputation as a guitarist, by no means totally
eclipsed by his brother's superlative skills. Of these men, only Taggart
recorded. By the time Josh White came to record in Chicago with
Taggart late in 1928, he was highly skilled in the facile finger-picking
style associated with the Greenville guitarists. He had traveled to
Chicago in the winter of 1924 with Arnold, whom he finally left to
join Taggart.

Taggart sang only spirituals on the street but at house parties he
would also sing blues, which would lend credence to the suggestion
that Blind Joe Amos's only issued title, "C&O Blues," recorded in the
summer of 1927, is by Taggart. By that date Taggart had had four couplings released on the same label and recorded yet another about the
same time as Amos. By 1928 Taggart joined Paramount and may later
have been seen by them as an answer to Blind Willie Johnson, appearing on Columbia. Interestingly, the first Paramount coupling has
Taggart teamed with a fiddler, who also adds a vocal harmony part.
The fiddler was obviously of the older tradition of Andrew Baxter
rather than of the blues tradition of Eddie Anthony. The whole has
a distinct "white" ring to it.

In his next session for Paramount later that year, Taggart is backed
by Josh White, who also sings the second vocal part. White's young
voice sounds highly accomplished for his age, and his guitar style is
mature and skilled. Criticized in the liner notes to an album containing these sides for having a "weak voice" which "is a handicap to the
record session," Josh was not yet fifteen years old.[4] By this date he
had acquired not only the high, clear voice—disliked by almost all
record collectors—which was to be his trademark for the rest of his
performing life but also the firm base of finger-picking skills which
he was to show in his 1932-33 secular recordings. He recorded on a
1930 Paramount session with Taggart, having recorded the previous
year with the Carver Boys, but Taggart's last Paramount session in 1931
was a solo performance.

By 1931 Man Arnold and Archie Jackson appear to have left Greenville and do not appear to have been regular residents. Gary Davis had
also left, but both Joe and Willie Walker were still around town. It
was there that W. R. Calaway and Art Satherley, A&R men for ARC,
located Josh White, who was recovering from a broken leg sustained

playing football. Following his recovery, he recorded a number of sides in 1932, fifteen of which were issued, the bulk as by Joshua White. His biographer states that "Josh remembers singing twenty-eight songs on three dates for which his mother received $100," but only twenty titles were recorded, some of them to be remade the following year. However, since five of the issued sides ran to more than one take, possibly a couple of the unissued sides did too, so that the emphatic recollection of twenty-eight titles might actually have been twenty-eight takes.

White's records deserve reassessment. They were clearly highly influential: both Buddy Moss and Blind Boy Fuller listened to them, Moss teamed up with him to record for ARC in 1935, and Fuller consciously utilized some of his fast guitar licks. White's "Low Cotton" was a frequently recalled number. Willie Trice remembered Fuller sitting in front of a phonograph, learning it by heart. J. B. Long recalled that it was one of the records which persuaded him to go into the record retailing business. While specifically referring to the back-breaking work of cotton picking, "Low Cotton" also had a further level of interpretation. "I've been picking low cotton. No high cotton can I see," was fully appreciated by farmers who found the bottom dropping out of the cotton market with prices scarcely worth the effort of picking their crops. The idea of "nine-cent cotton, ten-cent meat" and other variations to show low cotton prices are common in songs both white and black from the early Depression years. "Blood Red River," actually remade in 1933, despite its Greenville licks and pulled notes, shows guitar lines totally within the broader tradition of Carolina blues and highly suggestive of Fuller's playing in the guitar chorus. "Crying Blues," "Broad Players Blues," and "High Brown Cheater" have distinct traits of Blind Blake in the guitar playing, although clearly reflecting the fast finger-picking style of the Greenville bluesmen. The last title, more than any other of the 1932 sides, is strongly reminiscent of Blind Willie Walker, who was, in Josh White's estimation, the greatest of the East Coast guitarists.[5] Not only are there similarities in vocal delivery but the melody is that of Walker's "Dupree Blues"—admittedly traditional enough—recorded less than eighteen months earlier. "Bad Depression Blues" contains a guitar run reminiscent of Walker's "South Carolina Rag."

"Good Gal," reissued on album, is described by the liner-note writers as "a version of Charlie Spand's 1929 recording of the same title, on which White himself probably plays accompaniment. The solo version finds White playing in open E tuning and displaying the agile thumb-work and slick over-all technique that mark his accompaniments behind Walter Roland and Leroy Carr."[6] However, those accompaniments are two to three years hence; White was just eighteen when he recorded in 1932. The reverse of the original issue of "Good Gal" is "Greenville Sheik," quite a different sort of song and one specifically mentioned in his autobiography. "To avoid family trouble, 'Greenville Sheik' was the first of many recordings made from the early Thirties under the soubriquet of Pinewood Tom."[7] His biographer unfortunately assumed that it was issued soon after recording in April 1932. However, its release number shows that it was not issued for more than four years, by which time some two dozen titles had been released under that pseudonym. Issued on a number of ARC's subsidiary labels as 6-05-65—the sixty-fifth issue of May 1936—it was actually released last of all his recordings for the company! "Greenville Sheik" is an interesting song, gently assertive as one might expect from a young blood. He opens with "the Greenville Kid's my name, Folks, I'm tryin' to introduce myself to you," proclaiming himself "a young healthy kid . . . here . . . in this big city." Nowhere does he use the word *sheik*, so presumably ARC decided that the song might have greater appeal if they altered the title from "Greenville Kid," which would seem to be more accurate.

These sides sold well, for he was recalled in August 1933 for a further session at which he remade three of the four blues titles left unissued. The other two sides recorded then were religious, and perhaps it was no accident that they were titles recorded by Blind Willie Johnson at his first session in 1927. Although these were released, like his blues issues, as by Joshua White, those recorded at his next session some two months later were mostly issued as by Joshua White (The Singing Christian), which became the normal form of release for sacred sides. Beginning with the release of two sides from his March 1934 session, "Welfare Blues" and "Stormy Weather No. 1," Pinewood Tom became the artist credit he regularly used for blues. By that date he was living in New York and married there the same year, rarely traveling south to regions he had grown to detest. Although he recorded in New York with Leroy Carr (December 1934) and Walter Roland (March 1935), he was more successfully teamed with Buddy Moss in August 1935. We will never know whether ARC planned to keep this a permanent team, for Moss was removed from the music scene for rather more than six years and Josh recorded only two sides in 1936, which seemed to point in the new direction of his interests.

After Josh White, the best-known of the Greenville musicians was undoubtedly Gary Davis, although he had left town by the early 1920s.

By 1911, having played guitar for some eight years, he was playing there with a string band of six to eight pieces. He was then about Josh White's age when he recorded with Taggart. Adulthood came early to poor blacks in the South. Davis's early recollections were much like Josh White's, and having been asked to "tell us a bit about" South Carolina when he was interviewed in 1965, his immediate reply was that "in South Carolina they hung coloured people when they felt like it. In Georgia they staked them."[8] Certainly, once Davis had followed the common migration route to New York he had little cause to return South.

Back in 1911 the music he played was undoubtedly part of that broad regional string band tradition, although he was aware, in retrospect, that black secular music was undergoing a change. In response to a question as to when he first heard blues he replied: "That broke out in 1910. I couldn't tell you where it came from. I first heard them from a fellow coming down the road picking a guitar and playing what you call 'the blues.' When I started playing the guitar there was no such thing as a piece coming out called 'the blues.' They played other songs. The blues, they just begin to originate themselves."[9] This complements comments from other musicians who began to play in the first decade of this century. Davis, playing by 1903 at latest, clearly grew up in the pre-blues period and, as a teenager, became suddenly aware of the new music being brought into his region from elsewhere.

The string band in which Davis played from 1911 to about 1913 included Will Bonds, from whom Davis learned to play "Candy Man," as well as "a master guitar player." Although Davis yields precedence to Blind Blake as the greatest he ever heard on record, he was full of admiration for Willie Walker, brother of the Joe Walker young Josh White used to lead. It must have been a band of no small talent.

Gary Davis had been born on a farm between Clinton and Laurens, southeast of Greenville, to John and Evelina Davis on April 30, 1896. Out of eight children, only he and a younger brother survived a very tough early childhood. Brought up by his grandmother, as neither parent was competent to care for him, he learned to play harmonica, banjo, and guitar. He learned to play the latter in part from a neighbor, Craig Fowler,[10] but he also had an uncle who played guitar. By 1904 he owned his first guitar, a Washburn, and was singing in the Baptist church in Gray Court, on the Greenville road northwest of Laurens, as well as playing dances for both whites and blacks. Around 1906 his father was killed in Birmingham, Alabama, but by then he was quite independent. Playing as he did for dances and picnics in the country it was logical for him to join the Greenville string band once he moved to town. Much later in life he was to recall and record many of these early tunes, remembering the "old stomp down dances, you understand. Played on sets. They used to have them fiddle players. You see, around then I played for most all of them."[11]

Within a few years of residence in Greenville he applied for, and was granted, a place at the South Carolina Institution for the Education of the Deaf and the Blind at Cedar Springs, Spartanburg. His application was dated August 26, 1914, and he was admitted two days later as a "Beneficiary Pupil." According to his form, his blindness was nearly total, the result of being given "Medicine of Doctor who made a mistake." This sounds more like Davis's reason than a firm medical diagnosis, but one wonders who the "doctor" was and what type of medicine he had recommended. There was also a reference that Davis "cannot hear perfectly at times," although it seems never to have impaired his musical ability, and again one wonders if Davis simply might not have heard whenever it suited him. The application was signed by Evelina Cheek of Gray Court, perhaps someone with whom Davis sang at the Center Raven Baptist Church there, which he attended before his father's death, and by Clay Martin of Laurens, a relative.

In Spartanburg Davis probably played with local musicians, for he taught music in the school, although in 1939 he admitted to a Durham welfare worker that he never had learned to read music but "presumed it was like other reading," by which he meant Braille, having learned that at Cedar Springs in 1915. He arrived in Spartanburg too late to have played in the local string band, which included Roland Martin and Fiddlin' Martin, although it most probably outlived their departure. Davis certainly knew guitarist Simmie Dooley, who was also blind. Dooley was listed in the 1918 city directory as a musician, living then at 142 Short Centennial. A resident of Spartanburg until he died in 1961, Dooley probably lived there before 1918. As he was classified at that early date as a musician and not simply as "laborer," he must have been highly proficient to have been earning a living from his skills. When I spoke with Davis in 1971, trying to elicit details about his life in Durham in the 1930s by mentioning the names of bluesmen like the Trice brothers and Floyd Council, whom he knew, the one person he asked me about was Simmie Dooley.[12]

Despite his seeming good fortune, Davis left the blind school after six months. His main reason was that he did not like the food. He returned to Greenville in early 1915, and there, on June 17, 1919, he married an older local woman, Mary Hendrix, who was twenty-eight years old. Within five years the marriage had failed and he had left town. Davis was always bitter about these early days; according to Greenville bluesman Roosevelt Brooks, Mary "quit one blind man for another." Brooks ought to have known: the blind man involved was Joe Walker, for whom Brooks was the regular second guitarist. Davis was living in Asheville, North Carolina, in 1922 or 1923 and by 1926 was in Durham, with years of travel on the road behind him. Sometime during those years he had quit Greenville for good, taking with him the fast finger-picking guitar style which was to be so admired by the Durham bluesmen. Willie Trice recalled him as "the playingest man" he ever saw, who "never let a string be still."[13] More recently it was stated that Gary Davis "was the best and he knew it. He hardly ever had a good word for another guitar player. He was a merciless critic."[14] Under the circumstances, the man he described as being a "master guitar player" ought logically to have been the most influential of the Greenville guitarists, and so he was locally.

Blind Willie Walker never went on to the fame accorded Josh White and Gary Davis. Like Davis he was born in 1896; his parents came to town probably about the same date as Davis, but their place of origin and Willie's birthplace are not known. George and Lucy Walker were living on Elford Street in Greenville in 1913, but they might have been living there since late 1911. City directories were made up in the last months prior to the year of issue, and thus a late 1911 arrival would just have missed the 1912 edition. Gary Davis recalled playing in the string band with Willie Walker as early as 1911. Little else is known of Willie Walker for certain, except that he was blind from birth as were so many eastern musicians for whom the blues were but part of their repertoire.

Interestingly, Davis recalled Walker specifically as a bluesman, recalling that he played numbers like "Crow Jane." One could well believe Walker's version to have been definitive had it only been recorded, as evidenced by the superlative fingering and the clarity of his languid vocal delivery on his only issued coupling, which actually shows him to have been of a broader class of musician like, say, Blind Willie McTell or Blind Blake. It cannot have been a coincidence that they were all professionals. Josh White said that "the best was Blind Willie Walker from South Carolina. He was the best guitarist I've ever heard, even better than Blind Blake. Blake was fast but Walker was like Art Tatum. They didn't teach that kind of guitar. I don't know where he got it from—he was born blind in the first place—but this man played so much guitar it wasn't funny."[15] Like the majority of other professional performers, Walker had no other employment and he is named as a musician on his death certificate. He appears to have traveled and is listed as resident in Greenville in 1915, 1917 through 1919, 1924, 1931, and 1933, the year of his death, always on Glover, the same street as his parents. His father died there of pneumonia on December 23, 1928, but his mother was still alive there as late as 1958.[16]

On December 6, 1930, in his only recording session, Willie Walker recorded four sides for Columbia in Atlanta, perhaps because the Spartanburg guitarists Pink Anderson and Simmie Dooley had recorded some two-and-a-half years earlier for the same company in the same city. Interviewed in 1970 Pink Anderson, himself a professional performer all his life, quietly acknowledged Walker to have been the finest of all the Greenville-Spartanburg guitarists. Local musicians like Roosevelt Brooks, who knew Walker in the 1920s, played in his exceptionally fast style; however, no one seemed prepared to play pieces which were clearly locally known to be Walker's. Brooks, who by 1970 had lost most of his fingering ability, flatly refused to attempt Walker's "South Carolina Rag," as at first did "Baby" Tate, who remembered hearing Walker after he moved to town as a lad in 1926 and who was still an accomplished performer in the 1970s. Both men died without having recorded it. Even Gary Davis stated that he "didn't even learn (Walker)'s pieces," but Stefan Grossman was able to coax him to perform "Make Believe Stunt" and "Cincinnati Flow Rag," tunes which were locally accepted as being Willie Walker's. In the liner notes to the album on which these can be heard, Grossman states that "'Make Believe Stunt' . . . a rag in the key of A . . . is one of Rev. Davis' most exciting instrumentals. Some parts of this sound similar to 'Maple Leaf Rag.' However, the chord structure and feel of 'Make Believe Stunt' is quite unique."[17] Davis maintained that this number was Walker's, and its unique quality is probably not all Davis's, as doubtless he would be the first to confirm.

Eventually "South Carolina Rag" was recorded by John Jackson, a guitarist from the same tradition as Walker. Jackson's father knew Walker when the latter was living in Culpeper, Virginia, at one time. Walker came over to young Jackson's home to play guitar with his father, a tenant farmer in Rappahannock County, on the edge of the Blue Ridge Mountains. As John Jackson was born in 1924 and Walker was dead by early 1933, this was probably in the early 1930s. With no prompting, Jackson played me "South Carolina Rag" in 1972 as the one of Walker's numbers which he remembered. I urged him to record it whenever convenient and hope I was partly responsible for its appearance on album.[18]

In Greenville in 1970 a cassette of Willie Walker's only released coupling literally opened doors. Pete Lowry, Baby Tate, and I were trying to get some reaction from Roosevelt "Baby" Brooks, who, far from showing any interest in our enquiries, was more concerned with wearing off the effects of the previous day's drinking excesses until I pressed the cassette button on "South Carolina Rag." Quite literally he fell off his chair and, shaking and fumbling with excitement, grabbed Lowry's guitar from Tate and began to strum, simply carried away by the sound of Willie Walker, after some forty years. No average man could have unleashed such a strong emotion.

Walker was accompanied on his recordings by his regular second guitarist, Sam Brooks. Only "Dupree Blues" and "South Carolina Rag" were issued, early in 1931 at the peak of the Depression. The small initial pressing of 750 appears not to have been followed up and the general state of the record market meant that the other sides were never issued. Sadly the masters appear not to have survived, but we are fortunate that we have two takes of the rag for comparison and that all three have been made available on album.[19]

Happiest playing in the key of C, in which no local musician would challenge him, Walker was obviously supreme in the rag idiom. In the liner notes to both Walker numbers the writers state that the key of C "lent itself favorably to 4-chord ragtime progressions (C-A$_7$-D-G-C). Not only do ragtime chords follow easily from the C position but the pitch of such chords as they appear in the C progression is higher than that of the E or G ragtime progressions. For a sophisticaded [*sic*] guitarist, the higher pitch presents a brighter tone."[20] Walker was certainly sophisticated in his playing style, and his clear vocal delivery was a perfect complement to his delicate, yet strongly structured, guitar runs. The issued reverse of the rag was a ballad concerning one Frank Dupree, a South Carolinian from Abbeville, who robbed a jewelry store in Atlanta on December 15, 1921. Perhaps he gained notoriety by being the last man to be hanged in Georgia, on September 1, 1922, for the song rapidly entered the folk tradition, although Walker's version is indubitably the most accomplished: "As on 'Dupree Blues,' Walker's picking follows the 'East Coast tradition' in its lightning rapidity and fastidiousness. . . . (He) might be using a flatpick and picking the treble strings with the third and fourth fingers. This technique is very hard to master, and is extremely rare—if not unique—within the idiom. As we have projected their roles, Walker plays in the key of G with his guitar capoed at the fifth fret. Brooks plays in the key of C."[21]

How unfortunate that these two men recorded at such an inappropriate moment. Walker, unable to record again, died on March 4, 1933, aged thirty-seven, of congenital syphilis—most probably the initial reason for his blindness. We shall never know the full extent of his repertoire, but although there is no evidence that he performed gospel songs, there is no reason to doubt its range. Tate and Brooks, the "Two Babies from Greenville," as they used to call themselves, still played snatches of songs associated with Walker—a blues entitled "Honey What's the Matter Now" and, more in the medicine show tradition, "Way Down Yonder in Dixieland." Perhaps Walker's undoubted brilliance on record will convince critics that unrecorded musicians who left near-legendary local legacies of remembrances among people who knew them well were as accomplished as locals claimed. Perhaps then the myth that only the best recorded will be laid to rest.

A tightly knit group of musicians surrounded Willie Walker. Once he was teamed with Sam Brooks, Walker used no other accompanist. Small wonder that by 1930 they played so well together and that Brooks's dreamy vocal part to "Dupree Blues" sounds in some way an extension of Walker's own delivery. The high, almost falsetto "Oh babe" refrain was usual: local musicians recalled that Brooks could sing like a woman. A fine guitarist in his own right by all accounts, Sam Brooks was first cousin to the man he led. Oddly he is listed in the Columbia files as David Brooks. He survived Walker by many years: one story has him visiting his daughter in the small university town of Clemson, just west of Greenville, and dying there in 1964. Another story had him living into the 1970s, although it appears he is now deceased. In the 1970s, Sam Brooks's nephew "Baby" Brooks was playing with rather more verve and enthusiasm than skill, having given up playing in the mid-1960s. While his uncle played second guitar to Willie Walker, Roosevelt Brooks was the regular second guitarist to Willie's brother, Joe—yet another blind professional musician, listed like his brother as a musician in the city directory in 1931 and 1933 and resident there from 1926 to 1938 at least Joe Walker was the major influence on the young Josh White, and once Josh ceased to lead him, he teamed up with Baby Brooks, who had been born in the city on June 2, 1905, neatly halfway between the birthdates of older musicians like Gary Davis and Willie Walker and the younger men like Josh White and Baby Tate. Brooks recalled Man Arnold and Archie Jackson but spent most of his early years teamed with Joe Walker, occasionally joined by brother Tommy Walker on jug. Joe Walker was alive in Bucknerstown as late as 1969, although by 1972 everyone agreed that he was dead. Baby Tate called Brooks a "C-man" and warned, "Don't ever jump him in C now or he'll run all over you." Tate, who knew

Willie Walker and played with Joe Walker and Pink Anderson in their primes, clearly held a respect for Brooks's past playing.

One phase of the Greenville blues scene could be said to be ended by 1933, with the death of Willie Walker and Josh White's departure for New York. The remainder of the Walker-Brooks groups stayed, and Charles Henry "Baby" Tate joined them. He had lived in town since 1926, had seen Blind Blake and Blind Lemon Jefferson before he had left Georgia, and remembered a six-to-eight-piece string band still playing in Greenville when he arrived. He soon became a proficient guitarist and entertainer, a member of the first black group to broadcast over the city's first radio station, WFBC, located on the second floor of the Poinsett (now Jack Tar) Hotel in 1932. He had a Friday spot with the Carolina Blackbirds, which featured Tate's guitar and harp, the ukulele and tenor-steel guitar of McKinley Ellis, and Washboard Willie Young. Sometimes they were joined by Ellis's brother on upright bass. Playing to a substantially white audience they can rarely have featured blues, but the white audiences would have appreciated country instrumentals and probably not all of the music broadcast was of the variety which best suited Ellis, whose use of ukulele and pleasure in singing "Besame Mucho" and "Sheik of Araby" suggests a good deal of "blackface" music. By utter coincidence, Tate and Ellis met again in 1970 after many years apart and they were recorded, with Ellis playing a fine second guitar to Tate's lead.[22]

If that session was no more than a distant recollection and recreation of the music they had created in the 1930s, those years remained musically active around Greenville, although the main center for blues had shifted to Spartanburg. In the 1930s both Blind Boy Fuller and Brownie McGhee came to Greenville and Tate played with them. Tate even dated Fuller's sister in Wadesboro and claimed to have been offered the chance of a contract following Fuller's death in 1941. By that time, however, Tate had already enlisted in the army, which also prevented him recording in 1942 with Josh White in New York. At that time Tate lived next door to Daisy White (Josh's mother), and although Josh seldom returned to see her, he had known Tate since teenage days.

Tate's wartime service took him to North Africa, as well as to Italy. He was wounded in the D-Day landings, shipped back to recuperate at Fort McKay in Boston, and returned to Europe to be wounded yet again in the Battle of the Bulge before being discharged to civilian life. Because of the enjoyable times he had experienced playing guitar in English pubs around Poole and Southampton with an English Army friend on piano in the weeks before D-Day, he went out of his way in the summers of 1970 and 1972 to assist this English researcher! A fine guitarist, he moved to Spartanburg in 1954 where he quickly struck up a friendship with the older medicine show performer, Pink Anderson, and the remainder of his career is really part of that city. In that sense, he provides a convenient bridge between the two cities, and it is highly probable that there was a far greater link than can be documented, going back at least as far as Gary Davis and Simmie Dooley.

NOTES

1. Dena J. Epstein, *Sinful Tunes and Spirituals: Black Folk Music to the Civil War* (Urbana: University of Illinois Press, 1981), p. 147.
2. Eileen Southern, ed., *Readings in Black American Music* (New York: 1971), p. 117.
3. Robert Shelton, *The Josh White Song Book* (Chicago: Quadrangle Books, 1963), p. 19.
4. Bernard Klatzko, liner notes to *Blind Joe Taggart,* Herwin 204 (New York).
5. Max Jones, "Josh White (Part 2)," *Blues Unlimited* 56 (August, 1968): 16.
6. Stephen Calt and John Miller, liner notes to *Mama Let Me Lay It on You 1926-1936,* Yazoo L-1040 (New York).
7. Shelton, *Josh White,* p. 21.
8. Richard Noblett, Stephen Rye, and John Offord, "The Reverend Gary Davis," in *Nothing But the Blues,* ed. Mike Leadbitter (London: Hanover Press, 1971), p. 217.
9. Stefan Grossman, *Rev. Gary Davis: Blues Guitar* (New York: Oak Publications, 1974), p. 10.
10. Gerard J. Homan, "Rev. Gary Davis: The Early Years," *Blues World* 42 (Spring, 1972): 10. Grossman, *Rev. Gary Davis,* p. 14, names "Clara Fowles and her husband . . . Crete."
11. Grossman, *Rev. Gary Davis,* p. 9.
12. Gary Davis interviewed by the author, Brighton, England, August 4, 1971. I am indebted to Robert Tilling (August 22, 1983) for much early biographical data to 1919.
13. Willie Trice, interviewed by the author, Orange County, North Carolina, September 23, 1972.
14. Mike Joyce, "Dave van Ronk: Interview," *Cadence* 4 (August, 1978): 15.
15. Jones, "Josh White": 16.
16. Peter B. Lowry to the author, November 12, 1973.
17. Stefan Grossman to the author, April 15, 1974; idem., liner notes to *Rev. Gary Davis: Ragtime Guitar,* Transatlantic TRA 244 (London, England).

18. *John Jackson: Step It Up and Go,* Rounder 2019 (Somerville, Mass.: 1978).

19. *East Coast Blues 1926-1935,* Yazoo L-1013 (New York), and *Let's Go Riding,* Origin OJL-18 (Calif.), both have the same take of "South Carolina Rag." The alternate take appears on *Mama Let Me Lay It on You,* Yazoo 1040.

20. Stephen Calt, Nick Perls, and Michael Stewart, liner notes to *East Coast Blues,* Yazoo L-1013.

21. Ibid.

22. Bruce Bastin, notes to *Charles Henry "Baby" Tate,* Trix Records (Rosendale, N.Y.), to be released.

11

On Up the Road

Spartanburg, like Greenville, astride the busy routeway from Atlanta through Charlotte to the North Carolina tobacco towns, expanded rapidly in the first quarter of this century. In 1920 more than 70 percent of Spartanburg County's population was rural and the urban population was some 22,600. The best-known black secular performer was Pink Anderson, always more of a songster than a bluesman, who provides fascinating glimpses into those paradoxically disparate elements of the blues—the down-home performer and the established stage performer. However, a jazz-orientated reader might well be more aware that one of the classic female blues singers, with extensive experience on the theater circuits since the 1910s, was born in Spartanburg. She was Clara Smith, one-time challenger to Bessie Smith's popularity, who similarly appeared on Columbia Records between 1923 and 1932, almost identically paralleling her more famous contemporary. The feedback from stage performances into down-home music can never be accurately evaluated but the pattern clearly did exist. Perhaps one such event took place in Spartanburg in October 1917.

In August 1917 black troops quartered in Houston rioted as a result of discrimination against them. Seventeen civilians and an officer who attempted to quell the rioting were killed and there was considerable white backlash against the proposed quartering of black troops anywhere near southern towns. During the height of the concern the

War Department ordered the black 15th New York Infantry to Spartanburg's Camp Wadsworth. The outcry was immediate and the *New York Times* for August 31 carried a report that "the City of Spartanburg officially protested to the War Department against the sending of these troops, on the ground that trouble might result if the Fifteenth refused to accept the limited liberties accorded to the city's colored population. . . . Said Mayor Floyd to-night, 'with their northern ideas about race equality, they will probably expect to be treated like white men. . . . We shall treat them exactly as we treat our resident negroes.'" As the report ended with a statement to the effect that "the folks are having a hard time restraining themselves from going down to the railroad station and camping there so as to be sure to be on hand when the troop trains get in,"[1] they can scarcely have been seen by the troops as constituting a welcoming committee.

Colonel Hayward, their commanding officer, saw one way of easing the strain of potential confrontation: "Open air concerts, by the regimental band of the Division, were given two evenings a week from a band stand erected near the principal hotel of the town, and upon a great public square. Our Band [Jim Europe's] was conceded to be the best at Spartanburg, as it was later to be hailed as the best of the American Expeditionary Forces; and . . . the schedule (was) rewritten, so that the band of the 15th New York Infantry should play the concert of the first Saturday evening after our arrival. The program was carefully chosen. Drum-Major Noble Sissle, a true artist and our barytone (sic) soloist, sang delightfully." The initial mood of the crowd was "by no means reassuring"[2] but a good start to better race relations had been skillfully forged, and out of respect for the manner in which the black troops conducted themselves over the next two tense weeks, the unit was considered "disciplined" and embarked for France on October 24.

The presence of these well-disciplined black troops must have had some effect upon local blacks, if only because initially they must have feared a tightening of existing poor race relations. Apart from any sociopolitical attitudes it is difficult to imagine that Jim Europe's band cannot have had some other effects. His was, after all, the premier black society orchestra in New York. He had recorded ragtime for Victor Records in 1913—his own "Too Much Mustard" and Wilbur Sweatman's "Down Home Rag." The following year had seen recordings of "Castle House Rag" and "Castle Walk," publicized by the famous white ballroom dance team of Irene and Vernon Castle. If some regular bandsmen in Spartanburg were with him, especially Buddy Gilmore, who was to have considerable influence on European drummers, then quite probably some of Jim Europe's raggy tunes would have been played. Noble Sissle's "barytone" voice might well have been "delightful" on that evening, but he was soon to be teamed with the superb ragtime pianist Eubie Blake, recording as early as 1920, covering Mamie Smith's huge hit, "Crazy Blues," twice. It seems improbable that such a talented band, performing in the public square, would not have been heard by professional performers like Anderson and Simmie Dooley, and maybe even Gary Davis. In 1968 Gary Davis recorded "Hesitation Blues,"[3] one of Europe's better known recordings from 1919, on which Noble Sissle sang the verses.

However, the best known local performer, associated with Spartanburg all his professional life, was Pinkney Anderson. Born on February 12, 1900, in Laurens, almost forty miles to the south, Pink was four years younger than Gary Davis and from within a few miles of his birthplace. When Pink was about ten, he learned to play in open tuning with a knife from Joe Wicks, a neighbor. He rated the other local guitarists as men who could "just see-saw on a guitar" and left the country in 1915 to settle on 8th Street.[4] The following year he met Simmie Dooley, who was then teamed with "Henry," a guitarist from his home town of Hartwell, Georgia. In 1917 Pink joined "Doctor" W. R. Kerr's medicine show, staying with him for almost thirty years. Although Pink was already a good buck-dancer, having earned money back in Laurens dancing on the streets, Kerr taught him his life's trade as a showman. Much like the smaller minstrel shows, Kerr usually carried five or six people—musicians, comics, and dancers who would double. Pink "done it all," even in theaters and "nightclubs." After Henry left Simmie Dooley in 1918, Pink played with Dooley whenever he was in town. Talking of Willie Walker, Gary Davis stated that "him and Simmie Dooley both were good guitar players."[5] Davis's coupling of Dooley's name with that of Walker, for whom he had a high regard, testifies to Dooley's ability. In 1961 Pink recalled the tough training he had received quite literally at the hands of Dooley.[6] More than a dozen years later he still credited Dooley with teaching him all the chords—especially C-natural—which he had not learned from Wicks and remembered Dooley using a pocketknife as a slide on his high-necked guitar. He still ruefully recalled that Dooley "gave me the devil when I missed one." They played on the streets and at parties, and Pink also joined the local Spartanburg string band, which frequently played at the Textile Hall in Greenville as well. Somewhat earlier this band had included the father and older brother of Carl Martin, the multi-instrumentalist who recorded in the 1930s; both Fiddlin' Martin and his son Roland played violin and guitar. All were born in Spartanburg. Carl, born in 1900, moved just before he was old enough to join the band but played in similar units throughout the 1930s and, when he died, was a member of perhaps the only black string band still playing the professional circuit in recent years.

Pink Anderson played with the string band for seven or eight years, not quitting until the early 1930s. Like other such bands the personnel was fluid and musicians frequently doubled. It regularly comprised four or five pieces including fiddle, banjo, guitar, and bass. *Grover *Williams usually led on fiddle but also played guitar and bass. George *Bates sometimes played lead fiddle, although Pink led on occasion when both men played fiddle and once when they both played bass. James "Jim" *Williams played banjo, "Buck" played bass, and Pink played guitar. Occasionally they added another musician, infrequently a mandolin player or even a drummer. Pink recalled similar bands in Greenville and in Athens, Georgia, when he was there once with a show. He also saw Willie Walker playing on the streets in Greenville in the late 1920s, both alone and with Sam Brooks, although someone else was leading Walker at the time. Interestingly, he never knew Joe Walker and knew of Josh White only from his records. He saw Gary Davis in Greenville, as well as in many other locations, always traveling alone. He had seen Davis playing in Asheville but last saw him playing at Mt. Holly near Charlotte in 1922-23, when Pink was briefly resident there.

Pink played with the string band when not on the road with Kerr, but also continued to play with Dooley, who worked only one or two seasons on the medicine show circuit, with Doc Harper's show. Pink suggested that few shows wanted blind performers because of their special problems, but other blind performers like Willie McTell seemed unhampered. Pink's respect for Dooley's musical abilities is corroborated from a totally unexpected source. Writing about the highly influential gospel singer, Ira Tucker of the Spartanburg-based Dixie Hummingbirds, Tony Heilbut said that "as a little boy . . . he befriended an old blind singer, Blind Simmie. 'He passed in 1945, must have been eighty. Never did get any breaks. The whites had it covered, all you'd hear on the radio was hillbilly, and no scouts came in our neighborhood. But for blues he was the greatest.' "[7] Actually, Dooley lived until 1961 although, coincidentally, he died in his eightieth year. Even if no scouts came through the town, he did record one session in 1928.

Simeon Dooley, born July 5, 1881, in Hartwell, Georgia, a few miles across the Savannah River, was listed as a resident in Spartanburg by 1918 at least, significantly as a musician. Yet another professional blind musician, he remained there until his death on January 27, 1961, uncharitably listed on his death certificate as "unemployed," although he was 79. In 1928 he was living at 130 C.C.& O. Alley, presumably close to the railroad tracks: the initials stood for the Carolina, Clinchfield and Ohio Railroad, which had a terminus in Spartanburg from the main line from Elkhorn City, Kentucky. Planned as part of a link from Charleston to Cincinnati, it remained an important line joining other railroads like the Norfolk and Western, Baltimore and Ohio, and Seaboard. Its name was embodied into a blues by Dooley when he recorded that spring for Columbia.

Perhaps it was the manager of Alexander's Music Store in Spartanburg who made contact with Columbia's Atlanta agent, possibly Dan Hornsby. The white accordion player, Homer Christopher, who had been born in the Greenville-Spartanburg area about 1900, recalled a similar situation in Greenville. He cut two sides for Okeh Records in April 1926 after "a record salesman heard me play at a music store in Greenville, S.C. and booked me to make some records in Atlanta."[8] Christopher's guitarist partner slightly later was Raney Van Vin (or Van Vynckt), who was probably from Spartanburg, and together they recorded a "Spartanburg Blues" for Okeh in 1927. Someone came from Atlanta to collect Dooley and Anderson, and on Saturday, April 14, 1928, they recorded four titles at Columbia's mobile recording studio on Pryor Street in Atlanta.

They alternated singing stanzas, although Dooley understandably sang lead on his "C.C.& O. Blues." Issued under their own names, the first coupling was released in August with an initial pressing of 3,700 copies. Both numbers strongly feature the show circuit with Dooley's kazoo well in evidence. As he was forty-seven when he made these sides, he must be one of the oldest musicians in the blues world to have been commercially recorded at such an early date. The record sold well enough for a further pressing of 3,000 to be made. The other coupling was issued in mid-March 1929; an initial pressing of 3,475 was followed by a further one of 2,000. These were more bluesy and the railroad number features gently dovetailing guitars, while Dooley's vocal delivery is more blues-directed.

Columbia wanted Pink to return but didn't care for Simmie's voice. Without Dooley Pink refused to go. Perhaps Dooley disliked travel, for Pink stated that they twice turned down chances to travel with shows to California and Texas. Certainly travel was no obstacle for Pink, who traveled the entire Eastern Seaboard from Florida to Pennsylvania and inland to Kentucky and Tennessee with medicine shows. When in December 1930 Columbia next looked toward South Carolina for artists in a similar style, they secured Willie Walker and Sam Brooks, and also Lil McClintock, who even more readily fitted the pattern.

Dooley remained in town, posing occasional problems for the city directory compilers, who listed him as Semie and even Simel. His playing partner, Pink Anderson, was resident in 1918 at 140 Cantrell and two years later he was at 136 New, listed as a laborer and under the name of Pinkney for the first time. Later he was accurately listed as a musician, as he continued to work with W. R. Kerr's show until it ceased in 1945. While performing at the State Fair in Charlottesville, Virginia, he was recorded by Paul Clayton on May 29, 1950. Eight titles were recorded, mostly standards like "John Henry" and old show songs like "I've Got Mine," and the reverse of the album was of titles, appropriately, by Gary Davis. One of the Anderson songs was a recreation of one of the 1928 recordings, "Every Day in the Week," on which one Jumbo Lewis was added on washboard. Presumably he was a member of the show, and he might well have been the man who drummed with the Robinson Brothers' circus in the early 1930s. Theirs was one of the most popular shows through the Carolinas and Peg Leg Sam, who acted as straight man for Anderson on Kerr's show, played with them, as did many other show performers and bluesmen. A 1931 Chicago *Defender* carried the following: "Watervliet, N.Y. July 31. Darby Lewis, 28 (circus drummer) with the Robinson circus sideshow band, was sentenced to serve 6 months in Albany county penitentiary on charge of intoxication and disorderly conduct."[9] In view of Pink's involvement in running an illicit bar on his premises as late as 1970, well after he had suffered a serious stroke, Darby Lewis might well be the man who recorded with him in 1950. After all Lewis would only have been in his late forties and Pink's playing on the tracks show him to have been at his peak. His guitar lines are firm and highly accomplished, and his voice was the strongest and most assertive of all his recordings. Unfortunately he was not to be relocated and recorded more fully for more than a decade, although he was still then highly competent.

With Kerr's retirement Pink ran with other medicine shows, although he stayed less on the road. He worked for a while with Chief Thundercloud (Leo Kahdot), who had at one time a three-ring show and who purchased the Big Top from the Robinson Brothers' show when they went out of business. Although Kahdot ran a large show in Texas, Pink only worked his small one in North Carolina in later years, often with the harmonica player Peg Leg Sam. Pink also worked with Sam Williston's show, with Emmett Smith, and with Johnny Rickey's show out of Greenville. Spending more time now in town, Pink worked in a trio in the mid-1950s with Georgia-born Elmon "Keg Shorty" Bell on harmonica and Charley "Chilly Winds" Williams on washboard. Originally from Augusta, Georgia, Williams returned and died there about 1956. In 1957 heart trouble finally forced Pink into retirement. His old friend Simmie Dooley died in 1961 and he only continued to play with Baby Tate.

It was then that Sam Charters located Pink and fortunately recorded him in depth. Three albums were released—one of blues, one of medicine show songs, and one mainly of ballads.[10] The blues album included a number of Blind Boy Fuller's numbers learned from Tate, for Pink admitted that he "never did run up on him. I always did want to see him. He used to go up there around Salisbury, but everytime I'd go up there it seems like he'd be somewhere else." Indeed he learned most of his blues after he had teamed up with Tate in 1954, so that in a sense his album needs to be heard in the context of Baby Tate's recorded at the same time.[11] The release of the albums actually generated some work, and they played one unlikely gig in 1964 at Clemson University (then a College of Agriculture) down close to the Georgia state line. Later in the year Pink suffered the first of his strokes.

By 1970 when I first visited him he was seldom able or inclined to play. Nonetheless he commanded great respect locally and still ran the hottest crap game in town from his home, which saw other frequent visitors who came to sample his illicit booze or rent his back room by the hour. The story about how Pete Lowry and I drove up to his home, at the end of a dead-end alley, escorted by a local police car with its roof-light flashing belongs elsewhere and is amusing only in retrospect![12] One day Baby Brooks, whom Tate had brought over to his Spartanburg home just so that we could record him, vanished. Too late we discovered that Brooks had been absorbed into Pink's crap game, where he became blind drunk and was cleaned out. We found him days later when somehow he'd managed, by means unknown, to get back to his Taylors home. There was something about Pink Anderson which made one feel that he was the epitome of the indestructible "Travelin' Man" of whom he so joyously sang. One day when Anderson was sitting quietly in the corner of Baby Tate's house while Tate and Peg Leg Sam were recording, clearly wishing he was well enough to be able to join in, Sam was the first to remind me that "Pink had me playing with my tongue hanging out like a mule ploughing corn," he was so good. Had he heard that remark, Pink would have been glad of it as an epitaph.

As well as recording Pink so thoroughly, Charters also recorded Tate, on August 14, 1961. A few further titles were recorded the following year for the soundtrack of a film and subsequently issued on album.[13] Tate's album contains a number of songs reminiscent of Fuller, while "Dupree Blues," with its fast-fingered, distinctive Greenville licks, is most probably an unconscious recollection of Willie Walker. Otherwise Tate's influences were broader and reflect the major impact of other bluesmen of the 1940s and 1950s. Two tracks recorded in 1970 have been issued on album, including "Bad Gasoline" with Peg Leg Sam on harp.[14] On August 17, 1972, Tate died of a massive heart attack following several minor strokes.

The Spartanburg scene died with Tate, but not before he had sparked another area of research. Tate went out of his way to help Pete Lowry and me document the blues scene in the area, specifically locating McKinley Ellis and Baby Brooks. He also recalled Spartanburg guitarists Rufus *Strickland and Blind *Littlejohn, both of whom were deceased. Littlejohn played a steel National and died as late as 1969. Blind *Cooley was a singer from the town, last heard of in Greenville. *Jeff *Lark, also deceased, was a guitarist and harp player from Greenwood, South Carolina, while John "Jack" Hemphill, a guitarist from Brevard, North Carolina, lived in Spartanburg for a while but joined the church and moved to Dayton, Ohio. Before he moved he used to team up with another Brevard guitarist and play in Clayton, Georgia, a summer resort in Rabun County.[15] Best remembered of the unrecorded Spartanburg bluesmen was guitarist Larry Threaks, a cousin of Tate's, whom McKinley Ellis—who had heard neither Willie Walker nor Gary Davis—thought the best he'd ever heard. Born August 10, 1905, he died on June 26, 1970, about one month before Pete Lowry and I relocated Tate. Threaks again neatly encapsulated the local blues scene. Born in Laurens—like Gary Davis and Pink Anderson—he was raised in Greenville but lived and played in Spartanburg.

Oddly, in one instance blues from the Greenville area indiretly fed back into Georgia and once again involved a blind musician, this time a white man. Joe Parr from Lawrenceville was born blind in 1918 and learned guitar from "well, I'm going to have to say it—a black man. Babe Chaney was the one who showed me my chords. . . . I met him in Greenville, South Carolina."[16] They toured the North and Midwest together between 1951 and 1955. Parr remains a fine performer and his music retains the flavor of Chaney's blues instruction. His only issued recording, "Indian Chief Blues," shows little regionality, however.[17]

While the urban centers held the most influential "schools" of blues performers, rural areas also hid highly talented bluesmen. One county to the south of Spartanburg held musicians of considerable ability, some of whom recorded in the 1920s and 1930s, as well as others whose talents emerged only after 1970 entirely due to the initial efforts of Baby Tate. Union County may well have been closer to the norm despite possessing exceptional talent, although there cannot have been too many performers of the equal of Peg Leg Sam, let alone Henry Johnson. The recorded story commences earlier.

The first of the Union County musicians to record was yet another blind singer, Gussie Nesbitt. His early years run contrary to the general pattern: he was born in Spartanburg on January 12, 1910, and moved to Union (Union County) when he was a teenager. Nesbitt was a religious singer. He learned to play guitar by listening to records, not long before he commenced recording in 1930. Earlier that year he had written to Columbia Records in Atlanta, perhaps spurred on by the fact that the Spartanburg duo of Anderson and Dooley had recorded, and Columbia referred him back to the manager of Cooper's Furniture Store in Union, Burm Lawson. Possibly as part of the deal, Nesbitt purchased a guitar from the store and practiced in the back room. Here he met another singer-guitarist whom Lawson also intended to send to Atlanta, Lil McClintock. McClintock was from Clinton, a few miles from the birthplaces of Gary Davis and Pink Anderson, and was of their generation. Doubtless unbeknown to Lawson, a ballad about Delia Holmes, who was reputed to have been murdered in a gambling joint in Georgia about the turn of the century, had been collected in written form from McClintock as early as 1923.[18] The two musicians traveled together by train to Atlanta and recorded in succession on Thursday, December 4, 1930. Two days later the Greenville team of Walker and Brooks recorded there.

Two religious titles were released in January 1931 as by Blind Nesbit [*sic*], although only the then standard initial pressing of 750 copies was made. McClintock fared better: all four of his sides were issued, one coupling at the same time as Nesbitt's and a further issue in June 1931, both of 750 initial pressings.[19] His titles show a fascinating spread of music. Two titles are gospel numbers, but the two secular sides reflect a facet of black music all too seldom documented, possibly for self-explanatory reasons. "Don't Think I'm Santa Claus" has a "coon-song" refrain derived obviously from the minstrel stage, sung over the merest rudimentary guitar, played in plangent, possibly banjo-derived, accompaniment.[20] "Furniture Man" is sung and played in similar style, again with references to "coons," by which he clearly meant local blacks. The refrain mentions Mr. Cooper, which nicely publicized the store, but whether he was pleased with the opening stanza is doubtful. Anyway, McClintock was not to record again. In keeping with the minstrel quality of the song McClintock, calling himself "Mr. Brown," sang:

> What insurance has the poor man got with the furniture man?
> He'll take everything that you possess, from a bedstead to a frying pan.
> If there ever was a devil born without horns
> It must have been a furniture man.[21]

McClintock dropped from sight, but Nesbitt continued to travel and perform church music even though he mixed and played with local bluesmen in Union and in Charlotte, North Carolina. He remembered meeting many bluesmen, including Curley Weaver, Eddie Mapp, and Barbecue Bob when he recorded for Columbia; the latter was at a session held the day after Nesbitt's. He met the Texas bluesman Blind Lemon Jefferson in Alabama and Alabama guitarist Barefoot Bill in Texas. He knew Anderson and Dooley, Willie Walker and Josh White, and said of Peg Leg Sam that he "could do more with a harp than anyone I ever heard." He met Blind Boy Fuller in Wadesboro after he had begun to record and once heard Blind Blake in either Spartanburg or Charlotte; Baby Tate had heard of Blake in Charlotte.

The local bluesman whom Nesbitt knew best was guitarist Jack Gowdlock, who lived at Cross Keys, rather more than a dozen miles southwest of Union toward Laurens. Nesbitt would lead on guitar and often played slide while Gowdlock would "run chords . . . he really played." When Gowdlock traveled to Charlotte to record during Victor's extensive recording sessions of late May 1931, Nesbitt went with him, the session having been arranged by Burm Lawson. Nesbitt accompanied and sang with Gowdlock, who recorded four titles. The first two were gospel numbers and remain unissued, but the other two were blues and issued on Victor 23419, of which no known copy has survived. According to the Victor files, Nesbitt sang and played guitar on the gospel pair.[22] "I'm thinking, did I second him in anything that was rough [blues]. I don't think I did. I was with him on the religious; I wasn't on the other." We can hope that one day a copy will emerge.

"Poor Jane Blues" would appear to be the common "Crow Jane," which had been recorded nearly four years previously by the Charlotte bluesman Julius Daniels, also for Victor. "Rollin' Dough Blues" is not recalled by other Union County bluesmen and it would be interesting to know if it resembled in any way either of two quite different versions—Buddy Moss's "Dough Rolling Papa" or especially Sonny Jones's "Dough Roller" of 1939, the former from Georgia and the latter from just across the North Carolina state line. Gowdlock and his harmonica-playing brother *Sharron, who lived in their birthplace of Union, are deceased. Nesbitt, still living an active life in 1971 in church music, made one further recording session for Decca in 1935. Dan Hornsby arranged for him to travel to New York with a white singer from Anderson County, Scotty the Drifter.

The real strength of the Union County blues scene only became apparent through the untimely death of Baby Tate. In 1970 Tate unearthed a one-legged harmonica player who traveled with the last remaining medicine show. From Jonesville, southeast of Spartanburg, this remarkable performer at least lived to see broader recognition of his skills at festivals throughout the country before his death in 1977. Born Arthur Jackson, he was best known as Peg Leg Sam, having lost a leg when he fell from a freight train near Raleigh, North Carolina, in 1930. In 1970 Sam offered no suggestion that there might be any other fine musicians playing around his area. Total loyalty to Baby Tate prevented him mentioning that in Union he played with another superb guitarist, Henry Johnson, and that they still had a fifteen-minute radio show over WBCU Union, playing for a second-hand car dealer, who slotted in advertisements between numbers. The only known airshots reveal they were playing country blues and medicine show songs identical to the type that Sam and Pink Anderson used to play. Had Peg Leg Sam and Henry Johnson remained in obscurity, no one would ever have heard of Union County or its blues scene. It ought to remain an object lesson.

Peg Leg Sam was born "way back in the bushes" west of Jonesboro, on December 28, 1911. He lived all of his sixty-five years on the family ground. The countryside had changed little, although the cotton fields of his grandfather's time were now rough grazing. The old plantation house still stood—used as a hay store—and the slave houses remained, now unused, and some kudzu-covered. By 1921 or 1922 young Arthur Jackson had begun to play harmonica in the old "accordion" style, learning from two Jonesville men, *Butler *Jennings and *Biggar *Mapps. "Lost John" was the first piece he learned, but he had grown

up accustomed to music, for his mother, Emily Jackson, taught him
the older songs, both secular and spiritual, and she had been a good
organist and accordion player. A restless child, he ran away from home
when he was ten and joined the generation of freight-hoppers who,
like him, could never quite explain the compunction for travel. Spurred
on by curiosity, the avoidance of work to tie him to any one place,
and the love of the life of an itinerant entertainer, he commenced a
lifetime of travel. "I went on up into Ohio, caught the C O O. Then
I came back home again and stayed about a week. Plow time. I didn't
like to plow. Pickin' cotton time. I said, 'Uh oh, got to go again.'"[23]

As one might expect of such a man, he was a fascinating storyteller
who provided extensive coverage of his personal history, probably the
most detailed of any person traveling these rural entertainment circuits.[24] In 1937 he joined the medicine show circuit and for years acted
as straight man for Pink Anderson before taking over the role of "drag
man" himself, drawing crowds by his playing, singing, and patter to
await the pitch from the seller. With the larger shows which played
carnivals and fairs, as well as smaller shows which would set up in
a textile mill town on payday or at a tobacco warehouse during the
sales season, Sam lived the next thirty-five years, returning to the
Jackson farm during the winters. He spent his last few years there, after
Chief Thundercloud's show had ceased, farming for himself and
fishing, within sight of the land on which his grandparents were slaves.
He must have died one of the rare people utterly content with his life.

As a boy he danced to earn pocket change. He worked on Spring
Street in Greenville with Peg Leg Bates, "poppin' rags" at a shoe-shine
stand and dancing for the crowds. Bates went on to considerable fame
on the stage as a dancer and years later, in his plush resort hotel in
the mountains of upstate New York, warmly recalled his old days with
Sam. Sam's old "accordion" style harp playing gave way to the
"modern" style, as he realized it would be more likely to bring him
more money. By 1927 he was playing well, having learned much of
the new style from Elmon Bell, staying then in Spartanburg. Originally
from Atlanta, the son of a preacher, Bell sometimes played on medicine
shows with Pink Anderson, who rated him the best harp player he
knew.

The itinerant medicine show, possibly the only entertainment likely
to be available to poor blacks near remote Jonesville, had long intrigued
young Arthur Jackson. He remembered when he "first saw Pink it was
in 1917. He was working with a medicine show doctor in Jonesville,
showing over there. I was there too, in knee-britches! I wasn't but 11

years old, you know. He was about 17 or 18. I said, 'Lord, that's a bad man yonder.' " As he said, Pink "learned me all about the business."[25] The loss of his leg in 1930 made no difference to his hoboing. In 1936 he caught a train to Selma, Alabama, and worked his way back to Wilson, North Carolina, in time to head over to the tobacco warehouses in Rocky Mount during the sales season. There the boss for Fenner's Warehouse hired him for a daily fifteen-minute radio show during the season. It was to last twenty-five years, during which time Sam returned every season for four months to play around the warehouse and over the air. In later years he even appeared on Fenner's Friday Channel 9 Television show. With this firm base, Sam joined Emmett Smith's medicine show out of Chesnee, South Carolina, and ran with him off and on until Smith died in 1969. He reminisced:

> I worked with a heap of them. I worked with this'n what they call Thundercloud, worked with another, Jeffries, they call *him* Thundercloud. Worked with Smiley a long time. . . . I showed with Silas Green a long time; head comedian on there I was. . . . I used to work out of Nashville with Dr. Thompson's Jig Show. That was all through Memphis, Indiana. I was head comedian on that. He never did pay off though. He died. I was glad of it, he wasn't going to pay me nohow. Old Jeffries, he didn't pay me and he died. . . . The Chief [Thundercloud]'s a good pay-master. What he promise, you'll get it. Smiley. Name was Frank Kerr, white feller, you know. Work that day, he'd pay me. Work that night, he'd pay me again. Them two the best paymasters I ever worked with. Old Jeffries wouldn't pay Jesus Christ![26]

Small wonder that Pink Anderson stayed with Kerr until retirement and that Sam stayed loyally with Thundercloud, simply waiting each spring for him to come by and collect him for another tour. It happened every year until 1973 when the Chief failed to appear. The last medicine show was over.

Although Sam steered a solitary course, he knew and occasionally played with local bluesmen. He knew Willie Walker, Jack Hemphill, and McKinley Ellis and was introduced to Baby Tate in Greenville in the 1930s by another Union County guitarist, Arthur "Slim" Thomas, who joined the northward trek to Washington, D.C. He also recalled a guitarist from nearby Anderson County, *Jesse *Lawson, but it was with Henry "Rufe" Johnson that Sam was to strike up a playing relationship.

Henry Johnson was born in Union County on October 2, 1908, and until he was located in 1972 by Pete Lowry, had never traveled further afield than the adjoining Spartanburg and Chester counties. He typified a welter of parochial musicians who never had that urge for mobility which drove Sam. Indeed, a sense of calm was at the very core of this dignified man, whose quiet approach to his music belied his undoubted brilliance. His early upbringing was typical of a rural family tied to a tenanted farm although racial tension seems far less marked in the case of his family than was sometimes the case.

Roosevelt Johnson, his elder brother by some twelve years, was an excellent guitarist who had been playing for many years before Henry began to learn, about 1925. Although he became a superb player in open tuning, using a clasp-knife as a slide, he began playing in standard tuning wherein lay his prodigious finger-picking technique. He learned much from his brother and from Thelmon Johnson, a cousin, "who could really play one!" A far older guitarist from Union, J. T. Briggs, also helped him before he left town to go "above Spartanburg." The first song he learned was a powerful religious piece, "My Mother's Grave Must Be Found," and this pointed the direction of his music. For more than twenty-five years he played religious music but, like Gussie Nesbitt, saw nothing wrong in playing with secular performers. Remarkably, he was later to "cross over" to secular music and must be one of the few documented bluesmen to have commenced a musical career so firmly immersed in religious music. Henry's older brother by eight years, Jack, was a preacher and capable of "layin' it down like Paul in the Bible," before he died in 1941. Nevertheless, in his early years Henry acquired the name of "Rufe," which with some embarrassment he confirmed had been contracted from "Rooster." By 1933 he was also playing piano in church, having learned the rudiments from local party pianists like "Come By" Shelton and Tommy Foster. He sang regularly on radio with two quartets, the West Spring Friendly Four, an a capella group, over WSPA Spartanburg and the Silver Star Quartet over WBCU Union. He recalled seeing Gussie Nesbitt in Union, but otherwise his exposure to recording artists was nil, apart from the white Stapleton Brothers.

Mitchell and Mason Stapleton played guitar and mandolin and one of them was courting the daughter of the owner of the farm on which the Johnsons were tenants. They frequently played with Rufe and one day asked him to go with them possibly to record, in Charleston as he recalled. Almost certainly this was their recording date for Victor in Charlotte in May 1931, on the same day as Jack Gowdlock and Gussie Nesbitt. On four titles the brothers were joined by Roy Kingsmore on guitar and possibly mandolin. Perhaps that third guitarist's place was to have been filled by Rufe Johnson; after all, he was not required to sing. Interestingly, a Joe Johnson is credited as the writer of one of the titles. Certainly no racial prejudice existed among the Victor engineers for when they moved on to Louisville in June they recorded their established white country performer, Jimmie Rodgers, accompanied by blues guitarist Clifford Gibson. The following year in Dallas they recorded Jimmie Davis, a white Louisiana country singer who had recorded at those Charlotte sessions, accompanied by the Shreveport bluesman Oscar Woods.

Rufe continued to farm and play for the church. World War II made no difference. "2C's as close as I got. I was still followin' a mule." In 1952 he quit to take up a job as a porter in a hospital in Union and about the same time left the quartet scene with its personality conflicts and backbiting to play both secular and religious pieces. Sadly his spell of recognition was all too brief. Within eighteen months of his location in 1970 he was dead, from kidney failure brought on by a number of minor heart attacks. He had kept his illness a secret. His doctor told him not to travel, but he wasn't the first musician to ignore doctor's advice, and he died in February 1974 in the hospital in which he had just earned a long-service merit award. At least sufficient well-recorded material exists to fill out the picture of a superb musician.[27]

Another Union County musician who grew up in Spartanburg, later following the usual migration pattern north, was James "Guitar Slim" *Stephenson. Born on March 10, 1915, he grew up with music. He was playing pump organ by the age of five and an older brother played banjo. Within a few years Slim was playing piano and by the time he was thirteen was playing guitar at house parties and local "fling-dings," as well as in church. He listened to local bluesmen like Willie Walker, Pink Anderson, Baby Tate, and Peg Leg Sam and by the late 1920s joined John Davis's medicine show, traveling as far as Mississippi and Florida. He eventually settled in Greensboro, North Carolina, in 1953 where he still plays for parties and in the church. Located in 1974 he has played a number of festivals and can be heard on album.[28]

While some Union County musicians gravitated toward Spartanburg, some also moved to Charlotte, which acted as a major center for the northern section of South Carolina above Columbia. It was also the only significant recording center for bluesmen in the Southeast outside Atlanta. Union County musicians recorded there, but naturally it held its own blues scene and also attracted bluesmen from afar at the time of the recording sessions.

Charlotte lies close to the South Carolina state line halfway between Greenville and Winston-Salem. Geographically it is in the center of the Piedmont; commercially it sits on the northern end of the textiles industry axis. As with other major Piedmont urban centers its industrial expansion took place in this century and the 1920s saw the greatest period of population expansion, rising from some 46,000 to more than 83,000 by 1930. It just topped 100,000 by 1940. For some reason it became a major center used by Victor/RCA for locational recordings outside its northern studios. Numerous sessions took place between 1927 and 1938, when the recording location moved a few miles south to Rock Hill, South Carolina, although all black artists who recorded there were gospel groups.

Like Greenville and Spartanburg, Charlotte had a string band tradition at the turn of the century. A photograph in a 1946 *Downbeat* magazine of a black string band there in the 1890s showed C. T. "Pappy" Smith on clarinet, Bob Foster on mandolin, and Bob Matthews on guitar. A multi-instrumentalist on strings and reeds, Smith made his son his first violin and taught him to play. His son was the well-known jazz violinist Stuff Smith.[29] Other than that, the first documented evidence of a secular music scene came with the Victor recording sessions of August 1927.

More than 150 masters were cut on this tour, which commenced in Bristol, Tennessee, and ran through Charlotte to Savannah, Georgia, ending in late August. The Bristol sessions opened up a new world of white country music for Victor as they recorded the Carter Family and Jimmie Rodgers for the first time. In Charlotte the vast majority of sessions were by white artists but tucked between two Georgia Yellow Hammers sessions were three titles by the Georgia fiddle-guitar duo of Andrew and Jim Baxter, while the final session of the last day, August 16, was by the Virginia bluesman Luke Jordan. The Baxters had come because of their connection with the Yellow Hammers, but it is not clear how Jordan came to be there. Both are evaluated within their local contexts. One other artist who recorded at these sessions was Robert N. Page, once listed in discographies as being black, but his sole recorded coupling suggests he was a white singer, perhaps from that same borderline musical region as was Cedar Creek Sheik.

Paradoxically, the one known Charlotte bluesman was absent from the session. Julius Daniels actually only moved into Charlotte in 1938 but since 1912 had been living in Pineville, a small community some ten miles south, just above the state line. He had moved there at the age of ten with his parents, having been born in Denmark, South Carolina, halfway between Augusta and Charleston. He was one of the bluesmen with whom Gussie Nesbitt used to play. At the time of the Victor sessions in town in August 1927, Daniels had already recorded for them on February 19 of that year in Atlanta, and was therefore one of the earliest bluesmen in the Southeast to record and the first of the Carolina artists.

Daniels made ten takes of four titles in the temporary studio on the third floor at 35 South Forsythe Street, Atlanta. On three of the titles he was supported by another singer-guitarist, Bubba Lee Torrence, presumably already known to Daniels. They play as a team like Walker and Brooks and Gowdlock and Nesbitt. No Atlanta guitarist ever heard of Torrence, and he was never listed in the city directory. Indeed the name is rare there in any year but extremely common in Charlotte. The four songs cover a wide range, with the Appalachian folk influence notable on "Ninety-Nine Year Blues" with distinct banjo undertones in the guitar playing, somewhat reminiscent of Barbecue Bob in performance but not in style. Whereas he frails his twelve-string guitar in banjo fashion, Daniels deftly picks with considerable facility in typical Carolinas style. "My Mama Was a Sailor" is a strong blues with delightful twin guitars reminiscent more of a bluesier version of Walker and Brooks. On the strength of this title alone, Daniels was clearly a significant bluesman, a fine singer and very able musician. Interestingly, the coupled gospel sides are credited on the label as being arranged by "Mr. Daniels," an unusual address for a black artist. Daniels certainly deserves more recognition in view of the early date of these fine sides. We are fortunate that takes unissued at the time were later— unintentionally—made available by RCA from both this session and a follow-up in October 1927.[30]

For the second trip to Atlanta Daniels was accompanied by Wilbert Andrews. Presumably Andrews also came from Daniels's neighborhood as he too was unknown to Atlanta bluesmen. On that Monday they recorded four titles, three by Daniels with Andrews playing second guitar plus "Going Away Blues" performed by Andrews alone, which was never issued. All Daniels's songs were issued. "Can't Put the Bridle on That Mule This Morning" sounds to be from the common ground between white and black song. "Richmond Blues," the second title recorded, was covered nearly eight years later by Durham's Bull City Red during Blind Boy Fuller's first sessions, and it is difficult to draw a conclusion other than that the song was known to Red from Daniels's record. He shares two of Daniels's verses and his percussive guitar style is reminiscent of the Charlotte man's. In fact his "Richmond Blues" contains the line "white folks, white folks, don't work my brown so hard," which is more usually met in "Crow Jane Blues," which was Daniels's other title from the session, issued on the reverse of "Rich-

mond Blues." Daniels's "Crow Jane" is the earliest recorded version
of this traditional piece. Superbly sung over gentle guitars, it lacks the
remarkable individuality which Carl Martin was to bring to it but rates
as Daniels's finest vocal.

He was not to record again. Living in Charlotte on E. 1st Street he
held down a number of menial jobs such as gardener and laborer but
at the time of his death was a fireman, suggesting that although a heavy
drinker—according to his widow—he was clearly able to hold down
a responsible post. His death, on October 18, 1947, was the result of
myocardial failure brought on by syphillis, not by drink.

The next set of recordings in Charlotte were those of May 1931,
during which the Jack Gowdlock and Stapleton Brothers titles were
recorded. Only one other black secular coupling was made at those
sessions, albeit one of the more peculiar. As Hambone and Morrow,
James Albert and El Morrow recorded "Beans" and "Tippin' Out,"
accompanied by what sounds like homemade, guitar-like instruments.
"Beans" is a sermon-like fantasy on this staple diet of the poor and
would have been highly appropriate to a rural audience attending a
traveling show, but it is a remarkable choice for Victor to record, let
alone issue.[31] Nothing is known of either man.

RCA did not return to Charlotte to record black secular music until
June 1936. Ben Abney's few piano pieces are without much interest,
somewhat reminiscent of the Harlem stride school but nowhere as
effective.[32] The most interesting "blues" sides were made by Philip
McCutchen, issued as by Cedar Creek Sheik. "I Believe Somebody's
Been Ridin' My Mule" is thoroughly in the blues idiom, while "She's
Totin' Something Good" has something of the flavor of Blind Boy
Fuller's "Step It Up and Go," although preceding it. However, the other
titles aurally suggest a white performer. McCutchen was clearly an
interesting artist with a wide repertoire, some of medicine show origin,
akin to fellow South Carolinian, Chris Bouchillon. Apparently from
Andrews, near Charleston, McCutchen was last heard of in Rappahannock County, Virginia; at least, a white man of that name and reputedly
the same person was committed in the late 1930s to the Maryland state
insane asylum at Frederick, having leaped from the top of a telegraph
pole proclaiming that Christ would save him from injury. His optimism
was unfounded.

In February 1937 RCA returned, recording the Five Jinks, a male
vocal quartet of no blues interest but typical of the continuing interest
in black vocal groups which paralleled religious quartets and challenged
them after World War II in popularity. Two pianists were also

recorded. Curtis Henry's four sides suggest a Texas singer-pianist, but then we have no East Coast tradition against which to compare them. The other pianist, Walter Fuller, accompanied a rather boring vocalist, Scottie Nesbitt—no relation to Gussie. Fuller is obviously a pianist of some sophistication who tries to play "lowdown" and carefully follows the vocalist. Perhaps he was a band pianist. The Chicago *Defender* at various times in 1926 and 1927 mentioned a pianist who might have been Nesbitt's accompanist: the Six Musical Aces had Walter C. Fulford as leader and pianist and fifteen months later the Musical Aces still had Walter Fulford on piano.[33] A mid-1927 entry called the band "a mittle unit selling music in the dance field," stating that it hailed from Norfolk, Virginia.[34] Eddie Kelly's Washboard Band cut eight sides, but it is not known where they were from. One title was "Poole County Blues," although it should possibly have been Polk County, to the west of Charlotte. There is no Poole County in the state. The bluesiest of all their recordings, it features a shrill harmonica and washboard reminiscent of Jordan Webb and Robert Young, who played behind Brownie McGhee on his early recordings. Perhaps the one local bluesman to record at the sessions was the singer called "Roosevelt" Antrim on his first release but simply "Roosevelt" on his other. The name, and variations like Antrum, were not uncommon in the city in the 1930s. Accompanied by an unknown guitarist, playing remarkably like Blind Boy Fuller on some cuts, Antrim sounds to be an older singer with a manner perhaps consciously like Fuller's, who by that time would have been selling well. Anyway, at that time, Fuller was still to be heard playing on the streets in nearby Wadesboro from time to time.

It is not known who set up these sessions in Charlotte for none of the people scouted by Burm Lawson returned to record. Perhaps the agent was one Van Sills, who arranged the February 1936 session for Bluebird by the black Locke Brothers Rhythm Orchestra. They cut ten titles in a temporary studio set up on South Tryon Street and even named one of two instrumental titles after him—"Sills Stomp." White recording artist Bill Carlisle remembered that Sills headed the Bluebird distribution in Charlotte.[35] He also ran the Decca distribution, at least at a later date, being involved in an abortive session for the white Jordan Brothers in 1939.[36]

Bluebird was back the following year for its final recordings before moving to Rock Hill. In January 1938 they recorded six titles from the utterly obscure Virgil Childers. His "Dago Blues" is quite distinctive, his style unlike any other Carolina artist's although aurally of the region. "Red River Blues" has characteristics of Durham rather than the central

Piedmont and is one of the finest versions recorded. Here particularly he sounds an older singer. The session ended with two numbers in rural show style, "Travelin' Man" and "Preacher and the Bear," entirely within the tradition of Pink Anderson and Luke Jordan.[37] The two remaining titles were in popular vein, one being a version of "Somebody Stole My Girl" which could have been performed by a white singer.

It is interesting, if possibly irrelevant, to note the number of artists who recorded in Charlotte in the cross-over musical zone between black and white. For years Cedar Creek Sheik was considered to have been black. A local harmonica player, D. H. Bilbro from Chester (adjoining Union County), was thought from the playing on some of his recordings to have been black, but he was not. From "Somebody Stole My Jane" and "Who's That Knocking at My Door," Childers could well have been white, and Robert N. Page's true color still is not known. Among the white artists recorded there who made excellent use of black material were the Allen Brothers and Jimmie Davis.

The last sessions to be recorded in the city were made by Decca. On Monday, June 6, 1938, Kid Prince Moore and Shorty Bob Parker each cut six titles, accompanying one another. Until very recently, these sessions were assumed to have been made in New York, where Moore had already recorded nine titles for ARC in April of that year. Presumably Moore's Charlotte session was the work of Van Sills, but perhaps it was initially the result of the apparent connection between ARC and Decca with respect to Blind Willie McTell's 1936 Augusta session for Vocalion and Mayo Williams's follow-up in the next year. Williams contacted Blind Boy Fuller to record for Decca when he was recording for ARC.

At his first New York session on April 8, Moore recorded four titles, only one of which was issued. Five more titles, two remaining unissued, were cut a few days later. By some quirk of fate all five unissued titles survive, so his full recorded repertoire is to hand, and a most interesting one it is too.[38] In the three unissued titles from the first session he seems to have run the gamut of other popular recording artists' styles. "Pickin' Low Cotton" can have been of little interest to ARC as Josh White's version had been a heavy seller for the company three years earlier. "Bite Back Blues" has a vocal delivery much in the style of Blind Lemon Jefferson, although the guitar style strongly hints at the Carolinas. "Mississippi Water" spreads his sources. Perhaps this eclecticism caused ARC to have him return two days later to record two gospel songs which reveal a different facet of his range of material.

It has been stated that his "unusually sedate spirituals in the key of C offer comparison with East Coast techniques. On the eight bar 'Sign of Judgement,' Moore uses the free-thumbing approach of Georgia's [*sic*] Sylvester Weaver. . . . Instead of following a consistent pattern, the thumb works as an independent voice and a rhythmic tool to impart spontaneity and variety to his song. Even though many melody notes fall on the off-beat, Moore's phrases are always correctly resolved. . . . In 'Church Bells' the thumb does filler bass work behind the vocal passages, and the lower bass note generally falls on the off-beat, because of the close relationship of the voice and guitar. The melodic unison of the guitar and voice make his a decidedly 'country ' piece."[39] He cut his two final sides for ARC on the following day, a Saturday. The unissued title, "Market Street Rag," is an excellent East Coast rag performed much in the style of Blind Blake with hints of Blind Boy Fuller's "Rag, Mama, Rag." In view of the success of Fuller's rags recorded for the same company, it is rather surprising that Moore's fine rag was never released.

The range in Moore's Decca recordings is less impressive than in those for ARC, and the addition of Shorty Bob Parker's piano tends to obscure Moore's guitar work. However, piano-guitar duets were in vogue: Decca already had a successful pairing with Bill Gaither and Honey Hill. Aurally Parker is a much older man, sounding more like Peetie Wheatstraw, but there is some fine guitar from Moore on "Rain and Snow" and "So Cold in China," and a change of pace with the exuberant "Ridin' Dirty Motorsickle." The general pattern of Moore's vocal delivery is reminiscent of Blind Blake, most marked on "Ford V-8 Blues" and "Bear Meat Blues." On the latter and on the flip side of "Single Man Blues," the piano is better recorded and there are some gentle duet passages. Nothing is known of either man, but Moore's performances are such that he deserved a fuller appreciation.

Thus with Moore's Decca session in June and Blind Boy Fuller's Columbia session in October, 1938 saw the last commercially recorded blues in the Carolinas. Small wonder that by 1969 blues appeared to be simply music of the past.

NOTES

1. Arthur W. Little, *From Harlem to the Rhine: The Story of New York's Colored Volunteers* (New York: Covici-Friede, 1936), p. 49.

2. Ibid., pp. 55-56.

3. *Rev. Gary Davis: Lo I Be With You Always*, Kicking Mule SNDK 1 (London, England).

4. Pink Anderson interviewed by the author, Spartanburg, North Carolina, January 6, 1973.

5. Stefan Grossman, *Rev. Gary Davis: Blues Guitar* (New York, Oak Publications, 1974), p. 13.

6. Samuel B. Charters, liner notes to *Pink Anderson Volume 1: Carolina Blues Man*, Prestige-Bluesville 1038 (Bergenfield, N.J.).

7. Tony Heilbut, *The Gospel Sound* (New York: Simon and Schuster, 1971), p. 75.

8. Tony Russell, "Homer Christopher and the Rise and Fall of the Piano Accordion," *Old Time Music* 33 (Summer, 1979-Spring, 1980): 15.

9. Chicago *Defender,* August 1, 1931.

10. *Carolina Blues Man,* Prestige-Bluesville 1038; *Pink Anderson: Medicine Show Man,* Prestige-Bluesville 1051; *Pink Anderson: Ballad and Folksinger,* Bluesville 1071 (Bergenfield, N.J.). Album 1038 was recorded April 12, 1961, and 1051 on August 14, 1961. Michael Ruppli, *Prestige Jazz Records 1949-69* (Copenhagen, Denmark, 1972), pp. 197, 202.

11. *The Blues of Baby Tate: See What You Done Done,* Bluesville 1072 (Bergenfield, N.J.).

12. Bruce Bastin, "The Historical Research of Blues and Pre-Blues in the Southeastern United States," lecture to conference on Popular Music in the Americas at the University of Warwick, England, November 20, 1982.

13. *The Blues* (New York: Thomas J. Brandon, 1962); *The Blues,* Asch LP 101 (New York). The album includes two titles by Pink Anderson.

14. *Another Man Done Gone,* Flyright 528 (Bexhill-on-Sea, England, 1979).

15. Robert Springer, "The Blues Gives Them Inspiration You Know," *Blues Unlimited* 126 (September-October, 1977): 20.

16. George Mitchell, "The Street Singer," Atlanta *Gazette,* August 11, 1976.

17. *Georgia Grassroots Music Festival,* unnamed and unnumbered (City of Atlanta, 1978). This was a noncommercial issue.

18. Chapman J. Milling, "Delia Holmes: A Neglected Negro Ballad," *Southern Folklore Quarterly* 1 (December, 1937): 8; David Evans, "Lil McClintock," *Blues Unlimited* 40 (January, 1967): 11.

19. Dan Mahony, *Columbia 13/14000-D Series* (Stanhope, N.J.: Walter C. Allen, 1961), p. 56.

20. Richard Raichelson, "Lil McClintock's 'Don't You Think I'm Santa Claus,'" *John Edwards Memorial Foundation Quarterly* (August, 1970): 132–34.

21. Lil McClintock, "Furniture Man," issued on Columbia 14575-D (15016), recorded on December 4, 1930, in Atlanta.

22. Brian Rust, comp., *The Victor Master Book Volume 2 (1925-1936)* (Hatch End, England: by the author, 1969), p. 409.

23. Allen Tullos, "Born for Hard Luck," *Southern Exposure* 3 (Winter, 1976): 41.

24. Bruce Bastin, brochure notes to *The Last Medicine Show,* Flyright 507/508 (Bexhill-on-Sea, England). The albums contain a complete version of the show edited from consecutive days' performances, together with a full

transcription. Daniel W. Patterson and Allen Tullos, brochure notes to a film, *Born for Hard Luck: Peg Leg Sam Jackson* (Tom Davenport Films, Delaplane, Virginia), which includes video footage of the final 1972 medicine show. Alan Tullos and Glenn Hinson, "The Medicine Show in North Carolina," in *Patent Medicine in North Carolina,* ed. J. K. Crellin (Bailey, N.C.: The Country Doctor Museum, 1980).

25. Arthur Jackson interviewed by the author, Chapel Hill, North Carolina, March 17, 1973.

26. Ibid.

27. *Henry Johnson: Union County Flash,* Trix 3304 (Rosendale, N.Y., 1973).

28. David Newton, "Cotton, Dust, Experience Put Out Hollerin' Blues," Greensboro *Daily News*, August 18, 1977; *Greensboro Rounder: Guitar Slim,* Flyright 538 (Bexhill-on-Sea, England, 1979); *Memphis Piano Red: Guitar Slim—Play It a Long Time Daddy,* Ornament CH 7516 (Germany, 1981).

29. *Downbeat*, October 21, 1946; Stanley Dance, *The World of Swing* (1974; rpt., Da Capo Press, 1979), p. 176.

30. *Julius Daniels,* RCA (EP) RCX 7175 (England).

31. *Folk Song in America: Songs of Humor and Hilarity,* Library of Congress LBC 11 (Washington, D.C., 1977).

32. Abney was a resident of Charlotte on occasion between 1929 and 1939, initially listed as a driver.

33. Chicago *Defender,* October 2, 1926, December 24, 1927.

34. Chicago *Defender,* July 9, 1927, in George Winfield to Peter Carr, *You Don't Know Me But . . .* (London: Storyville Publications, 1978), p. 39.

35. Phil Melick, "More Jazz from Charlotte," *Storyville* 109 (October-November, 1983): 17; Tony Russell to the author, January 9, 1981.

36. Gaylan J. Mann, "The Jordan Brothers Band," *Old Time Music* 33 (Summer, 1979-Spring, 1980): 12–13.

37. The lyrics to "The Traveling Coon" had been collected in Durham in 1919. "The Preacher and the Bear," of minstrel origin, had been reported as a folk tale, with verses appended, from Virginia. Jan Philip Schinhan, ed., *The Frank C. Brown Collection of North Carolina Folklore,* vol. 5, *The Music of the Folksongs* (Durham: Duke University Press, 1962), p. 283.

38. Bruce Bastin, "Test Exists!" *Storyville* 82 (April-May, 1979): 130.

39. Stephen Calt, Nicks Perls, and Michael Stewart, liner notes to *Ten Years of Black Country Religion 1926–1936,* Yazoo L-1022 (New York).

12

Bull City Blues: Durham, North Carolina

Durham lies east of center in the powerful tobacco crescent of the North Carolina Piedmont towns, arcing from Winston-Salem in the west through Greensboro to Raleigh in the east. Smaller than these other centers, it became the focal point of a strong blues tradition. It was no accident that it emerged as such a center, irrespective of the fact that the recording industry in the 1930s paid it some attention. The 1939 state guide described it well.

> Durham (52,037 pop.) is a modern industrial city in the eastern Piedmont. The universal demand for tobacco, coupled with the business genius of the Duke family, is exemplified in the long rows of red-faced factories where thousands toil daily. . . . The great tobacco factories lie close to the heart of the business district and the railroad tracks that serve them cross up-town streets. . . . In South Durham is a section known as Hayti, where 12,000 Negroes live and operate their own business firms. . . . Often the air is permeated by the pungent scent of tobacco from the stemmeries, and the sweetish odor of tonka bean used in cigarette manufacture. . . . The hoarse bellow of the bull whistle at the American Tobacco factory reverberates over the town, joined by the shrieking blasts of the Liggett and Myers whistle. The iron gates of the factory gates are flung wide and an army of workers pours forth—men and women, white and colored. Buses and trucks, heavily laden, rumble along the thoroughfares. For an hour or two the streets are alive with the hurry and noise of a big city.[1]

The railroad tracks still criss-cross the city, but Hayti has gone and with it its blues tradition, although it remains scattered throughout the city and the surrounding counties.

Durham grew from a "country crossroads" with an 1865 population of fewer than 100 to the bustling community of the 1930s because of tobacco. The Duke family established the industry, culminating in the 1890 formation of the American Tobacco Company, guided by James B. "Buck" Duke. It became the city of Bull Durham tobacco—thus, logically, Bull City. Partly forced by antitrust legislation to diversify his interests, Duke spread his vast fortune in many directions; some reached the black sections of town. Unlike the planter-industrialists, the Dukes and other tobacco manufacturers were not members of the state's landed upper class and thus had less to gain from preserving the rigid racial system upon which the agricultural order was founded. Many blacks were employed in the tobacco factories. The jobs were highly sought-after and wages frequently far exceeded those of white-collar workers and professionals, like teachers.[2]

White business saw an advantage in both permitting and fostering black business, so that while in 1887 blacks owned but two plots in the city, by the mid-1930s their city holdings totalled more than $4,000,000 and business assets were almost twice that. The 1939 state guide proudly stated: "The Negroes have a college [today North Carolina Central] and operate business firms, including banks, a large insurance company, schools, newspapers, a library, and a hospital. . . . Gen. Julian S. Carr [another tobacco magnate] lent the Negro John Merrick money to start his business career, first as a barber then as a real estate investor. Washington Duke [father of the tobacco barons] gave the printing press used in publishing the first newspaper. White bankers helped organize the first bank."[3]

These early black businessmen provided an establishment basis for blacks with few parallels in the South. "John Merrick, who operated a barber shop for whites, and a young negro physician (set out) to provide a systematic and organised approach to aid . . . life assurance," explained two researchers into the role of black entrepreneurs in southern economics, and these two blacks were joined by "C. C. Spaulding, bringing to the position of general manager his experience as a grocer."[4] From such unlikely beginnings grew the largest black insurance company in the world, the North Carolina Mutual, commencing in 1898. In a paper read to the Durham Kiwanis in 1967, Spaulding's son acknowledged that here was white support to ensure success and saw that "one of the most interesting and practical results that have followed the growth and development of the North Carolina

Mutual has been the tempering of race relations."⁵ In a state which could boast the Wilmington riots in the same year that the Mutual was founded, this was no small matter and may well have contributed to the eventual black music scene, even if this was to be remote from most middle-class blacks.

The Mutual was but one of many prosperous black businesses. Major fraternities existed like the Royal Knights of King David, founded as early as 1893. Black business sections grew up on Parrish Street, where the Mutual block was situated, and Fayetteville, both sides of the Southern-Seaboard railroad line, and on Pettigrew Street. Also on Parrish, and still there, was the Farmers & Mechanics Bank, the first black bank. Thus the black business section, run by blacks, could get loans. Also on Pettigrew was the Biltmore Hotel, finally demolished in 1978 under urban renewal. Lathrop Alston, its manager, was a football star at North Carolina Central, then the North Carolina College for Negroes. Helped by Duke, the college provided a good education for blacks, while working-class students could work their way up through Hillside High School and Whitted High School. School ties became as important here as with Ivy League or Oxbridge.

The tobacco factories and textile mills provided jobs for blacks in abundance, all of which helped the musical community. The street scene was good and there was money to be made. Three massive tobacco factories were situated in Durham, one just north of Main Street to the north of Hayti, while the American Tobacco Company plant was just south of the railroad tracks on Blackwell and Pettigrew, on the edge of Hayti, and the Liggett and Myers plant was a short way to the west, on Duke and Pettigrew. Where blacks worked, black musicians earned. As this "army of workers" headed home at five o'clock every day, they marched in columns across the railroad tracks into Hayti and other communities, stopping traffic and looking for diversions. Gary Davis frequently situated himself on the corner of Pettigrew and Fayetteville, next to a woman's barbecue stall, to catch the workers in a generous mood.

Even middle-class blacks gave money, and many of these worked on Fayetteville. John Merrick, then president of North Carolina Mutual, suggested to a theater booker, F. K. Watkins of Atlanta, that he ought to open a theater in Durham. Watkins opened the Wonderland and a thriving theater-vaudeville business moved in. These theaters employed black pianists and a rich "school" grew up, attracted to Durham. Many musicians were paid for playing house parties, and some were even contracted to play. Pianists were expected to play certain houses on certain nights for a set payment; in the 1930s and 1940s this became very organized. Some musicians played only in homes and never on the streets. Gary Davis played at Wednesday night prayer meetings in private homes where the faithful gathered, having booked their musician.

Thus Durham was musically very active with black secular music available at a number of levels. Musicians were attracted by the ready money, and the city's socioeconomic opportunities permitted a standard of living superior to that of the average black in the South. Robert "Son" Mason, a blues guitarist from nearby Chatham County and the only black musician whose playing in the 1920s was such as to be named by the Chapel Hill sociologist and folklorist Guy Johnson,[6] commented that "them factories paid $12 or $15 a week. Long back then a man made $15 a week was making good money. . . . I just got tired of the country, I reckon. There was more in Durham. There weren't no factories out there, tobacco factories. Nothing but saw-mills and farms and I didn't want to do nothing like that."[7]

In the fall came the tobacco auctions at the Bull City warehouses, where farmers, with cash in hand for perhaps the first time since the previous year's auctions, were more inclined to pay for well-played and well-presented music. During the tobacco sales, every bluesman worth his salt came to town to try to make a little "change." Among the Durham guitarists, only Blind Boy Fuller, Sonny Terry, and Gary Davis could have been considered "professionals"; the other musicians were at best part-time and usually worked at some menial task. The prospect of a job lured them to Durham, together with the very real possibility that they could pick up some money from their music— not the hope of full-time musical employment. Around the warehouses good tips could be made. Musicians could earn ten or fifteen dollars, four to six times what they could earn at other jobs. This was certainly far above what the best factory jobs paid. Willie Trice often played there, remembering it as some of the most profitable work he ever did. Trice also made good money as a bootlegger for some local whites in the 1930s.

Almost every musician in and around Durham had some memory of an unknown, out-of-town performer at the warehouses. Richard Trice recalled a one-armed guitarist, traveling with a medicine show, who used a hook attached to the stump of his right arm to pick, and a one-man band (guitar-harmonica-tambourine-drums) whom J. B. Long also recalled seeing in 1938 when John Hammond and Goddard Lieberson were visiting. The Trice brothers in 1969 remembered a peg-legged harmonica player who played one harp through his nose while playing another in his mouth. Brownie McGhee had recalled him a dozen years earlier. He was the medicine show performer Peg Leg Sam, resident then in Rocky Mount and with whom, on different occasions, both Willie Trice and Brownie McGhee were to play in the 1970s. Sam commented that "any musician who was any good would come to Durham to play in the warehouses."[8]

Another country bluesman from Orange County, Jamie Alston, remembered another musician who "played blues, played all kinds of songs. . . . This guy was just about the same size as Blind Gary. A tall fellow. Can't think of his name . . . he wasn't blind. I heard him play a lot of times. Played by himself; at least he was when I saw him. 'Let Jesus lead you and the welfare feed you,' he was playing that. . . . Yeh, they stopped him playing. . . . The law stopped him."[9] Perhaps someone found the song offensive, but more probably it was simply that he did not have a permit to play on the streets. Police moved the audiences on anyway, usually in good humor, because of the narrow streets near the warehouses. Sonny Terry remembered a less good-humored occasion, which was by no means untypical: "Someone was always running us off but I'd just wait a little while and go back. I recall this one time in front of Currin's I was playing a little down from some white fiddlers. These cops come tellin' me to move on and this white man stepped out of the crowd just cussin'. He said, 'You son-of-a-bitches, what harm is this man doin'? He's just playin' a pretty harp for his money. How come you ain't botherin' them fellers ?' The police didn't bother me no more that day, but the next morning that man wasn't there and they run me off again."[10] By and large, however, provided they were careful where they played, most musicians kept clear of trouble and made good money.

Not all musicians went to play; some went to listen and learn. Jamie Alston would stay all night, as on occasion would Gary Davis, if he was paid. Jamie admitted, "I didn't play, I was just listening, trying to catch a source of the other's pieces. I'd come back, pick up my guitar and practice. Try to keep some of them in my head." He remembered paying Davis twenty-five cents in 1935 to play "Throwing Up My Hand," which he had just recorded. Davis always wanted payment before he played and wouldn't play for less.

If the tobacco warehouse scene was only seasonal, regular bluesmen and the part-timers played not only on the streets throughout the year but also in the cafés and barbershops around town, especially in Hayti. Just across the railroad tracks from the Bull City barbershop on Pettigrew was the Lincoln Café, a favorite haunt of musicians. Close by, in the city center, was a small newsstand, smokeshop, and beer joint, generally called the City Newsstand. A drummer-xylophone player named Ike Lindsey ran the place, and it featured live music into the 1960s. Blues guitarist Arthur Lyons, with whom Willie Trice often played at parties, was a regular there. Many others played there, including piano players like "Catman," James Norris, and Jesse Pratt, but the regular pianist was white—Arthur Pridgen at first and then Blind Sammy Fairclough. Washboard Sam (not the recording artist) played there regularly. A talented and regular buck dancer was Sam Dewey, but after Ike Lindsey died and the place closed, he moved to a factory job in Morristown, New Jersey. Arthur Lyons recalled that the repertoire of songs was wide, including both country songs, preferred by whites, and blues, played especially by the pianists. Many musicians would drop by, including guitarists Willie Trice and John Dee Holeman, who later teamed up together. During the war years soldiers from Camp Butler dropped by, and jazz musicians from touring bands, playing at the Biltmore Hotel or the Wonderland Theater, dropped by to jam, partly because the xylophone was there.

As the black scene on Pettigrew slowly died, so did the music elsewhere in the city. Like buck-dancer Sam Dewey, Washboard Sam moved to New Jersey, where he was killed in a bar fight in the mid-1960s. Arthur Pridgen died and Blind Sammy moved. Arthur Lyons, Jesse Pratt, Willie Trice, "Hambone," and John Holeman faded into the surrounding rural and urban fabrics until researchers located them a decade later. "Hambone" recalled: "I used to be a humdinger! Stay up all night, drink liquor and blow a harp! Yeah, and play a piano too. . . . I stopped in about '68, 'cause that's when I lost my health. But the old house-parties died out long before that."[11]

As well as the cafés, barbershops, and street locations, and the tobacco warehouses in the season, the other venue for musicians was the house party. Kip Lornell, who investigated the Durham blues scene in the 1930s in depth, determined two types of house party. The first kind "was organised by individuals who opened up their houses for a weekend night of dancing, drinking, and gambling. This type of house-party was not held at any one place on a regular basis, but in any one of the Black sections a house-party was usually going on each weekend at someone's home. These events were important because they provided a place where people could relax after a week of work. Informal house-parties were often called 'fish-fries' because the host often made extra money selling food and drinks."[12] Locally they were also known as "sellins," and the concept is an embellishment of the familiar 1920s rent party. The Library of Congress has on file an excellent photograph of a poster for one of the functions, taken possibly in Siler City, Chatham County, to the south of Durham (see illustration between pages 286–87). "Pickle-low" stood for piccolo, or jukebox, so one cannot say whether or not live music was featured.

If some house parties were ad hoc arrangements by individuals, "bootleggers ran the second type of house-party. These house-parties were staged every weekend at the same house or 'join' and were strictly a money-making venture for the bootleggers. They could sell their illegal alcohol and other concessions at their own joints at a great profit. Whereas at the informal house-parties blues players performed for tips and all the liquor they could drink, the bootleggers paid the musicians a set fee for playing from early evening until early the next morning." Outside the theater circuit this was the most profitable outlet for the Durham pianists during the late 1930s—men like Neil Parker, "Stovepipe," Hubert Sears, Murphy Evans, Duncan Garner, and Jesse Pratt, who remembered the "good times! Mighty seldom that people got to fighting too bad. The music sounded real good. You usta dance to the music we was playing. Hillian Davis usta play guitar with me. He could put a guitar behind his back, way up here. Kept playing it, dance with a girl, all at the same time! We got all our drinks free and about $15 or $20. We had to play from near about 8:00 until 3:00 or 4:00 in the morning."[13] It was for such a juke joint, the Shady Rest, that Duncan Garner's piano was "borrowed" from his parents. Run by Willie Trice's uncle, the Shady Rest was no doubt well stocked by Willie's bootlegger employers. Glenn Hinson creates an evocative picture of one of these functions:

> The party might be at a friend's place down in Buggy Bottom, or over at Peachtree Alley, or maybe out at Camel Grove. Or perhaps it's at one of the "houses" run by Minnie the Moocher, Big Mattie, or any of the other local bootleggers who worked in and out of Durham. The room you're in is large, with a few chairs off against the walls and a battered upright piano in the corner. A jar of moonshine for the musicians lays on the piano top. In a small room off to one side there's a table laden with barbeque, fried chicken and fish, chitlins, cakes, and maybe some ice cream, all for sale. Behind that, a woman pours bootleg from a jar into small glasses. There's a one-eyed man tinkling the keys on the piano—that would be Murphy Evans—a guitarist picking a rag lead, a second guitarist playing the blues lines, and a washboard player rubbing his board with thimbles on his fingers. As the night wears on, the musicians take breaks to dance or eat, and are replaced by others with banjos or harmonicas. The room is crammed with people dancing the "Charleston Strut" or the "Hollywood Skip." Every once in a while a man will break into a fast buck-dance, and the musicians will oblige him by stop-timing their music.[14]

Not all Durham blacks were interested in the music of the streets and the house parties. As Glenn Hinson shrewdly points out, "the musical preferences of Durham blacks in the twenties, thirties and forties were clearly split along class lines. The working-class blacks listened to the ragtime-flavored Piedmont blues. To this day, these people are quick to mention the names of Blind Boy Fuller, Big Son [Robert Mason], or Blind Gary, who 'could make that G'itar *talk* just like you and me!' These musicians 'belonged' to the people, and the blacks were proud to claim them. The middle-class blacks, on the other hand, listened to the nationally-known dance bands, who came and played one-night stands in the city. These blacks knew of the blues . . . but just weren't 'interested in that kind of stuff.' ''[15] As blacks gained access to non-oral forms of communication, their dependence on folk roots receded, although music retained in its various forms, secular and religious, remained a vital function in black communities. Blues was a social music wherever working-class blacks congregated.

> There was only one radio station in Durham during the thirties—WDNC. It played about one and one-half hours of black music each day; that music was entirely gospel and popular dance-band tunes. Although gospel songs appealed to a wide segment of the black community, they had no attraction at all for those who preferred the earthy, amoral blues. The dance-band tunes were, as Willie Trice remembers, "high-class stuff"; they were too professional, too smooth, and too irrelevent to the lives of the people. The theater was always an option, and there were two on Pettigrew Street owned by blacks. If silent movies were being shown, a blues pianist played the piano. When the stages were used for itinerant vaudeville acts and revues, they usually featured blues singers. . . . Whenever working-class blacks gathered for entertainment, the blues were not far away.[16]

Having usually graduated from high school, middle-class blacks were not limited to an oral culture. Music's main function became entertainment, and that was to be provided by the black jazz-dance bands, which employed professional musicians. They were themselves middle-class, and understandably blacks in other professional walks of life associated and identified with them. The few local swing bands were never as popular as the larger bands which would play Durham as they toured the South. The Bull City Nighthawks played around town as early as 1919, but the bands of Cab Calloway, Jimmie Lunceford, and Lucky Millinder drew crowds in the 1930s and 1940s. Calloway later recalled playing in Durham in 1931 at a tobacco warehouse with a rope down the middle, with whites on one side and blacks on the other.[17] English jazz critic Russell Davies, drawing on the diaries of one such itinerant jazzman, commented on another jazzband which played Durham: "The band of Joe 'King' Oliver played the Biltmore Hotel on Pettigrew in 1934. One of the reed players, Paul Barnes, noted in his diary that they had come in from South Carolina. Joe Oliver was in decline and it was a tough tour. Following fights in the audience on consecutive nights in Greenville, South Carolina, the diary cryptically commented: 'Orchestra leaves after dance' on June 21st. Although they played two nights at the Biltmore, the diary for July 3rd reported they were 'now deeply in debt.'"[18] Such bands played in the Armory during the tobacco season and in the empty warehouses in the winter. The admission charge of $1.10 meant that they played for a crowd of middle-class dancers.

It was at this group that radio broadcasting was aimed: "Norfley Whitted, (WDNC)'s Director of Negro Activities in the thirties, did a daily show entitled 'Studies in Brown'; he played what he described as 'popular' black music, from Duke Ellington to Paul Robeson. Further, he did a poetry show, reading selections from poets ranging from J. W. Johnson to Emerson. These two shows, except for a short period of live gospel music, were the extent of black radio programming in the area. In response to a question as to whether they ever played any blues records over the air, Whitted responded that they only did the blues performed by the swing bands."[19]

Willie Trice remembered broadcasting once over WPTF in Raleigh in 1932 but never in Durham. Interestingly, it was a live performance. "I didn't go the day they sent for me; I went over the next day. They let me play. I just played straight over the air. I played two songs, just in the studio. That was in 1932 . . . the only one."[20] He had written to the radio station, hoping to be able to perform, but in order to do so had to travel through Durham, past WDNC, in order to get to Raleigh to the east. This was also three years before the first recordings by Blind Boy Fuller and Gary Davis.

Durham's black newspaper reflected the attitude of black magazines and newspapers in ignoring the culture-transmitting role that blues played among working-class blacks during this shift from an oral to a literate culture. The only music mentioned in the columns of the *Carolina Times* was that of the dance bands, and the occasional classic female blues singer, like Trixie Smith. There was never a reference to the thriving blues community. Norfley Whitted had never heard of Blind Boy Fuller, a local bluesman who had made more than a hundred records in the five years after 1935, at exactly the period when Whitted was WDNC's programmer of black airplay. Lathrop Alston, manager of the Biltmore Hotel on Pettigrew from 1938, vaguely recalled Fuller but quickly dismissed him. " Blind Boy Fuller and them, see, they was just somethin' like this local, you know. And wasn't very popular. You'd just see somebody out there; you wouldn't probably ask who it was."[21]

With urban renewal, Hayti has vanished.[22] Large tracts of open, weed-infested land spread south of Pettigrew where once the hum of a vital community of thousands was heard. By 1973 a small section of Pettigrew remained. The Biltmore Hotel stood, and just up the street, the Bull City Barber Shop remained, where one of the barbers still recalled Gary Davis playing. A disused gas station provided a meeting place for derelicts, but also the older frequenters of the street would stop by, especially on Saturdays, to "shoot bull" as in the old days. Railroad tracks waited indifferently to transport goods—the Santa Fe, B&O, Southern and Seaboard, and a myriad of lines, whose letters offered a variety of possible decypherings. The music was gone. By 1978 even the Biltmore, last reminder of the years when Pettigrew had been *the* center for many Durham blacks, disappeared beneath the bulldozer. The stillness now belies the fact that the music, more persistent than the buildings which gave it occasional shelter, is still to be heard in pockets in and around the city. Only a weather-stained, painted name, Lincoln Café, high up on a building across from Pettigrew, gives any hint of the city's past and vital blues scene.

NOTES

1. Federal Works Agency, Works Project Administration, Federal Writers Project, *North Carolina: A Guide to the Old North State* (Chapel Hill: University of North Carolina Press, 1939), pp. 169–70.

2. Dwight B. Billings, Jr., *Planters and the Making of a "New South": Class, Politics, and Development in North Carolina 1865–1900* (Chapel Hill: University of North Carolina Press, 1979), p. 118.

3. Federal Writers Project, *North Carolina,* p. 17.

4. Harding B. Young and James M. Hund, "Negro Entrepreneurship in Southern Economic Development," in *Essays in Southern Economic Development,* ed. Melvin L. Greenhut and W. Tate Whitman (Chapel Hill: University of North Carolina, 1964), pp. 112, 123.

5. Asa T. Spaulding, "North Carolina Mutual and the Durham Community," paper read at the Durham Kiwanis Club, Durham, June 29, 1967, Duke University Pamphlet Collection. See also Walter B. Weare, *Black Business in the New South: A Social History of the North Carolina Mutual Life Assurance Company* (Urbana: University of Illinois Press, 1973).

6. Guy B. Johnson, *John Henry: Tracking Down a Negro Legend* (Chapel Hill: University of North Carolina Press, 1929), p. 125.

7. Christopher Lornell, "A Study of the Sociological Reasons Why Blacks Sing Blues through an Examination of the Secular Black Music Found in Two North Carolina Communities during the 1930s," (Master's thesis, University of North Carolina at Chapel Hill, 1976), p. 14.

8. Glenn Hinson, "The Bull City Blues," in *North Carolina Bicentennial Folklife Festival Program* (Chapel Hill, N.C.: Creative Printers, 1976), p. 20.

9. Jamie Alston, interviewed by the author, Orange County, North Carolina, November 16, 1972.

10. Kent Cooper, *The Harp Styles of Sonny Terry* (New York: Oak Publications, 1975), p. 21.

11. Hinson, "Bull City Blues," p. 10.

12. Lornell, "Study," p. 20.

13. Ibid., p. 21.

14. Hinson, "Bull City Blues," p. 46.

15. Glenn Hinson, "Blues and Big Swing: A Speculative Essay on the Nature of Class Structure and Music Preference in the Durham Black Community in the 20s, 30s and 40s," typescript, 1975, p. 2.

16. Ibid., pp. 9–10.

17. Cab Calloway and Bryant Rollins, *Me And Minnie the Moocher* (New York: Thomas Y. Crowell, 1976), pp. 122–23.

18. Russell Davies, B.B.C. radio broadcast, March 7, 1982, citing Paul Barnes's diary for 1934, held at the Jazz Museum, Tulane University, New Orleans, La.

19. Hinson "Blues and Big Swing," p. 12.

20. Bruce Bastin, "Willie Trice: North Carolina Bluesman, Part 2," *Talking Blues* 9–10 (n.d., 1979) p. 15. Revised and reprinted as "Nobody Didn't Show Me Nothin': Tracing the Musical Career of Orange County Bluesman Willie Trice," in *Studies in North Carolina Folklife,* ed. Daniel W. Patterson and Terry Zug (Chapel Hill: University of North Carolina Press, forthcoming).

21. Hinson, "Blues and Big Swing," pp. 13–14.

22. Bill Phillips, "Piedmont County Blues," *Southern Exposure* 2 (Spring-Summer, 1974): 56–62.

13

Blind Boy Fuller

Wadesboro, a small country market town in Anson County, North Carolina, lies close to the South Carolina state line to the southeast of Charlotte. One of ten children born to Calvin Allen and his wife Mary Jane (née Walker) from nearby Ansonville was a son, Fulton.[1] The family was not musical and young Fulton was the only one of the boys to play a guitar as a young man, but he was never serious about it until he was about 20.[2] One sister, Ethel, was reputed to be a fine guitar player,[3] and younger brother Jesse played a little in Fulton's style at a later date. The family does not seem to have been very close; as early as 1937 Fulton stated that his brother Sidney, living then in Burlington, North Carolina, was the only living relative of whom he knew.[4] Whether or not that was strictly true, Sidney and another brother, Clarence, were recalled by some of Fulton's musical associates, while his widow knew that brother Jesse was living in 1970 in Hamlet, North Carolina, near the family birthplace. In the same year two of his sisters, Annie Little and Viola Wilcox, were reported in Wadesboro and Lilesville, North Carolina, respectively. Other brothers, Calvin and James, are presumed dead.

Just when Fulton was born is a matter of some conjecture, as Anson County birth records date only from 1913, even then omitting the first names of black children. Statements from the North Carolina State Commission for the Blind, the state Social Security Board, and the

Durham County welfare records, all dating from 1937, give his date of birth as July 10, 1907, and there seems to be no reason to doubt them. His widow recalled his birthday as being in July, and although his death certificate, filed with the North Carolina State Board of Health, gives his age as thirty-two at the time of death in February 1941, thereby suggesting a 1909 birthdate, that of 1907 seems more probable, as there can have been little advantage in quoting his age as thirty instead of twenty-eight when applying for help in the summer of 1937.

Little is known of his early days in Wadesboro, but he reached fourth grade in school. Whilst still living there his mother died, and in the mid-1920s his father moved the family to nearby Rockingham, some twenty miles to the east and about seventy-five miles southeast of Charlotte. It was then that he met Cora Mae Martin, then only thirteen years old. The reserved nature he was to show in his later years was already visible at this early date. As Cora Mae stated, "We were not brought up in the same neighborhood and while together I learned very little about his past life." What was certain was that he married the young Martin girl when she was only fourteen, crossing over into South Carolina to Bennettsville in order that the ceremony could take place. This was in 1926, although Fulton's welfare file gives the date of the wedding as 1929, perhaps to avoid complications with a child bride.

While he was living in Rockingham he began to have trouble with his eyes. He went to see a doctor in Charlotte who allegedly told him that he had ulcers behind his eyes, the original damage having been caused by some form of snow-blindness. The physician's report of the eye examination produced for the Social Security Board in Durham in August 1937 is more specific.

Diagnosis: Eye condition primarily responsible for blindness.
  Right eye: phthisis bulbi
  Left eye: papilloma of the cornea evidently following old perforating ulcer.
Etiological factor responsible for primary eye condition: Probably gonorrhea conjunctivitis
Describe the appearance of eyes, including fundi.
  Right eye: fundi, phthisis bulbi, secondary glaucoma.
  Left eye: as above

Central Visual Acuity:	Without glasses.	With glasses.
Right eye:	Nil	Nil
Left eye:	Nil	Nil

Prognosis (Is there any likelihood that vision could be restored by operation or treatment?)   Nil
Recommendations.   Nil
Remarks. (When should applicant be reexamined?)   None.[5]

Clearly Banks Anderson, the McPherson Hospital eye physician, saw no hope of any chance of recovery of sight and yet, when Fulton left Rockingham in 1927, he still had his sight. It was not until some eighteen months after his marriage, sometime in 1927, that he began to lose his vision. By this time the couple had moved to Winston-Salem to find work. Fulton's brother Milton also lived in Winston-Salem, which might have been the reason for initially moving there.

Fulton first took a job as a laborer at a coal yard, but he cannot have been working long before he began to lose his sight and became heavily dependent on his young wife, not yet sixteen. Little surprise that later in Durham his welfare workers constantly made such comments as "applicant's devotion to Mrs. Allen and dependence upon her for use as a guide and constant care causes her to have to spend most of her time in the house rendering her unable to have a steady job."[6] Living first on 9th Street and later on 7th and Chestnut, he was close to the tobacco factories and warehouses where he was soon to be forced to play guitar and sing to make a meager living.

His welfare file described Fulton as "somewhat migratory." In 1929 he and Cora Mae left Winston-Salem, where they had been living in a hotel on Vine Street, and settled in Durham, living first at 606 Cameron, in the south of the town, where they stayed until 1934. At some time in that year they moved a short distance to Rock Street in the very south of the township, technically outside the corporation line limits. In December 1934 they moved to 115 Beamon,[7] a few blocks from the bustling intersection of Durham's "black bottom" life of Pettigrew and Fayetteville, in the southern limit of Hayti. By January 21, 1936, they had moved once more, this time further northeast onto one of the roads running off Pettigrew. Here, at 803 Colfax, Cora Mae first applied for blind assistance for Fulton. The last reference for relief under Cora Mae's name was in April 1936, and it was not until August 1937 that an entry occurs under Fulton's name, by which time they had moved next door to 805 Colfax. His application form for aid to the blind states: "Family live in the home of Mr. Clinton Martin. There are six people living in the house which is rented . . . located on an unpaved street in the vicinity of the Oak Grove Free Will Baptist Church. The section is residential. . . . The block on which the family live is comparatively quiet." At the time, Fulton's total personal possessions were listed in his welfare file as "owns a guitar."

Interviewed in 1972, Cora Mae stated that they had moved to Durham after leaving Winston-Salem but then moved to Danville, Virginia, where they "stayed a long time," moving then to Greensboro, North Carolina, for "about one month" before returning to Durham.

They were in Durham "a long time before he recorded." Presumably these residences were during the brief gap in the welfare files in 1936–37, but when completing the questionnaire for the Commission for the Blind, Fulton chose to omit them rather than complicate the picture. Nevertheless, his report stated that he "lived in several places," and there was no doubt as to the accuracy of that comment. However, a letter on file with the Welfare Department, dating from 1933, shows that he was known to them.

April 8, 1933

Mr. G. W. Proctor,
Chief of Police,   In Re: Fulton Allen (Col.)
Durham, N.C.   606 Cameron Alley, City.

Dear Mr. Proctor,
    If it meets with your approval, we are glad to recommend that the above named man be allowed to make music on the streets of Durham at a place designated by you.
    Assuring you that we are always glad to co-operate with you, I am
Yours very truly,
W. E. Stanley,
Supt. Public Welfare.[8]

Almost two years earlier Mr. Stanley had made a similar request, also to Mr. Proctor, on behalf of Gary Davis. What is interesting from these documents is the need for permission not only to "make music on the streets" but a "designated place." This fits well with the personal recollections of other musicians who knew Fulton and the blues scene in the 1930s; they stated that the police would move musicians on if they were blocking sidewalks or the street. Clearly certain areas were effectively proscribed by the law for performance; sadly they are not enumerated but obviously they included tobacco warehouses and much of the area of "black bottom."

Fulton was also quite obviously earning a living from his music in the early 1930s, and assuming he did spend most of the years from 1929 to 1934 on Cameron, his reasonably settled location would suggest that his situation was none too desperate. Whatever the reasons for moving to Hayti, most probably linked to both availability of persons to play for and police permission to play, Fulton came to the notice of a young white store manager, who had only just entered into the world of commercial phonograph records. In August 1934 he had seen his first groups recorded. His name was James Baxter Long.

The son of truck farmers from Hickory, North Carolina, Long was an ambitious man and by the early 1930s had become manager of one of the chain stores owned by the United Dollar Stores.[9] By 1934 he was manager of the store in the small but prosperous eastern seaboard tobacco town of Kinston, North Carolina. "I'd always loved music anyway and never did have it. Down in Kinston, the farmers were coming in selling tobacco. . . . I got this old phonograph out and began to pile a few records in. The more I played, the more they stayed. . . . So from that basis on I ordered a few records and they began to buy 'em and sell 'em there. Everybody thought that the radios'd kill the record business, but I satisfied so many people that I went ahead and ordered more and more."[10]

One day people began to come by asking for a record of a song about a wreck in Lumberton, to the south of Kinston, where seven tobacco farmers were killed when their car was struck by a train on a railroad crossing. After extensive checking Long found out that no such song had been recorded and received permission from the American Record Corporation, whose records he was selling, to find someone to record it. He checked with a Lumberton newspaper for the story and, together with a female journalist whom he hired to help him write the song, came up with "Lumberton Wreck." In order to locate a singer, he decided to hold a white talent contest. The Cauley Family won the fiddlers' convention, and between August 7 and 10 they recorded twenty-four tracks, including "Lumberton Wreck." Nevertheless, although Long chose a white group to record his song, on no other occasion was he involved with white artists, apart from Lake Howard, a neighbor of the Cauleys who had recorded with them.

Shrewdly noting that black quartet records sold well, Long also held a contest for black artists. "And I told (ARC) also about the quartet. They were selling a lot more quartets than I could get from Victor or the Bluebird then, and American, and so they said they'd take a quartet." Long's black talent contests were held at the Old Central Warehouse, which was bigger than the courthouse which he had originally booked. It was this other talent contest which pointed him in the direction for which he was to become better known, as the manager of Blind Boy Fuller.

When first recalling these 1934 talent contests, Long remembered only the two mentioned. Later he recalled also a blues contest, held on the same night as the quartets.[11] The winners of the quartet contest were Mitchell's Christian Singers, who went on to become one of the most consistent and heavily recorded black gospel groups of the 1930s. For many years the standard blues discography included an unusual ARC session listed as by Boll Weenie Bill, recorded in New York on August 22, 1934. In the ARC files, Boll Weenie Bill is listed as Boll Weevil Bill, and his four titles are listed with no division at the foot of the August 1934 Mitchell's Christian Singers session. They are credited as *vocal blues-guitar.* In 1979 Doug Seroff interviewed Lewis Herring, a member of Mitchell's group, who sang bass on their first session and who still lived in Kinston. Herring filled in detail about Long's initial involvement with the recording industry: "So the first night he had the White folks . . . a man and his children won the contest and got a chance to go to New York to make records. . . . Old Mansion Gospel Convention. That's the name they put on it. They had the White folks to the Courthouse this first night, on a Monday night. Well there was so many folks there at the Courthouse that they got scared. So we were to go Tuesday night. They put it off till Wednesday night and took us to a warehouse. We had boys from all over North Carolina and everywhere. Singers and guitar players and piano players."

According to Herring the concert took place in June 1934, but they did not hear from Long until August. As some members were unwilling to travel out of the state, there was a shake-up in Herring's group, the New Four Quartet, and members of Kinston's Harmonizing Four joined them, adding Willie Mitchell as manager. Louis "Panella" Davis was the only surviving member of Herring's original group; another Davis, Julius "Juke" Davis, joined them with the lead singer of the other group. Intriguing as this ARC material is, the main significance to this study is Herring's recollection that no artists other than Mitchell's group were in the studios when they were there. Seroff took up the story: "Mr. Herring dropped an off-the-cuff comment that during their sessions Juke Davis had sung a blues song and Louis Davis had accompanied him on guitar. The title Mr. Herring mentioned was 'Sugar Hill Blues,' which is one of the titles credited to Boll Weenie Bill. Herring told me that they had discussed the song(s) with the engineer and that they decided it would be a bad idea to release a Blues song that might be identified with the Gospel quartet."[12] Such a consideration rarely bothered other secular artists, who frequently recorded gospel sides under pseudonyms, but it would appear to identify Boll Weevil Bill.

Meanwhile, Long had been so successful with his store in Kinston that the company moved him to their larger store in the bustling tobacco center of Durham, at 2501 W. Club Boulevard, near the black eastern section of Hickstown. Long recalled that "as I went around the warehouse tryin' to see some of the farmers, get 'em to come to the store and trade you know, and I saw this blind fellow, colored boy, man, he had on a blanket-lined overall jumper. But he was cold—it was cold that day. But I heard him sing—he could sing. So somebody had to lead him around—I forget who it was. Anyway, I told him, I said, 'I'm down here at the United Dollar Store—department store. Come by and see me.'"[13] Blind Boy Fuller was brought out to Long's store, probably by George Washington (Bull City Red or Oh Red), where he was fitted out with some new clothes. Once again Long wrote to ARC to state that he "had some talent that they could use and what it was." Soon the first of many sessions was set up. In July 1935 Long, his wife and daughter, Blind Boy Fuller, Gary Davis, and Bull City Red set out for New York. "Every time I went up to New York," recalled Long, "well, somebody had never been up there. It was really a picnic." This first session for Fuller was linked to other sessions featuring the other two artists. Clearly Long was none too sure that Fuller alone would be successful; Gary Davis went along not only because he knew Fuller but also because of his guitar-playing skills. Red went along because he was often Fuller's lead on the streets.

Long's flair and actual knowledge of black music on records helped him from the start. He knew many blues songs in detail, as he would be expected to identify a song from a few of the lines sung by people who wanted to buy the disc from his store. He knew many popular, easily available blues and took care that his artists did not record too obvious a cover song, unless he chose specifically for them to do so. "Every song (Fuller) knew was some he had bought the record and learned from you see, and so I began to practice him a little bit, and Blind Gary. Oh, (Gary) could play the guitar up and down, any way in the world. . . . And then, he wanted to go if I could take Fuller and I had to have someone . . . George Washington and he loved to beat those spoons on a washboard."[14]

Although Long had dealt with W. C. Calaway as the Artists and Repertoire (A&R) manager for the 1934 sessions, the recording supervisor was Arthur Edward Satherley, known to all as Art Satherley. Since his arrival in the U.S.A. in 1913, he had found his way to Milwaukee, and when the Wisconsin Chair Company entered the record business about 1918, he found himself working in Grafton for Paramount Records. Satherley gained experience in marketing music to blacks and began to realize the potential of the rural market from another Paramount employee, A. C. Laibly. By the time he left Paramount in 1929, having been in charge of their New York studio, he had an enviable history of more than a decade in the record business, much of it with rural artists. After a brief stay with the QRS piano roll company, he joined Plaza Music, which soon became amalgamated to form the American Record Corporation. Hence Long's artists were fortunate to be in the studio with one of the most experienced A&R men, and a man who had a distinct sensitivity to the blues. More than one artist had a fond memory of "Uncle Art," of his efficiency and ability to put artists at their ease, without ever being patronizing.

For both Gary Davis and Fuller, recording held a greater fear than for most. Neither had recorded before and, being blind, neither was able to tell when the red light came on in the studio to inform the artists that it was time to end, so that a complete master could be cut. Either Long or Red had to touch the singer on the arm to notify him when to finish. Davis recalled, "We stayed on the corner of 133rd Street and 7th Avenue. . . . I didn't enjoy (the recording session) too well and I enjoyed it alright too. I couldn't hardly catch on to it until later on. They'd give you beer to drink but I didn't want any liquor."[15] Willie Trice, a close friend of both Fuller and Davis, recalled what they had told him about the session:

> Mr. Sadler [*sic*] said, when Mr. Long carried Fuller up there when he made records . . . said Gary was the playingest man he'd ever seen in his life . . . but Gary didn't know about making records, you know. He said it wasn't long enough. They stopped him and he said, 'What you stopping me for? It weren't long enough.' That messed that'n up and he had to play it over again. When he got through playing and they'd touched him to quit and he signed his songs off, he'd grab them and say, 'Is that'n all right?' He wanted to know they was all right and he was nervous too. He'd never done it before. Didn't sound it on the strings though, did it? Mr. [Satherley] just looked at him and he didn't miss a lick nowhere.[16]

Davis certainly sounded well enough at ease, but it is interesting to note that his first recorded number, "I'm Throwing Up My Hand," required a second take to obtain an issuable version, just as Trice had suggested.

The Boll Weevil Bill sides being unissued, this was the first recorded blues title by a Long artist to be issued. Davis recorded one further blues title for Long but no more. The two men clearly failed to get along together. Davis stated that "there was a difference between me and the 'man.' He paid the rest of them but he didn't want to give me all of mine. That was the difference between us. . . . They didn't give us nothing of what we should have got! Forty dollars for us and thirty-five dollars for Bull City Red." While money may well have been an issue, and certainly was when Long tried in vain to persuade Davis to record again in 1939, Willie Trice was probably closer to the reason. "Mr. Long didn't take him back on account of . . . Gary wanted to play spirituals. Mr. Long said Gary was kinda bull-headed. . . . Gary didn't know about making records." He certainly was single-minded and his religious convictions often told against him playing blues, so it was probably over the material to be recorded and over Davis's singing style that the two men first argued. Long reckoned that Davis's voice "had a strain in it and he didn't have nerve to go back again [to record] because he could play it if someone else was singing it . . . nobody could sing for him, he'd sing hisself."[17] This doesn't quite fit the facts, for not only did Davis play second guitar behind Bull City Red on three of his performances and back Fuller, but on "I Saw the Light," issued as by Blind Gary, he played the only guitar backing Red's vocal, and a virtuoso performance it is too, belying that notion that "nobody could sing for him." In 1970 Long stated that he had obtained clothes for Davis from his store, rehearsed him, and that Davis was paid $250 to $300—patently not so—waiving possible royalties for a lump sum at recording, as did most black artists at that time. He claimed that Davis's high, strangled voice meant that the records did not sell well and he therefore did not take him back to record. Certainly his sides from the 1935 sessions are extremely rare when compared with Fuller's from the same dates, but they were issued on fewer labels.

Fuller's role in the evolving fabric of the Carolina blues needs thorough revision. The older premise that Fuller was the originator of a style was drastically reviewed in *Crying for the Carolines,* where a case was made for him as a "master of eclecticism rather than the originator of a style; an artist who welded regional characteristics into a readily assimilable style."[18] It was plain at that time that Fuller had drawn heavily on other artists and on recorded examples, but it was not so evident that perhaps a chief source of his inspiration and certainly of his musical improvement had been Gary Davis.

Fuller was not blind until 1928 and only then became seriously involved with music. Cora Mae recalled him "messing with (music) a little before, but then that's all he did after." Earlier she remembered that "no one taught him to play. He just took it up on his own. He played by himself as far as I can recall." Fuller was aware that music was to be his one means of income, and "he'd sit down and rehearse that box—sometimes about all day long." Gary Davis never rated Fuller much as a musician. "When I first run across him he didn't know how to play but one piece and that was with a knife. He wanted to take some of my training. I'd sit down and he'd come up to my house every day and sit down and play. I taught him how to play. He would have been alright if I kept him under me long enough."[19] Willie Trice remembered that Davis taught Fuller to play in the key of A, and local bluesmen corroborated this, while many of Davis's guitar characteristics, such as the fast finger-picked runs and the powerful bass line, are to be found in Fuller's playing.

It is interesting to note how many references to Fuller's playing in the early mid-1930s are somewhat disparaging of his abilities. J. B. Long said that "every song he knew was some he bought the record and learned from . . . Blind Boy Fuller was a little timid 'cause (Gary Davis) was older than he was." Long pointed out that Fuller also had problems remembering his lines, confirmed by Willie Trice, who also suffered at his Decca session, although he had an excellent memory in later years. Perhaps the very act of recording worried the men. Long used to take Fuller and other artists to his home in Elon College for a few days to rehearse them thoroughly, but even that posed difficulties. "I usually brought them over . . . because by the time you'd get him ready to go to New York, he'd forgotten what he's singin'. And I'd take a piece of paper and write down 1, 2, 3, 4, so I could sit up there on the stool and just whisper what the next song was. 'Cause he'd mess it all up."[20]

There are many recorded examples from Fuller's work in which the influences of other popular blues recording artists of the day are to be heard. The guitar work of Blind Blake's "Black Dog Blues" of 1927 can be heard on Fuller's "Pistol Slapper Blues" of 1938, while Blake's "That Will Never Happen No More" has, as a second theme, one often used by Fuller. Blake epitomized the phenomenal facility of guitar playing so characteristic of the Piedmont styles, was a supreme ragtime guitarist, and one of the few admired by Gary Davis. Richard Trice, who closely copies Fuller's guitar style, clearly remembered Fuller listening carefully to Carl Martin's version of "Crow Jane," recorded in 1935. Although Fuller made no effort to attempt to record Martin's "finger-popping" style from this title, Martin's "Let's Have a New Deal" had a guitar bridge between the two parts of the third line in every verse which is strongly reminiscent of guitar passages in Fuller's "Why Don't My Baby Write to Me," recorded two years later in 1937.

Fuller in his turn was to become the most influential bluesman in the southeastern states, and there can be few bluesmen of the late 1930s and 1940s who hadn't heard his records. Much of what they heard was really Davis. If Fuller's influence was direct, via record rather than in person, Davis's influence was implicit rather than obvious.

Perhaps Long pointed out why Fuller has rated so little among blues collectors when he stated that Fuller "had the best thing, song line." Collectors tend to listen to the music rather than the lyrics, although ironically, early collectors of black secular music collected the lyrics and ignored the music. Many of Fuller's songs were bawdy, good-time numbers, but many contain fine imagery. As early as 1959 Charters saw Fuller as "a good blues singer and an exciting guitarist . . . able to bring to (the songs) a colorful imagination and an exciting vocal style.[21] It is interesting that most bluesmen performing his songs tend to play those with specific imagery rather than the double-entendre dance numbers which he recorded in such quantity.

Fuller's first group of recording sessions was obviously a considerable success. Almost entirely solo performances, his material was varied, comprising dance pieces like "Rag, Mama, Rag," risqué numbers like "I'm a Rattlesnakin' Daddy," and "Homesick and Lonesome Blues," which he commences playing slide guitar. On one session he was backed by Bull City Red on washboard, setting a pattern which Long was to adopt frequently for future sessions. On "Rag, Mama, Rag" and "Baby You Gotta Change Your Mind" he was backed by Gary Davis on guitar, as well as by Red's washboard. It is significant that not only were these the only titles on which Davis backed him but that Fuller allowed only one known guitarist to back him in the future—Floyd Council. Another precedent was that Long recorded twelve titles by Fuller, all of which were issued.

Long was not able to travel to New York for a further set of recordings until April 1936, when he was once again on vacation. This time Fuller performed alone and ten sides were issued. For the third batch of recordings, in February 1937, Long reverted to the initial pattern of accompanying washboard and guitar. Red led the group to New York but played only washboard and didn't record under his own name, perhaps because his earlier releases had not sold very well. Long hinted at another reason. "I didn't think Red could sing as well as he could play. But if you gave him about half a pint before he'd sing . . . he could sing something you could understand, but you had to have a little something to bring. He loved it. And Fuller wouldn't touch it at any price."[22] The guitarist this time was Floyd Council from nearby Chapel Hill, a truck driver who was well used to long distance travel.

At the time of these sessions, Council was working for Long, living out on his farm while his wife helped out in the Long home. Floyd first knew Fuller when living some twelve miles southwest of Durham in Chapel Hill, but only after Fuller's records had been issued. The same situation occurred with another Orange County guitarist, Willie Trice, who lived half-way between both men. The fact that Trice and Council, aware of each other's abilities and friends for some years, did not know of Fuller attests not only to limited communications facilities (people traveled very little) but also to the fact that Fuller was effectively unknown, even locally, until he began to record. This was not the case with Gary Davis, nor indeed with Floyd Council. In 1935 Fuller had simply been one of many bluesmen fortunate enough to be recorded. After 1935 the story took a different course.

At the February 1937 session, Fuller's recording of "Mamie" is an interesting example of how he recorded songs which were locally well-known. Willie Trice recalled it as the first blues that he learned to play, dating it no later than 1926, although it was the first song that he remembers hearing Fuller play.[23] Indeed, it could have been Council's lines in "I Don't Want No Hungry Woman," one of his six titles recorded during these sessions, which inspired similar images in Fuller's "Death Alley," recorded immediately before "Mamie." Council sang

> Now I'm going down in Tin Can Alley, and get as drunk as I can be,
> Yes . . . get drunk as I can be,
> Now don't want no hungry woman to lay her hands on me.[24]

This alley was in the rough black district of Chapel Hill's neighboring Carrboro, while Fuller's Death Alley was the local Hayti nickname for one of the short alleys running south of Durham's Pettigrew Street. Fuller would have known it well, having lived on Proctor Street, which linked many of them. This particular alley was notorious for its crudeness and variety of vices; pointless, violent death was a commonplace.

Floyd Council clearly suited Fuller's style and Long brought him back into the studio with Fuller later in the year. For Fuller, 1937 was to be not only a year of considerable activity—forty-nine titles were recorded, all of them eventually issued—but also the year in which he found himself inextricably caught up in the commercial aspects of the recording industry. Willie and Richard Trice, two young local bluesmen, became Fuller's firm friends soon after his recording debut. Having heard the records, Willie walked the six miles into Durham to meet Fuller. Some time after the ARC session with Council in February 1937, someone wrote on Fuller's behalf to Decca Records, asking if they would be interested in recording him. Why Fuller should have wanted to transfer when he was recording regularly for ARC is not known. Perhaps, like Gary Davis, he felt he was not receiving sufficient payment; perhaps he simply saw no reason why he shouldn't make money recording songs for another company. The outcome was that Decca wrote back to say that their agent, Mayo Williams, would be down to see him. Fuller asked the Trice brothers to be present, hoping that they might be asked to record as well. Williams arrived in Durham on Friday, July 9, and immediately the Trice brothers were auditioned. Willie remembered the day in detail. "I sat down and played two; Fuller played him one song. Fuller went inside and Mr.

Williams went in there with him. So Fuller called us in there and told us he was going to carry us with him."[25] They set off that night, arriving in New York at 2 AM. Later that morning Fuller woke Willie and they played on the streets for an hour. Whether or not Williams really wanted the Trices, he was probably pleased to have friends of Fuller along. Anyway, it would do no harm to record them. He was, after all, one of the most enterprising of talent scouts.

Fuller's session was held on Monday, July 12. Since he was now an experienced recording artist, the session held no problems for him, and he recorded ten songs. An electric storm blew up and there was a fear that Fuller might receive a shock through the microphone, so the engineers curtailed the session with two songs to go. On the following day the Trice brothers were recorded. Two titles had vocal and guitar by Richard, two had vocal and guitar by Willie, with Richard supporting on second guitar on one title, and two were vocal and guitar duets. Although Fuller's session went well, that of the Trices did not. It was stiflingly hot after the storm and there was no air-conditioning. Traffic noise meant that the windows could not be opened and the session progressed very slowly. Both were nervous, having never before recorded, which might account for the duets being recorded first—and remaining unissued! Willie also recalled that he was disturbed by Decca's habit of playing back a number (thereby destroying the mother) so that an artist could hear the weaknesses in a performance. Rather than improving his approach to the song, Willie found it highly disconcerting.

The duets were closely modeled on Buddy Moss's style, which perhaps contributed to their nonappearance on record. Willie recalled them as being "not the same song(s), but in the same swing; in the same key. If you'd heard Richard and me starting off you'd have thought it was Buddy Moss and Joshua White. . . . Buddy was about the leading guitarplayer on records, right before Fuller."[26] "Tennessee Town," the first of the duets, was the only song in which two takes were made. Perhaps as the session progressed slowly, they settled for one take, provided it was acceptable. The sensitivity of a session under the guidance of Art Satherley was patently lacking: these six titles took so long to make that Fuller had to return on the Wednesday to cut his final two sides and complete his contract. If the storm had been inconvenient and the Trices' recording session uncomfortable, it was nothing compared to the storm that broke once J. B. Long came to hear of the trip.

Decca issued "If You See My Pigmeat" coupled with "Why Don't My Baby Write to Me" on Decca 7330, and the two titles which had been delayed by the storm, "Weeping Willow" and "Corrine What Makes You Treat Me So," on Decca 7331. Long was understandably annoyed. After all, he had made Fuller's name well known and Decca "didn't get him when he wasn't known." "I understood they didn't give him nothin' hardly," he mused many years later. "Somebody said $150.00 . . . so I wrote 'em and asked 'em how did they get him to break a contract to record him. And I threatened to have to take steps to see that the records were not put out. On that basis, I just wrote 'em and told 'em that. 'Course, I didn't." The only records to be issued from the Decca sessions were the two Fuller couplings and the Willie Trice tracks, issued as by Welly Trice. The Fuller discs were swiftly withdrawn and are very scarce. Long seemed satisfied that Decca did not intend to issue the other Fuller sides, at least during his lifetime. The two Richard Trice sides were not issued until late 1939 or early 1940, as by Rich Trice. It is likely that they were not issued in 1937 because of the problem with Long, but why they should have been released at this late date is a mystery. Fuller's sides, including reissues of the original couplings, were released only after his death.

Long had pulled off a neat bluff with Decca, for he held no contract on Fuller: "No, I didn't have any of them tied up. The only thing that made me mad, when Decca took him. You see, they wouldn't have him until he got famous . . . and makin' the fastest-sellin' blues singer in the South at that time. And if they'd made me produce a contract, I wouldn't'a had one. I just told them that they had no authority to sign him up and they went along with it." Long assumed that money was the factor for going to record for Decca and "told (Fuller) that if that was all that was worryin' him over there [in Durham] . . . (I) got him a cheap car. He wanted to go somewhere all the time. Somebody'd drive him."[27] Willie Trice was one of the drivers.

If Long had no one "tied up" before the incident, he made sure it wouldn't happen again. Fuller was signed to a contract which none of his friends were allowed to see, and it bound him to Long for the rest of his life. Long made little of it, but Richard Trice remembered differently. "We come back [from New York]. . . . Wasn't but a week before Long went to see Fuller about making some more records and he found out Fuller done went and made records for Decca. [Long] got scared to death, 'cos it meant money for him too. He wanted to know who went with Fuller. He come right out there in the country and found us . . . that's when he tricked Fuller in his contract; tied him up so that his contract would never be out. See, I know a little personal 'bout Fuller, 'cos I was his friend. . . . Fuller couldn't see and he tricked him; wouldn't let Red see. Mr. Long had some bad days.

Anytime you do something wrong, brother, and it'll come right back to you. . . . Mr. Long didn't have to tie him up like that."[28] Fuller remained with Long, recording twice more in 1937, twice in 1938, once in 1939, and twice in 1940. At each of these trips to record, it seems that twelve tracks were called for; at only two of these sets of recordings were fewer issued and never less than ten. Fuller's exclusive artist contract for Okeh, dated March 4, 1940, was for a term of one year only but specified twenty-four recordings, with an option of one year. It is easy to make Long out to be a grasping manager, but this is probably far from the truth. Even the 1940 contract states that Fuller was due a flat payment of "$20.00 for each recording payable to J. B. Long," and there is little doubt that Fuller received the sum in full. Long wrote to Fuller's welfare authorities in 1939, stating that Fuller received $225.00 for his summer session for twelve tracks.

Just what drew Long to record bluesmen is not clear, but it surely wasn't money. Although the great chance to make money would have been from copyrights to songs, it was many years before he did even that. None of the early Fuller releases are credited with a writer, it was not until releases of the April 1938 session that any have Long's name on them, and they were released much later. Only two titles from the South Carolina session later in the year were credited to Long, and none of the titles from the Memphis session the following year were. Not until the March 1940 session were all titles credited to Long, including "Step It Up and Go," which he effectively rewrote for Fuller. Apart from the Decca sessions, none of Fuller's recordings ever had his name as writer on the record label. More than fifty of Fuller's songs had been issued before Long's name appeared as writer, after which some subsequent songs were presumably copyrighted in his name. He later said,"That's about the only big time that I could'a made some money out of it if I'd 'a had any of the things copyrighted, but I didn't know anything about copyrightin' back in those days." Long always claimed he never took any cut from Fuller's payments and only received expenses from ARC. "Starting way down in Kinston, I never asked a soul in the world for any part of what he was makin'. . . . I averaged about 250, $300 above all expenses . . . 'cause the car . . . if they'd a-sent 'em on a train or bus, wouldn't half of 'em get there." Long claimed that, where payments were made to him on record royalties, these had been arranged by W. C. Calaway, although he never seemed clear exactly what did happen. "I doubt if they were copyrighted because this fellow Calloway [*sic,*] I found out, when he was up there, he was gettin' that stuff and then Mr. Satherley was throwin' some to his friends."[29]

Whatever the actual turn of events, Richard Trice was accurate about Long contacting Fuller soon after the Decca session, for Fuller was back in New York in early September 1937 to record twelve more titles for ARC. This time he went alone with Long but was back before the end of the year, accompanied by a new instrumental voice—the harmonica of Sonny Terry. Perhaps Fuller had been less comfortable recording solo or perhaps Long felt that greater variety resulted from a varied instrumentation. Past discographies have always shown just Fuller and Terry to be present, but Floyd Council went along as well, recording behind Fuller on four tracks and meriting a session of his own, with Terry in support. Terry's harmonica added a distinctive tone to Fuller's material and his virtuoso attack marked him out as a certain future accompanist. On the fifth track of the session, "Ten O'Clock Peeper," Council is added on guitar and is also present on the last three tracks made on that day. Even the labels of these records state, "Blues singing with guitars." In 1970, when Council was first interviewed, he claimed to have made fifteen cuts with Fuller. A quick addition of the eight titles under his own name and the only three known then accompanying Fuller, in February 1937, suggested he was wrong. The evidence of these four hitherto unlisted accompaniments show him to have been entirely accurate.

Long allowed little time to pass before he again brought Fuller to the studio. Terry had so impressed that he was back, and they recorded in April 1938. They recorded eight titles at the first session and the pattern copied that of their previous session, with Terry present only on the first three sides. However, a harmonica is to be heard on the last track, "Mama Let Me Lay It On You, No. 2," which was a new version of a song recorded almost exactly two years previously. This harmonica is tentative, quite unlike the style of Sonny Terry, and is probably played by another blind harmonica player, Charlie Austin, of Wilson, North Carolina. Interviewed in 1972, Austin recalled this title as the only one he had made with Fuller—indeed, the only one he had ever made—giving both location and the year of recording accurately.[30] At the time of the claim, the record was scarce, I had not heard it, and the standard discography showed no harmonica present. When I heard the record, I realized Austin's claim was probably true. By that time, Austin had moved into the church and would not be further drawn on the topic. How he came to be on the session will probably never be known, but Fuller did know a blues guitarist from Wilson, Sonny Jones, and was known to have traveled there. This recording trip was the last at which Fuller recorded fewer than his contract stipulated—only ten in this instance. Hereafter he was held to, or refused to record beyond, the stipulated twelve on each trip. The first of these, held later in 1938, was a completely new venue—Columbia, South Carolina.

At ARC Satherley had taken over from Calaway, who had moved into the marketing side of the record business. He later sold "piccolos," or jukeboxes, and went into partnership in a motel in Augusta, Georgia, with Satherley's wife. Presumably it was Calaway's idea to hold this Fuller session at a mobile recording studio in a hotel in nearby Columbia. Certainly there appears to have been some confrontation with the musicians' union in New York. Long suggested that it was necessary to pay a union man to be present at the session there and to pay union dues if there were three recording in a group. This might explain why only Terry (and Austin) accompanied Fuller in April 1938, while for this October 1938 session in Columbia, Red was also present, as Long reactivated the washboard accompaniment. Long was emphatic that no one else took part, but a kazoo is plainly audible on "Jitterbug Rag." Fuller was not known to have played one at any time, and the Trice brothers were certain it was not he. Red accompanies Fuller on this title, leaving Terry free, so perhaps he plays it, which was Long's suggestion. However, the preliminaries to the session were involved, for when Long went to collect the artists for the trip, Red had not turned up, although informed of the time and date. This seems not inconsistent with other reports of Red, but Long was on a tight schedule and could not wait. Richard Trice asserted that Long went to collect another washboard player known to all as Washboard Sam, who played in a small bar in the center of Durham, and hired him on the spot. He drove back to collect Fuller and Terry only to find that Red had shown up. Trice suggested that since Long had paid Sam in advance, he took him along with Red. On the six titles featuring washboard recorded at the session, Red is clearly the player; it appears that Sam didn't fit well with Fuller. If Sam did go along, he may have played "gazoo," as the record label calls it. Two tracks earlier, on "Flyin' Airplane Blues," an unknown vocalist takes over from Fuller, who can be heard offering his usual exclamations of encouragement. It has always been cited that Red took over vocal duties here but if he is singing, his voice is not immediately identifiable. It is harsher than in 1935 and aurally different from the lead vocalist of the Brother George sessions nine months later in Memphis.

Whatever the minor details, some of Fuller's finest songs come from the session. Most interesting is the autobiographical "Big House Bound:"

I never will forget the day they transferred me to the county jail,
I never will forget the day they transferred me to the county jail.
I shot the woman I love, ain't got no one to come go my bail.

. . . .

Well I got nobody, Lord come go my bail.[31]

This was poetic license for Long did just that. He recalled that he

went over there and got him out of trouble that time. He shot his wife.
This was the most sensational thing I've ever seen . . . shot her leg. Didn't
hurt her that much, but I went over there when he called me and he said,
well, nobody would help him. . . . The prosecutin' attorney, Mr. Sumter
Brawley [?] lived across the street from us there and I was well acquainted
with him so I made the trip over the day of the trial. . . . I walked in and
he told me that his wife didn't sign the warrant and wasn't there. She
told her uncle about it. He went down and signed out a warrant. So that
was all I wanted. When I got in, I told the prosecutin' attorney when
the case was called . . . "His wife is not here to testify and the warrant
was taken out by her uncle which is circumstantial. It's not possible to
use it, see. It's hearsay." He said, "Well, tell the judge." . . . And the judge
says, "Case dismissed." Ha! And, boy, that busted the courtroom.[32]

It is almost certain that the shooting was accidental. Throughout their
marriage Fuller and Cora Mae were very close, and he depended a great
deal upon her. Numerous independent witnesses attest to this and two
welfare workers' reports will suffice.

The possibility of his getting a place on the project for the blind was
discussed with M. M. appeared reluctant about accepting any such
proposition, but inferred that he probably might if his wife could go long
with him as he was not willing to trust himself without her.

Her efforts at work are halted by M.'s desire to always have her with him.
Family ties seem to be strong and much companionship exists between
them. . . . At times M. has refused offers on music projects because he
felt that his wife could not be with him.[33]

On "Homesick and Lonesome Blues," the last title recorded at his first
batch, he sang that when he started out for New York, he "left little
Cora Mae cryin'." In his last months, when Fuller was incurably ill,
they moved from Murphy Street to Massey Avenue, to be closer to the
hospital where Fuller received treatment and where he was a patient.
Cora Mae would carry his food in, as hospital food made him sick.
To this day she has never remarried.

Stories exist around Durham of Fuller's use of a pistol. One involves
him being shortchanged in a drugstore, at which point he pulled out
his gun and carefully and deliberately emptied it at about head height,

all the time moving slowly round until he had moved through about 90°, and then calmly left. Presumably he was never again shortchanged! He kept the gun on him at all times and was known to have pulled it out in the house in practice and even to have discharged it with no intent to hit anyone. Perhaps he felt that being blind he was vulnerable, that his takings would be stolen on the street in the rough neighborhoods of Hayti. Whatever the circumstances, Cora Mae could hardly deny having been shot, and it would be known to her uncle, presumably the Clinton Martin in whose house on Colfax they were living in August 1937 and for some time after that.

Having held one successful recording session away from New York, Long next held one in Memphis. For Fuller, the outcome of this session was to be almost as traumatic as that following the Decca session, for the welfare department was finally to wake up to the fact that Fuller had an intermittent income from recording and close his case.

The combination of Fuller with Red and Sonny Terry was a winning one, so they all went to Memphis. As with the Columbia session, a degree of mystery surrounds this session, not the least of which centers on a second guitarist present on "You've Got Something There" and "Red's Got the Piccolo Blues," on both of which Red plays washboard. On July 29 Fuller cut his obligatory twelve titles, matrices MEM 101 through MEM 112, while the three following matrices were credited to Brother George and his Sanctified Singers, the probable personnel of which is discussed later. Matrices MEM 116, 117, and 118 were then recorded by singer-guitarist Sonny Jones, on the middle track of which he is backed by both Terry and Red. The logical suggestion is that Jones plays the second guitar on Fuller's sides: he was certainly present at the end of the session and was backed by Fuller's supporting instrumentalists.

When first interviewed in 1970, Long had no recollection of a Sonny Jones but by the time of his 1974 interview he had clearly thought about the session, although he is all too obviously hazy about the whole matter. "Aaah, Sonny Jones. I don't know. It did ring a bell with me. . . . Yeah, I went to Memphis. I'll tell you what it was. Somebody from that area came up there and they recorded a couple of numbers to see how he sounded. I didn't take him out there."[34] Perhaps Jones was around Memphis at the time and heard of the session. Perhaps he was traveling with a show. The main point is that Sonny Jones was well known to Fuller and had been for many years.

Recalling his trip to New York to record for Decca, Willie Trice remembered that Fuller had "carried someone else up there with him. Sonny Boy. Sonny Boy that played guitar. Dough Roller. I just called him Sonny Boy. His name was Sonny." However, it seems that Jones wouldn't pay Fuller the ten-dollar "agent's fee" he was asking for, so Fuller "said he wouldn't mess with him again."[35] At an earlier interview, Trice had recalled going one evening with Red to Fuller's home, where they met the man whose main song was what Trice then called "Bakery Shop Blues." Before Sonny Jones's name had even been mentioned, Trice quoted the first line of Jones's 1939 recording of "Dough Roller," the fourth title he recorded at Memphis. No one else from Durham recalled him, by name or from his records. Even Cora Mae failed to remember him, but she would have known only Fuller's close friends, like the Trices and Terry. In all probability Sonny Jones was from outside Durham, from nearby Wilson. A line in an obscure postwar blues recording on the Orchid label, probably from Baltimore, entitled "Leaving Homes Blues" by Sunny Jones, suggests that the singer is "goin' back to Wilson, N.C." Clearly a Carolina bluesman, and given a difference of a decade or so, it could well be the same man. Further, Baltimore was just one of many stopover cities on the East Coast migration route to New York.

Fuller certainly went to Wilson. Alden Bunn, a good blues guitarist from Bailey, just north of Wilson, who made a name for himself as Tarheel Slim in the postwar rhythm-and-blues field, remembered as a teenager that Fuller had been to Wilson, some seventy miles east of Durham, beyond Raleigh. J. B. Long recalled that Fuller "had a car, see . . . but somebody else drivin' it, you know. They gon' take care of it. He went down to Wilson. He'd make 25, $50 down there during tobacco season for a day or two, you know, and they moved around the tobacco market and they had a good thing."[36]

George Nickerson, a distant relative of Fuller's who moved to upstate New York, knew Fuller in the 1920s when he was living in Rockingham, and he was able to corroborate a number of deductions and surmises about Fuller's early life. He knew some of the musicians around Fuller's home town and clearly recalled Sonny Jones. Kip Lornell reported that "George saw Sonny on three separate occasions. The first time was around 1927 in Rockingham, when Sonny was visiting an uncle. George saw Sonny in Florida the next year. . . . The final meeting was in Charlotte in about 1930. He describes Sonny as being about Fuller's age, "a tall, brownskin guy, about 6' 3". He was real good looking."[37] Peg Leg Sam vaguely recalled a guitarist in Rocky Mount who had recorded, whom he thought was named Sonny Boy Williams, who went to Norfolk and played around New York. He was a slim man and Sam might well have confused the last name with better-known bluesmen. South Carolina bluesman Jack Gowdlock recorded a "Rollin' Dough Blues" in Charlotte in 1931, so perhaps it is the same song as that of Sonny Jones, although no copy has ever been found. At least, Jones's song has no connection with Buddy Moss's "Dough Rolling Papa" of 1934, beyond the motif, nor—more obviously—with Garfield Akers's "Dough Roller Blues" of 1930.

According to J. B. Long one record cut by Fuller at Memphis was probably never alloted a matrix number. An acetate was kept by Long, who took it to Kinston, where it became lost. Presumably a version of "Big Ball in Memphis" featuring vocal and guitar, some idea of its contents can be obtained from the only refrain that Long could recall, to the tune of "Bye Bye Blackbird": "Here I am, balls 'n all,/Throw your ass against the wall." Later in the day the tone in the studio changed, and the first of two Memphis sessions by Brother George and his Sanctified Singers took place.

The Brother George sides have always been identified as featuring Fuller, Terry, and Red on vocals, with Fuller on guitar. However, it is most unlikely that Fuller was present. Fuller had fulfilled his contractual agreement of twelve titles, and there is contemporary written evidence that he wanted to end the agreement.[38] Art Satherley's files on Fuller's recordings include no more than the dozen made under his own name. Brother George is Red—George Washington. His voice is recognizably that of the lead singer. Terry's voice can clearly be heard as the second vocalist, often in little more than an exhorting role. A third voice is sometimes to be heard, as on "I Feel Like Shoutin'" and "Jesus Touched Me." Even when this voice is heard, there is nothing to identify it aurally with Fuller. Sonny Jones was in the studio at the time and may well have contributed the occasional third vocal part, as well as the perfunctory, rhythmic guitar playing. None of these sides has a guitar part comparable to Fuller's on the 1940 Brother George sides.

One song that Long heard at the Memphis sessions was the first song recorded at Fuller's next session and became perhaps the song for which he is best known. Long recalled that "of course, I made 'Step It Up and Go' and heard a man down in Memphis, Tenn. And he came in there, but he was kind of a older fellow and his voice wasn't right but he made one about 'You Got to Touch It Up and Go.' . . . On the way back to Durham I was makin' it up 'Step It Up and Go' in place of 'Touch It Up and Go.' " A few days before the Fuller session, Charlie Burse had cut "Oil It Up and Go" for the same company; although it was never issued, it would appear to be the song to which Long referred.[39]

Whatever the minor issues concerning these recordings, the real problem arose only on Fuller's return to Durham, when the welfare department began to investigate his claim further. In June 1939 it had been determined that Fuller had been playing for money on the streets, although he denied that he had ever been told that it was "strictly against the rules. . . . He said that he had never been told of such a policy. He was asked if the form for application was not read to him but he said he 'disremembered.' He played last Saturday [June 16] in Raleigh at the City Market where he made $2.50. He said that he would have played some in Durham but people here always wanted him to play for nothing. He has promised not to beg on the street again.''[40]

Whether Fuller "disremembered" the rule or had been unaware of it, he made no effort to conceal that he played, unlike Gary Davis on occasion. By now the wheels had been set in motion and a placement agent, William Lewis, had followed matters up independently. In a report written the same day he said:

> A medical examination [in October 1938] by Dr. T. T. Jones revealed arrested syphillis and very bad kidneys and bladder. Dr. Jones declared Allen unable to work and said it would take long treatment to get him into good physical condition. . . .
> He was found to be under contract to J. B. Long . . . to receive $200.00 each time he made a trip to New York and recorded 12 selections. Inquiry indicated that because of the popularity of his records, Allen was getting only a small fraction of the legitimate returns on them while Mr. Long was "mopping up." Allen realized this himself but knew of no way of doing better. It was arranged that he would not sign another contract with Mr. Long on the expiration of the one he was then under, April 21, 1939. The recording company and Mr. Long were written. They were asked to cooperate with us in getting the man off public relief but neither replied. On the day the contract expired, both were again notified of the man's condition and advised that he was now free. A month later as we were about to conclude a contract with another company Mr. Long appeared and claimed that while Allen was free of his contract with him he was still bound to the American Recording Company, 1776 Broadway, New York. The Company was written in an effort to verify this but it simply referred us back to Mr. Lona [*sic*] and the matter is still undetermined. Both Frances E. Walker, local lawyer and member of the Lions Club, and Ludlow Rogers, local lawyer, have given advice in the case and Mr. Walker promised to help in any way possible.[41]

Despite all the apparent efforts made, Fuller still recorded for Long and ARC in mid-July in Memphis. Unfortunately, Lewis failed to mention the name of the other company with whom he hoped to have Fuller sign. One wonders if it might have been Decca! There the matter rested for a while as Lewis undertook "summer training at Chapel

Hill''[42] and before he could resume the case, Fuller had gone to Memphis. Despite Lewis's championing of Fuller's case, a student worker in 1939, Mrs. Bailey Watson West, who finally wrote the recommendation to terminate Fuller's award, wrote that ''at two different times Mr. Long had taken him and another blind boy to New York to make recordings. Fulton said that on the occasion of the first trip Mr. Long had given him $40.00. The last time he had made $200.00.'' This is proof that Long did pay Fuller whatever monies were due on his behalf and that, despite Fuller's fears to the contrary, Long was not cheating him. Mrs. West's final report stated: ''It is believed that Fulton's wife, who has become unemployed since the receipt of the B(lind) A(ssistance) check, could find work to do at this time. She was formerly employed in a tobacco factory and, since these factories are now opening, she could likely resume her work. In view of the fact that Fulton has had $425 cash in the past six months, it is recommended that his grant be terminated (from $23.00).''[43] Although from the standpoint of the welfare department, matters might seem to have been financially sound for Fuller, Cora Mae was increasingly needed to look after him. The termination of his grant led to his arrival ''in rather belligerent attitude'' in the caseworker's office the following month.[44]

March 1940 saw Fuller once more in the New York studios of ARC, where he recorded a further twelve titles, as per contract. Interestingly, two of these were released as by Brother George and his Sanctified Singers. Whether or not Fuller's continued illness affected his performance, the company chose to record four titles from him on each of three consecutive days; Fuller's titles on the first two days were followed by two titles from Sonny Terry. The established pattern continued whereby Terry and Red provided Fuller's accompaniment. ''Step It Up and Go,'' rewritten by Long, proved to be a massive country blues hit. Perhaps the termination of Fuller's grant gave rise directly to the lyrics of another song from that first day's recording:

I went to the pawnshop, Great God, my shoes in my hand,
I went to the pawnshop, Great God, my shoes in my hand.
Said, ''Give me a loan, Mr. Pawnshop man, and help me if you can.''

Said I called up in Burlington, asked my bossman to help me if he please,
Said I called up in Burlington, for my bossman to help me if he please.
    Said, ''Please hurry up and do something, Great God, I'm about to freeze.''

. . . .

Said I'm about to lose my home, I've gone and lost my car,
Said I'm about to lose my home, I've gone and lost my car.
Yes, I'm gwine down to the pawnshop, see if I can pawn my guitar.[45]

At some stage Fuller had moved briefly to Murphy Street and then on to Massey Avenue, close to the hospital. Long certainly helped Fuller on occasion, and Fuller had lost the car he once owned.

This time on the Brother George sides Fuller plays guitar, entirely in the manner of Gary Davis on "Twelve Gates to the City." On "You Can't Hide From the Lord" Fuller's guitar helps produce the most compelling of all the Brother George sides: he plays with all the subtlety and swing of Davis, while Terry, caught up in the excitement, takes over the lead in his distinctive, hoarse voice; Fuller sings the lower harmony. The rhythms are as interweaving and complex as those of a small congregation and make one wish they had recorded more. Possibly Satherley felt that the Memphis Brother George tracks lacked verve without Fuller, so that in New York he was to record ten blues plus two gospel sides. The slight change in personnel mattered little otherwise; the following year saw a Brother George session which didn't even include Red, who was after all "Brother George."

Terry's first sides under his own name were also recorded. On Terry's "Harmonica Stomp" Fuller plays guitar and can also be heard offering his usual "Yeh!" of encouragement. This is the only title on which Fuller backed another artist. Terry was adamant that Fuller was present, even if the title was not quite correct. After all, a guitar is present on only one of the four titles recorded. "I know the first one I ever made with [Fuller] . . . I made one myself and he played with me. It was the 'Harmonica Breakdown.'"[46]

All four of the Terry sides were listed in Fuller's contract. Besides the almost immediate issue of both Terry's records, six of Fuller's sides were listed for issue in April, including the Brother George coupling. Further Fuller couplings were listed in May and June, but for some reason "Passenger Train Woman" and "Good Feeling Blues" were held back and not issued until June 1941, well after his death. Before all the titles from these March sessions were issued, Long took him to the studio again, this time to Chicago, in June. Once more, Red and Terry went along.

Apart from one session back in New York with Brownie McGhee and Buddy Moss, all Long's remaining sessions were to be cut in Chicago. Fuller again recorded twelve titles, four as Brother George. Terry was again recorded and even one side of Fuller's, "I Don't Want No Skinny Woman," was credited to Blind Boy Fuller and Sonny Terry on issue. As with other sessions, much of Fuller's material was widely eclectic. "Skinny Woman" is based on Yank Rachell's "Gravel Road Woman" of 1934, while "Bye Bye Baby" derives from "Bill" Wilbur's 1935 "My Babe My Babe." One line from "Night Rambling Woman," taken from Victoria Spivey's first release in 1926, "Black Snake Blues," was to be prophetic, and it may not be entirely accidental that it was not only the last blues to be recorded at the session—and thereby the last blues ever recorded by Fuller—but that it came immediately after the religious songs headed by Georgia Tom Dorsey's "Precious Lord." "My left side jumps and my flesh begin to crawl,"[47] pointed to the limited future ahead of Fuller. Very ill now, he was not to survive the winter.[48]

Within a month of recording, Fuller was in hospital. The family doctor, C. S. Hicks, attended Fuller regularly from December 12, 1940, both in the hospital and at home, for Fuller discharged himself from the former. Although he was persuaded to return, there was nothing the medical staff could do for him, and he was sent back home. After this Fuller refused admission again. Dr. Hicks came by one Wednesday but had to return on the following day, February 13, 1941, to certify that Fuller had died at 5:00 P.M.

On his deathbed Fuller had sworn that, should he survive, like many another bluesman he would "cross over" to the church. Richard Trice was always to remember that, and although he modeled himself upon Fuller, he was to heed that advice himself in the late 1960s.

Fuller's death certificate, signed by Dr. Hicks on the Friday, showed that the immediate cause of death was "pyemia due to infected bladder and G.U. tract and perineum" and partly the aftermath of the July 1940 operation for "suprapubic cystotomy for stricture of urethra." Fuller was buried on Saturday, February 15, 1941, at the Grove Hill Cemetery by the McLaurin Funeral Home of 1108 Fayetteville, "where sympathy and efficiency go hand in hand." Even more efficient, the Durham civic authorities have made further use of the cemetery; the Fayetteville Street High School now stands on the grounds.

Blind Boy Fuller was dead. His name was to linger not only among bluesmen in the area but also among new generations of bluesmen, ever emerging in the South. For J. B. Long Fuller's death heralded the end of an era. With Fuller gone, he lost heart in the recording business, but before World War II he gave one more memorable name to the blues world and reactivated another—respectively, Brownie McGhee and Buddy Moss.

NOTES

1. Much of this detail comes from welfare department, Social Security, and blind assistance files for Durham, North Carolina, for which I am indebted to Bill Phillips. Rather than attempt to differentiate between them, I have simply listed them as "file" plus the date. Copies of all are in my possession.

2. Cora Mae Allen, interviewed by the author, Durham, November 19, 1972; Cora Mae Allen to author, April 5, 1970, and September 9, 1970.

3. Charles Henry "Baby" Tate, interviewed by the author, Spartanburg, South Carolina, August (undated), 1970.

4. File 1465, Fulton Allen, and 3252, Cora Mae Allen. Various dates.

5. Physician's report on eye examination for the Social Security Board, August 4, 1937, application number 21.

6. File 1465, August 4, 1937.

7. Ibid., but an undated city map states *Beaman,* while Cora Mae Allen, September 9, 1970, wrote *Beaumont.*

8. Ibid., April 8, 1935.

9. J. B. Long, interviewed by author, Elon College, North Carolina, July 31, 1970.

10. Kip Lornell, "J. B. Long," *Living Blues* 29 (September-October, 1976): 13.

11. Bruce Bastin, letter to *John Edwards Memorial Foundation Quarterly,* 9 (Summer 1973): 66.

12. Doug Seroff, "Sing Me That Old Song Again: Interview with Lewis Herring," *Blues Unlimited* 139 (Autumn 1980): 24–25, 11.

13. Lornell, "J. B. Long": 14.

14. Ibid.

15. Stefan Grossman, *Rev. Gary Davis* (New York: Oak Publications, 1974), p. 12.

16. Willie Trice interviewed by the author, Orange County, North Carolina, September 23, 1972.

17. Lornell, "J. B. Long": 14–15.

18. Bruce Bastin, *Crying for the Carolines* (London: Studio Vista, 1971), pp. 14–23.

19. Grossman, *Rev. Gary Davis,* p. 12.

20. Lornell, "J. B. Long": 14.

21. Samuel B. Charters, *The Country Blues* (London: Michael Joseph, 1960), p. 146.

22. Lornell, "J. B. Long": 22.

23. "Mamie" was probably well known throughout the Southeast. A convict group at Milledgeville, Georgia, recorded a version, AFS 259 B 2, for the Library of Congress in 1934.

24. Floyd Council (as The Devil's Daddy-In-Law), "I Don't Want No Hungry Woman," Vocalion 04643 (20640-1), recorded February 9, 1937, in New York.

25. Bruce Bastin, "Willie Trice: North Carolina Bluesman, Part 1," *Talking Blues* 8 (January-February-March 1978): 5.

26. Willie Trice, interviewed by the author, Orange County, North Carolina, September 22, 1972.

27. Lornell, "J. B. Long": 16–17.

28. Richard Trice, interviewed by the author, Orange County, North Carolina, September 22, 1972.

29. Lornell, "J. B. Long": 16, 18, 20.

30. Charlie Austin, interviewed by Ken Bass, Wilson, North Carolina, 1972; Ken Bass to author, June 15, 1972; Bruce Bastin and John Cowley, "Uncle Art's Logbook Blues," *Blues Unlimited* 108 (June-July 1974): 13.

31. Blind Boy Fuller, "Big House Bound," Vocalion 04897 (SC-25-1), recorded October 29, 1938, in Columbia, South Carolina.

32. Lornell, "J. B. Long": 17.

33. File 3252, April 21, 1936; File 1465, August 4, 1937.

34. Lornell, "J. B. Long": 18.

35. Willie Trice, September 22, 1972.

36. Lornell, "J. B. Long": 20.

37. Kip Lornell, "Albany Blues Pt 3," *Living Blues* 16 (Spring 1974): 30.

38. File 1465, June 21, 1939, August 7, 1939.

39. Lornell, "J. B. Long": 18. The Memphis Jug Band had recorded "Bottle It Up and Go" with Burse present on November 7, 1934, OK 8959.

40. File 1465, June 21. 1939.

41. Ibid.

42. Ibid., July 5, 1939.

43. Ibid., June 21, 1939.

44. Ibid., August 25, 1939.

45. Blind Boy Fuller, "Three Ball Blues," Vocalion 05440 (26600-A), recorded March 6, 1940, in New York.

46. Barry Elmes, "Sonny Terry and Brownie McGhee," *Living Blues* 13 (Summer 1973): 14.

47. Blind Boy Fuller, "Night Rambling Woman," OK 05785 (WC-3155-A), recorded June 19, 1940, in Chicago.

48. One oddity of this final session is the second harmonica on "Precious Lord," aurally by Jordan Webb, Brownie McGhee's harmonica player, although no evidence other than aural suggests the presence of a second such instrument.

14

Blind Gary Davis
in North Carolina

One of the prime direct influences on Blind Boy Fuller's musical development was Gary Davis, born in 1896 in South Carolina.[1] He left that state during or soon after World War I, but evidence is conflicting. Exactly when he came to live in Durham is not known. Applying for aid to the blind in July 1937, Davis stated that he lived there for twenty-one years, which would indicate he left South Carolina in 1916, but a 1934 welfare file entry stated that he had married a Greenville, South Carolina, woman "fifteen years ago and separated ten years."[2] The blind commission entry for July 21, 1937, was more detailed:

> Came to Durham 18 years ago and has lived here continuously ever since. M. came to Durham from Asheville, where he lived for 2 years.
> M. stated that he married at the age of 23. Has been separated from his wife, Mary, since 1924. Stated that he left her in Winston-Salem, N.C. Has had only one marriage. Reports that Mary has married again.[3]

However, even 1919 appears to be too early for Davis to have moved permanently into Durham, as he only married Mary Hendrix in June 1919.

By his own testimony, Davis was always on the road. Aaron Washington, a fellow musician with whom he used to play in Asheville, remembered him well: "Near as I can remember it was 1922 to 1923. When I first met him, he told me that he got blind in Greenville, South Carolina. . . . He was about 28 or 29 at the time. When I first met him

he had the guitar down to the depot station. I would imagine that he had just got off the train, he was just there in the waiting room. He had a guitar so I walked over and started a conversation with him. There was no one with him.'' Washington then set him up with accom-
• modation "right across the street from (me). Any kid he could get 'hold to, he would send word over to me that he wanted to go out. I would take him out. Along then his voice was really strong and he could sing good! . . . He would sit in the square and play the guitar, mostly he would hold the guitar right up close to his head. It got to the point where most everybody seemed to like him. Wouldn't hardly anybody pass him without throwing some money to him.'' They traveled to Chattanooga ("just would stay there overnight"), to Hendersonville and other small towns, and "played all over Asheville.'' Davis taught Washington to play spirituals: "Along about that time, I wasn't playing nothing but blues . . . I used to pick up his guitar, the first thing that I would hit was some kind of old blues. He wouldn't say nothing. By and by he asked me if I ever played any spiritual songs. I told him no. He told me that it might be a good idea if I did play spirituals because I would get just as much enjoyment out of it. Those few words followed me all the time and I decided to try.''[4]

Washington was from Williston, South Carolina, and had moved to Asheville by 1912 or 1913. He began playing guitar and joined a local string band by about 1919, which accounts for his initial interest in Davis. He left Asheville in 1926 to move to upstate New York, claiming that Davis remained in Asheville.

Although the date of Davis's move to Durham is uncertain, his welfare file there begins in 1931. The first entry is an obscure cable from Wilson, North Carolina, possibly from the superintendent of public welfare in that town:

> WILSON NC   253PM   APL 4 31
> W E STANLEY
> SUPT PUBLIC WELFARE DURHAM NC
> MEET GARY DAVIS BLIND AND DIRECT LATE NIGHT TRAIN
> JAS T BARNES[5]

Thus by 1931 he was in some way involved with the welfare departments and was known to be earning some money from his music, as the following police permission to perform in Durham some months later shows:

Mr. G. W. Proctor,
Chief of Police   July 16, 1931
Durham, N.C.   In re: Gairy Davis.-Col. [*sic*]

Dear Mr. Proctor,
    The above named man has requested a permit to play guitar and sing
in the colored section Friday, July 17th. If it meets with your approval,
I am glad to recommend that he be given a permit for this date only.
                                        Very truly yours,
                                        W. E. Stanley,
                                        Supt. Public Welfare.[6]

Local Orange County bluesman Willie Trice first knew Gary Davis in
1932; even then Davis was a remarkable musician, with more than
twenty years' experience. Trice never lost his awe at Davis's skills,
commenting that "he never let a string be still. . . . he could make a
piano of a guitar. . . . the playingest man I ever saw. . . . he could make
five hundred chords while I was trying to play two."[7]

Davis's first known address in Durham was in Hayti, at 410 Poplar,
where his landlady, Ella Whitaker, had lived since 1932, although Davis
is only shown as resident there in 1935. His mother, Belle Davis, had
been living at 410A Poplar since 1931. She worked in one of the
tobacco factories, so it is possible that she was a source of some financial support. His sister had also moved to Durham to find work and
married a local man, but by the late 1930s her whereabouts were
unknown. An uncle, William Sexton, had been living on Enterprise
Street but had taken little interest in Davis, and by July 1937 his
whereabouts too were unknown. Davis's half brother, Buddy Pinson,
also lived in Durham until in the 1920s he was bizarrely murdered—
stabbed by an angry girlfriend while peeling potatoes.[8]

Although his mother remained listed at the Poplar address in the city
directory until 1938, Davis's welfare file reported in December 1934
that he was living with a John King, who paid the rent, because his
"mother had died in June, left a little insurance but he had spent all
of that now."[9] Davis certainly appeared to be in an impoverished condition later in the year. "Man sleeps in the kitchen of a two room
duplex house. Home very poorly kept. House is in a dilapidated
condition."[10] However, the whole neighborhood had that reputation.
An independent if rather moralizing description of the street was given
in 1930:

Poplar Street is also parallel to the railroad with factories at the back.
There is no curbing, paving is poor and the sidewalk consists of dirty
paths. The houses are supposed for two families each and are very dingy

and dirty with no sign of care. Card games and loud swearing indicate the disorderly nature of the people who inhabit them. On Pettigrew are located cheap eating places, barber shops, grocery stores, a moving picture theater, a dance hall and several pool rooms. All loafing places affording an opportunity for demoralizing contacts with the baser elements for the unsophisticated country immigrant. The seasonal nature of the factory work in Durham causes great fluctuations in the volume of the population in this area. At one time the houses are all occupied, but the streets are vacant during the day. Everyone is at work. At another time the houses are well-filled and the streets crowded at all hours with loafing people. It is midwinter and the rent signs hang on many of the houses. It is spring and the people have left the city for work on the farms or in the North. The changes in the whole character of the neighborhood at different periods of the year is especially striking.[11]

A new worker took over Gary Davis's case in 1935 and suggested the possibility of "Blind Pension," adding that he "manages to make a few pennies playing a banjo."[12] In May 1935 his case was transferred to Raleigh under the Federal Emergency Relief Administration project. It did him little good and he was reported as stating that "they did not use him but three days last week in June and discharged him without pay. Man said he had to get back to Durham the best way he could. Stated that he borrowed money to go to Raleigh and was now in debt."[13] If this was the manner in which he was treated, it is hardly surprising that he harbored suspicions over money matters during his recording career. Considering Davis's musical skills and the department's acknowledgment that he "used to teach music at Cedar Spring's [*sic*] Blind School,"[14] it is understandable that "M. was disattisfied [*sic*] and did not stay but one week"[15] under the F.E.R.A. scheme, the more so if the type of work offered him related to the appraisal of a caseworker in May 1935, who decided that "M. can put bottoms in chairs and repair mattresses, etc. He would like work of this kind."[16] One doubts that Davis was wholeheartedly in favor of such work. Another caseworker was soon to report "that man was traveling with Mr. Fuller from Raleigh and earning $18.00 per week."[17] This report was made two weeks before Davis and Fuller, unbeknown to the welfare department, were to travel to New York with J. B. Long, to make their first recordings (see chapter 13).

At all times Davis felt that he had been cheated by Long: "I thought 50 dollars was some money. When I come to find out that he was getting the royalties and I wasn't getting but the 50 dollars. He had me covered on that you understand, but I waked up, you understand. He never got me no more." Sadly, that was only too true, although Long tried to tempt him back into the studio in 1939. To our great loss he did not record again until after World War II. In view of the scarcity of Davis's records in collectors' hands, one might question how well they sold and how much Long made from them if, indeed, he made anything at all. There appears to be more than a degree of hindsight in Davis's comment above, especially the reference to Long having him "covered."

Throughout his life Davis felt that he was being cheated. It is easy to see how a blind man might think that way: constantly moved on by the police, he was also an easy prey for anyone intending to steal from him. Blind from birth, he was independent enough never to need anyone to "lead" him on the streets. Nevertheless, the bitterness of constant harassment showed through at every interview. In 1965, asked if he ever played then in Harlem, Davis replied, " Well no. But I used to. That's where I got most of my robbing done. Every time I sit down, it seem like somebody take something from me. . . . You can call the police today and it will be a week today before the police come! When you ask the police for protection not a word. They won't allow you to have a gun or a pistol, not one in your house."[18] Even if he didn't think that a blind man with a gun might be dangerous, his contempt for the police was evident when he remarked that, playing on the streets in his early years, he "would get run off by the police more time than I can remember."[19] Davis's aggressive nature was well known in Durham. One welfare worker noted his out-spoken comments on his income: "'I don't like dog food, and must have good food to keep my body well.' . . . Summing up his present situation, these words were used: 'I am just sticking up side the wall now.'"[20] Another worker noticed that "he has a very aggressive manner . . . (and) a religious obsession which influences his activities in an almost impractical manner. He stated that he was far more interested in 'saving souls' than in remuneration for his services."[21] Yet another, making no further comment upon the incident although clearly disturbed by it, wrote that "all during the conversation, Gary was playing with a very large new pocket-knife. He would open it, run his fingers along the edge of the blade, then close it again."[22]

Perhaps this was the knife which featured in one "attempted robbing" in Durham which backfired seriously upon its perpetrator. Davis was playing and singing on the street when a passer-by put a dollar note into his hand. Another man, who happened to be passing in the opposite direction and knew Davis well, looked up at a woman he knew sitting on her steps listening to Davis, winked at her, and snatched the note from Davis's hand, laughing at the joke. Before he could explain that it was in fun, albeit rather foolish, Davis grabbed the man by one hand, pulled out a knife with the other, and began to stab him in the back and side, crying out that the Lord had allowed him to catch the thief and that this was to be his punishment. As he felt that it was divine retribution, it was some time before he could be prevailed upon to stop stabbing, at which time the wounded man collapsed. Although taken to hospital, he survived and apparently no charges were preferred. At this time, Davis was being carefully looked after by Willie Trice's cousin, Mary Hinton, daughter of his earlier landlady, Ella Whitaker. "Mrs. Hinton, landlady, is congenial and expresses interest in M.'s welfare. There is a degree of refinement in the home not in keeping with usual conditions existent in the block."[23]

There is no reference in the welfare files to Davis's 1935 recording session, but food orders in the amount of $4.00 per month continued to be given. An interesting note dated Christmas Eve 1935 exists from Mr. Stanley, superintendent of public welfare, to Mr. O'Briant of the Piggly Wiggly store in Durham, above which the welfare offices were situated. Clearly much welfare trade went through the store, one of the largest grocery chain stores in the South, and this note requested that Mr. O'Briant "please give Gary Davis $2.00 worth of food and charge it to my account." Whether or not this was a Christmas gift from the welfare department or simply from Stanley's own pocket is not known.

By April 1936, after more than a year, he was accepted as eligible to receive a blind pension. However, an entry the following month showed that his pension had been "held up in Washington." For some reason, Davis was not accepted for aid to the blind under the North Carolina State Commission for the Blind until July 1937, when a letter was written to him requesting that he file a formal application.[24] The rather unusual action of writing to a blind man can be understood in the light of one caseworker's experiences. "Visits have been made to the home but in view of the fact M. is a blind musician who plays a guitar on the streets and in public places he is always found outside the home."[25]

On July 13, 1937, Davis was examined by Dr. T. C. Kerns of McPherson Hospital, who confirmed that he had been blind since birth in both eyes. His further findings presumably led to Davis being accepted for an award under aid to the blind.

Eye condition primarily responsible for blindness.	Buphophtholmus
Secondary conditions.	Ulceration of cornea
Etiological factor responsible for primary eye condition.	Glaucoma
Prognosis.	Hopelessly blind
Remarks.	No need for another examination.[26]

The initial report on Davis by his first blind commission caseworker in the same month is enlightening: "M. has no income. When questioned about income, M. stated, 'They don't allow me to solicit.' . . . M's philosophy seems to be woven around his religious inclinations. Was ordained two months ago as a minister in Washington, N.C. Attends Mt. Vernon Baptist Church and is greatly concerned about 'work concerning saving souls.' He 'abstains from things that cause him to make errors in life.' Much ability is shown in his steel guitar which would be a source of income, but it appears that M. has scruples against this type of endeavor. When questioned about the guitar as a means of income, M. stated that he does not play the kind of music that meets public appeal since he became Christianized."[27]

That may well have been the case since his ordination but earlier, in 1935 if not later, he was well remembered by Orange County musicians, who often saw him on the streets or at warehouses.

About this time, by his own admission, Davis was playing blues. "Oh, yeh, I was a 'blues cat' then. What I mean by 'blues cat' is that I played blues and blues and blues again and again. I would go to parties, dances and things like that. Chittlin' struts and all that kind of stuff."[28] Willie Trice carried Davis to those parties in Orange County in his old T Model Roadster, along with Willie's girlfriend from South Carolina, where he was working on highway construction. They'd stayed all day, Davis had been in one of his querulous moods, and Willie had been somewhat uneasy. Ever loyal, he explained that Davis "had spells with his head, you know . . . he was taking B.C.'s then . . . he'd been drinking blackberry wine, that's what it was." Quick to recommend Davis's playing, Willie mused, "I never played with Gary but he let me use his guitar."[29]

Willie Trice recalled that the second time he met Davis "he just left a little party. . . . He had an old wooden guitar. The songs he played was mostly spiritual songs. He could play the others but he didn't do it often. He could play that guitar just like Joshua White, yes sir."[30] Willie also remembered that Davis could play piano. He carried him one day down to his home, which served as a country juke joint by the name of the Shady Rest, run by an uncle. "We had a piano in there. It was a dance hall then. We had a piano sitting over there in the corner and somebody hit a note on the piano and Gary says, 'Ain't that a piano?' I said, 'Yes,' and led him over to it. And he played the piano—played the same song he played on the guitar—sounded just like it. He liked an instrument he could carry with him." The piano belonged to the family of Duncan Garner, one of the best pianists in Durham, who eventually worked shows and vaudeville, actually appearing in a sketch at the Wonderland Theater in Durham in which Dewey "Pigmeat" Markham, one of the better-known black entertainers from those circuits, made his stage debut. One evening the Garner family returned home to find their piano missing, and presumably it was never recovered. That day, Duncan, Willie, and others had removed it by truck and taken it to the Shady Rest. There had been a piano at 410 Poplar where Davis lived.

Somewhere between 1932 when Willie Trice first knew him and 1937 when James Bailey, his perceptive blind commission worker, filed his initial report, Gary Davis had given up drink and moved wholeheartedly into the church. Perhaps this is why he was never anxious to talk at length of his earlier, preordination days. At his 1935 recording session J. B. Long had volunteered the information that "they'd give (them) beer to drink but (Gary) didn't want any liquor."[31] The date of the ordination has been given as 1933 in the past, but in a 1965 interview Davis stated that it was about 1936.

Interviewer:	Were you *Reverend* Gary Davis before you met Fuller?
Davis:	No.
Interviewer:	You were ordained after you met him?
Davis:	That's right.
Interviewer:	Could you give us any idea of when it was, about?
Davis:	Well it must be nearabouts as I can get it 39 years ago.
Interviewer:	Thirty-nine years ago?
Davis:	When I was ordained in Washington, North Carolina.[32]

James Bailey's report of July 21, 1937, mentioned that Davis had been ordained "two months ago . . . in Washington, N.C.,"[33] thus placing the date in May or at the very latest in early June 1937.

During the summer of 1939 there was considerable correspondence with reference to Davis obtaining a "Talking Bible," a set of records made especially for the blind. When the caseworker went to see him about this in December 1939, she found him "feeling rather badly." In the summer, prior to Fuller's Memphis session, J. B. Long had contacted Davis about recording again, but Davis had refused to go. Quite probably Long had contacted him as he felt that he might not be able to get Fuller to go if the welfare department was able to help Fuller transfer to another recording company, as seemed possible at one time. Long must certainly have been desperate, for Davis and he did not work together well. Davis's report stated that "worker learned that (he) had been offered a trip to New York during the summer to make records, but because he was not to be paid as much as he felt he was worth, he refused to go. He had learned subsequently that Blind Fuller received

$450 for his first trip and since he was offered only $40, or a possibility of $120, he did not feel that he should accept the offer."[34] One can appreciate that Davis felt he should be paid as much as Fuller, although $10 per performance (assuming that to have been Long's offer) was almost certainly what Long would have been empowered to offer to an effectively unknown artist, one whose earlier records on ARC had not sold. Certainly Fuller received nothing like Davis's suggested $450; indeed, the $225 that Long informed the welfare authorities that Fuller received is only half Davis's wishful thinking. The fact that Davis felt he was being misused might account for his wild overestimation of Fuller's receipts. In retrospect, Long's offer seems well in line with prevailing offers; Fuller, an established artist, was receiving under $20 per title. Davis must have been near the peak of his ability, so our loss can only be guessed at.

Davis was now beginning to spend more and more time away from home, often at revival meetings. In the summer of 1940 his caseworker reported that he "has stopped playing his guitar on the streets for money and claims to be a minister of the gospel."[35] The following summer, one of the workers called at his home "and found that he was still attending the Revival Meeting in Raleigh. He comes home every night with one of the 'Brothers' and he is not preaching. He gets his transportation and meals for going. (His landlady said) . . . 'His mind runs backwards, you know, and I believe it's because he has just thought about the Bible and Religion too much. . . . He sometimes wakes me up at two or three o'clock coming to bed, falling over a chair. He sits up and reads his Bible that late.' . . . He had actually caught fire one time, she said, and they had just seen him in time."[36]

His grant of twenty-four dollars, first given in July 1937, remained the same until June 1941, when the county was "averaging too much per grant," and his sum was reduced to twenty dollars. The cut brought an immediate response, and a student worker, Evanell Thomasson, caught his wrath: "'What I want's to know is how you expect me to live on that much money!' . . . He added that we had stopped him preaching and singing on the streets—and that since God had called him he just had to preach—and that he had to keep himself a little presentable so that he could do that. He said that people did not give him money for preaching like they used to because they knew that he got a grant and that they felt like he had as much as they did. . . . That started Gary on a sermon about being prepared to die. He took his text from 'Be ye also ready—' [*sic*] and went into a detailed sermon on trying to stay ready so that when your time came you could take your flight to glory."[37] If matters hadn't quite reached that point, the summer of 1941 was tough for the whole Davis household, and even Mary Hinton was found eligible for food stamps in August 1941.

Davis's inspiration at this time was probably reflected in his playing, to listen to the account of yet another student welfare worker, Laura Miller. In November 1941 she finally managed to find him at home, having called previously when he was playing either in Raleigh or Fuquay Springs. Davis was annoyed because he had remained at home all morning to see her but she didn't come until the afternoon. "He said that he understood but that he had to keep going because he was a preacher and had to try to save souls. . . . I asked Gary about his guitar; I'd seen him come in with it and wondered if he had been playing somewhere. He admitted he had been out playing but wouldn't say where. He said he would play for me if I wished and I urged him to play me a number. His ability as a guitarist is unbelievable. I have never heard better playing." Later, in her report, Mrs. Miller posed the question that so many others had done: "I wonder if he might be playing around some times to pick up a little change."[38]

In April 1942 he came into the welfare office to meet yet another caseworker who noted that "Gary said he was going down to a barber shop to play his guitar that day. Worker explained to Gary again that it would be necessary for him to stay within the barber shop rather than on the street for if he were to be on the street that would be begging and that it would be against the law. He replied that he understood this to be true and that he did not go on the street playing his guitar . . . his lack of hearing was the only thing holding him back from securing a regular preaching position."[39]

In December 1943 Davis married a Wake County woman and moved to Raleigh. In January 1944 he moved to the East Bronx in New York, living at 405 E. 169th Street, and continued to receive aid to the blind checks from North Carolina for a year. As of January 1944 he was henceforth considered to be a resident of New York.

Davis made one return trip to Durham during a very cold spell in February 1948, when he fell on the ice and "sprained" his wrist. He was again staying with Mary Hinton, who made an appointment for him to see a doctor and bought a ticket for his return to New York, using money that his wife, Annie, had sent. An X-ray was taken at Duke Hospital on February 9. He remembered the incident. "That was in North Carolina. I was carrying on a revival and I slipped down. I was going along one night and there was snow on the ground. . . . I didn't know it was broken until I went to a doctor the next morning . . . I lost the use of that hand a long time. I thought I was never going to play again—but I did!"[40] A revival is the most likely reason for his return to North Carolina in 1948 and there had been a heavy fall of snow at the time, delaying the welfare department, which took six days to answer Mary Hinton's call for help.

Whatever the event, Gary Davis's career now belonged to New York.

NOTES

1. All references in Davis's files held by the Durham County welfare authorities and the North Carolina Commission for the Blind give his date of birth as April 30, 1895. Eighteen ninety-six was first reported by Stefan Grossman, *Rev. Gary Davis* (New York: Oak Publications, 1974), p. 7. On his first wedding certificate (1919) Davis's date of birth is given as 1896. Robert Tilling to the author, July 17, 1980, and August 22, 1983.

2. File 282, Gary Davis, statement of James Whitaker, 716 Willard St., dated July 21, 1937; file 7380, Gary Davis, December 11, 1934.

3. File 282, July 21, 1937; Gerard J. Homan, "Rev. Gary Davis: The Early Years," *Blues World* 42 (Spring, 1972): 9, gives 1925 as the year Davis left South Carolina.

4. Kip Lornell, "Albany Blues, Part 2," *Living Blues* 15 (Winter, 1973–74): 26. Pink Anderson saw Davis in Mt. Holly near Charlotte in 1922–23 and in Asheville.

5. File 282, April 4, 1931. Davis learned "Bad Company Brought Me Here" from crippled Wilson guitarist Fate Locus. Richard Noblett, Stephen Rye, John Offord, "The Reverend Gary Davis," in *Nothing But the Blues,* ed. Mike Leadbitter (London: Hanover Books, 1971), pp. 218–19.

6. File 282, July 16, 1931.

7. Willie Trice, interviewed by the author, Orange County, North Carolina, September 23, 1972, and August 5, 1970.

8. Glenn Hinson, interviewed by the author, Durham, North Carolina, August 8, 1978.

9. File 7380, Gary Davis, December 11, 1934.

10. File 7380, December 11, 1934, December 13, 1934.

11. Hugh Penn Brinton, "The Negro in Durham" (Ph.D. diss., University of North Carolina at Chapel Hill, 1930), pp. 207–8.

12. File 7380, possibly January 21, 1935, but before May 1, 1935, when the case was transferred to the Federal Emergency Relief Administration.

13. Ibid., July 15, 1935.

14. File 7380, December 13, 1934.

15. File 55, Gary Davis, July 3, 1935.

16. Ibid., May 9, 1935.

17. File 7380, July 12, 1935.

18. Gary Davis, interviewed by S. T. Rye and R. A. Noblett, Romford, England, June 18, 1965. Transcript in author's collection.

19. Grossman, *Rev. Gary Davis,* p. 9.

20. File 282, July 21, 1937.

21. Ibid., undated but probably 1944.

22. Ibid., July 17, 1939. This was only five days after Blind Boy Fuller had recorded in Memphis, the session which Long had tried to persuade Davis to attend. Fuller can only have been back in Durham a day or so, as the session lasted three days.

23. Ibid., April 1937.

24. Ibid., July 1937. The letter has an underlined note, "Will be delivered by hand," and ends "With best wishes for your health and happiness, we are, Sincerely yours, Department of Public Welfare." With few exceptions, this is the tone of the department's dealings at all times in all observed files over some twenty years. Certain workers like James H. Bailey, Jr., showed efficiency and genuine concern.

25. Ibid., April 1937.

26. Ibid., July 13, 1937.

27. Ibid., July 21, 1937.

28. Grossman, *Rev. Gary Davis,* p. 12.

29. Willie Trice, September 23, 1972.

30. Bruce Bastin, "Willie Trice: North Carolina Bluesman, Part 2," *Talking Blues* 9/10 (1979): 12–13.

31. Kip Lornell, "J. B. Long," *Living Blues* 29 (September-October, 1976): 16.

32. Gary Davis, June 18, 1965.

33. File 282, July 21, 1937.

34. Ibid., December 11, 1939.

35. Ibid., July 12, 1940.

36. Ibid., probably May 15, 1941.

37. Ibid., probably July 29, 1941.

38. Ibid., November 3, 1941.

39. Ibid., April 13, 1942.

40. Grossman, *Rev. Gary Davis,* p. 16. However, on p. 125 Grossman states that "during his youth Rev. Davis broke his left wrist (the story of this incident is recounted in the interview) and it set in an unusual position. The hand was set somewhat to the left of the axis of the arm. This allowed him to play many unorthodox and difficult chord positions." In the interview (p. 16) Davis clearly states he broke his "right hand wrist. That was in North Carolina." Either Grossman made an error in transposing Davis's broken right wrist as an adult—he did not live in North Carolina in his youth—to his younger days, and to a different wrist, or he is mixing two different events. The former is more probable, as in the interview, Davis, in reply to Grossman's "Did you ever put down the guitar?" answered, "Well, for three years I didn't have no guitar, that's when I was a boy. There was a time also when I broke my right hand wrist. That was in North Carolina." In a letter to the author (July 10, 1985), Grossman stated that Davis's "left hand was definitely disfigured [which] resulted in some unorthodox chord fingerings that are especially noticed in his key of G arrangements, i.e. Samson and Delilah, Let Us Get Together. In

the 30's he did NOT [*sic*] record anything in G except for LORD SEARCH MY HEART which does not use these fingerings as it is played in G7 in the first position." Grossman also states here that he "felt that it was in the 40's that the left hand wrist was broken." The discrepancy remains, for Davis stated his right wrist was broken in North Carolina. Although the confusion may never be resolved, it is intriguing to contemplate Davis's virtuosity as a guitarist being partially the result of a childhood accident.

15

Brownie McGhee and Sonny Terry

Probably the best known bluesman to emerge from the Carolinas was actually born in Tennessee and didn't move to North Carolina with any permanence until the late 1930s, when he was in his mid-twenties. Walter Brown McGhee, known always as "Brownie," was born in Knoxville on November 30, 1914. At least, he'd always been led to assume that was the year of his birth, but the family Bible, on the fly-leaf of which all family data as to births and deaths had been entered in true rural tradition, had been lost in a fire. It was not until he applied for a passport to travel to England in 1958 that he discovered that the official date of birth was given as 1915.

Brownie's father, George Duffield "Duff" McGhee, worked as a farmer and a common laborer. He was a good worker and was taken on contract work by a construction firm, so he followed the jobs. Thus Brownie was born in Knoxville while his brother Granville was born two years later in Kingsport. He vividly remembered Kingsport more than sixty years later, for his father helped build the town. When they first moved there, they had no running water and had to rent use of a well for twenty-five cents a month. Brownie recalled that he "used to graze cows for twenty five cents a week on what is now called Broad Street."[1]

The McGhee family was musical. Brownie's father sang and played blues, and his mother had an old hand-cranked Victrola on which he heard records by Bessie Smith and Lonnie Johnson. Also, the family was fond of Jimmie Rodgers; "we had all of his records." Whenever his father's friends came round for a party or to play cards, the children were packed off to bed, but they heard the records when they were pretending to be asleep. Duff McGhee would play guitar at corn shuckings and country parties; he even played with a mixed group in which he was the vocalist, and Brownie clearly remembered that "my daddy did reels, rags and call sets." Brownie's uncle, John Evans, played fiddle at similar gatherings much in the mountain tradition. Evans fashioned Brownie's first instrument, a five-stringed banjo made from a marshmallow tin with a neck of seasoned poplar. Brownie himself made an instrument out of a Prince Albert tobacco tin and rubber bands when he was very young. Also, his father once bought him a toy ukulele. "My father always figured I had some rhythm."

Both boys went to school in Kingsport. Brownie graduated from Frederick Douglass High School in 1936, but Granville left in the ninth grade to take a job. One reason for Brownie's late graduation was that as a child he contracted poliomyelitis, which left him with a severely shortened right leg. As he could not walk fast enough to keep up with his friends, his brother made him a little cart in which to push him, until everybody stopped and Brownie could get out and join them. The cart was guided by a stick and Granville soon became known as "Stick" McGhee.

Unable to play as freely as other children, Brownie turned to music. In 1929 the family—without their mother, who had separated from Duff in 1922—moved into the country, where Brownie began to learn to play on the piano his father had bought for one of Brownie's sisters. The last few years during which he was in high school were musically very formative. There was plenty of music of all types to be heard in the country where he lived. "There was nothing out there but guitars and banjos, a few French harps [harmonicas], jews harps, and so on. . . . I had some cousins there who played pretty good hillbilly music. . . . Feller came out of North Carolina in one of my last years in high school. I never will forget him . . . called him T. T. Carter. He was a very good blues player.[2] During the 1930s, while still playing piano, he concentrated on learning to play guitar and molding a personal style. In his early years he finger picked, but in 1933-34 he learned to play with thumb and finger picks.

While still in high school Brownie played and sang for the Solomon Temple Baptist Church in Lenoir and with a gospel quartet, the Golden Voices, in Kingsport. He even began performing on weekends and during vacations for the white visitors at the summer resorts and the

Smokey Mountain Hotel. This taste for entertainment set him on his career once he left school. His instrument was by now the guitar— "fella can't carry a piano around on his back"—and he played "'most anywhere—picnics, dives, minstrel shows, even in buses and trains."[3] "I'd just go along the highway with my guitar over my shoulder, thumbing my way. An' when I got tired of thumbing in one direction, well, I'd just go 'cross the road and thumb my way back! . . . Up and down the roads, Virginia, Tennessee, North Carolina . . . that was my education."[4]

Brownie's mobility had been greatly increased by an operation on his crippled leg, performed in Knoxville General Hospital as part of President Roosevelt's March of Dimes campaign. Brownie was in the hospital for nine months; the operation was a considerable success. On separate occasions he recalled that "for nineteen years I had walked with a crutch and a cane and in 1937, I rid myself of that crutch and cane. I nearly took to hitch-hiking. . . . Today instead of having my foot five inches from the ground it's an inch and a quarter."[5]

For a while he continued to play around Sullivan County's Kingsport, often playing white country music—Stick playing guitar with Brownie on piano. They were joined by Lesley Riddle, who played guitar, mandolin, and piano and ran a successful venture working the riverboats for white drinking parties. Sullivan County was dry. Later Brownie recalled that Stick used to dance along with "a couple of girls with short dresses on" while Brownie and Lesley Riddle provided the music.

Despite the generally impoverished times of the 1930s, Brownie survived well, based for a while in Knoxville, where he ran two juke bands playing local engagements at roadhouses, jukes, and parties from his "Brownie's Alley." Obviously the band personnel varied as much as the instrumentation, but the units usually comprised two guitars, a string bass, possibly harmonica, and two washboards, "one on the belly, one on the horse," meaning that one washboard was played laid flat across the lap while another musician used two washboards strapped to a structure rather like a sawhorse, which he straddled as he played. One wonders if one of the units employed might have been the Tennessee Chocolate Drops, which included bluesmen Carl Martin and Howard Armstrong, who had recorded in Knoxville for Vocalion in 1930. Other known bluesmen certainly played in Brownie's bands. Leroy Dallas, an itinerant Alabama guitarist and singer who played regularly around Atlanta with a similar aggregation, the Star Band, played washboard in the Alley bands. He later moved to New York and recorded commercially in 1949, with Brownie backing him on guitar. Another washboard player was Robert Young, usually known as Washboard Slim, who was later to travel with McGhee and record with him in 1941. One of the harmonica players whom Brownie used was Eli Jordan Webb, originally from Nashville, then in his thirties. Clearly an itinerant, like so many black musicians in the 1930s, Webb moved to the rich tobacco town of Winston-Salem, North Carolina, and settled down. By chance, Webb was with Brownie when they were introduced to J. B. Long, who arranged for them to record in 1941.

By 1938 Brownie was on the move again, touring through the small townships of Tennessee, West Virginia, and western Virginia, often playing in coal-mining towns where the only effective currency was company scrip—credit notes which could only be traded for goods at company stores. A circular route from Bristol through Virginia to Winston-Salem brought Brownie to Jordan Webb's home town. Here the Reynolds tobacco firm, home of Camel cigarettes of GI fame, dominated the urban landscape. Brownie found plenty of work there, planning his own factory circuit to play for operatives when they came off shift. Presumably Webb played with him on occasion; a talented stonemason by all accounts, he was also a fine harmonica player. According to Brownie there was a city ordinance against begging on the streets. A search of city records in 1970 unearthed no formal legislation; perhaps, as in Durham, specific police permission was required to play on the streets, especially if it was likely to cause an obstruction. Good performers are always likely to draw a crowd, and possibly Brownie was considered a nuisance. Whatever the reason, a policeman asked him to leave town, which he did. However, he returned and was caught, spending a while in the city jail before talking himself out of a prolonged stay by leaving town for good. Jordan Webb elected to accompany him, and they left the tough neighborhood of the 11th Street "Bottom," the "Pond," and the corners of Fourth and Vine and Seventh and Patterson, which had provided McGhee with a steady income. It is remarkable to think that little more than a decade earlier Blind Boy Fuller had played the very same area and lived on Seventh and Chestnut—remarkable because Brownie's move took him to the very man who had made Fuller a household name among black record buyers and who was to launch Brownie on his recording career. In fact, some 1940s releases credit Brownie as "Blind Boy Fuller No. 2."

Brownie and Jordan Webb headed slowly eastward through Greensboro to Burlington, where they stayed in the local "black bottom." Through local blues players—Richard and Willie Trice and Buddy Moss—Brownie met Blind Boy Fuller's washboard player, George "Red" Washington, who introduced him to J. B. Long.

Brownie has never ceased to acknowledge that Long set him on his path to success. Likewise, Long appreciated Brownie's shrewdness and ability and called him "the smartest man I ever handled."[6]

Fuller had traveled to Chicago to record his last session in June 1940. For some time he had been very ill from the disease which was to kill him in February 1941, and it would have been clear to Long that he would have to seek a replacement blues singer. Blues singers in Chicago, however, were scarcely in small supply. Brownie graphically remembered that when Long first approached Okeh with the idea of recording him, the company told him, "Don't bother sending him up here, we got enough of them five bit blues singers."[7] Doubtless Lester Melrose had much of the scene buttoned up anyway, but Long's faith must have been strong and his influence not inconsiderable, for within two months of Fuller's session, Brownie McGhee was attending the first of innumerable recording sessions and setting himself a high standard from the beginning.

Just as he had traveled with Blind Boy Fuller and Sonny Terry, Red went with Brownie, acting as road manager. Long was determined to retain the sure-selling formula of guitar, harmonica, and washboard; Red would provide the same driving rhythm that he had brought to Fuller's records and Webb was a good enough harp player to fit Terry's role, although his playing, with its high pitch, owed more to the white country players. Four titles were cut at the initial session on August 6 and eight on the following day—a total of twelve, in keeping with Long's usual requirement per trip. Only two of those sides were never issued, although tests exist. "Step It Up and Go," covering Fuller's own version cut earlier in the year, features superb harmonica from Jordan Webb, but the balance of the washboard was perhaps too low. It was recut in 1941, without Webb, when McGhee returned to make a further dozen sides, by which time Fuller was dead. The remaining unissued title is the intriguing "Coal Miner Blues." Perhaps this is a personal song drawn from McGhee's own experience of travel among the mountain coalfields or perhaps it owes something to the song of the same title recorded by the white Carter Family.[8] A. P. Carter frequently traveled with Brownie's Knoxville friend, the light-skinned Lesley T. Riddle, in order to collect folksongs that he could work up into songs for Maybelle, Sara, and himself.[9] The whole session was a fine debut for Brownie. The first title, "Picking My Tomatoes," a jaunty, raggy piece with Red's washboard and Webb's shrill harp riffs, sets the scene nicely.[10] Long had shrewdly chosen a raggy number to commence the session, possibly because Fuller's rags always seemed to sell well, and he had lifted the number unashamedly from

Washboard Sam's "Diggin' My Potatoes," issued the previous year on Bluebird.

The majority of Fuller's June 1940 recordings had been issued in July and August, but four remained unissued by the time Brownie's were ready to be processed. Fuller's near-cracking voice on "Night Rambling Woman" was one reason for the delay. Fuller's record buyers had to be carried across to a new artist, so Brownie's "Pickin' My Tomatoes" was backed by Fuller's "Night Rambling Woman," showing a perceptive knowledge of the buying public who would be likely to purchase the record because of Fuller and perhaps come to like this new singer. In fact, Brownie's first two recordings were issued backed by titles from Fuller's last session: "Picking My Tomatoes" was issued in September 1940 and "Me and My Dog Blues" was issued in December 1940 backed by Fuller's "Bus Rider Blues." Couplings of Brownie's other titles followed at monthly intervals, so within four months of recording he had two issues on Okeh under his own name and shared two other Okeh records with Fuller. It is to Brownie's credit that no other initial releases of Fuller's records ever carried another artist on the reverse. However, Brownie's numbers actually owed little to Fuller and his lighter delivery marked a style of his own, so it is hardly surprising that when some of his records were issued—following Fuller's death—as by "Blind Boy Fuller No. 2" he was none too pleased and his father was most annoyed.

Brownie returned to Chicago in 1941, recording thirteen titles on May 22 and four gospel titles the following day under the well-tried pseudonym of Brother George and his Sanctified Singers. Aurally Jordan Webb is present at the session, and on "Key to My Door" Brownie can be heard exhorting "Slim" to play. The washboard is also Robert Young's more complicated contraption featuring cowbells and other gadgets rather than Red's regular board. Thus the Brother George trio of 1941 contained none of the men who recorded under that name in 1940.

The real reason for the precipitous return to the studio can be seen from Okeh's first release from the session, in July 1941. Although no top sides were then credited, it is obvious that the selling side was "Death of Blind Boy Fuller" by Brownie McGhee (Blind Boy Fuller No. 2). October saw a reversion, for the last time, to a coupling with a previously unissued cut by Fuller: "Key to My Door" was backed by Fuller's "Piccolo Rag." The Okeh executives must have had to search hard, for it was the only known unissued Fuller title, recorded in April 1938. By the time it was issued, Brownie was once again in the studio, this time in New York.

These October 1941 sessions included both washboard players, Robert Young and George Washington, and also both harmonica players, Jordan Webb and Sonny Terry. A most interesting addition was the Atlanta guitarist Buddy Moss, who was working for J. B. Long at the time. A number of sessions took place over two days under the names of Brownie McGhee, Buddy Moss, and Sonny Terry. This was Terry's first session since recording during the Fuller sessions, but none of his recordings were ever issued. The initial recordings of the session were by Moss, and the very first title, "You Need a Woman," was a superb solo version, his first recording in more than six years. From the first eight titles recorded by Brownie—again he recorded twelve—only two were ever issued. "Barbecue Any Old Time" is an uptempo number supported only by Robert Young on washboard, while "Workingman's Blues" added Sonny Terry to make up the old trio formula. It was the first recording to pair Brownie and Sonny. As their names are today inextricably linked, it is worth mentioning that Brownie had seen twenty-four sides issued before they teamed up on record. Oddly, the title chosen for the reverse of the disc was "Step It Up and Go, No. 2," the reworked Fuller song which had been rejected at the first McGhee session and which commenced the session in May 1941.

The following day, Thursday, October 23, saw them all back in the studio, with a very long nine-title session from Moss, who thus actually recorded one title more than Brownie. On the first two titles, "Joy Rag" and "Little Angel Blues," as well as two of the unissued titles from later in the session, Brownie harkened back to his Kingsport days and backed Moss on piano. The final title, "Unfinished Business," featured Moss alone. After Moss's run of nine titles, Brownie was back with his final four selections, for the last two of which Buddy Moss, having briefly rested, joined in on second guitar. "Back Home Blues" interestingly featured both harmonicas with contrasting styles, while "Swing, Soldier, Swing" featured both washboards and was clearly aimed at a market rather more "uptown" than the rags. The vocalist on the latter has never been identified, but aurally it is neither Moss nor McGhee.

The time and emphasis given to Buddy Moss at this recording session clearly indicate that Okeh and presumably also Long were most interested in giving Moss plenty of exposure and probably priority of place in recording. After all, Moss had been one of the best-selling blues artists of the mid-1930s for ARC and was quite evidently a superb performer. His keen intelligence and superb musicianship could so easily have placed him in a position similar to that of Brownie McGhee.

However, just when it appeared that he was likely to be able to return to his rightful place among recording blues artists, the outbreak of war proved catastrophic: within the year the Petrillo recording ban by the American Federation of Musicians closed recording studios, and the diversion of shellac to the war effort curtailed the release of records. Only an established artist, given good breaks, was going to survive. McGhee got them; Moss didn't.

Initially, Brownie's recordings from the October session were released following the usual pattern of one record per month. "Barbecue Any Old Time" and "Swing, Soldier, Swing" were issued in November. The December issue saw a reversion to the May session in Chicago for a coupling. The outbreak of war in January 1942 meant that no records were issued at all, while February saw release of the last issue for eight months, "Back Home Blues" and "It Must Be Love." With so many good sides remaining unissued due to the shortage of shellac, there was no 1942 recording session. Indeed, for almost half the year, there was no recording session for any American musician.

On August 1, 1942, James Caesar Petrillo, for the American Federation of Musicians, declared a ban on new recordings. The AFM feared that jukeboxes playing records were depriving musicians of work in bars and clubs which might otherwise employ "live" music.[11] Like all acts of generalization it was a two-edged weapon. The ban persisted until September 1943, when Decca gave in to the AFM demand of a royalty on all new recordings. Capitol followed suit in October, but Columbia and Victor held out until November 1944, when they were obliged to accede. When musicians were then able to return to the studio, popular music patterns were changing: vocalists were more significant and big bands were sliding into decline. By the mid-1940s a new range of minor, independent labels, often ignoring the process of union scale rates, had clearly seen where the new trends were leading and were getting there before the major labels even knew they existed. In the blues market especially, the major companies lost their hold and never reestablished it. In fairness, they probably cared very little. Black secular music began to be dominated by the independent producers, flexible in approach and often intuitive and visionary in a manner which the major corporations could neither match nor even tolerate. Petrillo can have had no possible concept that the action of the AFM in 1942–43 was to help revolutionize black secular music.

In early 1942, all this was far in the future for Brownie McGhee, although it was to play a very large part in his later life. In fact the events which led to Brownie's departure from the South for the attractions of the Big Apple began with John Hammond's 1938 Carnegie Hall concert, which had included Sonny Terry and Oh Red. The full story of Hammond's involvement in bringing black folk artists from North Carolina to appear at this concert is given in the following section but suffice it to say that Sonny Terry had made a very real impression on a number of persons. Someone—J. B. Long was unable to remember who—suggested that Sonny Terry attend a concert being given in the Constitutional Hall in Washington, D.C., which was to include Marian Anderson and Paul Robeson.[12] Long was unable to take time off from his shop in Burlington, and as Red had left Durham to work in the dockyards in Portsmouth, Virginia, Long suggested that Brownie should accompany Terry to the concert. Brownie backed him on stage, replacing the washboard support given by Red at the Carnegie Hall concert four years previously. While in Washington in May 1942 McGhee and Terry recorded for the Library of Congress with Huddie Leadbetter (Leadbelly); on these performances Alan Lomax, then assistant in charge of the Archive of Folk Song, announced that the recordings were made through the courtesy of John Hammond and James B. Long. Later McGhee and Terry accepted offers to play in New York.[13] Thus the famous duo was formed and they were not to return to the South for over thirty years. When they did return, it was partly in order to attend an arranged concert in Chapel Hill, where they again met Cora Mae Allen (Fuller's widow), and Richard and Willie Trice.

In 1942, with their departure from North Carolina, Long lost perhaps his last chance to plug the gap left with Fuller's death. With the war and the Petrillo ban, even Moss could not be used. By the time both were over, Long had lost all enthusiasm for trying to promote another artist. Moss was eventually to return to Atlanta, bitter about his lost opportunities and angry at their recollection. McGhee and Terry carried on as if nothing had happened. Living now in New York and playing to more fashionable audiences, they rapidly took advantage of the termination of the Petrillo ban to continue their recording career with a session for Savoy in December 1944. At their most optimistic moment they can have had no inkling where it would all lead them.

SONNY TERRY

Although today one immediately associates Sonny Terry with Brownie McGhee, they didn't meet until Terry was in his late twenties and they began to work regularly together only when Terry was in his thirtieth year. Born Saunders Terrell in Greensboro, North Carolina, on October 24, 1911, he moved later to Shelby, North Carolina, west of Charlotte.[14]

Dates of his move differ: earlier interviews suggested this was in 1915 but a very detailed interview in 1974 suggested 1922.[15] Terry certainly had vivid memories of his early days. When four or five years old he went on his father's wagon into Greensboro and saw a man playing on the street. "That fool could play too," he later recalled, "my father looked for me. . . . I done jumped off the wagon to where that man was, listening to that man play." His father played harmonica too but wouldn't buy his son one. Sonny used to play his father's in secret. He "used to come in from work, eat his supper, play four or five tunes and go to bed. I'd take a chair, reach up there and get it. I'd have to put it back cos he'd tear me up!" He was soon found out, but his mother came to his aid and asked him to play something. He played "Oh What a Beautiful City" so well that afterwards she would ask him to play it for her before she went to bed. He was later to play and sing that song as "Twelve Gates to the City" in 1940 for Okeh, one of the Brother George titles.

He heard music in Greensboro both from his father and other harmonica players: "My father worked hard but he liked to have his fun, too. He used to play harmonica at them Saturday night fish fries and some such things. He didn't never do no blues. I never heard no blues before I was about eighteen years old. He done buckdances, reels and jigs, stuff as that that you could dance to. He could play a harp with no hands, slide it along his lips. I remember seeing a fellow back then called John Map could do the same thing."[16] In 1974 he recalled two harmonica players, Melvin Mapp and his brother "Possum," who put his harmonica inside his mouth and played it. Presumably this was John Map. It appears to have been a common name among East Coast harp players. Eddie Mapp was a highly respected musician who lived a few miles east of Greensboro, Georgia; Biggar Mapps was a Jonesville, South Carolina, musician who taught Peg Leg Sam, who was also able to play harmonica inside his mouth like John Map.

When he was eleven Terry suffered an accident which seriously damaged an eye. Five years later he suffered an injury to the other eye, so that today he can see through only one eye, and then it is "like looking through a spider-web." Thus in 1927, when Terry planned to have his own farm, he was instead thrust into a new, harsh world. Although he worked a little on his father's farm—he could see just enough to plow a little when the cotton grew high—he really had only his music to fall back on. Before he lost the sight of his right eye, he had begun to play harmonica around Shelby and even played with a white group when he was about thirteen or fourteen. They used to come out to his house and pick him up, introducing him not only to

banjos, fiddles, and guitars but also to liquor. They often played fish
fries and Terry's specialty was "John Henry."

It was in Shelby that he first heard blues. "Several boys around there
played blues on their guitars. There was Slim Little John, who I played
with sometimes, and another guy called Meats Charlie. I even started
going with a woman called Dora Martin who was twenty years older'n
me. She sang the blues too. And she was a real good guitarist."[17] She
helped him learn the keys in which to play his harmonica along with
a guitar. He also broadcast over the radio in Gastonia and Charlotte
with two blues guitarists, recalling that he played numbers like "Lost
John" while they played blues like "Red River Blues." "I used to play
with a guy called Slim Littlejohn . . . a great big tall guy. Played with
a guy called Meef(?) Jolly both of them farmers. So long about Saturday night we would go to the fish fries and all play together. And ah
never forget we used to play together real smart."[18]

While Terry was living in Shelby, a number of his relatives died,
including his father, killed when his wagon and two mules were run
over by a truck-trailer which had suffered a blowout. He moved in
with his sister, Daisy, in Shelby and began playing with guitarist Bill
Leach. He also began to take off on his own and play on the streets
and at factories and warehouses in a wide circuit of small towns, and
he did his first stint with a medicine show.

"I took a job with this fellow they called Doc. He was a big, old
colored guy. He seen the way the crowds gathered around me, so one
day he asked me to join him on his medicine show."[19] The job worked
out well for a while, but eventually Doc began to cheat him. Many
years later Terry told a story about a crooked medicine show boss to
English collector Francis Wilford-Smith. Staying at Wilford-Smith's
house, Sonny noticed his white cat asleep on the floor and prodded
it with his stick, happily announcing that he could see it. Then the
memory came back to him, released by the sight of the patch of white.
He related the story, corroborated by Brownie McGhee, who had heard
it before, of how he was working for a show in the 1930s when the
boss refused to pay him what he had earned. Sonny went to get his
pistol, threatening to shoot the man. The boss didn't believe that he
could see him but forgot that he wore white trousers. Sonny promptly
shot him in the leg.[20] One wonders if it was Doc.

Terry's brother Jaboo had moved to Wadesboro, southeast of
Charlotte, and he went to visit him. Blind Boy Fuller's sisters, Annie
and Ethel, lived there, and many others of his family lived nearby in
Rockingham and Hamlet. Since Terry frequently went to town to play
at parties or on the streets at weekends, either solo or with a guitarist

like Fred Holmes,[21] it was logical that, should their visits coincide, these two blind musicians would meet. Terry remembered:

> I was playin' on one side of the street and he was on the other side. So I heard that whinin' guitar over there wailin', y'know. And he saw me over there. I had some little boy with me. . . . I said, "Go over and tell him to come over here." . . . By the time I found the one to tell him to bring him over, he had someone brought at me!
>
> So me and him got together, that was about 3:00. We played till about 6:00, and that way he first met me. He told me, he said, "Come to Durham, North Carolina." Said we may get to make a record together. I'd heard his records, y'know, and so by the seven or eight months I was there, I went on (to) Durham and got with him. I stayed with him about a year.[22]

At various interviews Terry suggested this meeting with Fuller was in 1933 or 1934, but if Terry met Fuller after he had recorded, and moved to Durham rather more than half a year later, and if Terry stayed with Fuller before he actually recorded with him in December 1937, the date of meeting was most probably early in 1937.

Fuller kept his word and introduced Terry to Long. Long remembered meeting Terry "through Fuller. He was over there playin' with him at his house. Or could it 'a been up at the warehouse? I'm not sure. I think it was over at his house."[23] It was at Fuller's house, and Terry recalled that Long "asked Fuller did he think that I was good enough to make a record. He said, 'Yeh!' That's why I liked Fuller. He's the one that got me started." In that same interview in 1974 Terry remembered that he had been unable to travel immediately to Durham with Fuller as he had to play in Fairmont, halfway between Rockingham and the coast. Terry then joined a "chief" on a medicine show around High Point and Greensboro, North Carolina, before returning to Jaboo in Wadesboro, where he played for a while. Only then did he head off for Durham.

Once there, Terry still returned to Shelby and sometimes brought Fuller with him. Terry's nephew, J. C. Burris, was born on a farm near Shelby in 1928; Burris's mother, Lou Daisy, was the sister who took Terry in after his father's tragic death. Burris recalled that he was "nine years old when Blind Boy Fuller came to the farm. I used to sit on his lap and light his pipe for him."[24]

In Durham Sonny Terry quickly became part of the music scene, although for a while he also sold liquor and worked in the factory for the blind across from Pettigrew Street, making "mattresses, bottom baskets and bottom chairs." Asked if Fuller had ever worked there Terry answered in disbelief, "Shit, no!" During the late 1930s Red used to stay at Fuller's house and sometimes played on the streets with

Terry, backing him on guitar, when Fuller was ill. Usually Terry played with Fuller on the streets and in the warehouses, but never in shops. Most money was to be made around the tobacco warehouses. Arriving at two or three in the afternoon, they could make perhaps ten dollars, enough for the week's groceries for all. They used to play south of Pettigrew, along Death Alley and Federal Street, close to Poplar, where Gary Davis lived. Like everyone, Terry had immense respect for Davis. "He was a tough man with a guitar. . . . The song I heard him sing on blues was 'Ice Pick Blues.' Man that was a killer. The guitar talked. . . . I loved him singing that song about Sampson and Delilah. Boy he could kill that." Like Willie Trice he always pronounced Davis's name as Gayree.

Soon came Terry's chance to record, and he traveled to New York just before Christmas 1937 with Fuller and Floyd Council. After that he appeared on titles from every subsequent Fuller session. By sheer coincidence, at the time when Fuller's first records with Terry as an accompanist were coming on the market, an entirely different event was being planned which was to change the direction of Terry's life. Jazz and blues enthusiast John Hammond "wanted to present a concert in New York which would bring together for the first time, before a musically sophisticated audience, Negro music from its raw beginnings to the latest jazz. The concert should include . . . country blues singers and shouters."[25]

Hammond eventually found a backer in the publication *New Masses,* which had printed examples of Lawrence Gellert's fieldwork in the Carolinas and Georgia. Hammond booked the Carnegie Hall—as Benny Goodman had played a most successful concert there—for December 23, 1938, and then set off in search of a show. Interested in Blind Boy Fuller, Hammond contacted J. B. Long and traveled down to meet him, accompanied by Goddard Lieberson, a pianist and student at the Eastman School of Music in Rochester, who was to become president of the CBS/Columbia group. They arrived to find Fuller in jail, an event about which he sang in "Big House Bound." However, as Hammond recalled, "next door lived a blind harmonica player named Sonny Terry, and as soon as we heard him play and shout his unique songs we decided he was a far superior performer. He definitely should be brought to New York for the concert."[26] Thus Fuller just missed fame from a different angle, and Terry became the first artist selected by Hammond for his famous Spirituals to Swing concert; it is just possible that if Fuller had not been in jail, they would not have met Terry.

The next artists Hammond booked were the gospel group with whom Long had commenced his recording career—Mitchell's Christian Singers. Long arranged for Red to take Terry to New York, and he accompanied Terry at the concert. In 1974 Terry reminisced that "back then" he was singing in a high falsetto voice and "didn't sing in natural voice until 1940," by which time he was recording for Okeh. Max Harrison, writing in a jazz magazine in 1967 about the recordings from the concert, described Red and Terry's "Mountain Blues" as "fascinating . . . stunted harmonica phrases and his outlandish falsetto voice coalescing into strange patterns of rhythm, colour and melody. Years later, pieces like this replaced in the affections of the blues public the sort of music represented by Ida Cox's' 'Fore Day Creep,'"[27] also recorded at the concert, on which she was backed by the traditional trumpet, trombone, and clarinet front line of a jazz band. Terry remembered it all with pride but was well aware at the time that it would have no impact upon his life down South. "It was a real nice concert. People yelled and clapped and went crazy over the music. Afterwards, me and Bull City Red took a bus back down to Durham. I commenced doing what I had always done, playing in the streets and at house parties and selling liquor."[28]

Before Red and Sonny caught the bus, Alan Lomax took Terry into the Havers Studio in New York to record on Christmas Eve, a Saturday, the day following the concert. It is not generally realised that Terry made a commercial recording session while in New York, cutting two sides for Columbia as Sanders Terry (Harmonica Player), doubtless thanks to Hammond. Clearly puzzled by the music they had recorded, Columbia issued the record in their classical series, no doubt accounting for its scarcity on collectors' shelves. Terry and Red had to wait until after Christmas for Terry to record two more solos, "Train Whistle Blues" and "New Love Blues," on December 28, at the same date as a Mitchell's Christian Singers session.[29]

The following summer Terry recorded behind Fuller in Memphis. This session resulted in him being dropped, like Fuller, from the welfare (or blind assistance) rolls. Fuller's welfare file contains a card, written to Terry's caseworker from J. B. Long, which shows not only Long's concern for his artists but also the fact that he clearly made no attempt to hide their earnings. Indeed, he obviously tried to work closely with the authorities.

Jamesville, N.C.
7-22-39

Dear Mr. Lewis,
Saunders Terry called me just after our return
from Memphis, Tennessee, and told me he had been cut
off—That is very hard to understand, as I told your
father to call me collect before we left if it was

not O.K. for him to go. Got him $25 and Fuller
what I told you, $225.00.

J. B. Long[30]

Terry went with Fuller to New York to record in March 1940, backing him on four of his blues titles and joining him to sing on the Brother
George coupling, playing harp on "Twelve Gates to the City," the song
his mother so much enjoyed. At the end of Fuller's first session on
March 5, Terry cut two sides which were issued the following month
under his own name, although Okeh was shrewd enough to add in
parentheses that he was "Blind Boy Fuller's Harmonica Player."
"Harmonica Blues" was Terry's version of "Rock Me," played and
sung solo in that high falsetto which he had used at Carnegie Hall. It
was rather odd that Long hadn't bothered to record him in Memphis,
in view of the concert the previous winter, but perhaps he had the
Columbia release in mind and did not wish to precipitate a controversy similar to that which he had provoked with Decca over Blind
Boy Fuller in 1937. For Terry's second title, Long used the same line-up
as at Carnegie Hall, adding Red on washboard. Credited to Sonny Terry
and Oh Red, "Harmonica and Washboard Breakdown" featured one
of Terry's more remarkable vocals, sung through the harp.

The pattern of recording was obviously sufficiently successful for
it to have been repeated the following day—four Fuller titles followed
by two by Terry. Remarkably, Fuller played guitar on Terry's first title,
"Harmonica Stomp," and it is quite evident that he played simply
because he wanted to play for his friend, not because Long asked him.
Fuller never otherwise recorded more than twelve titles, as the
Memphis Brother George session showed, and on no known occasion
did he back another artist. His sparse, often single-note runs drive the
number in a way that Red was unable to do alone, and, obviously carried along by the vitality and pace of the title, he joyously cried out
to Terry, "Play it now! Yeah, play!" It is one of Fuller's most successful
dance rags. The reverse side on issue was a slow "Harmonica and
Washboard Blues," which reverted to the duet of Terry and Red.
Released in May, this carried the even more explicit sub-credit in parentheses, "Blind Boy Fuller's Boys." The sides were speedily released;
half the sixteen recorded were issued in April and all were released
by June, by which time a further recording session had been planned.
Just before they left on that trip, Terry met Brownie McGhee for the
first time. "We were in Burlington . . . fixin' to leave for Chicago when
Red . . . brought Brownie around. That was the firs' time I met
Brownie. Yeah, saw him diff'rent times but we didn't start playin'
together 'til I came to New York."[31]

Fuller recorded with Terry and Red on June 19, 1940, Terry backing him on five and also singing on all four Brother George titles. In the middle of the session, Terry cut two more sides, released in August, which followed the pattern of the first coupling—one side solo and one with Red. Interestingly, all six of Terry's titles appear listed on Fuller's Okeh contract, which ran from March 4, 1940. Before the end of its one-year term Fuller was dead.

In October 1941, at the time of his accompaniments on the Brownie McGhee and Buddy Moss sessions, Sonny Terry cut four titles with Brownie's original harmonica player, Jordan Webb, with two washboard players present—Oh Red and Robert "Washboard Slim" Young. Unfortunately none were issued and no tests have survived, but the jive-sounding "What Do You Know, Joe" was entered in the company files as by Sonny Terry and Oh Red and Slim. Two washboards might seem unusual, but McGhee's "Swing, Soldier, Swing," recorded earlier that same day with both washboards present, was issued.

The outbreak of war could have meant the end of Terry's career also, had he not "got an offer to come up to Washington, D.C., to play at a school. Paul Robeson was giving it. Brownie wasn't doing nothing then so old J. B. Long told him to go along to help look after me, and maybe if they heard him they'd take him, too."[32] After the show they returned to Durham, but good fortune was with them. They were booked for a show in New York and then came a round of concerts with Woody Guthrie. This time they did not return but moved into a large house on downtown Sixth Avenue.

The rest of Sonny Terry's story properly fits the later chapter on migration to New York, and much is covered in the relevent sections dealing with Brownie McGhee. Their paths generally ran parallel, and they often recorded together with Brownie's pianist friends like Big Chief Ellis, Melvin Merritt, and Bob Gaddy, bass player Bobby Harris, and Brownie's brother, Stick. However, Terry's first sides were cut in 1944 for Moses Asch with Woody Guthrie accompanying on guitar. In 1946 a harmonica part was written into the Broadway production of "Finian's Rainbow" especially for Terry; the show opened on January 10, 1947, ran for 725 performances, and then went on the road for a further ten months. By 1955, he and Brownie were cast by Elia Kazan for Tennessee Williams's "Cat On A Hot Tin Roof" in New York's Morosco Theater, where they stayed until 1957.

The old Durham days seemed long gone, and they did not return until 1974, when they met old friends and Sonny asked to be taken round to some of the factories and warehouses outside which he had played nearly thirty years before. By that time the South had changed a good deal.

NOTES

1. Walter Brown McGhee, interviewed by Bill Millar, London, May, 1980. Transcript in author's collection. Unacknowledged McGhee quotations are from this interview.

2. Happy Traum, ed. *Guitar Styles of Brownie McGhee* (New York: Oak Publications, 1971), p. 8.

3. Tony Standish, "Sonny Terry and Brownie McGhee," *Jazz Journal* 11 (June, 1958): 3.

4. Paul Oliver, "Key to the Highway," *Jazz Monthly* 4 (April, 1958): 2.

5. Paul Crawford, "Blues Is Truth: Brownie McGhee in Conversation," *Guitar* 9 (January, 1981): 18; Traum, *Brownie McGhee,* p. 8.

6. J. B. Long, interviewed by the author, Elon College, North Carolina, March 24, 1973.

7. John Hansen to the author, December 20, 1973. The interview took place in New Zealand.

8. Archie Green, *Only a Miner* (Urbana: University of Illinois Press, 1972), p. 392, states, "We lack a precise clue as to whether the song itself was of black or white origin, although Maybelle Carter recalls it was obtained from a white man. But we do know that Negro miners came early to (Wise County)—the richest in Virginia." The Carter Family, "Coal Miner's Blues," Decca 5596 (64104-A), recorded June 8, 1938, in New York.

9. Kip Lornell, "I Used to Go Along and Help: Leslie Riddles [*sic*] Remembers Songhunting with A.P.," in John Atkins, *The Carter Family* (London: Old Time Music, 1973), pp. 34–35; Crawford, "Blues Is Truth," 18.

10. Both McGhee and Terry held Webb in high respect. McGhee recalled him as "a very good harmonica player, piano player, and singer too." Terry said, "Dance. He was everything. One man band." Long, too, had called him a one-man band. RGK [Bob Koester] and John Willhoft, "Billed Out and Bound to Go," *Jazz Report* (March, 1957): 8; J. B. Long, July 31, 1973.

11. Roland Gelatt, *The Fabulous Phonograph 1877-1977,* rev. 2nd ed. (London: Cassell, 1977), pp. 278–79; Oliver Read and Walter L. Welch, *From Tin Foil to Stereo: Evolution of the Phonograph,* rev. 2nd ed. (Indianapolis: Howard W. Sams, 1976), pp. 334–35, 397.

12. Traum, *Brownie McGhee,* p. 11, has McGhee stating that his "first professional job with Sonny Terry was with Paul Robeson in Riverside Stadium in Washington, D.C. I had met Leadbelly at this time. . . . While I was there, they made some records for the Library of Congress."

13. Millard Lampell invited him. Traum, *Brownie McGhee,* p. 11.

14. He has been named as Sanders, Saunders, and Sanford, Terry, Teddell and Terrell. On the Library of Congress disc 2491-B he was introduced as Sanders B. Terry. Early interviews place his birth "outside" or "near" Durham, North Carolina. Standish, "Terry and McGhee": 3; Samuel B. Charters, *The Country Blues* (London: Michael Joseph, 1960), p. 147. Later books and interviews state Greensboro, Georgia. I wonder if this might have been someone's initial error, repeated by all subsequent writers (including myself)

for Greensboro, North Carolina, which would have been "near" Durham. It would help to explain his eventual move to Durham and his tour with a medicine show out of Greensboro, North Carolina.

15. Sonny Terry interviewed by Glenn Hinson and Bill Phillips, Durham, October 1974. Transcript in the author's collection. All unacknowledged quotations and many facts concerning Terry are from this source.

16. Kent Cooper, ed. *The Harp Styles of Sonny Terry* (New York: Oak Publications, 1975), p. 8. This has a very full autobiography.

17. Cooper, *Harp Styles*, p. 12.

18. John Hansen to the author, December 20, 1973. Slim Littlejohn is almost certainly the guitarist, Blind Littlejohn, recalled by Greenville-Spartanburg bluesman, Baby Tate. Littlejohn died in 1969. Jolly is obviously the man named in Cooper as Meats Charlie. In the 1974 interview, his first name sounded more like Meech.

19. Cooper, *Harp Styles*, p. 17.

20. Francis Wilford-Smith to the author, March 28, 1979. Terry related it in 1960.

21. Other guitarists around Rockingham were "Jazz" McClain, James Henry Brown, and Henry Borski, according to George Nickerson, a relative of Fuller's. Nickerson's grandfather, a well-known old-time fiddler, taught Fuller to play a little. Kip Lornell, "Albany Blues, Pt. 3," *Living Blues* 16 (Spring, 1974): 30. A Rockingham singer, Wat Summers, was written into a short story by Phillips Russell: Charles P. Russell, "The Troubadour," reprinted from the *Smart Set* in *The Web-Foot Cadet* (np. nd.; about 1930).

22. Barry Elmes, "Sonny Terry and Brownie McGhee," *Living Blues* 13 (Summer, 1973): 14. Reprinted in Giles Oakley, *The Devil's Music: A History of the Blues* (London: British Broadcasting Corporation, 1976), p. 209.

23. Kip Lornell, "J. B. Long," *Living Blues* 29 (September-October, 1976): 15.

24. Tom Mazzolini, liner notes to *J. C. Burris: One of These Mornings,* Arhoolie 1075. Burris recorded in New York in 1958 with Terry and Stick McGhee.

25. John Hammond [with Irving Townsend], *John Hammond on Record, An Autobiography* (New York: Ridge Press/Summit Books, 1977), p. 199.

26. Ibid., p. 201.

27. Max Harrison, "The Spirituals to Swing Concerts," *Jazz Monthly* (November, 1967), in *A Jazz Retrospect,* ed. Max Harrison (Newton Abbot, England: David & Charles, 1976), p. 167.

28. Cooper, *Harp Styles*, p. 26.

29. Bruce Bastin and John Cowley, "Uncle Art's Logbook Blues," *Blues Unlimited* 108 (June-July, 1974): 16.

30. File 1465, Fulton Allen, July 22, 1939.

31. Standish, "Terry and McGhee": 4.

32. Cooper, *Harp Styles*, p. 26.

16

Other Blues in North Carolina

The shift from a pre-blues dance tradition to a blues tradition has been shown to have been a twentieth-century phenomenon in the southeastern states. In North Carolina and Virginia the tradition and the perseverence of older styles of music have been well documented. Both styles, pre-blues and blues, persisted in parallel in many communities, and many musicians were competent performers within both traditions. The black secular music traditions clearly responded to different socioeconomic stimuli. Whereas in Durham a strong blues tradition existed in the 1930s, in nearby Cedar Grove, Orange County, the older traditions of square dancing to string band music persisted.

Although the links and differences between these two traditions have been closely analyzed,[1] Orange County still remains a fascinating basis for closer study. For one thing, blacks have always been between a quarter and a third of the population in Orange County, and there was some slight racial mixing in music, rare or nonexistent in other regions of the state where blacks formed a greater percentage of the population. Thus strong white traditions remain reflected in aspects of the black tradition. For another, the county possessed quite distinct and separate "cells" of musicians, including both the string band tradition in Cedar Grove and a blues tradition in and around Chapel Hill, more closely identified with that of Durham. Blurring the borders of these cells are musicians like Jamie Alston, the only black member of a white country string band, who played blues guitar somewhat after the manner of Blind Boy Fuller and Carrboro-Chapel Hill musicians who were strongly influenced by the urban impact of the university and the popular string traditions of the 1930s, like the Chapel Hillbillies. Orange is also the county, other than Durham, in which the bulk of North Carolina research has been undertaken.

Before the 1920s and the advent of the phonograph record, Orange County abounded with musical talent, including many fine banjo players who more properly fit the period of pre-blues music.[2] Willie Trice's Uncle Luther, who died in 1933, was one whom Willie clearly recalled was "still playing when I was starting out. He played blues and could play rags. They didn't call them blues then, you know. . . . He called them 'reels.'"[3] Besides being an accomplished banjo player, Uncle Luke played slide guitar in open tuning like so many of his contemporaries in the transition period from pre-blues to blues. Luke's brother, Albert, played slide guitar and taught his young nephew, Willie, who even used a slide on a banjo to gain a bluesy effect. Willie's remark about reels preceding blues helps corroborate the relatively recent appearance of the latter.

Another musical family was the Masons. One of the finest banjo players by repute in the county was Duke Mason, who taught one of the remaining men, John Snipes. Duke's brother was the highly acclaimed Robert "Son" Mason. A fine twelve-string guitarist, Son usually played six-string. He settled in Durham and seldom returned to the county after Duke's death. After he retired he moved to Morrisville, Wake County, a small community between Durham and Raleigh. Duke's son, Henry, played both guitar and banjo.

Jamie Alston was also from a musical family. He was actually born in neighboring Chatham County, to the south, but moved to Orange County when he was six. His grandfather, Dave Alston, was a good banjo player and also taught John Snipes. He passed his skills on to his son, James, who became one of the best dance guitarists in the county and played regularly with John Snipes. James (Bud or Buddy to his friends) in turn passed on some of his talents to Jamie, who remembered his father "used to play guitar and I used to watch him. I learned how to play guitar when I was big enough to hold it in my lap. Daddy held the guitar and I'd stand up aside that guitar and play it. I couldn't hold it in my hands. . . . We used to play square dances."[4] Jamie's sister Minnie also played guitar.

The Baldwin family linked two of the Orange County bluesmen, Jamie Alston and *Wilbur Atwater. Will Baldwin, Wilbur's uncle, was rated by Alston and Atwater as the best banjo player in the county. He also taught John Snipes, who clearly picked up his knowledge from among the county's finest. Another Baldwin, Jamie's uncle Walker, often joined Buddy and Jamie Alston in sessions at John Snipes's house. Jamie's brother-in-law, Jim Baldwin, played a six-string tenor guitar or a banjo-guitar, performed in the early 1930s with Chapel Hill musicians like Thomas Stroud, and was rated by Jamie as the equal of Floyd Council, the only Chapel Hill musician to have been commercially recorded. Jim Baldwin died as late as October 1971 and Jamie Alston in August 1978.

Yet another Orange County musical family included folksinger and guitarist Elizabeth "Libba" Cotten, born in Chapel Hill about 1900. Her repertoire reflects the pre-blues dance pieces and tunes that were common in her girlhood. Her "unique" performance—for which she won the Burl Ives Award at the Wolftrap Theater in Vienna, Virginia, in July, 1972—is simply part of the traditional pre-blues reportoire common throughout much of the North Carolina Piedmont and to be heard in the music of Willie Trice and Wilbur Atwater of Orange County, Algia Mae Hinton of Johnson County, and Elester Anderson of Edgecombe County. Libba became a Cotten by marrying Henry, son of yet another fine banjo player and guitarist, Willie Cotten.

The strong banjo tradition does not end there. Bill *Britton, Floyd Snipes, and Mathew Hackney also played. Born in 1896, Matty also played guitar and mandolin, and his brother Cornelius played mandolin. Matty Hackney was a member of a black string band to the immediate south in Pittsboro, Chatham County. The band included Bill Henderson and sometimes another on guitar, an "Italian" on fiddle, and a banjo player.

Also from Pittsboro is Willie Brooks, whose family had lived there for years. A fine guitarist, capable of playing in any key, he plays one of two steel Nationals that he bought in the 1930s. He performs mostly blues, in a loose, improvisatory style, making up his own lyrics and often adding melody changes. Born in 1908, he too comes from the generation brought up on the changing music. From Goldston, to the southwest of Pittsboro, comes Howard Cotton, born in 1910, also from a family which has long lived in the area. He used to play banjo and still owns a guitar, which he usually plays in open tuning. He used to play parties, particularly in the 1940s, and was at one time very active in the local musical community. As the area around Pittsboro had long been dry, musicians traveled to other parts to play. Howard Cotton went to Sanford (Lee County); Willie Brooks often went to Chapel Hill, Durham, and Raleigh.

If the tradition of pre-blues music was strong in the southern half of Orange County, it was scarcely less impressive in the north, in and around Cedar Grove. Twenty-five miles from Durham, the area around Cedar Grove had a relatively poor farming population and an above-average percentage of tenant farmers, as opposed to the transient, more cosmopolitan workers in Durham.[5] This meant that in Cedar Grove the fiddle and banjo remained popular longer. Many musicians lived in nearby communities and traveled in to play at dances. These included Willie Criss (banjo-Hurdle Mills), Dink Bradshaw (banjo-Caswell), Bruin Moses (fiddle-Mebane), Minnick Poteat (banjo-Caswell), and Jimmy Nichols (banjo-Hurdle Mills). Near Browns Summitt, some ten miles north of Greensboro, were banjo players Arthur "Jelly-Roll" Smith, born in the 1890s, and the Pinnix brothers.

John Arch Thompson, his brothers, and their friends were the most important black musicians around Cedar Grove in the 1920s. Most of them were equally adept at playing both fiddle and banjo; John Arch, his brothers Jake and Walter, and a friend, Charlie White, could all double. Seven miles from where the Cedar Grove clan lived, in the Haw River area of Alamance County between Mebane and Greensboro, lived a further cell of banjo and fiddle players. Central to this group is the exceptional banjo player, Dink Roberts, who also plays guitar with a slide.[6] He was unusual in that he played blues on guitar, whereas most other banjo players (viz. John Snipes) are incapable of playing such music.

The parochial nature of these separate cells of musicians can be appreciated when it is realised that to John Snipes, Hillsboro is the nearest "big" town. It lies no more than ten miles north of Snipes's small cabin, where he has lived virtually all this century. Cedar Grove is only eleven miles northwest of Hillsboro, yet the whole Cedar Grove string band tradition was unknown to Snipes, himself a fine banjo player, much sought-after in his prime. At the time of his discovery he may well have been the most traditional of all the black banjo performers located in the area, his archaic, small, fretless banjo having an unmistakable sound.

There was a considerable overlap between white and black musicians in this music. One of the remaining Cedar Grove fiddlers, Joe Thompson, recalled that John Arch, Walter, and Jake Thompson (father and uncles respectively) "used to work around with a lot of white folks, just like it is in Cedar Grove now. Somehow they came in contact with Mr. Emp Wright and Mr. Bal Satherfield. They were extremely big-time fiddle and banjo players. That's who learned my daddy. After they got learned, then they started taking them to dances. . . . That was when my daddy was young, around eighteen or nineteen years old [he was born in the 1890s]."[7] John Snipes recalled only one fiddler with whom he played, and he was white. A white man also fixed his banjo, obtained about 1920 from his brother, Floyd Snipes. Willie Trice, born 1910, recalled a white father-son fiddle-guitar duet with whom he used to play when a young man; they lived on the adjoining farm. He never clearly recalled the name but it might have been Satterfield, perhaps a relative of the man mentioned by Joe Thompson.

By the 1930s two bands which added depth to this intriguing area of black-white musical interaction were performing around Chapel Hill. Carey Lloyd's white string band used black guitarist Jamie Alston, and the Chapel Hillbillies, a black group which played mostly for the white student body in Chapel Hill, included a fluctuating group of musicians. The cornerstone members were George Letlow (banjo, mandolin, and guitar), Tommy Stroud (guitar, mandolin, and banjo), Leo Stroud (percussion), and Albert Paylor (washboard). Other members included Albert's brother, James Paylor, on guitar, the Strouds' brother Clyde on tenor banjo, and J. T. Powell on string bass. Floyd Council was added for black functions, but apparently he brought a bluesier touch to the band, for he was absent from the usual fraternity functions. As a group, the Hillbillies survived well into the 1950s; a photograph from about 1955 shows at least a three-piece band, with a string bass player and Willie Hargraves on sax, performing for a white party.[8] They also played for white non-campus parties, including (well-paid) ones for C. A. Penn, then heir to the Lucky Strike tobacco fortune, and for Chapel Hill professor Paul Green, president of the National Folk Festival Association in the 1930s and noted for his plays portraying blacks in a folk setting.

According to Letlow, the Hillbillies came close to recording, probably in 1937. J. B. Long heard them and expressed an interest in recording them for the American Record Corporation. Their sort of music was popular throughout the 1930s, whether it was the corny music of the Hoosier Hotshots, who recorded for ARC among other companies, or the jazz-oriented, washboard-led groups of the Washboard Rhythm Kings, or even the guitar, mandolin, and bass trio from Raleigh, the popular Tobacco Tags, a white group that played over WPFT and, in 1937, added members from another local group, the Swingbillies, and thus broadened their musical base.

Letlow claimed that Floyd Council prevented the Chapel Hillbillies from recording, suggesting to Long that he be recorded instead. We will never know because neither Long nor Council gave a very clear account of how Council came to record; perhaps Letlow was referring to the February 1937 session when Council first accompanied Fuller to New York. But at all times Council was a highly respected musician. As late as 1973, when he was ill—a pathetic figure following a number of strokes—he was "Mister Floyd" to the neighborhood children and still treated with reverence by Gallie Farrington, a younger black harmonica player who lived nearby.

In and around Orange and Durham counties there was naturally a strong blues tradition, by no means solely marked by those few bluesmen who recorded. Jamie Alston remembered, "I used to go out to Chapel Hill and White Cross, play the club there."[9] At White Cross he played in Carey Lloyd's white string band, but he would also travel into Hillsboro and Durham to see and hear other musicians, trying to learn their tunes. Not all of his apparent copying came from either record or the seemingly obvious artist. One of his favorite pieces was "Step It Up and Go," one of Blind Boy Fuller's best-known numbers. Alston greatly admired Fuller and played a steel National guitar until his death in 1978, so one might be excused for presuming it was Fuller's version that he played. Presumption it would have been, for Alston was unaware of Fuller's recording. He learned quite a different version from Jim Price, a white country warehouse performer in Hillsboro. Alston's version is closer to white versions, such as that of Sam McGee.[10]

While Alston's repertoire reflects a broad background, some of it white, such ethnocentric differences are usually lost on the performers, for whom they are simply part of a traditional fabric, never totally fixed and always open to amendment in true folk tradition. *Wilbur Atwater's numbers are similar excellent examples.[11] A quiet, introspective man, Atwater was also from a musical family. Born on May 8, 1905, he has lived all his life in the southern section of Orange County, within a mile or so of where he lives now. Many in his family played instruments. *Rufe Atwater played fiddle; brother Tom, harmonica, and sister Betty, who played piano, married Charlie Farris, a guitar and harmonica player. His mother married again to banjo player Will Baldwin, whose brother Walker played both mandolin and guitar. Another Baldwin, *Dallas, plays guitar and lives out in the country. I was never able to meet him, for he was always "up the road." The Alston and Atwater clans, linked in marriage, were by no means all.

Tom and *Weldon *Rhodes played harmonica and John Snipes recalled another harp player who moved to Durham, Charlie *Poole. Snipes also recalled a guitarist from Chatham County who moved into the area, Johnny Minor. The name is well known in Chapel Hill as two pianists, brothers Jack and Junior Minor, played there. Another pianist was Dump Fair, still resident in Chapel Hill, who used to play guitar when younger, and Sam Perry, yet another pianist, died there about 1970.

In the rural eastern section of Orange County, close to Durham, lived another musical family. Richard and Willie Trice recorded in the 1930s, but the family was far broader. Luther (Luke) was one of three uncles who all influenced young Willie—Richard, being younger, came under the influence of his brother and Fuller. A paternal uncle was Albert Trice while Clarence Couch was a maternal uncle—both men guitarists.

> They was different. Albert . . . used a slide, a bottleneck, when he played some of his spiritual songs. I started out under him [about 1919]. . . . My uncle Clarence, my mother's brother, he used a knife. He could make some pretty music. He'd play that all out on the strings. My grandfather, her daddy, could play with all his fingers. He'd play notes, learned notes. [He could read.] He played guitar, never banjo. . . . My daddy, he raised tobacco then. We went down to a barn-raising and he had a little red guitar. He played spirituals; that's all he played. . . . My Uncle Albert had a guitar, large as a Gibson. He gave it to my daddy and she [Willie's mother, Lula Mae Couch] played. . . . She could play and when she got to pickin' we'd all sit on the floor. I said I had to get me one. . . . Yes, sir, she used to play.[12]

Second guitarist to Albert Trice was Bud Johnson, senile and mentally ill in 1970, but a fine player in his day. Marvin Lynn, a cousin of sorts to Willie, was in his estimation one of the finest guitarists in the region. He moved to New York, where he died in 1968, aged over seventy. Other cousins, all Trices, also played. Sandy was a competent blues guitarist, Ben played washboard and piano, Henry also played washboard but not so well. Mager, for whom Willie raised a number of crops in the 1930s, was also a good guitarist. Born in 1888, Mager would have played in the older style of, say, Albert Trice, but was no longer able to play when I met him.

As well as knowing the significant Durham bluesmen who recorded, the Trices also knew the other local bluesmen. Willie had known Floyd Council for seven years before Floyd recorded: "I met Floyd in Chapel Hill. The next time I see'd him was up in the country here. He played at a party with someone who played banjo and trap-drum. That was in 1930. Floyd was good then. They played around for parties, just the two of them."[13] Council's partner was almost certainly one of the Stroud brothers, most probably Tommy, who played in the Chapel Hillbillies. Even after they recorded in 1937, the Trice brothers continued to play with other more obscure local men. Willie played in a trio with guitarist Tom Rivers and washboard players C. T. "Babe"

Bennett, both of whom moved into the church. Rivers now lives in Washington, D.C., whereas Bennett remains in Durham and is in no way ashamed of his musical past.

In 1946 Richard moved to New Jersey, living in Summit, working for a storage company. He teamed up with a South Carolina guitarist, Lester Jackson, and the two began playing locally. On October 22, 1946, in New York City Richard recorded four sides for Savoy Records, two of which were issued as by Little Boy Fuller—not Richard's idea.[14] Actually, he plays more in the style of his brother than of Blind Boy Fuller. The recordings were very much in the country blues tradition at a time when country blues was not supposed to be commercially viable, but one should notice just how many country bluesmen from the East Coast states recorded in the greater New York area in the 1940s and early 1950s. In fact, Richard was called back to the Savoy studios on September 25, 1947, to cut four more titles, which included "Blood Red River Blues" and a remake of his Decca title, "Trembling Bed Springs Blues," which Richard did not know had ever been issued. All four have been recently issued on album.[15]

By 1948 Richard was back in Durham, once more teamed up with his brother. Together with local pianist James Horton they cut a sample 45 at radio station WTIK Durham for a white Californian named Tommy Little. A record on the Colonial label, seemingly of North Carolina origin, by Tommy Little and his Sunrise Rangers is a bluesy "High Geared Daddy" in the manner of Bill Carlisle. Perhaps this was Little's label, and perhaps the Trices' "Bed Springs Blues" and "Federal Street Boogie" were issued. Willie recalled that they had copies—whether pressings or acetates was never known—but that "the women-folks" got them. In 1952 or 1953 they again recorded "Federal Street Boogie," this time using Washboard Sam in support—the man Richard claims went to record with Fuller in Columbia in 1938. Only intended for their own use, the disc was lost. About this time, Richard gave up playing blues and moved toward the church. Willie looked around for a second guitarist and found him in John Dee Holeman. Born about 1930, Holeman was a far smoother musician; he also played with Arthur Lyons. Today he plays electric guitar with the light-skinned, jazz-influenced pianist, Quentin "Fritz" Holloway.

Willie Trice had given up playing in the mid-1960s until coaxed back by Pete Lowry in 1969. In the years until his death in December 1976, he practiced constantly, reworking his old material and writing new numbers, as well as recalling many early tunes. Having lost both legs through diabetes, he used playing as therapy, and in those last years he recorded enough that his place in recorded blues can be evaluated far more accurately than by those two meagre sides made in 1937.[16] He was a fine folk musician in the truest sense.

THE NORTH AND NORTHEAST

From the counties to the north and northeast of Durham and Orange County comes evidence of a similar spread of both pre-blues black secular music and blues, at least throughout the Piedmont region. Whether these traditions are as true of the coastal regions or the mountain region can only be conjectured. Brief studies from Edgecombe and Caldwell counties seem to justify the generalization. Edgecombe County, which has some claim to be part of the coastal complex, is a county with a heavier ratio of blacks to whites. Further generalization on the coastal region might be invalid, for no research has ever been undertaken, but if parallels with Virginia may be drawn, general premises will be found valid. The mountain region poses differences if only because black communities are few and the general number of blacks small. The Caldwell County black musicians are actually from a close-knit extended family group resulting from mixed marriages, but their approach to pre-blues music seems wholly within the known regional framework.

There seems little reason to doubt that the counties to the north—Granville, Vance, and Person—held similarly healthy black secular music traditions. Thomas Burt, who now lives in the south of Granville County, was born near Raleigh on August 17, 1900, and raised in Durham County. His father played accordion and called figures for local set dances. About 1914 Thomas began to play banjo, on a friend's homemade instrument. After briefly playing both organ and piano, he began to play guitar and then mastered fiddle and autoharp. Two brothers and a sister played guitar and with another brother who played ukulele, they began playing first for barn dances and then for parties in and around Durham, where Thomas came to know Fuller and Gary Davis. Like many other bluesmen Thomas now only performs spirituals, often accompanied by his wife, but his guitar playing, like Gary Davis's, is heavily blues-inflected, especially when he plays slide.

From near Henderson in adjoining Vance County comes Rassie Moore, now also a member of the church. Born in the Seven Paths township of neighboring Franklin County on May 14, 1915, he grew up well imbued with the reels and blues learned from the guitar playing of his father, his oldest brother, and other sharecroppers. A preacher since 1971, he frequently carries his guitar with him to services. Another Vance County bluesman with a considerable local reputation until his death at the end of the 1930s was Scrap Harris. Thought by some informants to have been as good a musician as Gary Davis, he played a twelve-string guitar in both finger-picking and slide styles, and he also played a homemade, twin-necked guitar. He may have been the unnamed man whom Jamie Alston remembered playing in Durham during the tobacco season. His reputation as a musician was such that many locals related stories to the effect that he had sold his soul to the devil. One informant stated that his guitar had to be buried alongside him because the devil was in it; another told the more usual story of the guitar playing on the wall after his death.

Little information has come down to us from the other Piedmont counties bordering Virginia, Warren, and Halifax, but that which has fits the general pattern. Robert House, who retired as chancellor of the University of North Carolina at Chapel Hill, recalled playing in a mixed trio as a young man in Warrenton. If this seems an unlikely occupation for an esteemed university chancellor, it might be that House didn't fit the "accepted" role and quite often played harmonica to his somewhat bewildered freshmen, to help them lose their nervousness at the sudden culture shock of transfer from farm to campus. In the mixed trio, which obviously only played for white functions, his sister played piano and they used a black fiddler. His suggestion that "music didn't know any social lines" was probably more indicative of House's personal approach than of the county at large but is clearly founded on some fact. He recalled black string bands, characteristically with a fiddle-guitar-banjo format although sometimes with a harmonica, which played for country dances, both black and white, in both Warren and Halifax counties. They played square dances and old-style quadrilles, with the specific dance etiquette of the period. He also recalled black accordion players in Halifax County, all now deceased, who played "tunes that you couldn't dance to."[17] Black accordion players were quite common: in the 1970s Kip Lornell located many, especially in Virginia but also in Chapel Hill, although in the community the music was played solely for the church. Among other Halifax County musicians who played for dances was banjo player Sid Dunstan, originally from Chapel Hill, whose brother Tom was town barber.

The bulk of the research undertaken outside Durham and Orange counties has been in a group of counties to the east of Raleigh—Edgecombe, Pitt, Wilson, and Nash. These extend along the Piedmont shelf—more conveniently Interstate Highway 95—into Halifax and Northampton counties and across into Virginia. Isolated and sometimes locally interlinked investigation has determined the same dualism in secular music: the early music of the reels and square dances and the later evolution of blues.

In this cellular approach to regionalism in North Carolina can be seen a mixture of fieldwork and evidence from commercially recorded music. In some cells, as in Durham, both are available. In the case of Charlotte-Mecklenburg County, this is entirely based on commercial recordings augmented by some written documentary evidence. In the case of this large cell east of Raleigh, virtually all evidence is from fieldwork. One known exception was singer-guitarist Alden Bunn, better known as Tarheel Slim. Born in 1924 into a second generation of blues musicians, he was from Bailey, on the boundary between Wilson and Nash counties, but his East Coast musical traits are eclectic rather than archetypal. He moved to New York in his early 20s, so his story is taken up in chapter 18.

It was not until 1970 that any evidence at all came to light that there were significant musicians in the area. John Henry Fortesque, better known by his local name of Guitar Shorty, played his big-bodied Kay guitar with a bottleneck on the streets in Wilson. His whole approach was highly idiomatic and seemingly spontaneous. Danny McLean, who first located Shorty, says that "he tunes his guitar standard except that the 4th string is raised to E; a 'cross-tuning,' EBGEAE. Were the 5th string raised to B it would be an E minor tuning but as it is, it is A^{9th}. He treats it as an EA^{7}B^7 progression, making an E chord but the raised 4th helps the steady bass and allows some one finger bars and bottleneck without much discord."[18] Despite frequent attempts to obtain factual information about Shorty's early life and influences, all that can be offered with any degree of certainty is that he was born about 1932 in the small coastal town of Belhaven, where he learned at least some of his playing style from an Uncle Wilbur. In a book which studied the place of music among black musicians, Valerie Wilmer described one occasion when she had gone to see Shorty. He "seemed blissfully unaware of the classic eight-bar, twelve-bar and sixteen-bar structures of the most common kinds of blues. He fragmented the time and switched from one pattern or chord sequence to another whenever the change sounded right to him, a cavalier attitude to form."[19] Her book went on to point out that such an attitude is now prevalent among progressive jazz musicians in "free-form" approaches to their music.

Among the least outrageous of Shorty's claims was that he had recorded in New York. This was dismissed along with less probable boasts—that he played with the Boston Symphony Orchestra and gave guitar instruction to the Beatles—so it came as somewhat of a shock to hear two untitled and anonymous acetates cut for Savoy in June 1952, indubitably by Shorty. In 1980, with the publication of the Savoy discography, these sides were ascribed to Hootin' Owl—by no means a poor indication of some of Shorty's falsetto mimicry.[20] Somehow he stayed alive until 1976.

Enquiries by Danny McLean and Ken Bass, who had located and worked with Guitar Shorty, led them into Pitt County around Bethel and Edgecombe County around Conetoe and Tarboro. From around Conetoe came Jack Jordan and Elester Anderson, from different musical generations but both capable of playing in the older, pre-blues style. Both recorded in that manner, although unfortunately Jordan was never satisfactorily recorded before he had a stroke. He was clearly once one of the finest guitarists in the area.

Born on Mae Wesley's farm in East Conetoe on August 31, 1908, Jack Jordan was unusual in that, one of eight children, he was the only one to play an instrument. He began to play around 1923 when he was fifteen and soon became accomplished enough to be in considerable demand for parties, dances, and even church functions. "Played all night long and all day Sunday. Wouldn't hardly stop. Loved to play then when I was young."[21] He recalled string bands, usually five-piece, using fiddle, mandolin, and guitar, playing for dances and picnics. "I was a boy then—just listened to them," although he played in some of the units by the late 1920s, even though they had largely died out by that date—far sooner, note, than around Cedar Grove. Jordan was emphatic that he never played for whites and was not aware that the string bands ever played for whites, but they may have done. During these early years in music, he was working full-time lumbering on a nearby logwood farm. The loss of an eye in 1932 had little effect. The following year he came across Gary Davis in Greenville, playing on the street, with three women singing along. He never played with him—"he was too bad for me !"—and like all others who saw Davis play, he was in awe of his playing technique. "You've got to have some fingers to do that," he mused, but it was as a finger-picker that Jordan was himself locally known. He started playing first in C-natural, that is, in open tuning, and also played in Spanish-Sevastopol. He played with local guitarists Ephen Lee, Joe Black, Ephen *Early, and Ephen Harris (possibly one of a well-known Pitt County family of guitarists), *Thelmon *Whitehurst, who followed the common migration route north to Washington, D.C., but occasionally returns to his native Greenville, and *Ken [t] *H[e]artsmith, from whom he learned some of his early technique. He remembered Johnnie Lee *Council and *Doc *Morley as harp players; Morley also played guitar.

Elester T. Anderson, also born near Conetoe, was of the generation of bluesmen who followed Jordan. Born October 25, 1925, he grew up in a strongly musical environment. At home he learned guitar from his father Isaiah, a brother Isaiah, Jr., (generally called "Zachmo"), and a maternal uncle, Jesse "Junie" Bradley. The latter especially played old country pieces, often in C, and when Elester Anderson played them, these were reminiscent of Libba Cotten and, according to Willie Trice, his uncle Albert Trice. Anderson began to learn to play when he was about thirteen, at which time his brother bought him a guitar and helped him to chord and play blues. At a time when Blind Boy Fuller was immensely popular, Zachmo picked up a good deal of his music from a chain gang, as "he got into a little trouble and he went to the road for three months. He came back playing just like Blind Boy Fuller play."[22] Logically Fuller remained Elester's chief influence. Within three or four years Elester was playing dances around Tarboro with Jesse Anderson, a cousin, on harmonica. Along with guitarists *Buzz and *Fan Harris, the Andersons were among the best known in the area. They built up a sufficient reputation to be offered a stint on a medicine show in Greenville, but they never accepted.

The Harris brothers were from Pitt County and highly respected. Despite having only three fingers on his chording hand, Buzz Harris was acclaimed by most of the surviving musicians. Frequently playing in Spanish tuning, he usually played second guitar to Fan. A feature of Buzz's playing was to use a dime under his finger to act as a slide. Fan Harris, too, had a considerable local reputation, but by the time he was located in 1970 he was rather senile and was able to play very little. One impressive song was "Georgia Woman," rather in the manner of Carolina Slim, who recorded it for Savoy in 1951. Slim's real name was Ed Harris. He was from Caswell County and known to have spent some time in the Durham area, so he may have been known personally to Fan Harris, or even related to the clan.

Elester Anderson recalled many other local musicians with whom he used to play. Guitarists included Joe Black, *Doss Howard, who also played piano, Roy Thigpen, Ephen Lee and Jack Jordan, "North Peppi," and a distant cousin, Willie John Anderson, who died aged seventeen. Other men played both harp and guitar—*Booster *James, who had his harp fitted to the body of the guitar, *Alonzo "Lonzie" *Williams, and George Higgs. He knew another harmonica player from Greenville only as Shorty, and knew Peg Leg Sam when he was living in Rocky Mount. Shorty is quite probably Elmon "Keg Shorty" Bell, who taught Peg Leg Sam. Once in Greenville, playing at the tobacco market, he ran across a guitarist whom he knew only as Jimmy but smilingly recalled that "I wouldn'ta liked to have come on behind him, 'cos he was good!" Although he largely quit playing in the 1950s, he was still a member of a more modern band as late as 1968 in Greenville. Back playing his older blues, he played occasional concerts in Chapel Hill and Durham in the mid-1970s and was recorded by Trix Records frequently between 1972 and 1979, including sessions with George Higgs on harp in 1979 and a trio session with his sons playing electric bass and drums in an interesting set of Fuller's material, sounding as Fuller might himself have sounded had he survived into the postwar period. Anderson died on May 9, 1980, but his music remains unissued.

Other than Joe Jordan, the sole surviving member of the black string band tradition was Joe Black, but it was never possible to interview him in any depth for not only was he then becoming senile and forgetful but some local white farmers proved to be as hostile as anyone I'd met during fieldwork research into black music. Born on the Howell farm south of Bethel in 1898, Black also started off playing in open tuning, in Sevastopol. A contemporary guitarist was Josh (possibly Doss) Howard, and Black performed with Junie Bradley, Elester Anderson's uncle, on second guitar. A member of the string band recalled by Jack Jordan, Black named Dave *Woodward, a guitarist, and 'Frank' as other members. The band generally comprised fiddle, mandolin, and guitar, and Joe played guitar whenever he was present. Although he was unable to express the type of music played, there seems to be little doubt that it was similar to that played by other black string bands in the period before and during the 1920s.

Another Pitt County guitarist known to Jordan, Black, and Anderson was Willie Bell. Born about 1903 in Ayden, just south of Greenville, he was playing by about 1915. He too started out as a finger picker in C, like Jordan and Junie Bradley, but he never played with a slide, again like Jordan. He played parties and dances but always on his own. He had once played blues regularly but when interviewed in 1973 resignedly informed me that he had not played in years as "the Devil got me now. Done broke up my sound."[23]

Apart from Greenville, the entire area seems to have been well off the major travel routes, although now close to Interstate Highway 95. The older route north ran from Raleigh along Highway 1. Few itinerant musicians seem to have ventured into the country, although Jack Jordan recalled a migrant ten-string guitarist about 1929. He was emphatic that Blind Boy Fuller never visited his area around Bethel and Conetoe. A measure of the remoteness is given by Joe Black, who first heard blues when he saw Bessie Smith in Rocky Mount. For him to have recalled her name, and indeed to have bothered to travel into Rocky Mount, suggests some sort of publicity, so this must have been after she first recorded in 1923. He probably never traveled further afield.

Bessie Smith is known to have played in Durham from July 29–31, 1926, and a poster for an appearance in Wilson was ordered on August 14, 1926, so she probably played there within a month or so. Perhaps, then, she also played nearby Rocky Mount about this time.[24]

Rocky Mount, on the border of Edgecombe and Nash counties, provides a small but locally significant center for tobacco marketing and local agriculture. The one well-known performer who spent some time here was Peg Leg Sam, who is discussed earlier in detail. Many musicians recall him with respect, and perhaps one mark of that respect is another man's attempt to emulate his style. One such harmonica player who lived for many years in Rocky Mount was Roosevelt May. Born in Halifax County on February 26, 1915, he learned to play harp in his early teens, partly from an uncle who used to play in the single-noted accordion style, and remembered many tunes played in the chordal, cross-harp manner characteristic of Carolina harp blowing. He met Peg Leg Sam about 1945, and his influence was such that when May came to make probably the only commercial blues record made in the Carolinas in the post-war period, he chose one of Sam's "standards," "Greasy Greens." Recorded for the Hub label in Raleigh about 1968, the session included another song closely associated with Sam, "Bad Liquor Made Me Leave My Happy Home," which remains unissued. In the early 1970s, May moved back to Halifax County, to the picturesquely named community of Moonlight near Scotland Neck, where he died in October 1978.

From Northampton County, near Rich Square, comes Percy Lassiter, born in 1908 and still performing pre-blues tunes. His older brother, Otis, taught him to play about 1921, after which they played regularly together, Otis playing second to Percy's lead. They performed at house parties and country dances, and in the streets in nearby towns, playing both older tunes and blues learned from phonograph records by Blind Boy Fuller and Blind Lemon Jefferson. Otis moved into the church and today Percy only plays for friends, but in view of the almost nonexistent evidence concerning black secular music in the coastal region, he remains important in helping to establish the premise that there was little significant difference in style in this region from that of the Piedmont. There was known to have been a strong black fiddle tradition in the northeastern part of the state: a black fiddler known only as Alvin reputedly taught most of the white players in Gates County, on the edge of Dismal Swamp. It seems that at one time the fiddlers traveled from all over the county to meet and play on Christmas Day.

Tobacco warehouse, Durham, North Carolina, 1940 (from the collection of the Library of Congress, courtesy of the Southern Historical Collection, University of North Carolina at Chapel Hill).

OPENS SEPTEMBER 22ND

ROYCROFT WAREHOUSE

HENRY T. ROYCROFT

JOHN K. ROYCROFT

MARVIN A. ROYCROFT

JOHN C. CURRIN

Star Brick

and

Big Four Warehouses

ARTHUR L. CARVER

WADE M. CURRIN

CARL H. COZART

BIG BULL WAREHOUSE

O. M. PERRY

S. T. MANGUM

G. A. WEBSTER

PLANTER'S WAREHOUSE

O. B. UMSTEAD

G. E. FARABOW

L. T. O'BRIANT

BANNER WAREHOUSE

W. L. PROCTOR

W. H. DANIEL

LIBERTY WAREHOUSES

Nos. 1 and 2

F. G. SATTERFIELD

WALKER STONE

G. T. CUNNINGHAM

J. S. SATTERFIELD

Tobacco market ads, Durham, North Carolina, 1936 (courtesy of the Perkins Library, Duke University, Durham, North Carolina).

Sign advertising a Pickle Low [piccolo, or jukebox] party, Siler City, North Carolina (from the collection of the Library of Congress, courtesy of the Southern Historical Collection, University of North Carolina at Chapel Hill).

DeLUXE SHOWS
of America
"All That the Name Implies"
Will Grace The Midway At The
Bigger and Better

American Legion Tobacco Festival And Fair
SEPTEMBER 21-26

See Sonny Boy Campbell's Diving Sensations, consisting of five people, beautiful girls, clowns, etc., with Sonny Boy Campbell doing a full ganor from a height of 110 feet.

MONKEY SPEEDWAY—Monkeys Racing of their own free will
TEN-IN-ONE—Consisting of freaks, funny people, short and fat, etc.

One Ring Circus
REVUE—With girls dancing in their native way

Crime Show And Minstrel Show

The Rides Consist of: Merry-go-round, Whip, Rid-E-O, Twin Ferris Wheel, Chair-o-plane, Lindy-loop, Loop-o-plane, Caterpillar. Also Three Kiddies rides, consisting of Ponies, Automobiles and a Baby Ferris Wheel.

Poster for Deluxe Shows, Durham Tobacco Festival and Fair, 1936 (courtesy of the Perkins Library, Duke University, Durham, North Carolina).

Peg Leg Sam [Arthur Jackson] 1973 (courtesy of Kip Lornell).

Baby [Charles] Tate and Peg Leg Sam, 1970 (courtesy of Peter B. Lowry).

Blind Boy Fuller, mid-1930s (courtesy of
Paul Oliver).

J. B. Long in front of his store in Kinston, North Carolina, ca. 1934, standing before the
largest consignment of 78 rpm phonograph records ever delivered in the state to date
(from the author's collection).

Reverend Gary Davis (courtesy of Robert Tilling).

Brownie McGhee and Lesley Riddle, early 1930s (courtesy of Lesley Riddle and Kip Lornell).

Sonny Terry in front of a tobacco warehouse, Durham, North Carolina, 1974 (courtesy of Bill Boyarsky).

Richard Trice, 1946-47 (courtesy of Richard Trice and Peter B. Lowry).

John Snipes (courtesy of Bill Phillips).

Guitar Shorty, 1973 (courtesy of Kip Lornell).

Willie Moore (courtesy of Kip Lornell).

Elester Anderson, 1973 (courtesy of Kip Lornell).

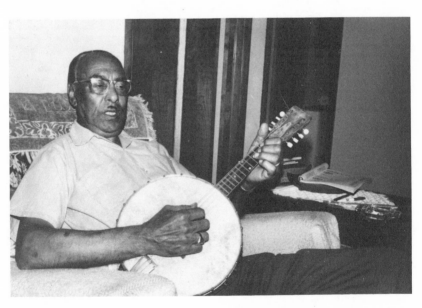

George Letlow, a member of the Chapel Hillbillies, ca. 1974 (courtesy of Kip Lornell).

If anyone exemplifies the perseverence of the older, pre-blues style of the region, it is Algia Mae Hinton of Johnson County, immediately southwest of Wilson County and south of Raleigh. Born August 29, 1929, she was raised in the O'Neal Township in a musical environment. Many members of her immediate family played reels, spirituals, and blues. Her mother, Ollie, was such a proficient performer on guitar, autoharp, harmonica, accordion, and jaw harp that tales persist of her selling her soul to the devil, a commonly documented facet of folk music.[25] One of the youngest of fourteen children, she grew up to find that many in her nuclear and extended family were already playing for house parties and frolics. Only one of Ollie's children failed to play. Algia Mae's maternal uncle played guitar, an aunt played guitar and banjo, and cousins and brothers-in-law were also musicians. Clearly the Hinton family was part of the early string band tradition, and its roots have been traced even further to the southwest, into Moore County, no longer in the traditional Piedmont region but into the coastal plain.

Between Pinehurst and Carthage until well into the 1940s there was an active black string band so well known that other black musicians traveled to the area to participate. Rumor has it that Blind Blake played there, apparently driven in by car. Some claim he stayed in Pinehurst, others that he stayed in Durham and returned to Pinehurst. Incidentally, Blake was reported to have been seen in Wilson.

Further to the east, well within the coastal plain, lies Lenoir County with Kinston as the county seat. Here J. B. Long first became interested in locating black talent rather than simply selling it over the counter of his store, and there was clearly plenty of talent by the time he organized his talent contests in 1934. Willie Moore was born in Kinston on April 22, 1918, and by the early 1930s was beginning to learn to play guitar, taught partly by his father and partly by other local amateur musicians. "They weren't no educated group," he recalled to Kip Lornell; "they weren't playing for no money, just for house parties, drinks and so on. Of course, there were quite a number of those boys who played guitar, such as Black Cat, Francis Suggs, Leo Hamilton, George Weasly, and Mr. Needs on violin . . . but they never proved anything."[26]

In the mountains a far more complex social situation prevailed, as blacks were in a minority or effectively nonexistent. One fascinating pocket of traditional music remains in Caldwell County, embodied in the performances of such musicians as Elizabeth "Babe" Reid, Cora Phillips, Etta Baker, and Theopolis "The" Phillips. Part of a highly complex social community, deriving from mixed marriage and intermarriage between Reid and Phillips families, their music is not distinctly black but offers an intricate insight into the blending of traditions.

Mixed marriages were by no means uncommon in the hill country, and the Phillips family stems from one. The grandfather was a quarter black on his mother's side and he married a white girl. In 1931, The married into the Reid family, taking twenty-four-year-old Cora as wife. She and Babe Reid were cousins in a remarkable musical family. Babe's mother, Mattie Moore, and Cora's father, Boone Reid, were brother and sister and among the county's finest musicians, Mattie on banjo and Boone on fiddle, banjo, and guitar. All eight of Boone's children learned to play. Babe began in 1922 when she was twelve, learning from her mother to play banjo but switching to guitar on hearing her cousin Cora and half-sister, Etta Baker. It was hardly surprising that when Babe and Cora grew up they married musicians—Fred Reid and The Phillips. The is dead and Fred no longer plays but the women still play. Stephan Michelson describes their style:

> Etta Baker and Babe Reid play guitar with thumb and one finger ("Travis" picking). Cora Phillips plays with thumb and two fingers, The with thumb and three fingers. The frails the banjo, but Babe, Fred and Etta pick it, all with one finger. The also does "Carter licks" on the banjo—brushing his index finger back and forth across the strings. As a result, Babe's and Etta's playing relies more on their thumb than do the others'. Etta's beat is heavier, Cora's treble more delicate, and The's playing is less regular, the least thumb orientated. Unlike most players who rely so much on thumb dexterity, Babe and Etta keep their thumbs stiff and bent away from the hand. . . . The basic guitar style is often called "Cotton [*sic*] picking" after Elizabeth Cotton (who actually plays a right-handed guitar left-handed, playing the bass with her fingers, the treble with her thumb). It is "traditional" music from the black hills of Western Carolina and identical, as the participants remember it, to that they heard from their grandparents. There is little improvisation.[27]

Although a series of separate cells or schools of musicians existed throughout the North Carolina Piedmont in the northern section of the state, overlapping into the mountains on the west and into the coastal plain to the east, from counties as far apart as Caldwell and Orange, Johnson and Edgecombe, it does seem that they were no more than part of a tradition of pre-blues, finger-picked music which was far more widespread.

THE BLUES SCENE TODAY

It would be presumptuous to write anything approaching a conclusion to a history of blues in North Carolina. In the late 1970s the state became aware of its black musical heritage and the persistence of a strong blues tradition. The Office of Folklife Programs at the North Carolina Department of Cultural Resources has played a major part in this process of making people more aware of their heritage. Since 1974 it has brought folk artists into schools to perform, including many black artists like John Snipes, who before his "discovery" in 1972 had never played before white adults, let alone a classroom of white children. Since 1976 Durham has housed the North Carolina Folklife Festival, reputedly seen that year by 100,000 persons. In 1978 the North Carolina Museum of History, through the Department of Cultural Resources, commenced a traveling exhibition lasting from September 30 until August 1979, depicting The Black Presence in North Carolina. It comprised four sections: Black Leadership, Black Religion, Black Literature, and Black Music, all to about 1900.[28] In 1978 the city of Durham held a specific event to celebrate the place of blues in the history of the city; the daily paper carried a heading which read, "Bull City Blues: A Durham Tradition."[29] Thanks to the success of the annual Folklife Festival, local papers started picking up stories of blues singers in other towns and proudly wrote them up. The forty-second annual National Folk Festival, held at Wolf Trap Farm, Virginia, in June 1980, highlighted blues from North Carolina performed by Thomas and Pauline Burt, Etta Baker, Algia Mae Hinton, John Holeman, Fritz Holloway, and James Stephenson.

The story is far from concluded. In view of the unprecedented interest taken in black music in the state, it might be as well to make some comment upon the above events, leaving the more detailed story to be taken up when appropriate by someone more closely involved with current events. Maybe, as so much of the fieldwork stems from Glenn Hinson, the task should be his.

The 1978 Folklife Festival on the Eno River on the north side of Durham included many traditional black musicians grouped into three regions—coast, Piedmont, and mountain. Cora Phillips and Babe Reid represented the mountain region but understandably more black artists represented the other two. The Piedmont was represented by:

Elizabeth Cotten	guitar, banjo	Chapel Hill	Orange County
James F. Borders	bones	Statesville	Iredell
Thomas and	blues/		
Pauline Burt	gospel guitar	Creedmoor	Granville
John Dee Holeman	guitar	Durham	Durham
Quentin Holloway	piano	Greensboro	Guilford
Odell Johnson	gospel guitar	Durham	Durham
Arthur Lyons	guitar	Durham	Durham
Rev. Rassie Moore	gospel guitar	Henderson	Vance

James *Stephens	guitar, piano	Greensboro	Guilford
Guitar Bill and	blues/		
Hattie Thompson	gospel guitar	Durham	Durham

The coast region was represented by:

Elester T. Anderson and			Edgecombe
Lester Anderson, Jr.	guitars	Speed	County
Algia Mae Hinton	guitar		Johnston
Joe Mitchell Holley	harmonica	Corapeake	Gates
Percy Lassiter, Sr.	guitar	Rich Square	Northampton
Roosevelt May	harmonica	Moonlight	Halifax
Fred "Junior" O'Neal	guitar		Johnston
Buddy Person	guitar	Carthage	Moore

By any standards that is a remarkable presentation. As representative of a music thought to have been dead a decade earlier, it clearly underlines the strong persistence of the traditions in the state.

The town newspapers took up the story of that summer's festival. In one issue the *Halifax County This Week* stressed "Folklife Festival to attract people from a number of cultures," an aspect frequently overlooked, while another headlined "Folklife Festival to feature Scotland Neck harmonica player," Roosevelt May.[30] The Fayetteville *Times,* taking its details from a press release covered by many papers throughout the state, made considerable mention of bones player James Borders,[31] who was pictured elsewhere playing along with white country fiddler Homer Sherrill from South Carolina.[32] Under the heading "Music from Caldwell's Hills," the Lenoir *News Topic* carried an article on Cora Phillips.[33] The Charlotte *Observer* pictured Thomas Burt with the heading "Singing the Blues,"[34] and the local Selma paper concentrated on Algia Mae Hinton and Fred O'Neal from Johnston County.[35] The Raleigh *Times,* writing of Thomas Burt, called him an "old time blues guitarist one of a dwindling breed."[36]

Newspaper reports on aspects of blues were an innovation and had probably not occurred before the small blues festival held as part of the Fine Arts Festival at the University of North Carolina at Chapel Hill in March 1973. Reports were to be found in the local papers,[37] but an article on Piedmont blues in the *Daily Tar Heel,* the campus paper, in November 1972 was probably the first.[38]

The policy of awareness and acceptance has been very recent, but it was no less refreshing to note Durham's acknowledgment of its bluesmen and wish to "honor these musicians for the important role they have played in Durham's history."[39] This took place on February 18, 1978, and among artists who had attended the Folklife Festival were "Other Honored Guests," among them Richard Trice and Cora

Mae Allen. Beamed over local radio and television, the editorial of the city's *Morning Herald* the following day firmly stressed that "Durham has every right to brag about the country blues music which found a fertile spawning ground here years ago."[40] So it does and it is good to see it proud of the music before it had vanished forever.

NOTES

1. Pre-blues music was first briefly described in Bruce Bastin, "Back Before the Blues Were Blues: Pre-Blues Secular Music in North Carolina," *Sing Out!* 24 (July-August, 1975): 13–16; Christopher Lornell, "Pre-Blues Black Music in Piedmont North Carolina," *North Carolina Folklore Journal* 23 (February, 1975): 26–32; idem., "A Study of the Sociological Reasons Why Blacks Sing Blues Through an Examination of the Secular Black Music Found in Two North Carolina Communities during the 1930s" (Master's thesis, University of North Carolina, 1976). Further detail was given in Glenn Hinson, brochure notes to *Eight-Hand Sets and Holy Steps: Traditional Black Music of North Carolina,* Crossroads LP 101 (Raleigh, 1978), which has examples of the playing of many artists cited.

2. Bruce Bastin, brochure notes to *Orange County Special,* Flyright 506 (Bexhill-on-Sea, England, 1974).

3. Bruce Bastin, "Willie Trice: North Carolina Bluesman, Part 1," *Talking Blues* 8 (January-February-March, 1978): 3, revised and reprinted as "Nobody Didn't Show Me Nothin': Tracing the Musical Career of Orange County Bluesman Willie Trice," in *Studies in North Carolina Folklife,* ed. Daniel W. Patterson and Terry Zug (Chapel Hill: University of North Carolina Press, forthcoming).

4. Jamie Alston, interviewed by the author, Orange County, North Carolina, November 16, 1972.

5. George Vukan, *Geographical Survey of Orange County* (Chapel Hill: Institute for Research in Social Science, 1948), p. 48, cited in Lornell, "Why Blacks Sing Blues," p. 30.

6. Bastin, "Pre-Blues Secular Music": 13–16; Cecelia Conway and Tommy Thompson, "Talking Banjo," *Southern Exposure* 2 (Spring-Summer, 1974): 63–66.

7. Lornell, "Why Blacks Sing Blues," p. 41.

8. Kip Lornell, "The Chapel Hillbillies," *Living Blues* 24 (November-December, 1975): 8, 45.

9. Jamie Alston, interviewed by author, Orange County, North Carolina, November 16, 1972.

10. Sam McGee, "Boogie," *Milk 'Em in the Evening Blues,* Folkways FTS 31007 (New York).

11. *Orange County Special,* Flyright 506; *Ain't Gonna Rain No More: An Historical Survey of Pre-Blues and Blues in Piedmont North Carolina,*

Rounder 2016 (Somerville, Mass., 1979). The latter includes titles by various Orange County performers; both albums include titles by Jamie Alston.

12. Bastin, "Willie Trice": 3.

13. Willie Trice, interviewed by the author, Orange County, North Carolina, September 22, 1972.

14. Michael Ruppli and Bob Porter, *The Savoy Label: A Discography* (Westport, Conn.: Greenwood Press, 1980), p. 29.

15. *Southern Blues: Roots of Rock 'N Roll,* vol. 11, Savoy SJL-2255 (New Jersey, 1981); Bob Porter to the author, August 22, 1981.

16. A full discography of Willie Trice is in Bruce Bastin, "Willie Trice: North Carolina Bluesman, Part 2," *Talking Blues* 9-10 (n.d. 1979): 16-17.

17. Robert House, interviewed by the author, Chapel Hill, North Carolina, January 16, 1973. Black accordionist Clarence Clay, from South Boston, Halifax County, was recorded in Philadelphia (see chap. 18). Tom Carter, researching white fiddle music, located a black accordionist in adjoining Person County (Carter in conversation to the author, 1972).

18. Danny McLean, liner notes to *Guitar Shorty: Carolina Slide Guitar,* Flyright 500 (Bexhill-on-Sea, England, 1972).

19. Valerie Wilmer, *As Serious As Your Life* (London: Allison & Busby, 1977), p. 9. See also idem., "Guitar Shorty: An Appreciation and Memory," *Blues Unlimited* 120 (July-August, 1976): 20-21; *Melody Maker,* September 2, 1972, p. 27; Valerie Wilmer, *The Face of Black Music* (New York: De Capo, 1976).

20. Ruppli and Porter, *The Savoy Label,* p. 75.

21. Jack Jordan, interviewed by the author and Pete Lowry, Bethel, North Carolina, October 2, 1972.

22. Elester T. Anderson, interviewed by the author, Tarboro, North Carolina, March 11, 1973.

23. Willie Bell, interviewed by the author, Bethel, North Carolina, March 10, 1973.

24. Doug Seroff, "Blues Itineraries," *Whiskey, Woman, And . . .* 11 (June, 1983): n.p.

25. Bruce Bastin, "The Devil's Goin' to Get You," *North Carolina Folklore Journal* 21 (November, 1973): 189-94.

26. Kip Lornell, "Willie Moore," *Living Blues* 2 (Summer, 1971): 15.

27. Stephan Michelson, liner notes to *Music from the Hills of Caldwell County,* Physical PR 12-001 (Silver Spring, Md.). Some of Etta Baker's songs are transcribed and annotated in Happy Traum, *Finger-Picking Styles for the Guitar* (New York: Oak Publications, 1967), and her playing style is further described in Robert Gear, *Bottleneck and Open Guitar Tunings* (Cambridge, Mass.: Daisy Rivers, 1975).

28. *The Black Presence in North Carolina* (Raleigh: North Carolina Museum of History, 1978). I was asked to write the section on Black Music, pp. 41-52, which was reprinted with annotations in *North Carolina Folklore Journal* 27 (May, 1979): 3-19. A revised version gives greater detail on fieldwork in

"Back before the Blues: Black Music in North Carolina," in *Afro-American Culture, European Perspectives*, ed. Robert B. Stepto and John Barnie (Westport, Conn.: Greenwood Press, forthcoming).

29. "Bull City Blues: A Durham Tradition," Durham *Morning Herald*, February 5, 1978.

30. "Folklife Festival to Attract People from a Number of Cultures," *Halifax County This Week*, June 29, 1978; "Folklife Festival to Feature Scotland Neck Harmonica Player," ibid., June 22, 1978.

31. Fayetteville *Times*, June 16, 1978. Other examples included the Greenville *Reflector*, June 18, 1978, and the Lenoir *News Topic*, July 4, 1978.

32. Raleigh *North Carolina Leader*, July 13, 1978.

33. "Music from Caldwell's Hills," Lenoir *News Topic*, July 13, 1978.

34. "Singing the Blues," Charlotte *Observer*, July 3, 1978.

35. Selma *Johnstonian-Sun*, June 29, 1978.

36. "Old Time Blues Guitarist One of a Dwindling Breed," Raleigh *Times*, June 14, 1978.

37. Bruce Bastin, "Classic Bluesmen Still Coming On and They're Right Here," *North Carolina Anvil*, April 7, 1973; "The Dying Art of the Blues," Chapel Hill *Daily Tar Heel*, March 29, 1973.

38. "The Blues as Sung in the Piedmont," *Daily Tar Heel*, November 6, 1972.

39. Glenn Hinson, *Black 'n Blues: A Celebration of Blues and Jazz in Durham"* (Durham, N.C.: Durham Human Relations Commission, 1978).

40. "Let's Accentuate Durham's Positives," Durham *Morning Herald*, March 29, 1978.

17

Goin' to Richmond: Virginia and the Northern Border Regions

Virginia is the northernmost state on the East Coast to have had extensive early blues and black pre-blues traditions, although until the late 1970s very little had ever been documented. Socioeconomically, Virginia stands somewhat apart from the Carolinas and Georgia. While Maryland and Virginia held 70 percent of all slaves in the late seventeenth century, by the 1860s the total had dropped to 15 percent. The black population increase in Virginia remained lower than in the three major states to the south, rising by only 60,000 to 690,000 between 1880 and 1920, by which time many had made the move north. Unlike Georgia and particularly South Carolina, only a quarter of all farms in the state were operated by "non native whites."[1] Cotton was less important than in the other southeastern states: at the turn of the century, production was less than 1 percent of that for Georgia. Tobacco was the crop, which was not to suffer until the late 1920s and the early years of the Depression, when North Carolina and Georgia tobacco— boosted by boll weevil damage to cotton—began to affect sales.

Dena Epstein provided detailed documentation of black secular music in Virginia before the 1860s,[2] while further detailed documentation of the music in the state was conducted in the late 1970s by the Blue Ridge Institute at Ferrum College, mostly by Kip Lornell, who makes the following pertinent comment about the persistence of the non-blues secular tradition: "Many of Virginia's black banjo players grew up in an era when the differences between black and white folk music were less clearly defined. They tended to see their music as 'rural' or 'country' and they did not impose the racial connotations on music that it has today. Most of the banjo tunes by black performers that have been collected in Virginia cross racial lines—that is, they cannot be labelled black or white"[3] He found that many musicians, including all the banjo players located, had retained their instruments, although the social institutions which offered them performance outlets have died away. The counties of Franklin, Patrick, and Henry, bordering the Piedmont and the Blue Ridge foothills, have long maintained strong black and white string band traditions. In Martinsville a local black physician held an annual all-black fiddlers contest in the auditorium of his hospital from 1928 to 1945, and there were many similarities with events at Fort Valley, Georgia, in the 1940s.

Lornell recorded more obvious persistencies of pre-blues harmonica, such as "Buckdance" and "Fox Chase" from Sanford Collins and James Applewhite respectively, showing—in the case of the former—both its significance as an accompaniment to dancers and its alliterative use in musically describing a host of sounds. Quite coincidentally these two men underpin the generally unseen but undeniable interplays within the broad fabric of black East Coast secular music. Both live in Norfolk, which offers economic pull factors with the industry attendant on the shipyards and port facilities. Both were born in North Carolina—Collins in Belhaven in 1919 and Applewhite in Rocky Mount in 1929. Collins moved to the Norfolk area in the late 1940s, following the postwar boom; Applewhite finally settled there after living in many places, including Washington, D.C. Collins played harmonica since childhood; Applewhite's greatest influence was his uncle, medicine show performer Peg Leg Sam.

As well as recording excellent banjo players performing pre-blues numbers, Lornell also uncovered hitherto unknown traditions of fife-and-drum bands and accordion playing. In retrospect, and together with research undertaken in North Carolina and Georgia, it comes as no real surprise that such traditions did exist, but that they have done so until such a late date, when no other hint of their existence this century had come to light, really is remarkable. The accordion tradition was strong along the coastal waterways north of Newport News. The northern neck, including Northumberland County, is very remote and had been culturally separate, until the last twenty years or so brought the construction of a bridge and the removal of tolls. The community includes the Menhadden fishermen, among whom the worksong tradition is a living memory. Across the Potomac, in rural Maryland, ring dances were being performed as late as 1975. Today in Northampton County only a few younger blacks perform on accordion and then only in church. In the summer of 1981 Lornell located more accordion players in Amherst and Nelson counties, especially in the Massies Mill section close to Lovingston. Again the music is primarily religious. The main performer, Walter Toms, died only about 1970.[4]

Few Virginia bluesmen were recorded during the peak of commercial activity in the 1920s and 1930s, and only one recorded there on location. There were no portable studios set up regularly as in Charlotte and Atlanta, and bluesmen like Carl Martin became known only after they had left the state and recorded elsewhere. Reece Du Pree's "Norfolk Blues" has the line "I've got a gal in Norfolk," which might pinpoint the origins of one of the fine country blues guitarists who accompany the Georgia singer. Recorded in February 1924 in New York it predated Ed Andrew's Atlanta recording by some six to eight weeks.

The one bluesman to record in Virginia cut four sides for Okeh on October 3, 1929, tucked away among a number of sessions by vocal quartets and gospel groups. Two titles found him in the Bubbling-Over Five, a small band with soprano sax, violin, piano, and banjo-guitar, and on "Don't Mistreat Your Good Boy-Friend" he has an extended opening solo on a slow blues which has much of the flavor of a jug band. Two harmonica instrumentals, accompanied by a pianist who appears not to have performed regularly with the harp player, were issued as by Blues Birdhead. One side was reissued on Velvetone as by Harmonica Tim, which is no more helpful. However, a 1931 *Norfolk Journal and Guide* mentioned "James Simons, known around and about as 'Birdhead' had made a name for himself with his performance on the harmonica. He makes it laugh, cry, smile or sigh."[5]

Charles Rey, Okeh's Richmond distributor, had scouted for Blues Birdhead, and quite possibly a local dealer located perhaps the best-known and most respected of Virginia bluesmen, Luke Jordan from Lynchburg. He recorded the first of his ten sides for Victor in Charlotte on August 16, 1927. They sold well, and "Church Bell Blues" from his second coupling remains his best-remembered song. In November 1929 Victor brought him to New York, where he cut six more sides, of which two remain unissued while one coupling has yet to be found. Jordan was born in either Appomattox or Campbell County about 1890 and lived in Lynchburg from his late teens until his death in the early-mid 1940s. Without peer there as a singer and guitarist, he appears to have been a professional performer and was never known to have held a regular job. Using his Gibson guitar Jordan taught many other guitarists of his and the following generation. Two informants were "followers"—Brown Pollard and Percy Brown. Pollard, Brown, and other local bluesmen interviewed described a significant local blues scene, of which Luke Jordan was the only one to record.

Brown Pollard was born in Amherst County in 1897 and is thus of the same generation as Jordan, although Pollard maintained that Jordan was his main influence. Interestingly, although everyone in Lynchburg knew of Luke Jordan, outside in the country they all knew Brown Pollard. Jordan was known to have a good voice, but Brown was thought to be the better guitarist. Indeed, Brown taught Jordan "Church Bell Blues" but was unable to recall from which source he had come by the song. Located in 1969, Pollard had quit playing some ten years earlier but still had a fine voice and, according to Percy Brown's mother, still was able to play guitar on occasions. Pollard's brother, Manuel Brown, was recorded in May 1975.

Percy Brown, like Pollard, lived in Lynchburg. In Pollard's view, Brown was "working up to be the best in the area," ready to challenge Jordan, and the general opinion of other local residents was that Brown was an excellent "commentor." The Brown family was a complex musical unit, with virtually everyone proficient on an instrument. Of four children—Norris, Robert, Percy, and Noel—only Percy survived to be interviewed. Noel had the reputation of being the finest local mandolinist. Percy played tenor banjo, guitar, and fiddle—in order of proficiency—but was also known to have played piano, mandolin, saxophone, and drums.[6]

Other local guitarists, all now presumed dead, included Luke Stratton from Lynchburg, Otis Sheldon from the country outside Lynchburg, Noah Booker from Concord (Campbell County), Julius Rose, and Walter Johnson, best recalled for his bottleneck playing. Still alive were Murt Carter from Lynchburg, Grover West of Lynchburg, originally from High Point, North Carolina, and Stanley Taliaferro—usually called Jim Crane—a second-generation bluesman in his fifties. Clayton Horsley, a younger bluesman recorded in 1977 in Lynchburg, was born in 1929 and raised in Amherst County. His main influence came from the records of Blind Boy Fuller, but his style reflects a more idiomatic approach rather than that of a simple copyist. From a musical family in which his brother and two sisters also played guitar, Horsley used to play at house parties and gatherings, but family responsibilities forced him to stop.

Lornell's research uncovered two bluesmen from neighboring Bedford County. James Lowry was active in the area in the 1950s, during which time he was recorded over radio station WBLT in Bedford. WBLT began broadcasting in 1953, and Lowry had a regular program for some months in that year. Initially the station used local talent for live shows but before the end of the year had switched almost exclusively to discs and transcriptions. Lowry was in his forties when his sides were cut, three of which appear on album.[7] Most interesting is "Tampa Blues," marred only by a poor quality guitar. The song was known to Bedford and Campbell county musicians dating back to the 1930s, is unknown further north than Charlottesville, is common in Amherst County, and known to the Foddrells in Patrick County in the south. Brown Pollard claimed to have originated it, but this could not be substantiated. One commercial recording is known, made in 1943 by Skoodle Dum Doo and Sheffield for the Regis label in New Jersey. Aurally, and from the writer credit to Richard, the former is Seth Richard, who recorded two sides, one of them "Skoodledum Blues," for Columbia in 1928. Until "Tampa Blues" turned up in fieldwork, clearly a native of south-central Virginia, it had been assumed in some way to have been linked to Florida. Aurally an East Coast location for Seth Richard is appropriate and hearing the Regis version, Brown Pollard declared the singer/guitarist to have been from around Lynchburg. Possibly Richard might be the mysterious twelve-stringed guitarist from Charlottesville, generally known locally as Hopper Grass. A younger bluesman from Bedford is Richard Wright, born in 1949. He learned his "Peaksville Boogie," named after a rural section of his town, from his father, William Wright, who had learned his music from older men around Bedford, like Johnny Younger, Glascoe Younger, and Robert Saunders, as well as from the phonograph records of Buddy Moss and Blind Boy Fuller.

The blues tradition remains alive in the southern counties of central Virginia in the competent hands of Turner and Marvin Foddrell and John Tinsley. The Foddrells, fine singer-guitarists from Stuart (Patrick County), come from a very musical family; their father, Posey, was a well-respected musician.[8] They have received some exposure at festivals and have been recorded in depth, their first releases being on the Blue Ridge Institute's albums. For a man born in 1928 Turner Foddrell has considerable traditional talent. Specializing in instrumentals like "Slow Drag," he nonetheless has a highly idiomatic "Going Up to the Country," lyrically different but melodically the same song as "Born in the Country" by Willie Moore, a Kinston, North Carolina, bluesman.[9] Younger by five years, Marvin Foddrell bases his songs more on recorded tradition.

Born in the Chestnut Mountain section of Franklin County on February 10, 1920, John Tinsley grew up in the scattered black community within the predominently white population, which possessed a very strong string band tradition. None of his close relatives were musically inclined, so when he was about twelve John began to learn to play blues from neighbors, Bob and Fred Holland. When Blind Boy Fuller began to record in 1935, Tinsley's future musical inspiration was set, even though blues were only to be heard "live" between square dance sets on Friday and Saturday nights when the crowd was resting. In 1949 Tinsley moved to Bassett in adjoining Henry County, where he met Dee Stone, a mechanic at a local garage who ran the small Mutual record company in Martinsville as a side interest. Since Stone specialized in early bluegrass and white country music, it was surprisingly imaginative of him to approach Tinsley with the idea of recording. It was probably some form of custom pressing, for Tinsley paid Stone for the privilege and received some 150 copies of the record— possibly the total pressing as only four or five copies have survived. Cut in Mt. Airy, North Carolina, "Keep your hands off 'Er She Don't Bear Touching" is an excellent two-guitar rag in C by Tinsley and Holland, strongly reminiscent of the duets of Blind Boy Fuller and Floyd Council.[10] Recorded for the Blue Ridge Institute's project in 1977, "Penitentiary Blues" relates Tinsley's experiences of a six-month jail sentence. The following year he cut an album in Rocky Mount, Franklin County, performing both his own numbers and others absorbed into his style, like Fuller's "Rattlesnake Daddy" and Buddy Moss's "Dead and Gone."[11] His tough childhood was reflected in "When I was a Child" where "my father didn't want me, my mother had to put me down." On some titles his vocal and guitar are supported by his son on piano and a young black harp player, J. P. Young.

Also from Franklin County are Archie Edwards and the highly individual Lewis "Rabbit" Muse, who is really a stage-show or street performer rather than a bluesman but who gives an unexpected blues edge to "Jailhouse Blues," where he plays ukelele to a loose aggregation of stock blues phrases. "Rabbit Stomp" is more typical, an amusing hokum piece with scat singing. Muse recorded an album for Outlet Records in Rocky Mount, Virginia. Born in 1908, he belies his age. Archie Edwards, born in Rocky Mount in 1918, remains an excellent singer and guitarist. He moved to Washington, D.C., and his place is more appropriately assessed there.

The Richardson family of Gretna, Pittsylvania County, exemplifies the role of strong family traditions in the preservation of a blues tradition in south Virginia. Herbert Richardson, born in 1919, and his son William, born in 1945, play a broad variety of music together, and their two-guitar instrumental "Tell Me Baby" is a good regional example. When a young man, Herbert learned from his father, John Richardson, and a brother, Otis, and subsequently taught William.

OTHER BLUESMEN FROM THE COMMERCIAL PERIOD

Aside from the Mississippi bluesmen, the guitarist in the Paramount catalogue perhaps most highly rated among blues collectors was Virginian William Moore. He was born on March 3, 1893, in Tappahannock, Essex County, on the middle of the three peninsulas north of the James River. Here he worked as a barber—hence his "Barbershop Rag"—and also farmed to supplement his income. Until the 1940s he spent his life in either Tappahannock or Warsaw, where he had a second barbershop. Soon after World War II he moved to Warrenton to be with his son and died there on November 22, 1951.

Moore played around Richmond County for local dances. Contemporaries recalled his ability on guitar less than his skills at playing fiddle and piano. Despite the remoteness of the region he is fully within the picking tradition of the Carolina-Georgia ragtime performers, for in "Raggin' the Blues" "a brief four-bar break uses the progression $C-C_7-F-A-A^b_6$, a staple of Carolina and Georgia rags. As in "Barbershop Rag" Moore employs his unique picking trademark—the rapid succession of three ascending notes effected on different strings, by the thumb, followed by the first and second fingers."[12]

Moore's reputation came from the 1928 Paramount sides made in Chicago—uniformly fine performances. Eight sides were released on four records: the first coupling, "Barbershop Rag" and "Tillie Lee," was first advertised in the Chicago *Defender* on May 5, 1928; the third coupling was first advertised there on July 28, 1928, but the company must have thought carefully before releasing "Old Country Rock" and "Raggin' the Blues," brilliant though they are, for they were first advertised in the Chicago *Defender* on June 8, 1929, some eighteen months after they had been recorded. Their release as by William Moore as opposed to the earlier three by Bill Moore gave rise to some speculation among collectors that these were different men, but sixteen lead sheets were submitted at the same time by Chicago Music to the Library of Congress's copyright office on May 31, 1928, in Moore's name. Eight of the titles correspond with the issued sides, all drawn from a matrix block covering 20309 through 20324, representing sixteen matrices. As sixteen titles were submitted together for copyright, it is almost certain that they represent the complete session(s). They offer a much greater insight into Moore's repertoire and deserve to be listed in full. All compositions are words and melody except where noted, these being the four instrumentals. The name credit was to William (Bill) Moore, except for "I Got Mine," which was credited to William Moore, and the final coupling issued, which was submitted in the names of Moore and Williams.

E 693002	Tillie Lee		(Paramount 12613)
E 693003	Silas Green from New Orleans		
E 693004	One Way Gal		(Paramount 12648)
E 693005	How the Sun Do Shine		
E 693007	Catfish Woman Blues		
E 693010	Ragtime Millionaire		(Paramount 12636)
E 693011	Chicken Feathers		
E 693012	Rough and Ready Blues		
E 693013	Midnight Blues		(Paramount 12636)
E 693015	Raggin' Dem Blues [*sic*]	(melody)	(Paramount 12761)
E 693017	Old Country Rock	(melody)	(Paramount 12761)
E 693018	I Got Mine		
E 693019	Barbershop Rag	(melody)	(Paramount 12613)
E 693020	Stranger Blues		
E 693022	Unfortunate Blues		
E 693023	Ragtime Crazy	(melody)	(Paramount 12648)[13]

One Virginia bluesman whose life spanned the commercial recordings of the 1930s to the revival period of the 1970s was Carl Martin. He was born in Big Stone Gap on April 15, 1906, but about the turn of the century his parents had moved in from Spartanburg, South Carolina, where his father probably played with the local string band. Carl recalled that he "played violin and guitar. He played a violin all the time, mostly played at parties around there; he'd get out with the fellows and play. They used to call him Fiddlin' Martin. . . . My brother was a musician too. He was a wizard—played violin, all stringed instruments—named Roland Martin. He was six years older than me."[14] "It was a coal-mining region. Fellows would come through there with a guitar—mining men—and they'd stop over at our house and I'd watch them play. I was just a little boy, and I learned to pick up a piece or two."[15] Numerous accounts by both black and white musicians testify to the part played by itinerant black workers in disseminating music in the mountain region.

In 1918 the family moved to Knoxville, Tennessee, where Roland had a string band. "They had a bass fiddle, had mandolin, violins . . . all had instruments, so I learned to play different ones being around them. . . . Played for both white and colored . . . all through Virginia and West Virginia, Kentucky, and all down South. The string band worked every day . . . stand on corners, on vacant lots—all different places—play all day. Play for medicine shows. That was right around World War I, 1918 or so. We played on sidewalks, streets, in stores, anywhere."[16] Young Carl played bass fiddle at first, then guitar, and finally violin with the band until he formed his own unit in the 1920s with multi-instrumentalist Howard Armstrong from Lafayette, Tennessee.

In Knoxville on April 3, 1930, Armstrong and the Martins recorded for Vocalion as the Tennessee Chocolate Drops. Their instrumentals, "Knox County Stomp" and "Vine Street Drag," were reissued in the white 5000 series, more discretely credited to the Tennessee Trio. The original name was the band's idea, not the record company's, and anyone feeling that it is somewhat Uncle Tommish has never met Howard Armstrong. A prouder, more dignified and imposing personality among bluesmen would be difficult to name. He recalled the recording session in some detail: "The fellows (the record company) sent out there, they were professional men. . . . The fellow came in from Knoxville and he said anybody here that played music . . . (had) a chance. So everybody you know back then—everybody wanted to get out and make a record. Everybody heard you and you wanted to be heard. . . . So we practiced for about a week or two . . . and they set up in the big St. James Hotel, and we went up there."[17] On the record Armstrong played fiddle, although he more regularly played mandolin or guitar in the band. Carl Martin played "bass violin," while Roland Martin played guitar. Vocalion had been to Knoxville the previous summer, in August, when they recorded Leola Manning, whom they again recorded in 1930, and a singer guitarist, Will Bennett, from nearby Loudon.

Soon after the Vocalion session, Armstrong and Martin were joined by Spartanburg guitarist, Ted Bogan, who clearly recalled his admiration for the local guitarist, Willie Walker. They then added Bill Ballenger on bass fiddle and called themselves the Four Keys, working through West Virginia, Ohio, Pennsylvania, and Michigan, finally settling in Chicago in 1932, where they played bars and clubs. By the mid-1930s the three were recording at various times: Bogan and Armstrong recorded in 1934 for Bluebird, Armstrong adopting the name of Louie Bluie; Carl Martin recorded as an accompanist as well as under his own name, showing himself to have been a highly accomplished and sophisticated guitarist, somewhat in the manner of Big Bill Broonzy. His 1935 "Crow Jane" is one of the most idiomatic, but his pretty picking can be heard on other discs from the same period.[18]

In 1966 Carl Martin was recorded with a Chicago string band, and the old trio was brought together as Martin, Bogan, and Armstrong. Two good albums give an excellent idea of their repertoire.[19] Perhaps one track on their first Flying Fish album sums up fifty years of playing music for a wide and varied audience of every possible racial background. No other band could possibly revive an old Hawaiian pop song like "You'll Never Find Another Kanaka Like Me" without sounding either maudlin or satirical.

The region of Carl Martin's birthplace is the narrow triangle of the extreme western tip of Virginia, bounded by Kentucky in the north and Tennessee in the south, in which Kingsport and Bristol were the nearest urban centers. Guitarist Lesley T. Riddle lived in Kingsport during much of the 1920s. He was born June 13, 1905, in Burnsville, mid-way between Asheville and Johnson City, Tennessee, to which he moved as a boy. He associated with Brownie McGhee before he set off first to settle briefly in North Carolina and then to move, like many other southern bluesmen, to upstate New York, where he settled in Rochester in 1942.

Perhaps Riddle's major claim to some recognition is that he was also closely associated with A. P. Carter of the Carter Family, arguably the most influential white group to record. Black Kingsport musician John Henry Lyons told Carter that Riddle could play guitar and knew a number of songs, and for a few years after 1934 they went on the road "about 15 times" to collect songs. Although the light-skinned Riddle recalled that they "never did get any songs from colored folks,"[20] A. P. Carter did visit Brownie McGhee and stayed the night, much to his father's concern that the neighbors would be upset! More significant to blues in Virginia is that Riddle knew the obscure guitar duet Tarter and Gay, who came from that same western triangle of the state.

Stephen Tarter was from either Carl Martin's birthplace—Big Stone Gap—or Gate City, which was Harry Gay's home town. Their sole recorded coupling was made in 1928; "Unknown Blues" and "Brownie's Blues" are completely within the East Coast tradition, with delicate, interwoven guitar lines.[21] Tarter's voice is clear and his lines are well enunciated in the manner of Willie Walker, while the guitars of "Unknown Blues," in C, are strongly reminiscent of Walker and Brooks of "South Carolina Rag." They clearly shared a common tradition and were of the same generation; Riddle recalled them as being aged about thirty when they recorded. They had been playing around Kingsport for two or three years before they came to his notice. "They played professionally for many years. . . . Steve was one of the finest instrumentalists that I ever heard. . . . Steve could play anything.

Anything that he heard sung or played he could go home and play it. He could play guitar, banjo, mandolin, fiddle, anything that had strings on. . . . He could rag his guitar just like you rag a piano. Steve's father, I think, was a musician. I used to hear Steve talk about how his father could play fiddle, mandolin, and guitar, just like he did. That's probably where Steve picked it up." Riddle remembered a party on Wynolia Street, in Kingsport, held by a doctor. "Steve got me to go over there and play with him. Harry wasn't around that night. . . . I would play second behind Steve. Once in a while, on a blues or something that I knew I would sing and Steve would follow me. He used to take "Unknown Blues" and play it a little faster, put it up a little bit. He could play it fast, slow, any kind of way. . . . I never heard him play with no steel [slide]. I imagine that he could."[22] Even though Tarter more usually played mandolin, Riddle rated him the finest guitarist he ever saw. Tarter taught Gay "everything that he knew on guitar," so Gay played second guitar on the record, on which Tarter sang. It was a popular record locally.

Tarter and Gay were the only black artists recorded by Victor in Bristol in 1928. Victor's 1927 Bristol recording session also produced only one record by a black artist, El Watson. Tarter and Gay traveled to Bristol to audition as a result of publicity generated in their home town of Johnson City,[23] but perhaps, unlike El Watson, they were not prepared to travel to New York to record further. One lone recording session for Columbia took place in Johnson City on October 24, 1929, producing a coupling by harmonica player Ellis Williams, with guitar accompaniment, plus a spoons player added on "Buttermilk Blues." Nothing further is known about any of the men.

TIDEWATER BLUES

The Virginia tidewater region is a tidal, coastal zone almost one hundred miles wide. While the more remote sections continue to harbor very old traditions, the large urban centers of Newport News and Norfolk have always exerted a powerful influence, extending far beyond the surrounding countryside. During and immediately after both world wars jobs became available, and blacks flocked in from the Carolinas and Georgia. Bluesmen came to town as well. Buddy Moss moved in briefly about 1951, while the last known location of Durham washboard player Oh Red was Portsmouth or Norfolk, where he worked in the shipyards. However, there was already a thriving blues scene in the urban centers as well as across Chesapeake Bay around Cape Charles and in the Delmarva Peninsula.

Guitarist Alec Seward was born in Newport News on March 16, 1901, and began to play his brother's guitar at an early age. He remembered that itinerant potato pickers around Norfolk had helped teach him to play, and he felt that many of these had moved to Baltimore. Seward himself left the region in 1922 to settle in New York in 1924; he remained there until his death in 1972. Many fine guitarists lived around Norfolk and Cape Charles. In the 1940s, when Seward returned briefly to Norfolk, he met Willie Carl and tried to persuade him to return to New York with him. Georgia bluesman Roy Dunn, working on a freighter out of Norfolk, also knew Willie Carl, then living in Cape Charles.

Besides having an active blues scene, Norfolk has for years been a center of quartet singing, both secular and sacred. The seminal Norfolk Jazz (or Jubilee) Quartet had three extensive recording sessions for Okeh in 1921, recorded no more from September 1921 to April 1923, then switched to Paramount, for whom they recorded in every year in the 1920s except 1928. The gap in recordings and switch in company can be explained by an article in the *Norfolk Journal and Guide:* "Estelle Jones, 19 years old . . . had driven a knife into the heart of James (Buddy) Butts, her lover, famous tenor and member of Norfolk Jazz Quartette. At the time of his death the quartet was under contract with Okeh Record Company."[24] Butts was a founding member of the group, one of the city's most influential tenors, and with his death came the termination of the Okeh contract and the need to reorganize with a new tenor lead before a further contract could be sought. If nothing else, this shows that the risk of a violent end was not the prerogative of the bluesman.

Black quartet contests were held in tidewater Virginia, notably in Norfolk, during the 1920s and 1930s. Performances were a capella with syncopations and four-part harmony. Rarely reissued on album and only now being investigated by researchers like Doug Seroff, Ray Funk, and Kip Lornell, these groups shared a significant and parallel—sometimes overlapping—popularity with blues. Two examples are to be found on an album of Tidewater Blues, programmed by Lornell as part of the Blue Ridge Institute project, on which far more detailed notes about the region and the artists can be found.[25]

Musicians moved north from the tidewater region; Caroline County's John Cephas spends most of his time in Washington, D.C., where he was born. Philadelphia, too, became a favorite center. Carl Hodges from Saluda, Middlesex County, between Newport News and Tappahannock, moved there about 1960, aged about twenty-seven, and worked there for two years before returning. While he was there he met other immigrant musicians and was introduced by Maryland songster Bill Jackson to researcher Pete Welding, who recorded him in 1961. "Blues all Round" showed him to be a guitarist firmly in the mainstream of Piedmont country blues.[26] Hodges remembered his early days for Kip Lornell. He learned some of his guitar skills from his grandfather, Carl Hodges, Sr., and other Middlesex County bluesmen like Eli Roman and Roy Jackson as well as Goucester County bluesman Benny Sparks. Carl well remembered days before roads were paved: "There wasn't much chance to get nowhere lest you hitch up the wagon and drive somewhere. Couldn't go far that way. They didn't have dances like they have today, beer joints, nothing like that. So, mostly the places you did play was for house parties. That was the biggest sport then anyway."[27] Hodges continues to play local gigs.

Henry Harris, born in Warren, Albemarle County, on March 25, 1915, learned from both string band music and blues when he was young. Uncles William and Charlie Harris played fiddle and banjo respectively and older brother Nathan played guitar for local dances. By the time Henry was playing in the late 1920s, he was trying to copy guitar players in these strings bands. Hence his repertoire remains strongest on instrumentals like "Albemarle County Rag" and "Motorcycle Swing," the latter explained by his early work for a motorcycle company in Richmond after 1925 and his passion for the machines to this day.

Corner Morris, born in Suffolk, Nansemond County, near the Dismal Swamp, on May 22, 1905, began playing about 1920. Many of his pieces are pre-blues learned from a cousin, James Moore, and neighbors Sam Scott and Gavin Jones. His picking style, as on "Going Down the Road Feeling Bad," has much of the country dance tradition about it.

In 1941, under the auspices of the Hampton Institute, Roscoe Lewis undertook to document local black folklore and recorded one superb singer, whose name is sadly not known to us. Identified only as "Big Boy," he recorded some sacred songs, a version of "John Henry," and a truly remarkable four-and-a-half-minute "Blues."[28] His voice is strong and his guitar technique really thrilling. Part railroad song and part cante fable, it calls to mind Jimmie Strothers's "Richmond Blues," less from content than the singer's ability to weave continual themes into his performance, never to lose momentum. Other than the recordings made at Fort Valley in the early 1940s, Lewis's recording is the only example of noncommercial blues recorded in the Southeast in those years.

Not all musicians moved north, but with the exception of Blues Birdhead, none of those who remained ever recorded commercially. Other local bluesmen were recorded in the 1970s, the most heavily recorded being Pernell Charity from Waverly, Sussex County, southeast of Petersburg, where he was born on November 20, 1920.

Apart from six months spent in New York, Charity lived there all his life. Both he and an older brother, Otis, learned to play guitar: "The first one I played, I made it out of an old cigar box. I just took it up myself. I saw quite a few different ones that were playing and I watched them make different chords and different songs. The first song that I did was one that I made up, 'Mama Told Me.' I played that one in the streets, people started to paying me nickels and dimes and I started picking up more songs."[29] Among the "few different ones" that Pernell saw playing was J. C. Jones, by repute the best local guitarist. Sam Jones—no relative—who was a close friend of Pernell recalled that "J. C. could play rings round anyone here, including Pernell." J. C. Jones, who used to play in the local urban center of Petersburg, moved north to New Jersey. Petersburg also sported guitarists Irving Green and Charlie "Guitar Slim" Jones. John Woods was a harmonica player from nearby Richmond; Wilbur Barrett, Sam Jones's cousin, still lives in Petersburg "someplace" and is a good harmonica player too. Waverly pianist *Fisher *Beale moved to Baltimore. *Bow Tie *Green and *Albert *Brooks played washboard in small groups. By 1971 Otis Charity had ceased to play, Pernell played only at home, and Sam Jones had joined the church, where he continued to sing and play.

In the 1930s and 1940s, however, Pernell Charity and Sam Jones—who was five days younger—were blues partners. Jones recalled that "Pernell taught me some guitar music. I was playing with three fingers and my thumb and Pernell taught me to play with four fingers and my thumb. . . . We got to play parties and dances . . . off and on for about five or six years." Sam Jones became a proficient musician about 1936 and then bought his first guitar in Williamsburg, where he was working on a C.C.C. camp. Two uncles were musicians; James Williams taught him to play blues on guitar while Joseph Taylor "was about the ukelele [*sic*] king around here."[30]

Pernell Charity recorded between 1971 and 1975 but died of cancer on April 12, 1979, before achieving any acclaim for his music.[31] An eclectic artist whose main influence was Blind Boy Fuller, he must have been typical of a vast number of parochial bluesmen who traveled little, learning from local musicians and transients as well as from phonograph record. His blues are often tinged by later popular bluesmen like Lightning Hopkins.

THE NORTHERN BORDERS

One little-known bluesman who doubtless typified many other black musicians who moved into West Virginia was guitarist Dave Dickerson. Born at Tip Top, Tazewell County, Virginia, on May 4, 1913, he lived only a few miles from the state line and actually attended the black Genoa High School in Bluefield, West Virginia, for ten years. By 1934 he was resident in West Virginia, working for a construction company in Bluefield. As a child he had listened to blues and learned many songs from record; his family bought Paramounts—especially Blind Lemon Jefferson—by mail order. Even in his late years he recalled anxiously awaiting the arrival of the mailman in order that new acquisitions could be learned. He used to play for friends during his years working for U.S. Steel at mines like Thorpe and Filbert but was not located until 1966 when Roddy Moore, who heads the Blue Ridge Institute, met him. Just as he was beginning to play regularly at a coffeehouse in Blacksburg, he fell ill and gave up playing. On his only issued song, "When the War Is Over," he plays twelve-stringed guitar in a very traditional East Coast style, with a smooth vocal delivery.[32]

White musicians like Dick Justice and Frank Hutchison of Logan County, West Virginia, testified to the impact of black music on their playing styles and those of their contemporaries. Hutchison heard blues about 1904–5 from a man believed to have been Henry Vaughn; "when he was seven or eight a railroad crew came through the area and Frank would go down to the tracks to listen to a negro worker play blues on his guitar."[33] Sherman Lawson, a fiddler who recorded with Hutchison in 1928, learned from a crippled black musician named Bill Hunt, who had moved into the area some time before 1910. He taught Hutchison "Worried Blues," which he twice recorded for Okeh.[34] At one time Dave Dickerson played with a black string band in Gary, West Virginia, which played for dances and house parties. Gary is within twenty miles of the southern edge of Logan County. Howard Armstrong's Four Keys was another black band that played the area, and Armstrong remembered Hutchison because of his ability to play blues. "I remember him so well, because in those days very few whites would even deign to play blues. . . . He was a harp-blowing man. Really bad."[35] An Okeh publicity photograph shows Hutchison with rack harmonica.

Blues can also be documented north of Bluefield, in Summers County. One Virginia immigrant who settled there in Meadow Creek was retired railroad worker Elva Johnson. He was from "a little place called Hardware 'bout twenty-five miles [north] of Buckingham Courthouse. . . . in Old Virginia''[36] and went to work on the Chesapeake and Ohio Railroad, where he met guitarist Bill Williams, himself originally from Richmond, Virginia. Johnson learned from the highly skilled Williams, who at one time ran with Blind Blake, and also learned track-lining songs on the railroad. He finally retired at the age of seventy-six and began to play such festivals as the excellent John Henry Folk Festival near Charleston, West Virginia.[37] Another performer at this and similar small festivals in his later years was Uncle Homer Walker, a fine clawhammer banjo player, whose musical repertoire almost entirely predated blues. From Summers County, where he was born on February 15, 1898, he more recently moved to Glen Lyn, Virginia, just below Bluefield. Walker was able to trace his knowledge of the banjo back to slavery times, for he had learned from his grandfather, who had been a slave. One of the fast-shrinking body of performers who played predominently pre-blues music, he died in 1980.[38]

While the majority of known black musicians in West Virginia who fit into the pattern of the East Coast blues and pre-blues styles are from the southern counties, Clarence Tross is from the tiny community of Durgon, Hardy County, north of the Shenandoah Valley, in the very northeast of the state. Born in 1884, he learned to play banjo from his father, Andy Tross, who lived until 1910. Born about 1850, Andy Tross—like Homer Walker's grandfather—had been a slave, and it is possible that their banjo playing represents the oldest tradition to have been located in the 1970s. Tross recalled that in the local music tradition around the turn of the century "it was mostly the colored men played accordion. They played for dances around here. Fiddle, banjo, accordion—all used to play for dances."[39] This fits the general overall pattern of the string band tradition before the advent of the guitar. Clarence Tross made his own banjo, and his uncle, Moses Tross, a fine fiddler, also made his own instrument. Andy Tross used to play beef bones as an accompaniment to dancing; "beating the bones" probably closely paralleled the function of drum.

Hardy County, West Virginia, is on a similar latitude with north Virginia and Washington, D.C. Across the Shenandoah Valley and the Shenandoah National Park is Rappahanock County, where the best-known of all East Coast performers still playing at festivals was born in 1924. John Jackson grew up in a musical environment. "Everybody in my family played music. My father ₚlayed guitar and banjo, my mother played French harp [harmonica] and accordion, and all my brothers and sisters played something or other. I never could learn much about my father's style, though, because he played left-handed. He didn't change the strings, he just turned the guitar upside down and played it like that. I was four or five when I started to play, and I used to copy my brother a bit, but it was really a convict on the chain gang by the name of 'Happy' that started me to playing."[40] In his notes to an album of Jackson's blues and country dance tunes, Chuck Perdue had rather more to say about Happy. He was a "water boy on a chain gang crew that was cutting highway 29–211 through the mountains near John's home, about 1933–34. John says . . . he plays the best guitar he has ever heard—somewhat in the styles of Blind Blake but much better."[41] From him John Jackson learned several songs as well as how to play guitar in Spanish tuning. He also well remembers buying records from an itinerant salesman who brought round a buggyload. By 1950 he was living close to Washington, D.C., in Fairfax where Perdue located him, since which time he has toured extensively, including trips to Europe.

Elsewhere the influence of black secular music on whites in the Appalachians and the foothills has been documented. In his excellent book on Tennessee country music Charles Wolfe cites two significant white artists who recalled early black influences. Uncle Dave Macon learned songs from blacks around McMinnville as a child—he was born in 1890—and "much of their music found its way into his vocal style."[42] Charlie Bowman, born 1889, who played with the Hill Billies led by Al Hopkins, learned some of the song "Nine Pound Hammer" from black railroad construction gangs in East Tennessee about 1905. William "Blackie" Cool, a West Virginia guitarist who spent many childhood years working through the coalfields, "learned a lot from an old friend of mine, an old black guy. . . . He was one of the prettiest players ever I saw. . . . I just went crazy over that kind of playing."[43] Wolfe also touched on a critical factor on the restrictions and oral spread of traditional music in the mountains. "Often the highest praise a fiddler could receive was 'best in the county,' for in an age of poor roads and rough, hilly country, the width of a county often meant a hard day's journey."[44]

Away from the mountains the black banjo tradition, like that of the string band, has disappeared from north Virginia. Nonetheless the songster tradition epitomized by John Jackson—as opposed to the straight blues tradition—has been found in Maryland and Delaware. There is a case to be made for the persistence of this aspect of black secular music in the northern limits of the indigenous sounds of the southeastern blues states, as opposed to the Deep South, where a stronger, more elemental blues tradition persisted. John Jackson from north Virginia, Bill Jackson (no relative) from Maryland, and Frank Hovington from Delaware—especially Bill and Frank—share many characteristics.

Bill Jackson was born in Granite City, Maryland, a small town just west of Baltimore, on February 22, 1906. At the age of fifteen he began to learn to play guitar from an older neighbor, Jim Fuller, reputed to have been one of the finest local musicians and reported in the mid-1970s to have been living in Baltimore. Pete Welding, who located Bill Jackson, took up the story: "After six months rudimentary instruction from Fuller, Jackson struck out on his own and began playing at the house parties, community work parties, back country suppers and dances that comprised the region's social life. Small three-or-four piece string groups made up of guitar, banjo, mandolin and fiddle would play reels, jigs, and breakdowns for the dancers at these affairs. These small bands and individual performers would play and sing blues, banjo pieces, and railroad songs."[45] Jackson worked for several years on the Baltimore & Ohio Railroad before moving to Philadelphia, where he almost recorded in 1928 for Victor, whose studios were just across the river in Camden, New Jersey. The two songs he was requested to perform, "Long Steel Rail" and "Old Rounder Blues," had to wait until 1962 to be recorded by Welding, then involved in recording black folk artists in the city. Recorded years after Jackson had ceased to perform in public, the sides serve simply to underline the fact that he must once have been a highly proficient musician.

Frank Hovington was another in this tradition—to my mind one of the finest songsters to have been recorded during the 1970s, an excellent bluesman in the East Coast tradition. Talking about Bill Jackson, Welding described this distinctive blues style as "one that is characterized by a carefully controlled emotionality; a deliberate, more sedate handling of vocal and instrumental techniques; a very conscious awareness of and adherence to formal elements; and an extremely high caliber of musicianship, especially as regards the complexity of instrumental accompaniment." This could have been a tailor-made description of Frank Hovington in action.

Born in Reading, Pennsylvania, on January 9, 1919, young Franklin eventually accompanied his mother to join his father, who worked on a small farm near Frederica, Delaware. A neighbor, Adam Greenfield, so impressed Frank with his banjo and guitar playing that he bought his first banjo at the age of eleven and was playing guitar four years later in 1934. Greenfield was originally from New Bern, North Carolina, and had traveled as a Pullman porter before finally settling at Anders Lake, near the Hovington farm. However, another musician really taught Frank how to play—William Walker, who had come from Suffolk, Virginia, and was probably born in the decade after Green-field. Walker used a two-fingered style. About 1939 Walker left to live in Alexandria, a suburb of Washington, D.C. As well as playing guitar behind Walker, usually accompanying his banjo, Frank Hovington played with a number of other local musicians, who are described in the detailed notes to the one album of his music. The concluding note that I then wrote remains true: "While his music may never feed him, nothing can take away his dignity and pride in it. It is the music of yesterday, not renovated after serious plastic surgery but unselfconsciously played by a fine songster, steeped in a tradition which is as much part of him as is the countryside about him."[46] He was recorded once more, in 1980, but he was no longer playing regularly and the quality of his music showed it.[47] On June 21, 1982, Frank Hovington died and was buried at Gibbs Memorial Gardens, near Camden, Delaware.[48]

NOTES

1. *Blue Book of Southern Progress* (Baltimore, Md., 1923), p. 67.

2. Dena J. Epstein, *Sinful Tunes and Spirituals: Black Folk Music to the Civil War* (Urbana: University of Illinois Press, 1981).

3. Kip Lornell, brochure notes to *Virginia Traditions: Non-Blues Secular Black Music,* Blue Ridge Institute BRI–011 (Ferrum, Va., 1978).

4. Lornell to the author, August 17, 1981; *Blue Ridge Institute Newsletter* 4 (December, 1981): 8.

5. "Gay Evening Enjoyed at February Frolic with Tux Club," Norfolk *Journal and Guide,* February 16, 1931.

6. Don Kent, conversation with the author, August 1976; Don Kent, "On the Trail of Luke Jordan," *Blues Unlimited* 66 (October, 1969): 4–5.

7. *Western Piedmont Blues,* Blue Ridge Institute BRI–003 (Ferrum, Va., 1978).

8. Frank Weston, " 'I First Got Started When I Was Eight Years Old,' " *Blues Unlimited* 140 (Spring, 1981): 31–32.

9. *Another Man Done Gone,* Flyright 528 (Bexhill-on-Sea, England, 1979).

10. *Home Again Blues,* Mamlish S–3799 (New York).

11. John E. Tinsley, *Country Blues Roots Revisited,* Outlet STLP–1012 (Rocky Mount, Va.). See also Frank Weston and Sylvia Pitcher, "John Tinsley," *Blues Unlimited* 142 (Summer, 1982): 26–29, and John Tinsley, *Sunrise Blues,* Swingmaster LP 2014 (Groningen, Netherlands, 1982).

12. Stephen Calt, Nick Perls, and Michael Stewart, liner notes to *East Coast Blues 1926–1935,* Yazoo L–1013 (New York).

13. Library of Congress Copyright Office, Washington, D.C.; John H. Cowley to the author, January 21, 1979.

14. Pink Anderson from Spartanburg called Blind Roland Martin a "great musician".

15. Pete Welding, "An Interview with Carl Martin," *78 Quarterly* 1 (1968): n.p., reprinted in Pete Welding, "Carl Martin 1906–1979," *Living Blues* 43 (Summer, 1979): 29. A hypothesis concerning one guitarist whom Martin might have heard is in Dave Moore, "Carl Martin, Billy Bird and the Poor Boys," *Blues Link* 5 (n.d. [1974–1975]); 12–13. See also Robert Tilling, "Carl Martin: a Brief Appreciation," *Blues Magazine* (Canada) 2 (December, 1976): 16–18.

16. Welding, "Carl Martin": 29.

17. J. Roderick Moore and Kip Lornell, "On Tour with a Black String Band: Howard Armstrong and Carl Martin Reminisce," *Goldenseal* 2 (October–December, 1976): 47.

18. *East Coast Blues,* Yazoo L–1013. "Crow Jane" is transcribed in Thom Larson, "Carl Martin's *Jane Crow,*" *Blues Magazine* (Canada) 3 (February, 1977): 34–35.

19. Martin, Bogan & Armstrong, *Barnyard Dance,* Rounder 2003 (Somerville, Mass., 1972). *Martin, Bogan & Armstrong,* Flying Fish 003 (Chicago, 1974).

20. Kip Lornell, " 'I Used to go Along and Help: Leslie Riddles [*sic*] Remembers Songhunting with A. P. Carter," in *The Carter Family,* ed. John Atkins (London: Old Time Music, 1973), p. 35. See also Kip Lornell, "Brownie's Buddy: Leslie Riddles," *Living Blues* 12 (Spring, 1973): 20–23.

21. *East Coast Blues,* Yazoo L–1013.

22. Kip Lornell, "Tarter and Gay," *Living Blues* 27 (May-June, 1976): 18.

23. Kip Lornell, "Spatial Perspectives on the Field Recording of Traditional American Music: A Case Study from Tennessee in 1928," *Tennessee Folklore Society Bulletin* 46 (1981): 157.

24. "Drives Knife in Lover's Heart and Cooly Goes Home," Norfolk *Journal and Guide,* August 19, 1922, courtesy Doug Seroff.

25. *Virginia Traditions: Tidewater Blues,* Blue Ridge Institute BRI 006 (Ferrum, Va., 1982).

26. *Blues Scene U.S.A.* vol. 3, Storyville 670.181 (Denmark).

27. Kip Lornell, brochure notes to *Virginia Traditions: Tidewater Blues,* p. 5. Two titles by Carl Hodges, and the subsequent artists cited from this region, are also represented on this album.

28. Kip Lornell to the author, December 16, 1976, and March 6, 1979; Big Boy, "Blues," on *Virginia Traditions: Tidewater Blues,* BRI 006 (Ferrum, Va.: Blue Ridge Institute, 1982).

29. Kip Lornell, "Down in Virginia: Sam Jones and Pernell Charity," *Living Blues* 13 (Summer, 1973): 26.

30. Ibid.: 25–26.

31. Pernell Charity, *The Virginian,* Trix 3309 (Rosendale, N.Y.). Alternative versions of two songs are on *Virginia Traditions: Tidewater Blues.*

32. Dave Dickerson, "When the War is Over," *Another Man Done Gone,* Flyright 528.

33. Mark Wilson, brochure notes to *Frank Hutchinson: The Train That Carried My Girl from Town,* Rounder 1007 (Somerville, Mass.).

34. Sherman Lawson, interviewed by Mike Seeger in Switzer, West Virginia, August 2, 1964; "Hutch: Sherman Lawson Interview," *Old Time Music* 11 (Winter, 1973–74 [*sic*]): 7.

35. Moore and Lornell, "On Tour": 51.

36. Jeff Titon, "Elva Johnson," *Talking Blues* 7 (October-November-December, 1977): 2.

37. Kip Lornell to the author, March 11, 1977; Kent Cooper, "John Henry Folk Festival," *Living Blues* 29 (September-October, 1976): 28.

38. Edward J. Cabbell, "Uncle Homer Walker," *Goldenseal* 6 (July-September, 1980): 70–71; Amy O'Neal, "Blues Heritage Gathering," *Living Blues* 22 (July-August, 1975): 6.

39. Kip Lornell and J. Roderick Moore, "Clarence Tross: Hardy County Banjoist," *Goldenseal* 2 (July-September, 1976): 8.

40. Bill Pollack, "John Jackson's Good-Time Blues," *Living Blues* 37 (March-April, 1978): 26.

41. Chuck Perdue, liner notes to John Jackson, *Blues and Country Dance Tunes from Virginia,* Arhoolie F1025 (El Cerrito, Calif.).

42. Charles K. Wolfe, *Tennessee Strings: The Story of Country Music in Tennessee* (Knoxville: University of Tennessee Press, 1977), p. 33.

43. Sam Rizetta, " 'Whoop it Up a Little Bit': The Life and Music of Blackie Cool," *Goldenseal* 7 (Fall, 1981): 64.

44. Wolfe, *Tennessee Strings,* p. 20.

45. Pete Welding, brochure notes to *Long Steel Rail: Blues by Maryland Songster Bill Jackson,* Testament T–201 (Calif.).

46. Bruce Bastin, brochure notes to Frank Hovington, *Lonesome Road Blues,* Flyright 522 (Bexhill-on-Sea, England, 1976). Two other songs recorded at that time are on albums in the Library of Congress Folk Music in America series: *Songs of Migration and Immigration,* vol. 6, LBC 6, *Songs of Childhood,* vol. 13, LBC 13 (Washington, D.C. 1977).

47. *The Introduction to Living Country Blues USA,* L + R Records 42.030 (German, 1981), (one track only); Guitar Frank and Guitar Slim, *Living Country Blues,* vol. 8, *Lonesome Home Blues,* L + R Records 42.038 (Germany, 1982).

48. Philadelphia *Enquirer,* June 30, 1982; Winnie Hovington to the author, July 7, 1982.

18

Going Up the Country: The Migration North

WASHINGTON, D.C.

Washington, D.C., provided a logical stopover for southern blacks in the process of moving further north. For many it became a permanent or semi-permanent base, hence it became the first major city with a black majority population. The southeast part of the city, down to the Anacostia River, is predominantly black. Many bluesmen brought their music to the city, but despite the location in the city of the Archive of Folk Song at the Library of Congress and more recently the American Folklife Center, plus annual Smithsonian Folk Festivals and the National Folk Festivals held at Vienna, Virginia, no formal attempt has ever been undertaken to investigate black folk music in Washington.

Research into the movements of bluesmen in southern states has uncovered men who moved to D.C. at some time in their lives, like Thelmon Whitehurst from Greenville, North Carolina. Henry Johnson from Union, South Carolina, recalled a guitarist, Arthur "Slim" Thomas, who moved there—not the same man as Guitar Slim from Union, who settled eventually in Greensboro, North Carolina. In the mid-1960s, a local white resident, Ed Morris, located bluesman Buddy Boy Jenkins, who had clearly come in from the Carolinas. Morris had become friendly with ex-Charleston guitarist Ed Green, an older

songster and bluesman, who had roomed in D.C. since about 1950.
Jenkins befriended Green but was a secretive man. Morris described
him as "nomadic (changing residence almost daily, it seemed), cynical,
and untrusting with a perpetual chip on his shoulder. . . . Once, we
did get him to travel with us to a party at John Jackson's house. On
this occasion, (a) tape was made. . . . When finished singing, he
withdrew into general testiness and overindulgence in alcohol. A man
apparently guarding something he felt worth hiding, Buddy Boy Jenkins
was impossible to interview. . . . We have nothing less general than
the East Coast (probably the Carolinas) for his stomping grounds."[1]
That might serve as an epitaph to many bluesmen, unknown outside
their small band of friends, who were past their peak as performers,
irretrievably damaged by a combination of alcohol and poverty. The
party tape, however, survived. Slightly the worse for drink and clearly
the worse for living a rough existence, Jenkins nonetheless came across
as a performer who once must have been proficient. The most significant number was a version of "Greasy Greens," sung in just the same
manner as the Rocky Mount, North Carolina, harmonica player, Peg
Leg Sam. Sam's version is highly distinctive; Jenkins's phrasing and use
of certain stanzas suggest that he heard him. Nothing more could have
been made of this had it not been for a chance remark by another North
Carolina bluesman, Elester Anderson, of Tarboro, just to the east of
Rocky Mount. Trying one day to recall some of the older bluesmen,
he was playing harmonica with a younger cousin, Juke-Boy Anderson,
on guitar. Suddenly Elester said, "That's how Buddy Jenkins used to
play. You know how Buddy Jenkins could play 'cos your brother
would play just like Buddy Jenkins. He and Buddy Jenkins played just
about all the time."[2] Then, Buddy Jenkins was merely another
bluesman about whom, in all probability, nothing more would ever
be known. More than four years later I heard the Buddy Boy Jenkins
tape and it is difficult to conclude but that they were the same man,
especially as a favorite unnamed ragtime tune of Jenkins was the same
as one that Bethel's Jack Jordan used to play.

If Washington, D.C., became the home for untraceable bluesmen like
Whitehurst and itinerant vagrants like Jenkins, it remains the home
for other fine bluesmen like Archie Edwards and John Cephas. Edwards
was born in 1918 in Rocky Mount, Virginia, in Franklin County—
within a few miles and two years of John Tinsley. Highly regarded
around the city, he nonetheless did not record until 1980. Despite
guitar and vocal inflections more reminiscent of Blind Lemon Jefferson, his cover of Jefferson's "Balky Mule Blues," issued as "Bear Cat

Mama Blues'' on a sampler album, reveals distinctive touches of East Coast guitar and a high degree of playing competence. A far better idea of his repertoire and range can be obtained from a full album in the same series.[3] Drawing widely on source material, he remains a fine musician and singer completely in the regional style. Other artists' songs swiftly become his own, but he has an impressive range of his own songs with no obvious recorded source. The album title track, among others, shows him to be a fine, raggy, finger-picker; he also plays exciting slide guitar, as on "I Called My Baby Long Distance." Until recently little more than a well-kept and well-respected secret, Edwards's music can now be heard, for he is a member of the local "Traveling Blues Workshop."

John Cephas was born in Washington, D.C., on September 4, 1930, but raised in Bowling Green (Caroline County), Virginia, between Fredericksburg and Richmond, in the Virginia tidewater region. Growing interested in music at the age of ten he learned his first chords on guitar from an aunt and from local bluesmen Haley Dorsey and James and David Talifarro, as well as from record.[4] Recording in 1980 he recalled plenty of music in the country. "When I come along, we didn't have too much else to do. . . . We sit aroun' and play guitars on the weekend. That's the only real entertainment we had, really you know. Of course, some people had record players an' stuff like that, but I guess it was more fun gettin' out there an' drink home-brew an' corn-liquor an' havin' that stompin' music."[5]

Understandably Cephas returned to Washington to find work and now holds down a well-paid job as a carpenter, living in the city during the week and returning to Bowling Green at weekends, neatly encapsulating the pull factors of work in the big city for rural dwellers. For a while he played with pianist Big Chief Ellis, who settled in the southeast of the city. Originally from Alabama, Ellis had recorded in New York in the 1940s with East Coast musicians like Brownie McGhee, so Cephas's clean, economical, but firm guitar lines suited him well. They gigged locally and appeared at the 1975 National Folk Festival, but after Chief's untimely death in December 1977 Cephas joined up with a young black harmonica player, Phil Wiggins, with whom he had been playing since 1975 in a trio called the Barrelhouse Rockers. Playing traditionally, in a manner belying his twenty-six years, Wiggins offers an effective accompaniment, never burying Cephas's delicate guitar shadings. Their album reveals an indelible stamp of the East Coast, especially on the indigenous pieces. Cephas's playing has an uncanny resemblance to Frank Hovington's, notably on titles like

"I Ain't Got No Lovin' Baby Now," which Hovington also recorded. Cephas's "Richmond Blues" is exactly in the style of Bull City Red's 1935 version.

Another version had been recorded three years earlier, a duet with fellow Virginia guitarist John Woolfork, from Caroline County. He also performs an excellent "Reno Factory," which has recorded parallels only in Virginia, and an intriguing "West Carey Street Blues," which seems to be based on one of Blind Lemon's most frequently copied songs, "One Time Blues" of 1927. Actually it is closer to two other Virginia recordings: played slowly, Cephas's version is melodically closest to "West Kinney Street Blues" by the enigmatic Skoodle-Dum-Doo and Sheffield, recorded for Regis in 1943, but it shares the last three stanzas with not only Lemon's version but also James Lowry's 1953 version, "Karo Street Blues," from Bedford, Virginia. Lemon's East Cairo Street became Karo Street for Lowry, while West Kinney is a street in Newark, New Jersey—topical, as it was recorded there. Cephas names it West Karo at times in his song, mistranscribed as West Carey. One wonders how he came to know the song, for although it has an harmonica accompaniment like the Regis version, Cephas's timing and approach to the song suggest that was not the source but clearly neither was Lemon's. His "Eyesight to the Blind" is very closely based on the New York-located Larks' version recorded for Apollo in 1951 (when it reached number five in the rhythm and blues charts), whose lead singer and guitarist was the North Carolina-born Tarheel Slim. In 1981 Cephas and Wiggins first toured with the American Folk Blues Festival to Europe, adding a fresh sound to the more commonplace sounds of amplified Chicago.

BALTIMORE

If Washington, D.C., is a logical stopover for northward-migrating blacks, so too is Baltimore, although as a blues center it has been totally ignored. No fieldwork has ever been undertaken there, and the only information to hand of the undoubted blues scene has come from other bluesmen who recalled incidents in passing. Virginia guitarist Pernell Charity recalled that local pianist *Fisher *Beale had moved there, and Jim Fuller, the teacher of Maryland songster Bill Jackson, was traced to central Baltimore. The black communities of the Oyster and Colt 45 areas posed problems to a researcher with no firm leads, but one guitarist there with a solid reputation was John Henry *Key, living in the southwest of the city. Baltimore is also reputed to have sported the Orchid label, one rare issue of which featured the vocal and guitar of a Sunny Jones, probably the Sonny Jones who recorded in 1939; only two copies are known of it. On "Leaving Home Blues" he sings about returning to Wilson, North Carolina. Apart from these few fractured gleanings of a Baltimore blues scene, nothing more is known.

PHILADELPHIA

Philadelphia may well have no more significance as a blues center on the migration route north, but it has provided greater documentary evidence. Not only was there a record industry there in the 1940s and 1950s but extensive research was undertaken there by one of the most thorough and indefatigable American researchers, Pete Welding, and his published findings enable us, to some extent, to fill out the background of Philadelphia as a blues center.

Morris Ballen owned Gotham Records, one of the most important on the eastern scene, and was involved with other smaller labels. Most Gotham issues were of gospel artists, but there was an excellent representation of country blues from various sources. Ten titles, many of them in the East Coast style, were recorded for Gotham by Dan Pickett, the most prolific of the label's bluesmen. It has been suggested that Pickett was from Alabama and that he might be the same man who recorded in 1937 for Decca as Charlie Pickett. The Gotham "Ride to Your Funeral in a V-8" is based directly on Buddy Moss's song, "Lemon Man" has strong Durham undertones, and on "Number Writer," on which he is joined by a second guitarist, the two-guitar accompaniment is typical of the East Coast.

One of the last Gotham blues issues was by a Carolina bluesman, Doug Quattlebaum. "Lizzie Lou" owes more to the emerging rock-n-roll of the southern whites—not forgetting that Philadelphia was to become a significant center for this music—but "Don't Be Funny Baby" is a strong blues, with forceful vocal delivery, tough lyrics, and acoustic country blues guitar. Especially in the bridges, the guitar fits the East Coast pattern, even if the vocal line is less evidently regional. Quattlebaum was not recorded again until 1961 when, as Pete Welding explained, "A friend told me of a singer-guitarist he had heard operating off an ice cream truck in the Negro commercial district of South Philadelphia. Parking his Mister Softee Truck by the sidewalk, he would plug his guitar and a cheap microphone into a small amplifier he had rigged up on the truck body. Once set up, he would then launch into a song program, much of the material of a frankly popular nature with an occasional stirring blues thrown in."[6] With a name like Quattlebaum he was easy enough to locate for a recording session, and an album was cut for the pioneering Bluesville label. Although he used a steel National and played several of Blind Boy Fuller's numbers, his influences were broader, and he evinces a less obvious regionalism than other bluesmen who moved to the city. Born in Florence, South Carolina, in 1927, he moved to Philadelphia, where his father-in-law taught him to play guitar, in 1941. He also learned a little from his step-father, a brother of bluesman Arthur Crudup, but he seems largely to be self-taught, as his idiosyncratic touch suggests.

Welding also found a blind singer from Florida, Connie Williams, playing both accordion and guitar on the streets in south Philadelphia.[7] Born in 1915 in southern Florida, Williams had attended the St. Petersburg School for the Blind, and there he improved his musical abilities. By the early 1930s he was on the road, singing and playing for a living. He settled in Philadelphia in 1935, although he continued occasionally to travel. One important teaming was with Gary Davis in New York, and some gospel numbers, like "Crossed the Separated Line," recorded from Williams by Welding, clearly show this. He was probably most at home playing gospel songs; Frank Hovington warmly recalled Williams singing with a gospel quartet, as he was a frequent visitor to his mother's African Methodist Episcopal church in Frederica, Maryland. Hovington also remembered running across Connie Williams in Philadelphia in the 1940s.

Williams was one of the few blacks outside Louisiana still playing accordion for a living: on some titles on his album he plays accordion. Welding produced a whole album featuring two black gospel street singers, one of whom plays accordion accompaniment.[8] Clarence Clay and William Scott had been singing and playing in Philadelphia's city-center commercial district for thirteen years by the time Welding located them. Both were from Virginia, where they were born in the 1920s; Clay—the accordionist—is from South Boston (Halifax County). The accordion was a popular instrument in Virginia and across into North Carolina.[9] Another Virginian recorded by Welding in Philadelphia was guitarist Carl Hodges, who has now returned to his home state.[10]

Quite clearly, an important blues tradition existed in the city, doubtless dating from a period far earlier than this scant documentary evidence suggests. Like Baltimore, it served as a distinct base, not simply as a jumping-off point on the way to the New York metropolis. During and after World War II this vast urban complex emerged as the center for many fine Piedmont bluesmen, the terminus of a major migration route directly parallel to that from Mississippi via Memphis and St. Louis to Chicago.

NEW JERSEY–NEW YORK

The movement of blacks into New York City was well established by the turn of the century, although Harlem as such had still to emerge. In 1900 some 60,000 blacks lived in the city, mostly in Manhattan, and by 1910 a boom was under way as the black population topped 90,000. Fewer than 25 percent had been born in New York state; "Virginia, North Carolina, South Carolina, Georgia and Florida, in perfect geographical order, were the major southern sources of New York's migrant population."[11] This sudden influx of southern blacks was almost entirely rural. By 1920 two-thirds of Manhattan's black population lived in Harlem, then extending approximately from 130th Street on the south to 144th Street on the north, and stretching west of Fifth to Eighth Avenue.[12] Between 1910 and 1920 that population had swollen by 66 percent. It more than doubled in the following decade so that by 1930 New York City held more blacks than the combined Negro populations of Birmingham, Memphis, and St. Louis, all of which were of enormous significance in the regional development of blues. By 1930 the figures of black in-migrants to the city from their states of origin almost exactly repeated the pattern of two decades earlier; only the Carolinas have reversed in importance.[13]

Negro In-Migration, New York City 1930

Virginia	44,471
South Carolina	33,765
North Carolina	26,120
Georgia	19,546
Florida	8,249

In his pioneering study of human geography in the South, published in 1932, Rupert Vance highlighted some reasons for this demographic shift. "The Negro . . . has suddenly become the most mobile figure on the Southern map. The shutting off of immigration and the resultant high wages have reallocated marginal black tenants bewilderingly contending with the gyrations of weather, weevil and cotton prices in Alabama and Georgia black belts."[14] Poor blacks in states to the north of these also suffered similar troubles and, rather than face them out, moved. However, movement was not continuous and was subject to fluctuation as returning migrants left the industrial northeast. "Migration, the escape outlet for lack of jobs, shows an irregular tendency to decline over the period [1930-60]; the decade 1940-50 interrupted the trend . . . with further improvements in the loss ratio for 1960-70."[15] Agricultural adjustment and the growth of mechanization, the removal of past provincialism through rising educational levels, and an increase in the number of cities with populations in excess of half a million all contributed to these fluctuations.

Documented evidence reveals an established blues scene in New York during the period of its maximum black population influx. There was money to be earned by musicians, so musicians came, and many New York black jazz musicians of this period came from the Southeast.[16] A number of artists, clearly of southeastern origins, recorded in the greater New York area in the 1920s. Out on Long Island QRS recorded Georgia harmonica player Eddie Mapp in the company of Slim Barton and James Moore, neither men known to Mapp's friends of that time. In 1928 Seth Richard recorded for Columbia; research in Virginia strongly suggests that he was from around Bedford County. As Skoodle-Dum-Doo, the title of one of the 1928 sides, he recorded in New Jersey in 1943. The guitar-harmonica combination of Bobby Leecan and Robert Cooksey suggests a southeastern origin. While their song titles suggest a number of states, they may have been based across the river in Philadelphia for a while, as "South Street Stomp," "South Street Blues," and "Philadelphia Cut-Out" indicate. Maybe Leecan's "Macon Georgia Cut-Out"—assuming that he is the Blind Bobby Baker credited on the Pathe-Perfect issues—correctly places his origin. In 1926-27 they recorded quite extensively for Victor at their Camden, New Jersey, studios. They were certainly active around New York in 1927, backing singers Helen Baxter and Margaret Johnson, and were clearly resident there the previous year, for an incident involving them appeared in the New York *Amsterdam News.* Jazz researcher Walter Allen wrote that "there was a feature story about the killing of one member of the Jazzing Three which toured the pool halls, cafes and restaurants of Harlem to pick up money by playing for the patrons. The trio was broken up when an unknown assailant's bullet killed Luny Van Story, age 35, of 221 West 140th Street. Robert Leecan, 28, of 140 West 133 St. was injured. Robert "Rabbit Foot" Cooksey, 32, of 155 West 123 St. was not hurt. The trio played harmonica banjo and guitar."[17] Cooksey was around New York as early as 1924-25, when he accompanied Viola McCoy and Sara Martin, and was still there in 1928, recording for Victor behind El Watson, presumably another southeastern singer in view of his earlier session for Victor in Bristol, Tennessee.

One of the major bluesmen to settle in the city was South Carolina's Josh White, although by the time he reached New York he was far removed from being the typical rural southern bluesman. His final recorded coupling for ARC in 1936 was "No More Ball and Chain" and "Silicosis Is Killin' Me," and he was about to enter his phase of vociferous social protest, seeing his songs as vehicles for a wider response. Writing the liner notes to the album on which "Silicosis Is Killin' Me" was reissued, that terrier of social injustice Archie Green states that "although I have never tried to force blues into the mold of conscious protest, I have long felt that work blues inferred positive socio-political statements. . . . "Silicosis Is Killin' Me" . . . about industrial death, seems to be the ultimate negation of life. Yet for me the very act of composition and the meaningful recorded performance together imply that laborers need not be senselessly murdered in tunnel construction. . . . Essentially, I hear work blues with optimistic ears."[18] One might well say that Archie Green has no other, but Josh White would have been well pleased that this indefatigable man chose his song to make the point. However, it was not the cry of an impoverished southern black that one was to hear, for Josh White opened at the Cafe Society Downtown in Manhattan in 1939 at $100 a week and by 1947 was earning $750 a week there.

About 1938 White had cut his hand on a milk-bottle so badly that he had to re-learn how to play the guitar, which he already played incorrectly—"upside down." This partly accounts for the gap in his recording career.[19] A session in March 1940 produced a three-disc album set for Musicraft and a twelve-inch disc for Blue Note. The set was entitled *Night Life in New York;* the music was rather better than one might have expected. Despite the presence of a completely unnecessary upright-bass player, a refugee from numerous swing band sessions, "Prison Bound" and "Hard Time Blues" still retain some fine guitar licks, indicative of Greenville and his early 1930s sides. On the Blue Note, the bassist is joined by his old band leader Sidney Bechet, with whom he'd recorded in 1932. Bechet's inclusion, playing clarinet, underlines the shift to the white nightclub circuit. Later in the year, Columbia issued a controversial album set entitled *Chain Gang.* Despite fervent opposition from social activists, who thought the material degrading to blacks, and claims by Lawrence Gellert that Josh was using his material, John Hammond saw to the album's release. It might well have gained, in the words of Josh's biographer, "wide critical success," but it had nothing to do with grassroots secular music.

In 1941 White was back in the studio to record for Columbia with another clarinetist, Ed Hall, and later there was a session with the Almanac Singers (including Pete Seeger and possibly Woody Guthrie). By now well into his social protest phase, in 1941 Josh cut a session for Keynote which pointed the direction which was to bring him before a subcommittee of the Committee on Un-American Activities in September 1950 on grounds of Communist affiliations.

The Keynote session produced another three-disc album set, this time entitled *Southern Exposure: An Album of Jim Crow Blues.* Titles like "Jim Crow Train" and "Bad Housing Blues" reflect its social nature, and in the liner notes, radical black writer Richard Wright sees what he terms "the 'other side' of the blues. . . . 'non-commercial' because of its social militancy. . . . Where the Negro cannot go, his blue songs have gone, affirming kinship in a nation teeming with indifferences, creating unity and solidarity where distance once reigned."[20] Even without appreciating that the writer credits of all six titles are to Cuney-White,[21] one senses the conscious hand of intellectual liberalism. Actually, to the "Crow Jane" melody, "Defense Factory Blues" has some good guitar with strong regional characteristics, but it was probably the last direct link with the skilled young Greenville teenager whose early 1930s sides were remembered by many East Coast bluesmen, not for their social protest content but for the clear diction and fast fingering.

One shrewd bluesman who had seen a better life beckon from the Big Apple was Brownie McGhee. In 1942 he and Sonny Terry moved to New York, where they became popular playing in white folk clubs and recording on the small labels which proliferated after 1943. They became involved in the white revivalist movement of the Seegers, Guthrie, Cisco Houston, and the New Lost City Ramblers, while selling heavily to a black record-buying audience which spread well beyond the Northeast. It was a rare combination, and among collectors and less discerning critics they have been largely castigated on the former count and ignored on the latter.

Before they achieved international fame, money was as hard to come by as in North Carolina. Brownie still had his big Gibson J.200 guitar, which he had bought on the proceeds of his first recording sessions, and with an amplifier it stood him in good stead working on the streets. The Depression, which had almost ruined the record industry, had receded. Record sales were approaching the old 1927 peak of 104 million records sold until, as Roland Gelatt states in his magnificent history of the phonograph, "price cuts, jukeboxes, and intensive promotion by three highly competitive companies served to swell and quicken the phonograph's return to public favor. When the figures were compiled for 1941, the industry rubbed its eyes with amazement and found that 127,000,000 discs had been sold that year."[22] Then the war in Europe spread to include the United States, and Brownie McGhee's hope that the latest boom and his Okeh contract would chart him to success collapsed. In April 1942 the War Production Board ordered a 70-percent cut in the nonmilitary use of shellac—the basic ingredient of a record. Most shellac came from India, a British colony under serious threat of Japanese invasion.

On the heels of the shellac restrictions came a recording ban. By 1939 some 225,000 jukeboxes were using 13 million records. James Caesar Petrillo, an ex-trombonist and president of the American Federation of Musicians, feared that by 1942 the numbers of jukeboxes might reach 400,000 and, at the June 1942 Dallas convention, called for militant action. Every AFM local was instructed to inform members that they were to refuse all recording engagements after July 31, 1942. Interestingly, when Petrillo had been playing in Art Kahn's 1926 orchestra he recorded for Columbia. Two of the titles were "What a Man!" and "He's the Last Word."[23] For bluesmen like Buddy Moss that was to be true.

After restrictions on the use of shellac were relaxed and the Petrillo ban ended by late 1943, independent record companies blossomed forth. Arnold Shaw, in his highly informative and readable book on the post-war rhythm-and-blues years, explained that "although wartime prosperity generated a higher level for blacks and wartime psychology favored public desegregation . . . home entertainment was still a staple of Negro life. As black income levels rose, there was a growing demand for records, and not the white records and artists produced by the major companies."[24] The new independents were run by whites with attitudes far removed from those of the majors. These men were succinctly described by an old record company executive in Shaw's book: "Ralph Bass was one of a group of men who were white and intelligent, even learned, and who became so involved in R & B they went black—and I mean *Black*. They talked black, affected black mannerisms, and some of them married black women. . . . Paul Reiner of Black & White Records, Herman Lubinsky of Savoy, Freddy Mendelsohn of Regent and Herald, Leonard Chess of Chess and Checkers [*sic*], Jerry Wexler of Atlantic, Art Rupe of Specialty—all of them were bright, well read if not erudite, and all of them became so profoundly enmeshed in R & B, they literally changed color. And all of them happened to be Jewish."[25] Lubinsky established Savoy, the first significant independent rhythm-and-blues label, in 1942 and almost immediately began to challenge the major-dominated charts. While the "hits" would be of the newer music, Savoy nonetheless decided that there was a sufficiently large market for the traditional blues sounds. Lubinsky, never a man to invest where there was no return, clearly endorsed the action. It should be noted that the *Billboard* yearbook for 1943 lists many "sepia" reissues by the major companies—presumably because of the AFM recording ban—but with

Savoy still preoccupied with gospel, the only independent record company to feature among "Records Released" that year was Joe Davis's Beacon label.

Brownie McGhee and Sonny Terry began recording for Savoy in 1944 but did not have a hit until after a second Petrillo ban in 1948. That spring they recorded "My Fault." Only then was McGhee able to arrange a contract. He had been introduced to Savoy by Sam Manning, a Trinidad-born band leader who had recorded for many labels in a span of twenty years, commencing with Paramount in 1924 and recording mainly for Okeh and Columbia during the 1920s. He had an active dramatic career on Broadway and Drury Lane,[26] and was involved in the Pan-African Movement, serving on the executive committee of the International African Friends of Abyssinia in 1935 with Marcus Garvey's first wife as treasurer, and Jomo Kenyatta as honorary secretary.[27] Brownie McGhee well remembered Manning, who reportedly died in Africa, in 1967:[28] "I had talked to Sam Manning before, he was a shrewd West Indian guy. He said, 'Brownie, I'll get you a recording date, you give me 25 per cent of your money.' I said, 'alright, you get it.' He was right there in Harlem. He got me an audition for Savoy. Herman Loebinsky [*sic*]. He wanted me to try out for four sides. I got it all down in my little diary how much I got. I didn't get much! December 12, 1944, WOR Studios, New York."[29] As the pianist and bass player brought in by Lubinsky couldn't fit with McGhee, he recorded these sides with only Sonny Terry in accompaniment. They are all fine country blues reflecting nothing of the movement to the slicker city. Six titles were issued from the session, two of them as by Sonny Terry. "I Don't" was also made but remains unissued.[30] Following the two Terry sides, it was probably technically by Terry.

In next ten years McGhee recorded for more than a dozen small labels. Although by no means all performances were in the adopted Carolina blues style, many of his 1946 sides for Alert were, and he reworked Fuller's "Three Ball Blues" as "Pawnshop Blues" for Disc in 1947 and covered "My Bulldog Blues" the following year for the Sittin' In With label. There were more fine sides in 1952 for Bob Shad's SIW and Jax labels and a fine unaccompanied coupling for Par. He also appeared as guitarist on a wide array of sessions, often with East Coast musicians like Leroy Dallas, Bobby Harris, and Alonzo Scales, or others who readily played in their style, like Ralph Willis and Big Chief Ellis. He performed with nonregional units, backing female shouter Big Maybelle on Savoy, and teamed up again with Leadbelly for Disc backed by jazz bassist George "Pops" Foster, who had been on many of his

Alert sides, and Harlem stride pianist Willie "The Lion" Smith. In 1946 pianist Dan Burley, then business editor of the *Amsterdam News,* recorded him for Rudi Blesh's Circle label in the form of a rent-party group, using the ubiquitous Pops Foster on bass and Brownie's brother on second guitar.

Recording for Moses Asch's Folkways label in 1955 effectively shifted Brownie and Sonny—as they became universally known—away from black listening audiences to white, both for recording and performing. Their "folk" period began, but they are always capable of laying down a fine Piedmont blues in the very best tradition, and their prodigious recorded output is studded with examples. Although their subsequent careers lie outside the limiting scope of this study, there can be no doubt that through their music a vast number of people have been exposed to some of the vigorous music which has grown out of the fabric of Piedmont blues. To Paul Oliver in 1958, Brownie described himself as "a damn good entertainer." No one could argue with that modest self-assessment.

One of those in the small camaraderie which Brownie built up of largely East Coast bluesmen in New York was his brother, Stick. Christened Granville, he was rather more than two years Brownie's junior. From Kingsport, Tennessee, he moved about 1940 to Portsmouth, Virginia, to stay with a sister. With the advent of war, Stick found himself in boot camp in St. Petersburg, where he wrote a song popular among his draftee friends with the refrain, "Drinkin' wine, motherfucker, drinkin' wine, pass the bottle to me," which was to become his passport to minor success later in New York. First, however, he served a four-year stint in the army in the Pacific theater of the war, during which he received a slight hand wound which fortunately did not affect his guitar playing. The guitar returned with him, engraved with the names of every city he had visited there, so that he preferred to be called "Globetrotter" McGhee. Brownie, however, never cared for it, partly because he felt responsible for his brother acquiring the name "Stick."

Stick arrived in New York shortly before the Circle session in June 1946. He and Brownie then worked on the boot camp song, altering the lyrics to make them nonsensical—everyone knew what was intended anyway—and brought in Horace Holmes to write down the melody line. On the strength of the song Mayo Williams cut a session for his own Harlem label in 1947 just with Stick and a bass player. A superb "Baby Baby Blues" with excellent East Coast guitar was backed by the bowdlerized "Drinkin' Wine Spo-Dee-O-Dee." Stick continued to work in the Village, making cosmetics for an old friend from

Kingsport, when the rapidly arising Atlantic label decided to record "Drinkin' Wine."

Herb Abramson cut it in February 1949 at a studio on 57th Street using Brownie and Big Chief Ellis in support. Brownie did not think that Pops Foster had been on bass, for otherwise "it would have been a much more elegant session."[31] It was an instant success, staying in the charts for twenty-two weeks and reaching third place in the *Billboard* rhythm-and-blues charts. Selling over 300,000 discs, it was Atlantic's first rhythm-and-blues hit and set the future direction of the company.[32]

On the strength of the Atlantic hit, Williams leased the Harlem version to Decca, but it is rare among collectors. Stick never quite had the same success again—although a 1951 song made second place in the charts—despite four more sessions for Atlantic, three for King, and sessions for other labels, including Savoy. On some he was backed by Brownie and on two, including his last—for Herald in 1960—he was accompanied by Sonny Terry. He contracted cancer and died in New York on August 15, 1961.

One of the older bluesmen with whom Brownie McGhee recorded, Leroy Dallas, cut a few sides for Bob Shad's SIW label in 1949. Acting on a tip from McGhee, researcher Pete Welding located Dallas in Brooklyn in 1962, but by then he was unable to repeat his earlier sides with any success. Born in Mobile, Alabama, on December 12, 1910, he moved to Memphis in 1924. Six years later, aged twenty, he was on the road with Frank Edwards, whom he met in Mobile. Although Edwards's highly personal style did not suit Dallas—or anyone else for that matter—he nevertheless learned from him. Edwards "played very, very slow, with a drag. He never did have the rhythm that I cared for," he recalled, but "after I learned different keys and chords from Frank, then I figured out the rhythm for myself."[33] Edwards, usually playing only harmonica, and Dallas teamed up with Georgia Slim and played with the Star Band in Atlanta. In 1943 Dallas moved to New York, where he recorded with Brownie McGhee and Big Chief Ellis, another Alabaman, who was managing a bar, the Big Apple at 135th and 7th Avenue, in which McGhee used to play. Interestingly, this bar was owned by Adolph Thenstead, a Jamaican pianist, whose Mentor Boys had provided the backing for Sam Manning's 1927 Okeh session. An extant airshot of WNYC's Jazz Festival of February 19, 1949, has McGhee introducing his piano player as "Big Boy Ellis from Birmingham, just a new discovery, famous with the blues." They were the only bluesmen on the program. Backing Leroy Dallas on "Your Sweet Man's Blues," Ellis and McGhee enable him to show his Piedmont influences; he makes a nod of appreciation toward Frank Edwards's slower 1941 version for Okeh. Also on Dallas's "Your Sweet Man's Blues" is bass player Bobby Harris from South Carolina. His real name was Herman *Caseay and he recorded for many of the same small labels as did McGhee—Derby, Jackson, and Par.

Another Alabama artist, often backed by Brownie McGhee, who managed to absorb much of the East Coast guitar styling was Ralph Willis, who lived for a while in the 1930s in North Carolina, perhaps near Winston-Salem. Born in 1910 he moved to New York in the 1930s, living for a while on 110th Street. Like McGhee, he recorded for many small labels between 1944 and 1953. His first coupling for Regis included a slightly Fullerish "Worried Blues," although his languid vocal delivery is far removed from Fuller's. An uninhibited performer, he excelled in bawdy numbers like the Regis flip, "Comb Your Kitty Kat," while a 1951 recording of "Income Tax Blues" is strongly reminiscent of Tommy McClennan. His first release was as Ralph ('Bama) Willis, and later releases were as Alabama Slim and Ralph Willis's Alabama Trio, but two 1948 Savoy couplings were issued for some reason as by Washboard Pete and Sleepy Joe's Washboard Band. Supported by McGhee's guitar, he cut a fine cover of Luke Jordan's "Church Bell Blues," a gentle "Blues Blues Blues," and a delicate "Tell Me Pretty Baby" (two takes), all refuting with immense clarity the rumor that the older East Coast blues style was dead. His final sides— with McGhee and Terry—were cut for King in 1953, remarkably seeing issue in both England and France.

One musician with whom McGhee was associated in New York was Gary Davis, whose careers in Greenville and Durham have been outlined earlier. By the time he arrived in New York in January 1944, he was singing only gospel material. Not until later, under the coaxing of Stefan Grossman, did he begin to record secular music that he had heard in his youth. Whether one listens to Davis's 1935 sides or to those from his period of "rediscovery," the living sound of the Piedmont tradition is always there. The "holy blues" of his "Miss Gibson" guitar, to which he frequently talked while playing, live on a wealth of recordings. In January 1949 he recorded sides for Harry Lim's Continental label—which first recorded Big Chief Ellis—resulting in Davis's sole postwar 78 rpm disc, one side of which was a stunning near-blues.[34] Hints of his Greenville days frequently show through, as on "Jesus Knows How Much We Can Bear,"[35] on which, having told Miss Gibson to "get out of here," he takes off on a superb example of the delicate ragtime guitar style, not unlike Willie Walker's runs on "South Carolina Rag." Later albums feature instrumentals as well as serious attempts to record his earliest repertoire, like "Cincinnati Flow Rag" and "Make Believe Stunt."[36]

Davis was truly one of the supreme talents to have emerged from the Piedmont tradition. A detailed documentation of his life in New York has been compiled and awaits publication,[37] and some of his songs, guitar styles, and techniques have been analyzed.[38] One intriguing aspect of his career involves unissued sides recorded in 1949 and the early 1950s. Brownie McGhee recalled recording for Continental with Davis,[39] while Big Chief Ellis recorded with both, separately and together, for Bob Shad.[40] It is highly probable that some of Shad's sides exist, for previously unissued material by other artists has been made available on album over more recent years.

Brownie McGhee and Gary Davis were but two of the East Coast bluesmen who had already recorded by the time they had moved to New York. McGhee's Durham friend, Richard Trice, was another. Georgia harmonica player Buster Brown had been recorded at the Fort Valley Festival in 1943 when he was twenty-eight. He moved to New York as late as 1959 and recorded almost immediately for Bobby Robinson's Fire label. Robinson was no stranger to hits, but Buster Brown's "Fannie Mae" reached number one in the national rhythm-and-blues charts just before Christmas 1959 and stayed for a remarkable twenty-five weeks, the twelfth longest-lasting disc ever. It then crossed over to the pop charts, staying there a further seventeen weeks.[41] Somehow the New York producers always managed to retain a down-home sound to their sessions, even using session men and out-of-work jazzmen as accompanists. Buster Brown's tough, raw vocals and swinging country harp fitted oddly with the riffing saxes and punchy rhythm sections, but he was understandably never able to reproduce his initial colossal success, even though "Sugar Babe" reached number nineteen in 1962. After Robinson let him go he made a series of recordings for small labels, even cutting sessions for Checker in Chicago, but alcohol had begun to take its toll. His last release was in 1972 and by January 1976 he was dead, buried back in Georgia. It would be fairer to remember him as the fine country harp player, whooping and driving over the infectious, bouncy "Good News" cut for Fire in 1960.

One guitarist who had been recorded in 1935 actually set up in New York in opposition to the club circuit run by Brownie McGhee, and according to Alec Seward, both men operated in quite distinct territories. He was Gabriel Brown, whom Alan Lomax and Zora Neale Hurston had recorded on behalf of the Library of Congress in Florida and about whom Lomax had written that he was "better even than

Leadbelly." According to Lomax, Hurston "used him in her earlier shows in Harlem as a singer and an actor [in] . . . a ballad opera based in a turpentine camp and brought the singers up to New York." Presumably this was the "musical comedy" *Polk County,* which was set in a saw mill, but her biographer states that she began work on that show "in the spring on 1944."[42] By that time, Brown was living in Asbury Park, New Jersey, and had signed contracts with Joe Davis's Beacon Record label, one of the flourishing independents. The second recording session with Gabriel Brown actually took place during the period of the American Federation of Musicians' recording ban—although it was a union session, as were all of Davis's sessions—which meant that Gabriel Brown was already living and recording in the North when Hurston wrote him into *Polk County,* but the show might help explain why Davis recorded four further sessions between September 1944 and July 1945.

The very detailed story of these sessions can be found in the brochure and album notes to two albums, each of which features sixteen of Brown's solo recordings, the first covering 1943–45, the second 1944–52.[43] Brown's last commercial release was from a 1952 session, an inordinately late date for a thoroughly uncompromising country blues. By the time Brownie McGhee had recorded for Savoy in December 1944, Gabriel Brown had cut four sessions for Davis, and the sales of his sides can only have acted as an incentive for other small operators to try for a slice of the action. Brown's later years are shrouded in obscurity, but he returned to Florida, where he died in the early 1970s, drowned in a boating accident.

Many of the bluesmen who moved to New York in the postwar period were to make their first recordings there, some to go on to greater fame and others to return to obscurity. One of the younger set of musicians who went on to make a name for himself was guitarist Alden Bunn, later known as Tarheel Slim. Born on September 24, 1924, in Bailey, North Carolina, some twenty-five miles southwest of Rocky Mount, he began playing about 1937 when Blind Boy Fuller was at his peak. He listened avidly to his records—his mother bought every new release that she could—but never saw him play. He had even traveled to a fair in Oxford where Fuller was due to perform, but found him absent because of illness—almost certainly the one which brought about his death. Bunn played with local gospel groups around Wilson, where he had his own group, broadcasting over WPTF in Raleigh five days a week. He gigged in Rocky Mount with medicine show harmonica player Peg Leg Sam, whom he was not to meet again until 1973 at the University of North Carolina's blues festival. Having locally booked the Selah Jubilee Singers in 1947, he came to the notice of their leader, Thurman Ruth: "We were doing a concert in a place out from Wilson, N.C. one night, and Allen [*sic*] Bunn's group was on the show. . . . He had a beautiful voice and played a lot of guitar. So I asked him would he like to become a member of the Selahs. . . . So he told me, 'Well, when my tobacco season is over, I'll be glad to join.'"[44]

For some eight years Bunn was associated with the Selah Jubilee Singers or with Ruth's groups, for Ruth left the Selahs and their name in Raleigh and took to New York a new group, which included Eugene Mumford, recently released from prison in Durham. Ruth and Mumford were to become seminal vocal group singers. With Bunn, they recorded under a number of names and on one day, October 5, 1950, recorded sessions under different names for four companies: as the Selah Singers for Jubilee, as the Southern Harmonaires for Apollo, both in New York, as the Jubilators for Regal, and as the Four Barons for Savoy, in Linden and Newark, New Jersey, respectively. Best known as the Larks, they sang secular songs: "Eyesight to the Blind" has fine lyrics and excellent Carolina blues guitar, with strong Fuller overtones. Really a strong country blues release, with vocal part harmony, it reached number five on the 1951 rhythm-and-blues charts.[45] It set the pattern for Bunn's recording activities. He recorded the following year for the same company with Sonny Terry and Big Chief Ellis, covering Fuller's 1937 "Put You Back in Jail" as "Baby I'm Going to Throw You Out." Nineteen fifty-four saw an excellent "Too Much Competition," rather closer to McGhee than to Fuller, released on Red Robin as by Allen Baum. The reverse featured a vocal group and steered him toward the more lucrative popular market. He teamed up with Anna Lee Sanford, whom he married, and as Tarheel Slim and Little Ann they finally had a good seller, "It's Too Late," for Bobby Robinson in 1958. The following year Slim cut two driving rhythm-and-blues sides with the excellent Jimmy Spruill on guitar, but he was not to record blues again until the 1970s, when he was located by Pete Lowry and recorded for Trix, accompanied by Brownie McGhee and Big Chief Ellis on some titles.[46] He played a few festivals, notably Chapel Hill in March 1973 and Philadelphia in 1974, but died of cancer on August 21, 1977.

Another bluesman who recorded quite extensively in New York was Virginia guitarist Alec Seward, born in Newport News on March 16, 1901. Although he settled in New York as early as 1924, he had played little until he took lessons with Brownie McGhee, who had set up his "Home of the Blues" teaching guitar on 125th Street. Seward lived on 123rd and was his first pupil, but Brownie told Paul Oliver that

"he didn't study enough; didn't come more than three times a week."
Seward's first recording was made on the same day in 1947 that Stick
McGhee cut "Drinkin' Wine" for Harlem, and over the next few years
he recorded for four different labels, as well as recording with Sonny
Terry on Elektra. On some of the latter, Woody Guthrie is present and
they better fit the slowly burgeoning folk boom than they do the traditional blues which Seward recorded earlier, assisted by guitarist Louis
Hayes, a rough-voiced singer from Asheville, North Carolina. Their
duets occasionally consciously reflect Fuller but more usually simply
depict the broader pattern of Piedmont blues. No records were ever
issued under their own names but always under colorful pseudonyms
like Blues King, the Blues Boys, the Back Porch Boys, Guitar Slim and
Jelly Belly, or Slim Seward and Fat Boy Hayes. Many of their best sides
for Tru-Blue and, surprisingly, MGM—such as "Bad Acting Woman"—
appear on album. Disillusioned with the music scene, Seward quit
playing in 1957 but, thanks to Sonny Terry, recorded for Bluesville
in 1965, making one pleasant album.[47] He died on May 11, 1972.

One elusive bluesman whose records sold well in the early 1950s
was Carolina Slim. Recording for Savoy, between July 1950 and June
1952, he had releases also on Acorn and Sharp—an album— which
were part of the Savoy combine. These last two labels called him
Carolina Slim whereas the Savoy issues call him either Jammin' Jim
or Lazy Slim Jim. He also made two sessions in 1951-52 for King
Records, released as by Country Paul, with writer credits variously to
Paul Harris and Paul Howard, rather than to E. Harris as on Savoy.
King and Savoy may have been equally correct, for his real name was
Edward P. Harris. He was born on August 22, 1923, in Leasburg, Casell
County, North Carolina, some thirty miles northwest of Durham and
quite close to the Virginia border below Danville. His father, a local
songster, taught him to play guitar, and he spent most of his life as
an itinerant musician throughout the South and Southwest before he
reportedly settled in Newark, New Jersey, in the early 1950s. His
recording career was relatively extensive, if shortlived; he had twenty-
four titles issued on 78 rpm discs and three more later on album. He
died in Newark's St. James' Hospital on October 22, 1953, of a heart
attack, having been admitted for back surgery.[48]

Harris's blues reflect a wide range of influences from Lightning
Hopkins imitations as on "Black Chariot Blues" to Blind Boy Fuller
copies like "Shake Boogie," complete with "tweaking" across the
bridge. Fuller-like guitar phrases also occur in numbers otherwise not
associated with him, like near the end of "Blues Go Away From Me."

Richard Trice once saw him in Durham, recalling him a tall man of the stature of Floyd Council, and he thought that he might have been a local man. Since he is otherwise recalled as having played with Fuller in Durham, perhaps some of Fuller's influence was direct. Many of Harris's numbers were firmly in the regional mold; his first recorded number, "Mama's Boogie" with bottleneck guitar and a second guitarist, is a good example.

Two other fine bluesmen emerged from nowhere to record, then immediately dropped from sight, yet remain among the finest exponents of the regional style. Boy Green recorded for Regis, and his fine voice and excellent picking are well exposed on "A and B Blues," the flip of which, "Play My Jukebox," possibly unconsciously hints at the recently ended Petrillo ban. Alec Seward mentioned an East Side guitarist, who has never been located, by the name of Willie Green, who might have been the same man. A Willie Green recorded two titles for the Enrica label about 1959 and a man of the same name recorded two unissued sides for Savoy in May 1962.[49] Dennis McMillon, who recorded four titles in 1949 for Fred Mendelsohn's Regal label in Linden, New Jersey, came from North Carolina. Knowing that Mendelsohn had recorded bluesmen in Atlanta earlier in the year, his maid recommended McMillon, stating that he needed ten dollars busfare to get back home.[50] McMillon received his busfare plus an additional forty dollars for the session, for three titles of which we are fortunate to have alternative takes to compare.[51] On "Woke Up One Morning" he plays beautiful slide guitar while the party-dance number, "Paper Wooden Daddy," with its obscure double-entendre, has lyric affinities with Fuller's "I'm a Rattlesnakin' Daddy." Someone told Willie Trice that McMillon was from Burlington, where the city directory contains a host of McMillons—and variations—for that might not have been the correct spelling. It is certainly a northern North Carolina name and is unknown, for instance, in Charlotte.

The foregoing roster of bluesmen who recorded in the city did not end abruptly. Later bluesmen had broader horizons and were less obviously transporters of an oral tradition with clear regional origins. Nonetheless, the music of their birthplaces found its way into their music. Larry Johnson came from Georgia in 1959, having left Navy service, and in 1966 at the age of twenty-seven, was recording blues highly reminiscent of Blind Boy Fuller's, who was selling heavily at the date of Johnson's birth in Atlanta. He recorded an album with a young guitarist from Alabama, Henry "Hank" Adkins, which he followed with solo material for Bobby Robinson, including covers of

Fuller's "So Sweet" and "Step It Up and Go," as well as an instrumental, "Carolina Boogie," in similar vein.[52] About 1970 he cut a further album, playing much in the style of Gary Davis, from whom he learned and for whom he had a great regard. "My Game Blues" is an excellent example of the regional style.[53]

Larry Johnson brought other East Coast bluesmen to the attention of a broader audience. Guitarist Charles Walker came in via Newark in the 1950s, having been born in Macon, Georgia, on July 26, 1922. His father had been a bluesman in Atlanta, going by the name of Bo-Weevil. Lee Roy Little, a pianist from Virginia, had played with Walker ever since 1959, and they had recorded—often together—for a number of small labels. Pianist John Acey Goudelock was from Gaffney, South Carolina, and guitarist Joe Richardson from North Carolina. Tenor sax player Noble Watts had come in from Florida, and although Watts's successes in the late 1950s for the Baton label were rhythm-and-blues instrumentals, they often had a distinct down-home feel. As late as 1961 the small Cee Jay label recorded a female singer, Betty James, backed by two superb acoustic blues guitarists who were obviously from the Southeast, one of whom might have been Tarheel Slim. "I'm a Little Mixed Up" and "Help Me to Find My Love" are clear indications that the regional style persisted, even on commercial release, long after many had thought fit to see it buried. Its commercial appeal was such that the disc was leased by Chess in Chicago and the former title was even issued on album, in both the U.S.A. and England.[54]

Another female singer and guitarist from the southeast was Marylyn Scott. In 1945 in Charlotte, North Carolina, she made one obscure coupling for the Free label, on which she was backed by a small modern jazz combo with two saxophones. There is little of regional interest but on "Straighten Him Out" it is just possible to hear snatches of her acoustic guitar. Herbert Reeder, who played tenor saxophone on the session, knew nothing of the singer, whom he "hadn't seen before and hasn't seen since."[55] This session presumably led to a session for Regent, in the rhythm-and-blues vein, backed by Johnny Otis's Orchestra with his regular guitarist, Pete Lewis. Her true ability can only be heard on a rare Lance release which remained undiscovered until 1972, on which she is billed as "Marylin [*sic*] Scott and Her Guitar."[56] One side has a fairly standard, albeit East Coast, guitar boogie, but "I Got What My Daddy Likes" is one of the finest postwar blues from the Piedmont. Her guitar playing is excellent, and her bawdy lyrics outdo the original from which it was taken, Lucille Bogan's

"That's What My Baby Likes" from 1935. Its down-home appeal lies in its very informality, with men in the studio passing comments and laughing outright in slightly embarrassed amusement at lines like

> He flips my flap-jacks clear across the table,
> He feeds all the horses in my little stable,
> I got what my baby likes . . .

She appears also to have recorded for Regent-Savoy as a gospel singer under the name of Mary Deloatch (Deloach). Her fine voice can be heard to good effect on the driving "The Lord's Gospel Train," with excellent piano accompaniment, recorded at her last session in 1951. An earlier session that year had been held in Atlanta, but she disappeared from sight, leaving a Norfolk, Virginia, address in the Savoy files.[57]

FURTHER NORTH

The New Jersey–New York metropolis was not the ultimate goal for all blacks migrating north from the southeastern states. Many stopped off en route at major urban centers, many came to the city and moved on, others bypassed it completely.

William P. Bryant, a guitarist, was born in Rocky Mount, North Carolina, where he knew and played with Alden Bunn (Tarheel Slim) before moving north in 1947. He moved from Newark to Boston, where he set up a barbershop which for years was the hangout for jazz guitarists like Kenny Burrell, Wes Montgomery, and George Benson. Bryant grew up flat-picking in the local style under the influence of records by Josh White, Moss, and Fuller, whose "Black and Tan" he covered in his only issued recording, made on Labor Day 1969.[58]

In Boston Bryant taught a guitarist from Florida, Alvin Hankerson. Born in Fort Lauderdale in 1923, Hankerson was only three when a hurricane destroyed his home, killed his mother, and removed the tip of his right thumb, providing his nickname, Nub or Nubbit. He joined his father on a farm at Waynesboro, Georgia, but by 1939 he moved north, settling in the Roxbury district of Boston. Although he had sung with a large swing band and recorded—as yet undiscovered—soon after he reached Boston, his first issued recording was not until 1962, when he cut for Skippy White's Bluestown label: released as by Guitar Nubbit, "Evil Woman Blues" is entirely East Coast in style. His most remarkable number was "Georgia Chain Gang," with highly personal lyrics over a boogie rhythm—perhaps the last country blues to describe this rural institution, linking with strong voodoo ties of "Doctor Buzzard." A further coupling in 1965, with a drummer added to emphasize the rhythm, included the up-tempo "Big Leg Woman," using lyrics of Blind Boy Fuller's that Baby Tate often liked to use. Hankerson played a few local clubs, then suffered a mental breakdown and subsequently played very little.[59]

While the New York–New Jersey conurbation exerted an overriding pull factor on migration north from the southeastern states, Detroit, with its highly paid motor industry, was also very tempting. A fascinating blues center spawning John Lee Hooker among a welter of lesser-known men, it also possessed highly idiosyncratic record producers like Joe Von Battle, Bernie Besman, and Jack Brown of Fortune. Most of the Detroit bluesmen hailed from the deep South around Mississippi, but a few were from the Southeast. Best documented is Robert Richard, who recorded in 1948 for Von Battle's JVB label, although some sides were leased to King. He also played harp on others' records. Powerful down-home blues they were, but they were not especially reminiscent of his Georgia background. He was born in Cartersville, northwest of Atlanta, on October 4, 1924, and learned to play guitar and harmonica from an uncle, with whom he went to live when his father died in 1934. In 1942 he moved to Detroit, where his brother Howard, also a guitarist, was living, and soon began to mix with the bluesmen along Hastings Street, core of the city's blues scene. In the mid-1970s he recorded an album, playing both guitar and harmonica; his southern roots are often in evidence, especially in his harp playing.[60]

An obscure Detroit bluesman who recorded in the 1950s but was still to be seen around the city a decade later was Henry Smith. Two sides leased to Dot Records of Gallatin, Tennessee, mask his origins in the general stamp of Detroit blues. "Kansas City Blues," an instrumental recorded for Von Battle and issued only on album in 1977, again offers no obvious regional trait, but the liner notes state that "his style can be considered one of the smoothest ever to be placed on tape by Von Battle."[61] Perhaps the reason lies in Smith's only other release, on Fortune. On one side he simply backs a boogie piano instrumental, which offers him no chance to show his ability, but on the reverse, "Dog Me Blues," his only solo performance reveals all the traits of the style associated with the northeastern part of North Carolina around Durham and suggests that this is indigenous, not from record.

Clearly there must have been blues scenes involving country artists in many of the northern cities, but virtually no work has been done in any cities other than Chicago and Detroit. However, in the early 1970s, Kip Lornell uncovered a number of bluesmen around his home town of Delmar, just outside Albany, New York. Many musicians had come in over the years from Alabama, Mississippi and Texas, but a high percentage were from the Southeast. Willie Moore, who moved from North Carolina to Albany in 1949, was the first to be located. A rough preliminary recording session was arranged in November 1970, but unfortunately Moore died of cancer on May 2, 1971, before the planned recording session proper could take place. Thus the only material available comes from that rough session, but we are fortunate to have even this. Two sides issued on album afford a glimpse of how Willie "Cowboy" Moore—according to his obituary notice—must have sounded in his prime.[62]

A Georgia guitarist, Buddy Durham, led Lornell to other Albany musicians. Edward Lee Durham was born in Ashburn, Georgia, halfway between Cordele and Tifton, some 150 miles south of Macon, in 1915. He only began to play about 1936, when he learned a blues in C-natural from an uncle, Tom McCray, but he recalled two other local bluesmen. "My uncle was pretty good but he didn't make no records, didn't none of them ever make no records. There was a guitar picker around (Ashburn) named J. C. Woodard . . . he could make you tremble all over! He also had a boy playing with him, what they called M.C. They was about my age. It was somewhere in Roosevelt's time. They lived between Ashburn and Tifton." By the time Durham had moved to Albany in 1955, he had pretty well given up playing. Although severely burned on the hands in a fire in 1967, he was still able to record in 1973. His voice was well past its peak, but his playing was strongly regional, as on "Goin' Back to Tifton."[63]

Another Georgia bluesman in Albany was Leroy Holmes. Born on April 8, 1921, near Woodbine, between Jacksonville and Brunswick, he commenced playing about 1938 and, as he recalled, "the guy that got me most interested was Pete Hutchinson. I used to hang around joints with him but he was about fifteen years older than me. One of the important things about the music was that it was an access to the girls . . . usually the guy that played the guitar got the most attention."[64] Holmes never recorded. Roy Hunt, Leroy Clark, and Emmit Lang were but three other guitarists from around Woodbine whom he recalled. Another man also moved to Albany, only to return south to Florida in 1956.

John Carter, a harmonica player, was raised in Key West, his parents having moved there from Nassau in the Bahamas, where he was born on September 27, 1914. Discharged from the army in 1945 he remained musically active around Albany for some years, running with a guitarist who might have been Dennis McMillon, who recorded for Regal:

Gabriel Brown, ca. 1943-44 (courtesy of Lucille Davis Bell).

Brownie McGhee, ca. 1948 (courtesy Wilbert and Mattie Ellis and Peter B. Lowry).

Stick McGhee, ca. 1948 (courtesy of Wilbert "Big Chief" Ellis and Peter B. Lowry).

Guitar Slim [James Stephenson] (courtesy of Kip Lornell).

Clarence Tross (courtesy of Carl Fleischhauer)

Frank Hovington, 1976 (courtesy of Bengt Olsson).

Alec Seward, 1970 (courtesy of Peter B. Lowry).

Jackson Jordan (courtesy of Kip Lornell), Tarheel Slim [Alden Bunn] ca. 1961 (courtesy of Peter B. Lowry), and Aaron Washington, 1973 (courtesy of Kip Lornell).

"McMillan, a little short guy, brown skin about like me. He wasn't from around here. . . . He said that he made a record but I never did hear it. He was a hell of a nice quiet guy. This McMillan could play! He left sometime around 1950 or so."[65]

Lornell also located two South Carolina musicians who spanned a wide range of black secular music. Elias "Mac" McKenzie was born in Charleston on May 15, 1915 and around 1918 his family moved to New York City. There he learned to play violin, performing in "tramp bands" in the mid-1930s.[66] "They used to play the kazoo and wear funny clothes, beat washboards. Those are the bands that I used to be with. I had my own little five piece band on the side. We used to play a lot of club dates and parties." In 1940 he moved to Albany, where he eventually gave up music, commenting acidly that "nowadays you have to be a Julliard graduate." Closer to the jazz scene than blues, he was, in his own words, "raised up with the blues singers, Bessie Smith, Ma Rainey, all of them."[67] Aaron Washington was born at Williston, South Carolina, east of Augusta, on January 2, 1902. He learned to play guitar from his uncle, Matt Washington. "When I picked up my first little tune, I must have been about nine years old. . . . The first tune I played was on two strings. That old tune was 'Georgie Buck Is Dead.' I used to play that one in 'vassapool or natural, either. . . . Back then you could hear the old people play fiddles, guitars, banjos and accordion too. Mostly it was string music . . . you see the blues, the regular blues, didn't start until quite a few years after I was a kid. I don't know exactly what year, but I would say it was the '20s at least. I don't remember no blues singers before I was 20 years old."[68] About 1912 Washington moved to Asheville, North Carolina, where he was a member of a string band by 1919. He worked there with Gary Davis and was certainly playing blues by the time he left in 1926, settling in Catskill, New York, south of Albany, where there was little music. By the time he moved into Albany in the early 1950s, although the scene around Green Street was still very active, he took little part. Coaxed into recording by Kip Lornell, he performed a repertoire which remained predominantly pre-blues.

It is unfortunate that no enterprising blues researcher investigated cities like Buffalo, Rochester, and Pittsburgh,[69] as they might well have maintained significant cells of southern musicians lured north by greater economic opportunity. By this late date it is unlikely that anything like a comprehensive survey can ever be undertaken, but all evidence points to the fact that southern folk, having moved to northern cities, brought their music with them. That music also persisted against the odds for much longer than had been presumed. In

1970, writing in answer to the rhetorical question "Is there a Folk in the City?" as a follow-up of the classic statements on folk culture by Robert Redfield and George Foster,[70] folklorist Richard M. Dorson warned that many songs "may belong to an inactive memory culture rather than to a vigorous living growth."[71] With the passage of time, that warning was, of course, apt, but at the time he was writing, the blues styles that built up the pattern of Piedmont blues and spread into the northern cities were clearly still part of a persistent living growth. Even if no longer "vigorous" within the community, they were some distance from being part of an "inactive memory culture." However, during the late 1970s so many of these carriers of the tradition died that Dorson's foreboding is now a reality.

NOTES

1. Ed Morris, quoted by Bruce Bastin, brochure notes to *Another Man Done Gone,* Flyright 528 (Bexhill-on-Sea, England, 1979), p. 7.

2. Elester T. Anderson, interviewed by the author, Conetoe, North Carolina, March 11, 1973.

3. Archie Edwards, "Bear Cat Mama Blues," *The Introduction to Living Country Blues USA,* L+R Records LS 42.030 (West Germany, 1981); *The Road is Rough and Rocky: Living Country Blues USA, Vol. 6,* L+R Records LR 42.036 (West Germany, 1982).

4. Kip Lornell cites James Talifarro; Axel Küstner cites David Tallafarro. They might be the same man. The name has a variety of spellings in Virginia and North Carolina.

5. Axel Küstner, liner notes to *Bowling Green John and Harmonica Phil Wiggins From Virginia,* L+R Records LR 42.031 (West Germany, 1981). LS 42.030—see note 3—includes "Reno Factory." See also John Cephus and John Woolfork, "Richmond Blues," *Virginia Traditions: Tidewater Blues,* Blue Ridge Institute BR 1006 (Ferrum, Va., 1982).

6. Pete Welding, liner notes to *Doug Quattlebaum: Softee Man Blues,* Prestige 1065 (Bergenfield, N.J.). Another Florence, South Carolina, bluesman recorded an album in Pennsylvania—Nyles Jones, *My South, My Blues,* Gemini 7101 (Pittsburgh, Pa).

7. *Blind Connie Williams: Philadelphia Street Singer,* Testament T-2225 (Calif.).

8. *The Blues of Clarence Clay and William Scott: The New Gospel Keys,* Prestige-Bluesville 1066 (Bergenfield, N.J.).

9. Kip Lornell to the author, November 21, 1975.

10. Hodges can be heard on *Ramblin' on My Mind: A Collection of Classic Train and Travel Blues,* Milestone MLP-3002 (Calif.), and *Blues Scene U.S.A.* vol. 3, Storyville SLP-181 (Denmark). Both include tracks by Connie Williams

and Maryland songster Bill Jackson. The latter also has one title by Doug Quattlebaum.

11. Kelly Miller, "The Economic Handicap of the Negro in the North," *The Annals of the American Academy of Political and Social Science* 27 (May, 1906): 547, in Gilbert Osofsky, *Harlem, The Making of a Ghetto: Negro New York, 1890–1930* (New York: Harper & Row, 1963), p. 304. See also Ira Katzenlson, *Black Men, White Cities: Race Politics and Migration in the United States 1900–30 and Britain 1948–68* (London: Oxford University Press, 1973), pp. 62–85.

12. Osofsky, *Harlem,* p. 123.

13. Ibid, pp. 128–29.

14. Rupert B. Vance, *Human Geography of the South: A Study in Regional Resources and Human Adequacy* (Chapel Hill: University of North Carolina Press, 1932), pp. 279–80.

15. John L. Fulmer, "Trends in Population and Employment in the South from 1930 to 1960 and Their Economic Significance," in *Essays in Southern Development,* ed. Marvin L. Greenhut and W. Tate Whitman (Chapel Hill: University of North Carolina Press, 1964), p. 225.

16. John Chilton, *Who's Who of Jazz* (London: Bloomsbury Book Shop, 1970). Of specific relevence is idem., *A Jazz Nursery: The Story of the Jenkins Orphanage Bands* (London: Bloomsbury Book Shop, 1980), as many of these Charleston, South Carolina, musicians became renowned jazzmen.

17. New York *Amsterdam News,* March 3, 1926, in *Record Research* 93 (November, 1968): 15.

18. Archie Green, liner notes to *Hard Times,* Rounder 4007 (Somerville, Mass.).

19. Robert Shelton, *The Josh White Song Book* (Chicago: Quadrangle Books, 1963), p. 24; Francis Wilford-Smith to the author, July 18, 1983.

20. Richard Wright, notes to *Southern Exposure,* Keynote album set 107. A good example of his writing is in idem., *Twelve Million Black Voices* (London: Lindsay Drummond, 1947).

21. Waring Cuney was a black poet and member of the Harlem Renaissance. Marion Berghahn, *Images of Africanism in Pan-American Literature* (London: Macmillan, 1977), pp. 129–30. Abbey Arthur Johnson and Ronald Maberry Johnson, *Propaganda and Aesthetics: The Literary Politics of Afro-American Magazines in the Twentieth Century* (Amherst: University of Massachusetts Press, 1979), p. 115, state that Cuney wrote about "desperate folk . . . the working class," which is what Josh White's songs reflect.

22. Roland Gelatt, *The Fabulous Phonograph 1877–1977,* rev. 2nd ed. (London: Cassell, 1977), pp. 276, 278–79.

23. Brian Rust, *The American Dance Band Discography,* vol. 1 (New Rochelle, N.Y.: Arlington House, 1975), pp. 903–4.

24. Arnold Shaw, *Honkers and Shouters: The Golden Years of Rhythm and Blues* (New York: Collier, 1978), p. 179.

25. Johnny Sippel in Shaw, *Honkers and Shouters,* p. 343.

26. Richard K. Spottswood to the author, October 2, 1981.

27. Imanuel Giess, *The Pan-African Movement* (London: Methuen, 1974), p. 355.

28. Jeffrey P. Green to the author, September 3, 1981; John Cowley to the author, December 29, 1983.

29. Paul Crawford, "Blues is Truth: Brownie McGhee in Conversation," *Guitar* 9 (January, 1981): 21.

30. Michael Ruppli and Bob Porter, *The Savoy Label: A Discography* (Westport, Conn.: The Greenwood Press, 1980), p. 19.

31. Walter Brown McGhee, interviewed by Bill Millar, May, 1980.

32. Joel C. Whitburn, *Top Rhythm and Blues Records 1949–71* (Wis.: Record Research, 1973), p. 68; Shaw, *Honkers and Shouters*, pp. 372–73; *Drinkin' Wine Spo-Dee-O-Dee*, Crown Prince IG-401, (Sweden, 1981).

33. Pete Welding, "Leroy Dallas," in *Nothing But the Blues*, ed. Mike Leadbitter (London: Hanover Books, 1971), p. 221.

34. Gary Davis, "I'm Gonna Meet You at the Station," *Folk Blues*, Continental CLP 16003 (New York).

35. *Blind Gary Davis/Short Stuff Macon*, Xtra 1009 (London).

36. *Rev. Gary Davis: Ragtime Guitar*, Transatlantic TRA 244 (London).

37. Robert Tilling to the author, February 6, 1981.

38. Stefan Grossman, *Rev. Gary Davis: Blues Guitar* (New York: Oak Publications, 1974).

39. Paul Oliver, "Key to the Highway," *Jazz Monthly* 4 (April, 1958).

40. Wilbur Ellis in conversation with the author, August 1974; Bob Rusch, "Big Chief Ellis: Oral History," *Cadence* 3 (March, 1978): 6.

41. Whitburn, *Top Rhythm and Blues*, p. 19.

42. Alan Lomax to the author, June 28, 1983; Robert Hemenway, *Zora Neale Hurston: A Literary Biography* (Urbana: University of Illinois Press, 1977), pp. 212, 298–99.

43. Bruce Bastin, brochure notes to *Gabriel Brown and His Guitar*, Flyright 591 (Bexhill-on-Sea, England, 1981), and *Gabriel Brown 1944–1952*, Krazy Kat 785 (Crawley, England, 1984), which contains eleven otherwise unissued titles.

44. Doug Seroff, "The Whole Truth About T. Ruth, Part 1," *Whiskey, Women, and . . .* 9 (July, 1982), n.p. For a discography see part 3 of the article in Ibid. 10 (November 1982), n.p.

45. Whitburn, *Top Rhythm and Blues*, p. 60. The Larks even appeared in a 1949 film, *Waiting for the Sunrise*, Jean-Claude Arnaudon, *Dictionnaire du Blues* (Paris: Filipacchi, 1977), p. 242.

46. Tarheel Slim, *No Time At All*, Trix 3310 (Rosendale, N.Y., 1975).

47. Guitar Slim and Jelly Belly, *Carolina Blues*, Arhoolie R2005 (Calif.). One title—avoiding duplication—is to be found on each of *Blues 'N' Trouble*, Arhoolie F1006 (only the 1980 revised pressing which differs from earlier pressings) and *Blues 'N' Trouble*, vol. 2, Arhoolie F1012. *The Blues of Alec Seward: Creepin' Blues*, Bluesville 1076, (Bergenfield, N.J.).

48. Sheldon Harris, *Blues Who's Who* (New Rochelle, N.Y.: Arlington House, 1979), p. 212.

49. Ruppli and Porter, *The Savoy Label,* p. 180.

50. Mike Rowe, "Fred Mendelsohn," *Blues Unlimited* 36 (September, 1966): 5.

51. Dennis McMillon, "Poor Little Angel Girl," *Livin' With the Blues,* Savoy MG1600 (New York); *Sugar Mama Blues 1949,* Biograph BLP 12009 (New York). Two takes of two other songs are on Biograph 12009.

52. Larry Johnson and Hank Adkins, *Larry and Hank,* Prestige 7472 (Bergenfield, N.J.); Larry Johnson, *Presenting the Country Blues,* Blue Horizon 7-63851 (London).

53. Larry Johnson, *Fast and Funky,* Blue Goose 2001 (New York); Tom Pomposello, "Larry Johnson Interview," *Living Blues* 16 (Spring, 1974): 16–22.

54. *The Blues,* vol. 4, Argo 4042; Pye CRL 4003 (London).

55. Phil Melick, "More Jazz from Charlotte," *Storyville* 109 (October-November, 1983): 19.

56. Simon Napier, "Lance Records," *Blues Unlimited* 101 (May, 1973): 13. I located the only known second-hand copy—as opposed to dealer stock—in northeastern North Carolina in March 1973.

57. George Moonoogian to the author, May 13, 1980.

58. Bill Bryant, "Black and Tan," *Another Man Done Gone,* Flyright 528 (Bexhill-on-Sea, England, 1979).

59. Neil Paterson, "Guitar Nubbit," in *Nothing But the Blues,* ed. Mike Leadbitter (London: Hanover Books, 1971), pp. 216–7; Victor Pearlin, "Skippy White," *Blues Unlimited* 84 (September, 1971); 13. A lyric transcript of "Georgia Chain Gang" is in *Jefferson* (Sweden) 46 (Winter, 1979): 34–35.

60. Robert Richard, *Banty Rooster Blues,* Barrelhouse BH 010 (Chicago, 1977).

61. George Paulus, liner notes to *Blues Guitar Killers: Detroit 1950s,* Barrelhouse BH 012 (Chicago, 1977).

62. *Another Man Done Gone,* Flyright 528.

63. Kip Lornell, "Albany Blues, Part Two," *Living Blues* 15 (Winter, 1973–1974): 22; *Goin' Back to Tifton,* Flyright 509 (Bexhill-on-Sea, England, 1974).

64. Lornell, "Albany Blues, Part Two": 23.

65. Kip Lornell, "Albany Blues, Part Three," *Living Blues* 16 (Spring, 1974): 29.

66. The best known "tramp band" is undoubtedly the one featured in the film *Stormy Weather* (Twentieth Century-Fox, 1943). See Dr. Klaus Stratemann, *Negro Bands on Film,* vol. 1, *Big Band 1928-1950* (Lübbeck, Germany: Verlag Uhle & Kleimann, 1981), pp. 27–28, for details, and for suggested personnel, *Storyville* 108 (August-September, 1983): 217–19, and 109 (October-November, 1983): 28–29.

67. Kip Lornell, "Albany Blues," *Living Blues* 14 (Autumn, 1973): 25–26.

68. Lornell, "Albany Blues, Part Two": 25–26. Aaron Washington and Buddy Durham are two musicians whose reasons for moving north are in Christopher Lornell, "The Effects of Social and Economic Changes on the Uses of Blues," *John Edwards Memorial Foundation Quarterly* 11 (Spring, 1975): 43–48.

69. Peter J. Corrigan, "Rochester Blues: Joe Beard, Sidney Blue," *Living Blues* 43 (Summer, 1979): 26–27. Mississippi bluesman Son House was rediscovered in Rochester.

70. Robert Redfield, "The Folk Society," *The American Journal of Sociology* 52 (January, 1947): 293–308; George M. Foster, "What is Folk Culture?" *American Anthropologist* 55 (1953): 159–72.

71. Richard M. Dorson, "Is There a Folk in the City?" *Journal of American Folklore* 83 (April-June, 1970): 208.

19

Tricks Ain't Walkin' No More

Blues as we know it had no conscious origins and similarly has no conscious end. Specific factors gave rise to blues and continued over a given period as a result of similar and related factors, but the music has largely now vanished, in any meaningful regional folk sense. Music changes and the very essence of folk music is based on that facility.

While this study is effectively a collation of known materials concerning the history of the blues tradition in the Southeast, it was never meant to be exhaustive of all aspects of the music. That the origins of blues are attributable to psycho-social-historical factors has been argued in detail elsewhere,[1] and this study merely posits the conclusion and places it firmly in the twentieth century for the Southeast.

Twenty years ago few people outside a small circle of collectors were really interested in blues. The music was certainly not part of the tradition of accepted oral history, itself in its infancy. Since then, a broader focus has been taken, and academic institutions, at one time—with remarkably few exceptions—utterly disinterested, have taken an interest for a variety of reasons. Detailed, if limited, in-depth study has highlighted early misconceptions and, understandably, new directions and interests have extended our knowledge and brought the richness and diversity of blues into better perspective.

Current research into gospel music and black quartets, secular and spiritual—which may point the new research direction of the 1980s—

has shown that blues was not the only secular music of interest to blacks at a time when blues was popular. Discovery in the 1970s of evidence of a network of older dance traditions—not just in the Southeast—of what has been termed "pre-blues" music added a further dimension. The term, partially accurate, fails to inform that it actually persisted throughout the period of commercial blues interest and did not simply pre-date it. Popular black secular music did not follow a simple chronological and stylistic path for all.

Over the past two decades, various approaches to the music have emerged which would not have been considered earlier. Today blues is accepted as a force in popular culture and popular music, which would seem to assure future detailed research. Writers in the field of American popular song acknowledge the input from black secular music,[2] as do those who assess the phenomenon of rock-and-roll. The impact of the latter upon Western society was such as to afford it closer scrutiny than is usual for a music of recent origins. Doubtless other aspects of black secular music, parallel to and growing out of blues, will provoke investigation. We hope that the efforts of organizations like the International Association for the Study of Popular Music,[3] among less co-ordinated research, will see that coverage does not come too late.

Constantly we find that parallel or related studies shed new light upon our assessment and interpretation of blues. At this point it is worth repeating that our assessment of the music must be based on aural appreciation. Writing on the impact of technology on British folksong, Kenneth Goldstein confirms that "when it comes to understanding . . . performance style, there is no real substitute for live performance or sound recordings of it,"[4] and this is no less true for blues, although we must now look to sound recordings in almost every instance.

In his study of orality and literacy, Walter Ong emphasizes that "the basic orality of language is permanent. . . . Oral expression can exist and mostly has existed without any writing at all, writing never without orality."[5] It is perhaps appropriate to state that of some 3,000 languages spoken today, only "some 78" have a written literature.[6]

As the music is constantly changing so are our perspectives and evaluations of it. Dena Epstein has pointed out erroneous myths about black folk music,[7] while elsewhere it is suggested that "all the significant early sources treating Afro-American cultural development. . . . can benefit from a kind of reassessment, reinterpretation, and reaffirmation [sic]."[8] Citing this suggestion, Peter Lowry asks us "to examine the possibility that extant etic definitions of blues are flawed, and that they have produced further bias in our understanding of an important form of black American music."[9] Any fieldworker who has collected blues knows that much of the music is clearly "that to which people danced, partied, and otherwise occupied and enjoyed much of their non-church free time on weekends." Lowry postulates that "if there is catharsis in blues, it lies in the phenomenon of 'Saturday nighting,' and not within the song or the performer."[10]

As blues has a function within its social context, however one views that function, there can be no escaping the fact that once removed from that setting, it is obliged to make adjustments. The performers' artistic awareness of what they are creating assuredly spells the very end of that music as folk song. The process of prolonged exposure to a different culture must necessitate either change or petrifaction. One inescapable product is what might be described as "tourist blues,"[11] which some musicians—by no means only on European tours—provide. By its very nature the Southeast has fared better than Chicago. Perhaps it is merely that the music has changed, but it points out the underlying premise of this entire study—that blues was a socially-based music which could not thrive healthily outside its natural environment. Even as we recognize the blues' massive role as a popular music among blacks, we should recall Paul Oliver's caveat that "there are still those for whom the blues has no significance at all."[12]

Blues, then, is a musical language and, like language, is subject to sudden change. George Steiner's comment on shifts in the use of language is just as pertinent to the music under study here. "Language is . . . most plausibly an interpenetration of the reflective with the creative along an 'interface' of which we have no formal model, it changes as rapidly and in as many ways as human experience itself."[13] We have glimpsed just one mode of expression resulting from changing experiences among one group of people.

NOTES

1. Bruce Bastin, "The Origins of a Blues Tradition in the Southeastern States" (Master's thesis, University of North Carolina at Chapel Hill, 1973).

2. Alec Wilder, *American Popular Song: The Great Innovators* (New York: Oxford University Press, 1972), and Myron P. Matlaw, ed., *American Popular Entertainment* (Westport, Conn.: Greenwood Press, 1979).

3. The International Association for the Study of Popular Music (IASPM) is based at Göteborg University (Sweden) and Exeter University (England). *Popular Music,* vol. 1 (1982) and vol. 2 (1983), have been published by Cam-

bridge University Press. See also Berndt Ostendorf, *Ethnicity and Popular Music,* Working Paper 2, IASPM [1983].

4. Kenneth S. Goldstein, "The Impact of Recording Technology on the British Folksong Revival," in *Folk Music and Modern Sound,* ed. William Ferris and Mary L. Hart (Jackson: University Press of Mississippi, 1982), p. 9.

5. Walter J. Ong, *Orality and Literacy: The Technologizing of the Word* (London: Methuen, 1982), pp. 7–8.

6. Munro E. Edmonson, *Lore: An Introduction to the Science of Folklore and Literature* (New York: Holt, Rinehart & Winston, 1971), p. 332, in Ong, *Orality and Literacy,* p. 7.

7. Dena J. Epstein, "Myths about Black Folk Music," in *Folk Music,* ed. Ferris and Hart, p. 152.

8. Adrienne Lanier Seward, "The Legacy of Early Afro-American Folklore Scholarship," in *The Handbook of American Folklore* (Bloomington: Indiana University Press, 1983), p. 50.

9. Peter B. Lowry, "Hard Times, Bad Luck and Trouble: A Fallacy about Blues," paper given to the American Folklore Society, Nashville, Tennessee, October, 1983. Typescript, p. 9.

10. Ibid., p. 8.

11. Bruce Bastin, "The International Impact of Blues," paper given to the conference on Salute to Memphis Music, Memphis State University, Tennessee, August, 1980. Typescript, p. 11.

12. Paul Oliver, *The Story of the Blues* (London: Barrie & Rockliff, 1969), p. 6.

13. George Steiner, *After Babel: Aspects of Language and Translation* (London: Oxford University Press, 1975), p. 19.

General Index

Because different sources provide different versions of musicians' names, this index includes all variations in spelling and/or epithet.

Tune Index

Books in the Series Music in American Life

Only a Miner: Studies in Recorded Coal-Mining Songs   *Archie Green*

Great Day Coming: Folk Music and the American Left   *R. Serge Denisoff*

John Philip Sousa: A Descriptive Catalog of His Works   *Paul E. Bierley*

The Hell-Bound Train: A Cowboy Songbook   *Glenn Ohrlin*

Oh, Didn't He Ramble: The Life Story of Lee Collins, as Told to Mary Collins
Edited by Frank J. Gillis and John W. Miner

American Labor Songs of the Nineteenth Century   *Philip S. Foner*

Stars of Country Music: Uncle Dave Macon to Johnny Rodriguez
Edited by Bill C. Malone and Judith McCulloh

Git Along, Little Dogies: Songs and Songmakers of the American West
John I. White

A Texas-Mexican *Cancionero:* Folksongs of the Lower Border
Américo Paredes

San Antonio Rose: The Life and Music of Bob Wills   *Charles R. Townsend*

Early Downhome Blues: A Musical and Cultural Analysis   *Jeff Todd Titon*

An Ives Celebration: Papers and Panels of the Charles Ives Centennial Festival-
Conference   *Edited by H. Wiley Hitchcock and Vivian Perlis*

Sinful Tunes and Spirituals: Black Folk Music to the Civil War   *Dena J. Epstein*

Joe Scott, the Woodsman-Songmaker   *Edward D. Ives*

Jimmie Rodgers: The Life and Times of America's Blue Yodeler
Nolan Porterfield

Early American Music Engraving and Printing: A History of Music Publishing in
America from 1787 to 1825, with Commentary on Earlier and Later
Practices   *Richard J. Wolfe*

Sing a Sad Song: The Life of Hank Williams   *Roger M. Williams*

Long Steel Rail: The Railroad in American Folksong   *Norm Cohen*

Resources of American Music History: A Directory of Source Materials from
Colonial Times to World War II   *D. W. Krummel, Jean Geil, Doris J. Dyen, and
Deane L. Root*

Tenement Songs: The Popular Music of the Jewish Immigrants   *Mark Slobin*

Ozark Folksongs   *Vance Randolph; edited and abridged by Norm Cohen*

Oscar Sonneck and American Music   *Edited by William Lichtenwanger*

Bluegrass Breakdown: The Making of the Old Southern Sound
Robert Cantwell

Bluegrass: A History   *Neil V. Rosenberg*

Music at the White House: A History of the American Spirit   *Elise K. Kirk*

Red River Blues: The Blues Tradition in the Southeast   *Bruce Bastin*

Good Friends and Bad Enemies: Robert Winslow Gordon and the Study of
American Folksong   *Debora Kodish*

Fiddlin' Georgia Crazy: Fiddlin' John Carson, His Real World, and the World
of His Songs   *Gene Wiggins*

America's Music: From the Pilgrims to the Present (Revised Third Edition)
Gilbert Chase

Secular Music in Colonial Annapolis: The Tuesday Club, 1745–56
John Barry Talley

Bibliographical Handbook of American Music   *D. W. Krummel*

Goin' to Kansas City   *Nathan W. Pearson, Jr.*

"Susanna," "Jeanie," and "The Old Folks at Home": The Songs of Stephen C. Foster
from His Time to Ours (Second Edition)   *William W. Austin*

Songprints: The Musical Experience of Five Shoshone Women   *Judith Vander*

"Happy in the Service of the Lord": Afro-American Gospel Quartets in
Memphis   *Kip Lornell*

Paul Hindemith in the United States   *Luther Noss*

"My Song Is My Weapon": People's Songs, American Communism, and the Politics
of Culture, 1930–50   *Robbie Lieberman*

Chosen Voices: The Story of the American Cantorate   *Mark Slobin*

Theodore Thomas: America's Conductor and Builder of Orchestras, 1835–1905
Ezra Schabas

"The Whorehouse Bells Were Ringing" and Other Songs Cowboys Sing
Guy Logsdon

Crazeology: The Autobiography of a Chicago Jazzman   *Bud Freeman, as Told to
Robert Wolf*

Discoursing Sweet Music: Brass Bands and Community Life in Turn-of-the-Century
Pennsylvania   *Kenneth Kreitner*

Mormonism and Music: A History   *Michael Hicks*

Voices of the Jazz Age: Profiles of Eight Vintage Jazzmen   *Chip Deffaa*

Milton Brown and the Founding of Western Swing   *Cary Ginell, with special assistance from Roy Lee Brown*

Santiago de Murcia's "Códice Saldívar No. 4": A Treasury of Secular Guitar Music from Baroque Mexico   *Craig H. Russell*

The Sound of the Dove: Singing in Appalachian Primitive Baptist Churches *Beverly Bush Patterson*

Heartland Excursions: Ethnomusicological Reflections on Schools of Music *Bruno Nettl*

Doowop: The Chicago Scene   *Robert Pruter*

Blue Rhythms: Six Lives in Rhythm and Blues   *Chip Deffaa*